Character Design
Collection
HeroineS

3dtotal Publishing

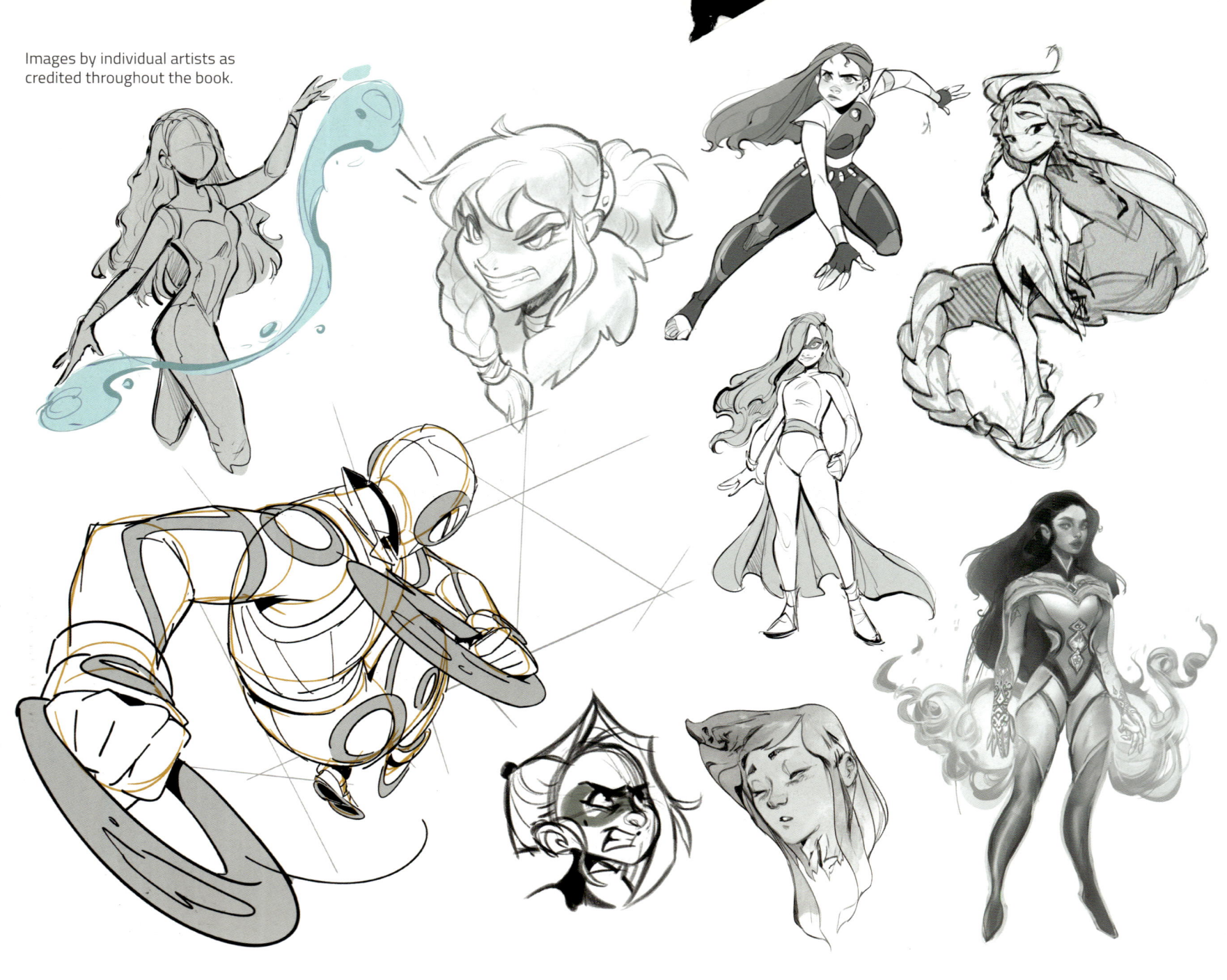

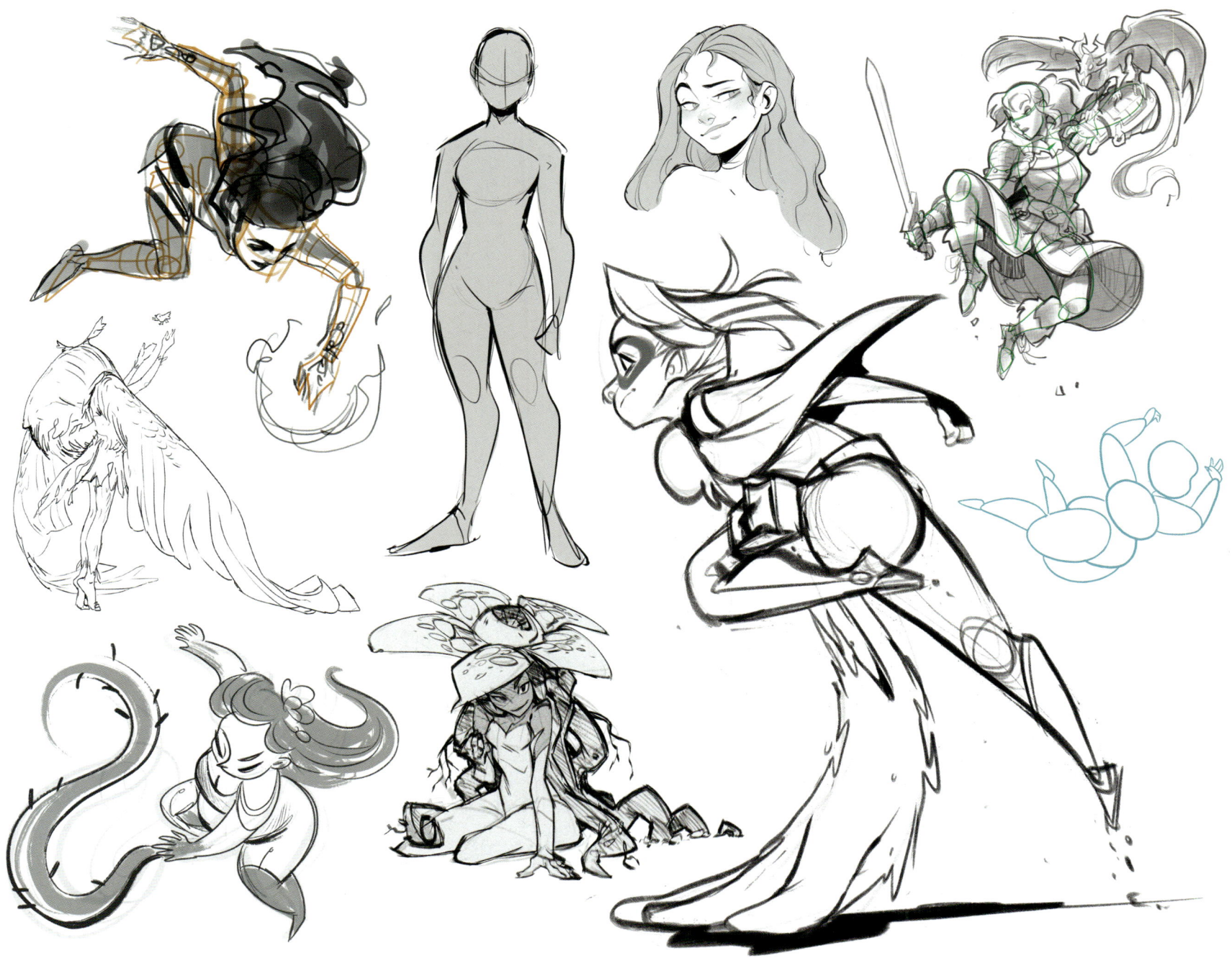

3dtotalPublishing

Correspondence: publishing@3dtotal.com
Website: www.3dtotal.com

Every effort has been made to ensure the credits and
contact information listed are present and correct. In
the case of any errors that have occurred, the publisher
respectfully directs readers to the www.3dtotalpublishing.
com website for any updated information and/or corrections.

First published in the United Kingdom, 2021, by
3dtotal Publishing.

Address: 3dtotal.com Ltd, 29 Foregate Street, Worcester,
WR1 1DS, United Kingdom.

Soft cover ISBN: 978-1-912843-26-8
Printing & binding: Gutenberg Press Ltd (Malta)
www.gutenberg.com.mt

Visit www.3dtotalpublishing.com for a complete list of
available book titles.

Managing Director: Tom Greenway
Studio Manager: Simon Morse
Lead Designer: Fiona Tarbet
Lead Editor: Samantha Rigby
Editor: Philippa Barker
Designer: Joseph Cartwright

Cover images by individual artists
as credited throughout the book.

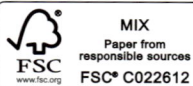

One tree planted for every book sold

From 2020, 3dtotal Publishing pledged to plant one tree for every book sold by partnering with and donating the appropriate amounts to re-foresting charities. This is one of the first steps in our ambition to become a carbon-neutral company with carbon-neutral publications, giving our customers the knowledge that by buying from 3dtotal Publishing, they are working with us to balance the environmental damage caused by the publishing, shipping, and retail industries.

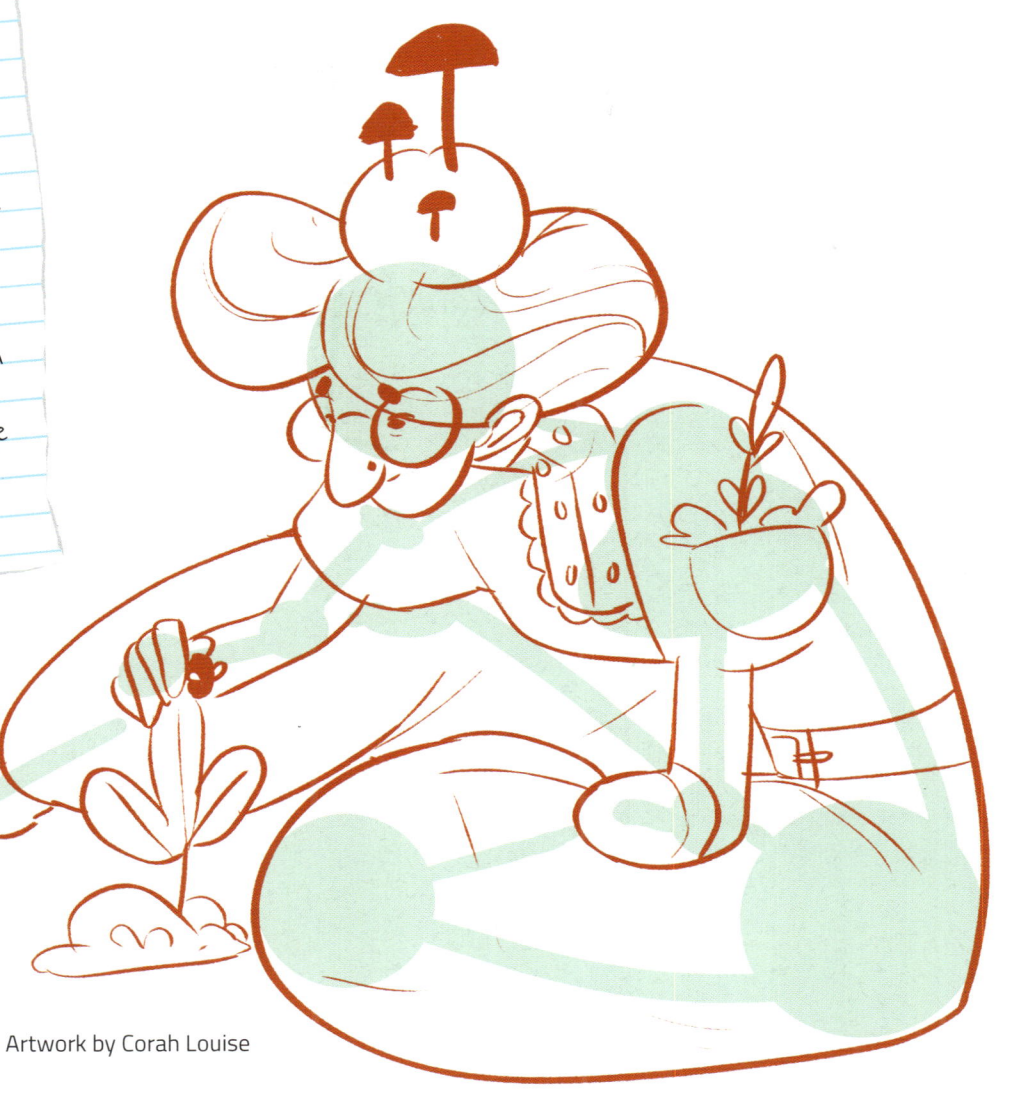

Artwork by Corah Louise

CONTENTS

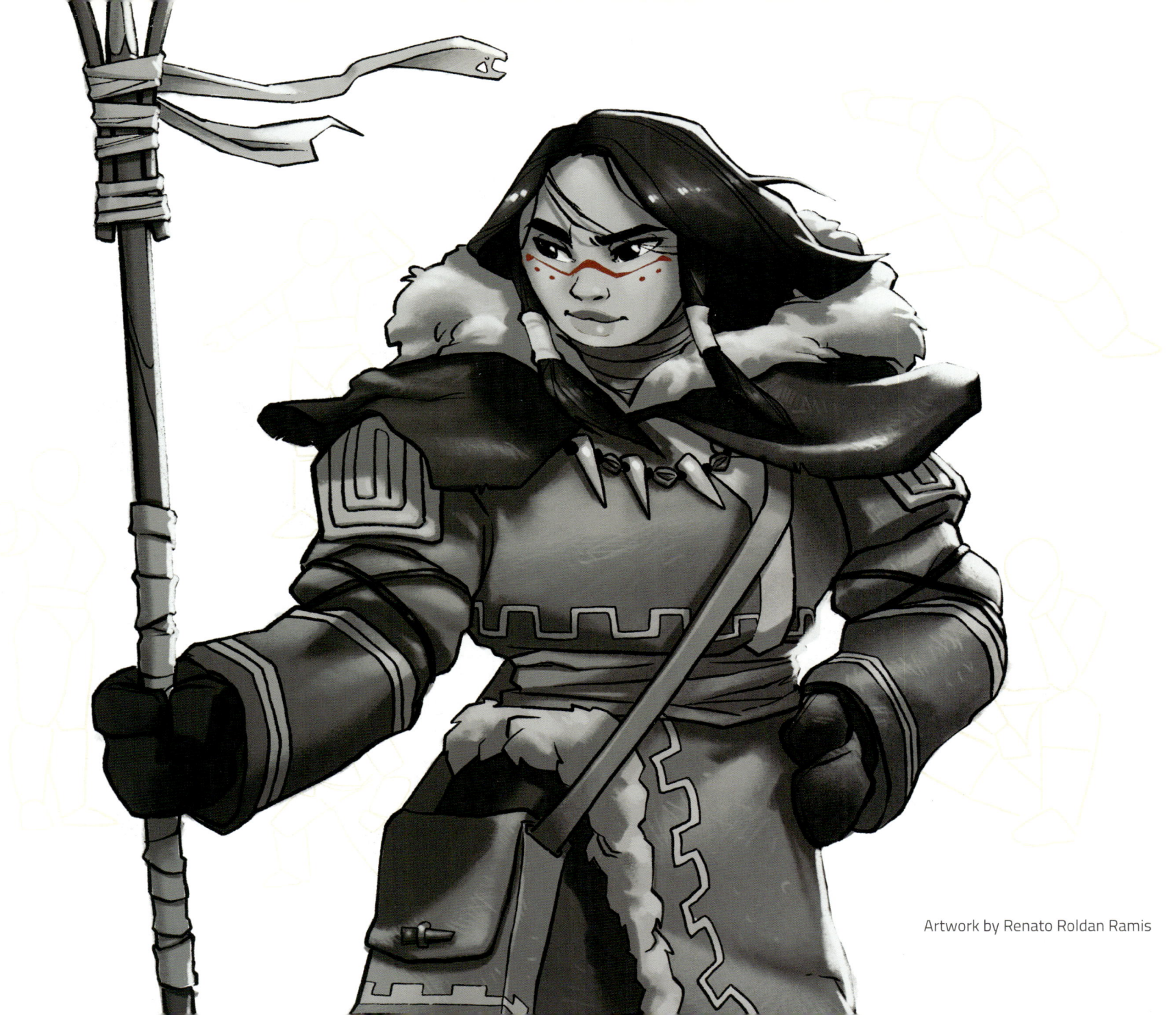

Artwork by Renato Roldan Ramis

Introduction

At the heart of every great story you will find great characters. Many of the TV shows, films, games, and comics we love are made memorable thanks to iconic, engaging character design. While there are a range of roles and types, the heroine character is more important and popular than ever. From crime-fighting superheroines to enchanting princesses, magical fantasy warriors to pioneering heroines from the past, it is an art form revered the world over. Our favorite heroines remain with us long after the closing credits or final page.

In this book, fifty professional character artists from the animation, illustration, comic, and game industries share a fascinating, behind-the-scenes look into the creative process that goes into building a compelling heroine design. Browse their rough sketches and initial thumbnails as they explore early ideas, alongside outfit variations and facial expressions that help to develop the character and their story. As well as a chosen design, each artist shares a range of dynamic pose explorations with basic shape overlays – a constructive resource for mapping out how the heroine will move and exist in her environment.

We hope this book provides a valuable and inspirational resource, enriching your understanding of how to develop ideas for a character, as well as providing inspiration for an abundance of fierce, confident, kick-ass heroines for the next generation.

Philippa Barker
Editor, 3dtotal Publishing

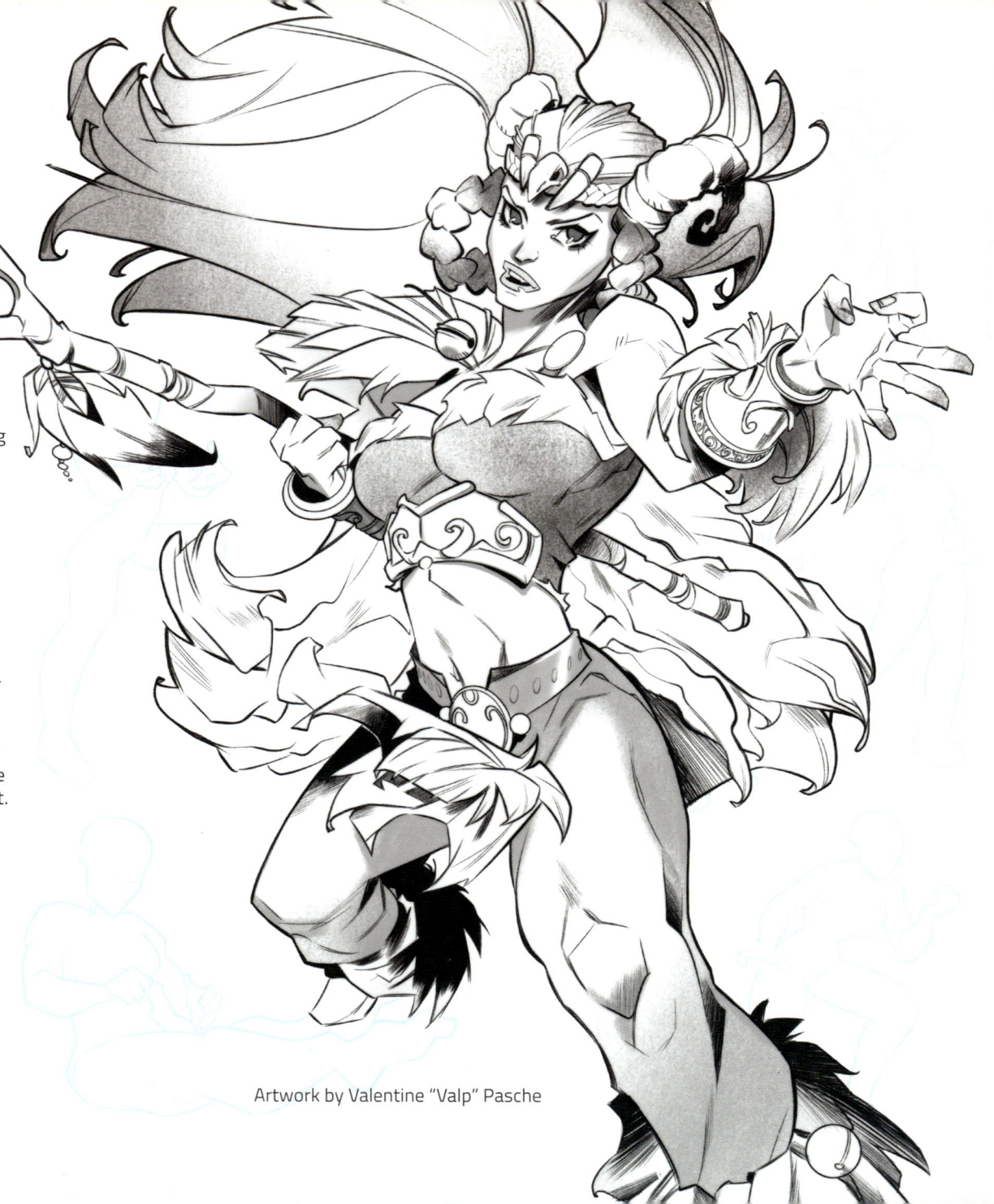

Artwork by Valentine "Valp" Pasche

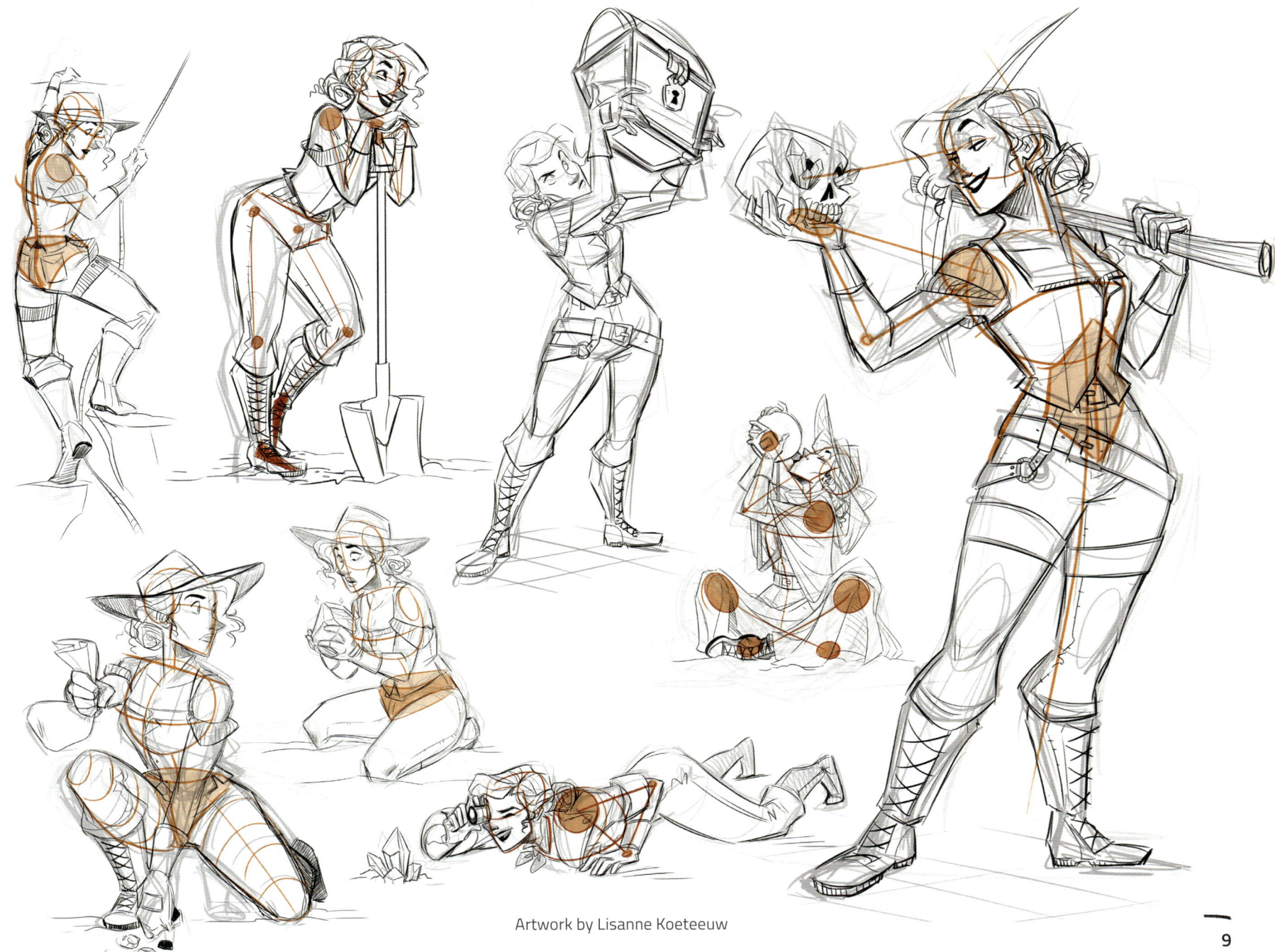

Artwork by Lisanne Koeteeuw

Dragon trainer

THIS SKETCHBOOK BELONGS TO: Martin Abel

Orla lives in a faraway kingdom where she is part of an elite army that train dragons. She readies the dragons for hunting, as well as for battle, where they fight loyally alongside her to defend the kingdom from attack. She has an unbreakable bond with the creatures she works with and is very knowledgeable and skilled in how to care for them. Brave, patient, and intelligent, Orla knows the risks that come with her line of work, but believes to her core that this is her calling.

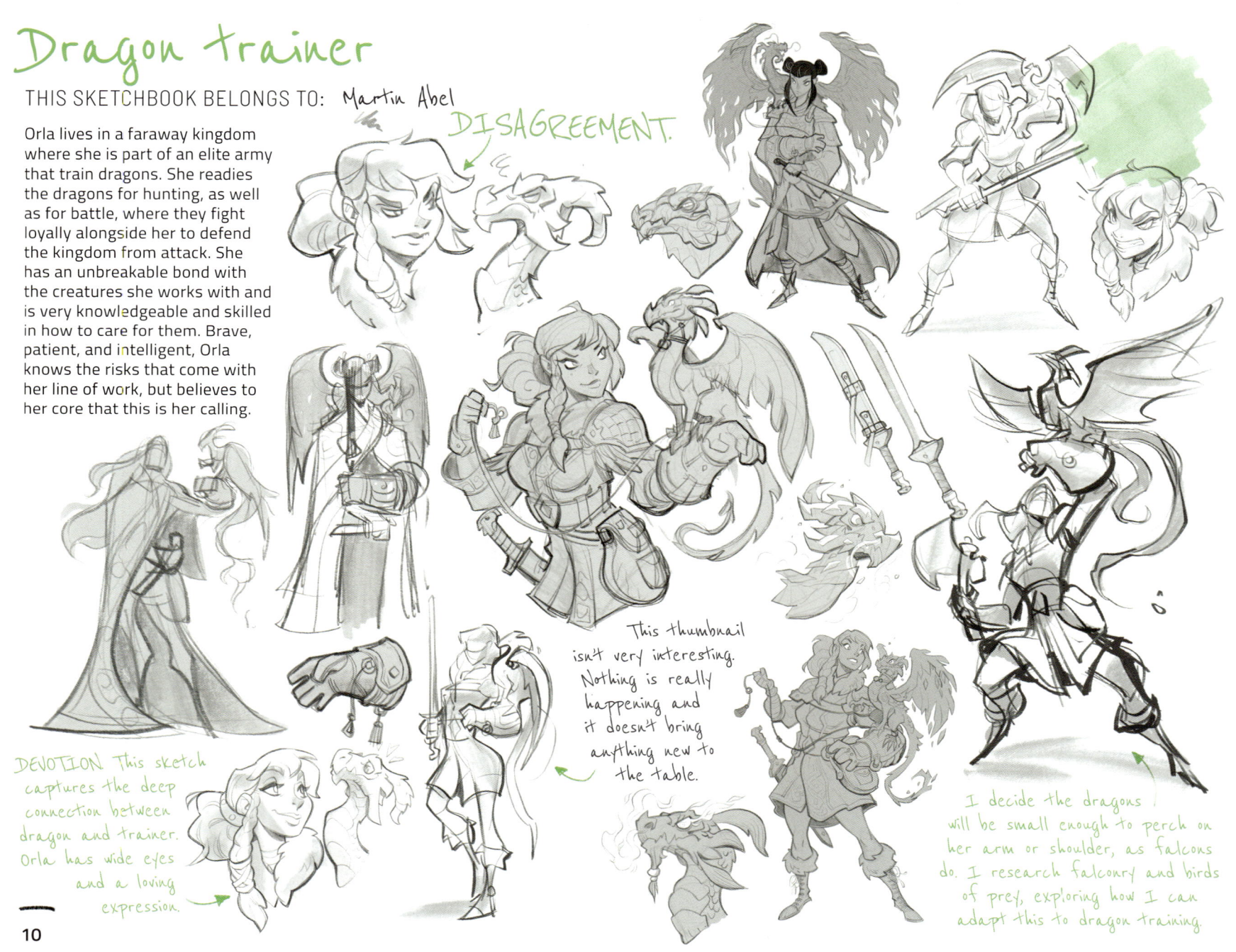

DISAGREEMENT.

DEVOTION. This sketch captures the deep connection between dragon and trainer. Orla has wide eyes and a loving expression.

This thumbnail isn't very interesting. Nothing is really happening and it doesn't bring anything new to the table.

I decide the dragons will be small enough to perch on her arm or shoulder, as falcons do. I research falconry and birds of prey, exploring how I can adapt this to dragon training.

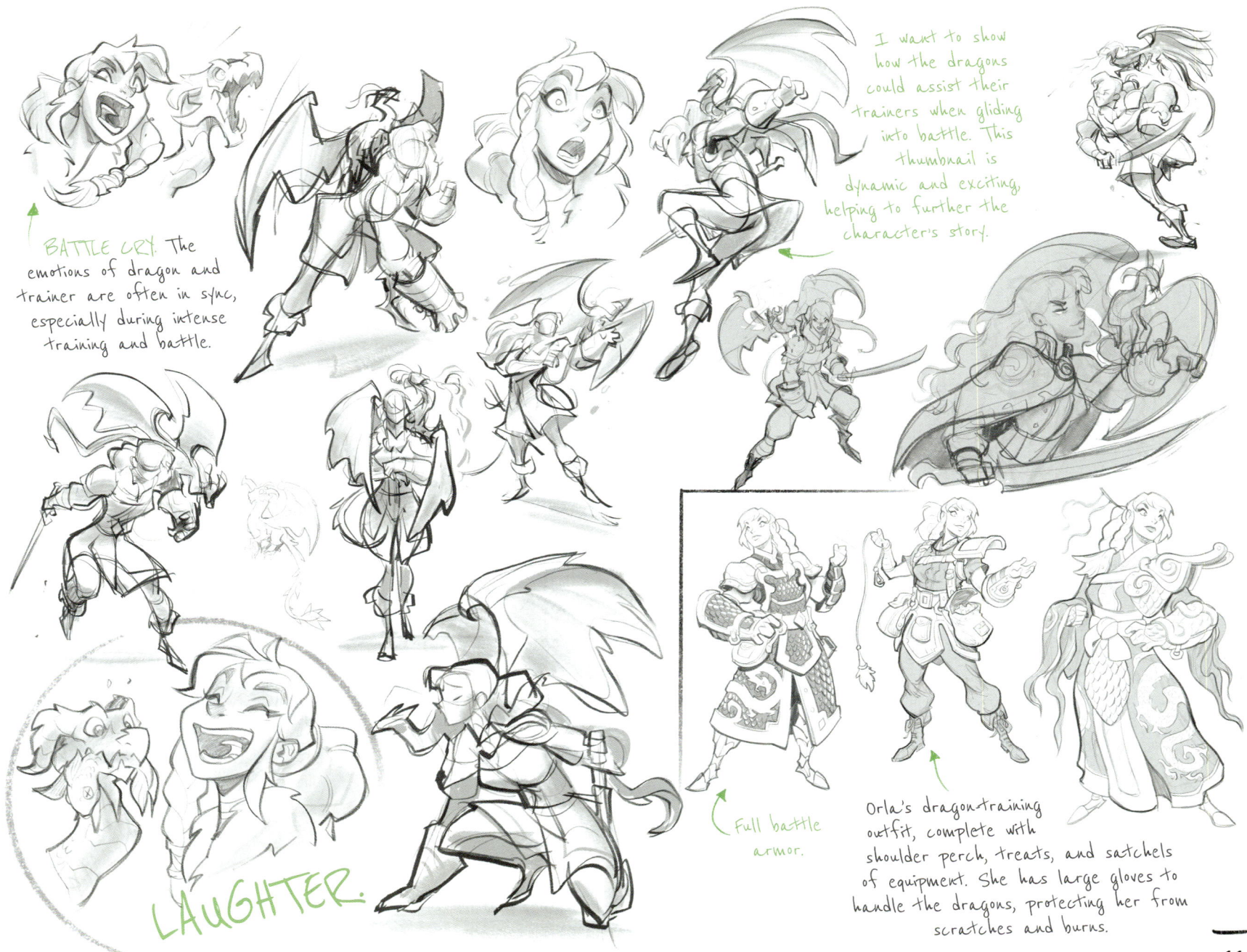

BATTLE CRY. The emotions of dragon and trainer are often in sync, especially during intense training and battle.

I want to show how the dragons could assist their trainers when gliding into battle. This thumbnail is dynamic and exciting, helping to further the character's story.

LAUGHTER.

Full battle armor.

Orla's dragon-training outfit, complete with shoulder perch, treats, and satchels of equipment. She has large gloves to handle the dragons, protecting her from scratches and burns.

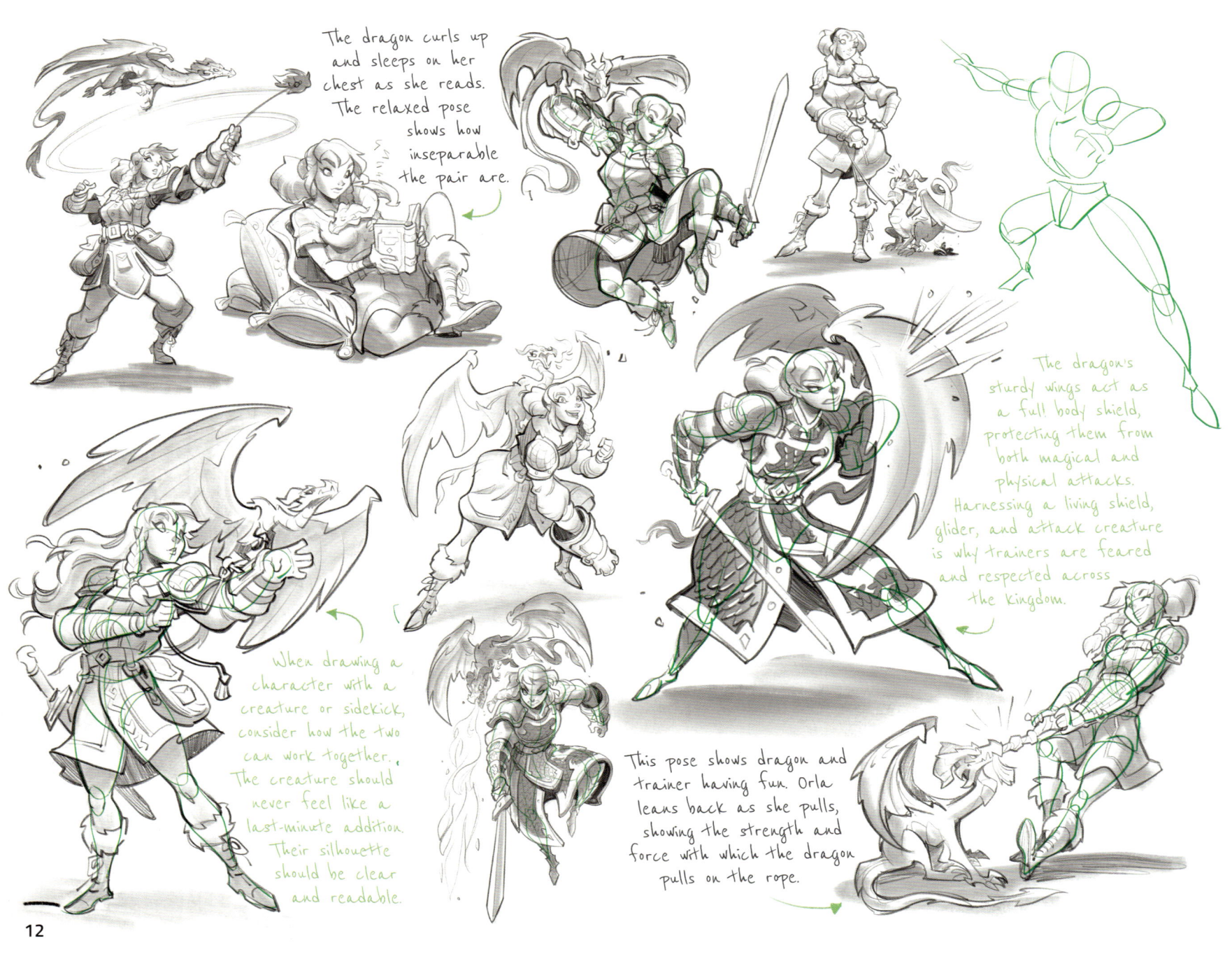

The dragon curls up and sleeps on her chest as she reads. The relaxed pose shows how inseparable the pair are.

The dragon's sturdy wings act as a full body shield, protecting them from both magical and physical attacks. Harnessing a living shield, glider, and attack creature is why trainers are feared and respected across the kingdom.

When drawing a character with a creature or sidekick, consider how the two can work together. The creature should never feel like a last-minute addition. Their silhouette should be clear and readable.

This pose shows dragon and trainer having fun. Orla leans back as she pulls, showing the strength and force with which the dragon pulls on the rope.

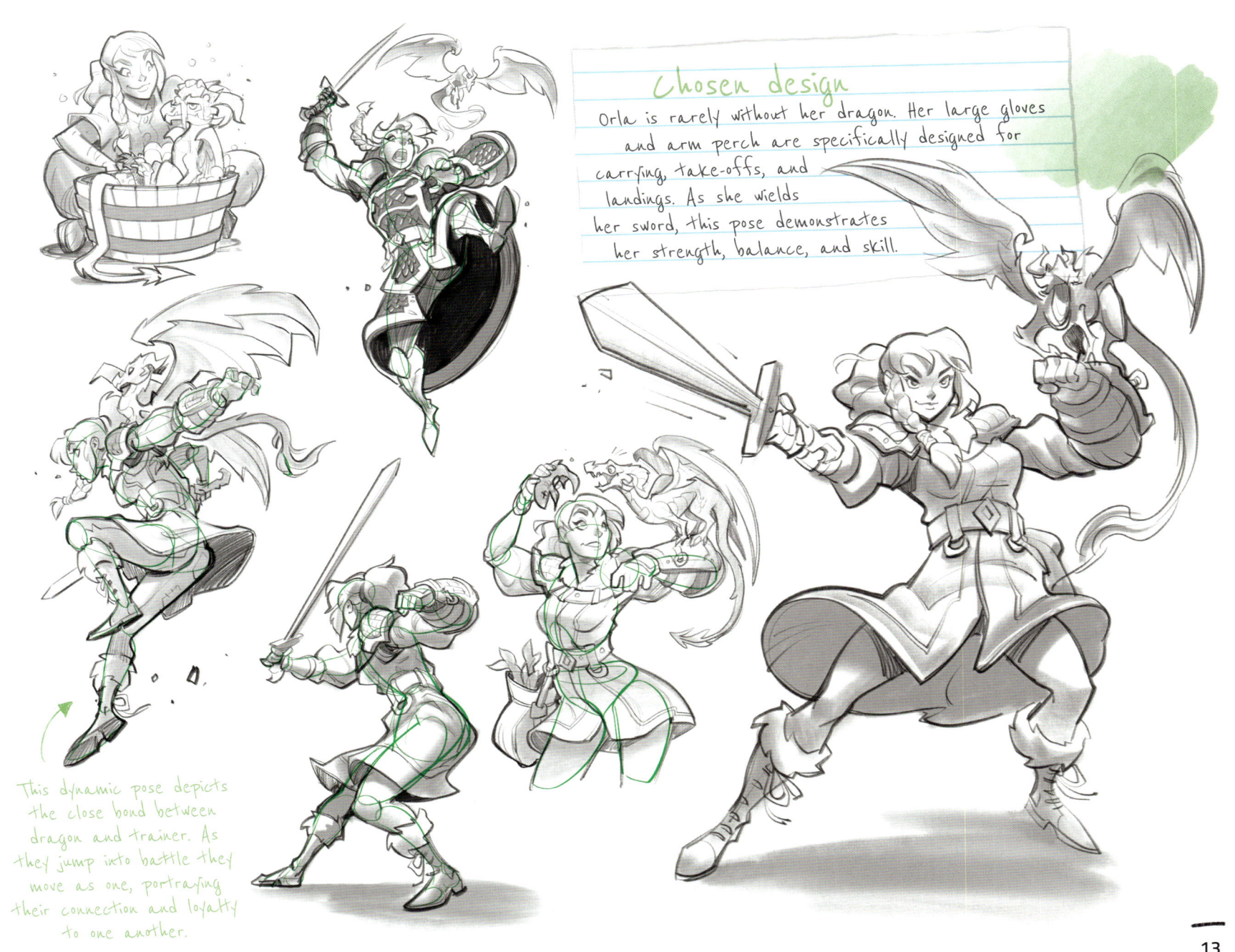

Chosen design

Orla is rarely without her dragon. Her large gloves and arm perch are specifically designed for carrying, take-offs, and landings. As she wields her sword, this pose demonstrates her strength, balance, and skill.

This dynamic pose depicts the close bond between dragon and trainer. As they jump into battle they move as one, portraying their connection and loyalty to one another.

Vampire hunter

THIS SKETCHBOOK BELONGS TO: Chris Ables

Sigrid has trained as a vampire hunter from a young age. Vampiric history, lethal combat skills, and the responsibility of being a soldier in the war against evil forces have been dutifully passed down to her through her maternal grandmother's line. With her steely gaze and intimidating physical presence that invokes sturdiness and strength, she shows her enemies that she is a skilled, focused, and tenacious warrior. She cares little about validation because she has already proven herself.

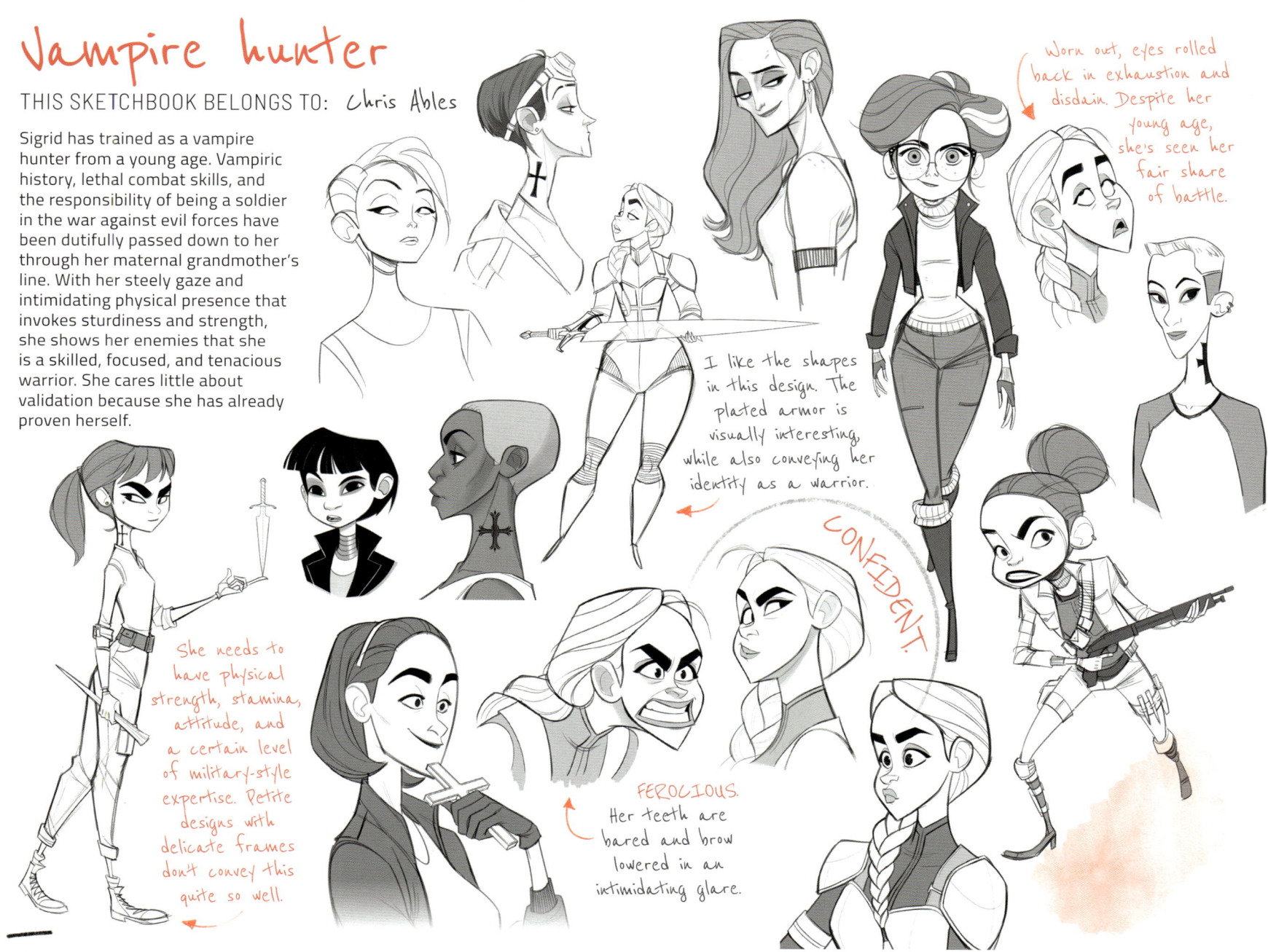

Worn out, eyes rolled back in exhaustion and disdain. Despite her young age, she's seen her fair share of battle.

I like the shapes in this design. The plated armor is visually interesting, while also conveying her identity as a warrior.

CONFIDENT.

She needs to have physical strength, stamina, attitude, and a certain level of military-style expertise. Petite designs with delicate frames don't convey this quite so well.

FEROCIOUS. Her teeth are bared and brow lowered in an intimidating glare.

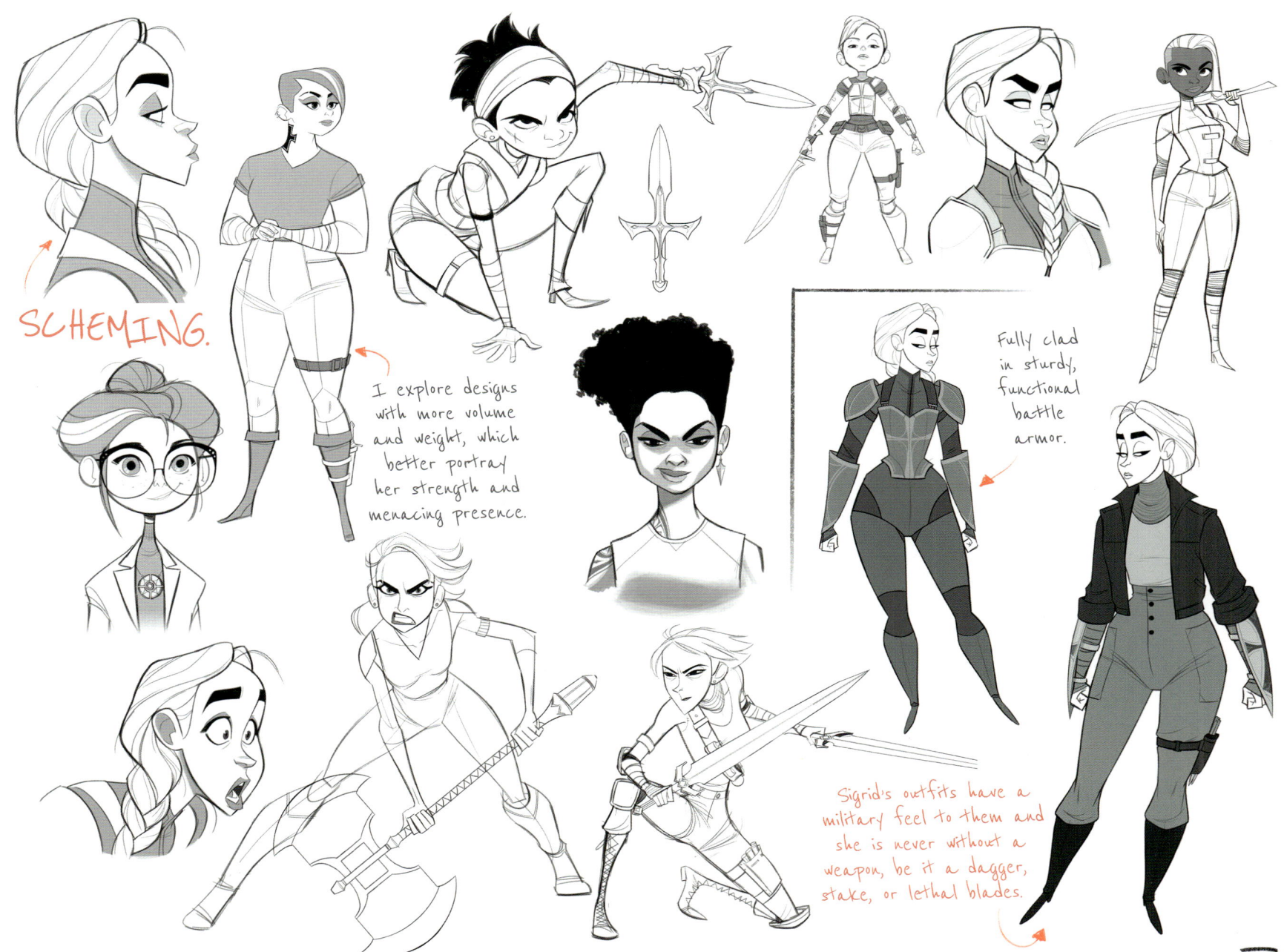

SCHEMING.

I explore designs with more volume and weight, which better portray her strength and menacing presence.

Fully clad in sturdy, functional battle armor.

Sigrid's outfits have a military feel to them and she is never without a weapon, be it a dagger, stake, or lethal blades.

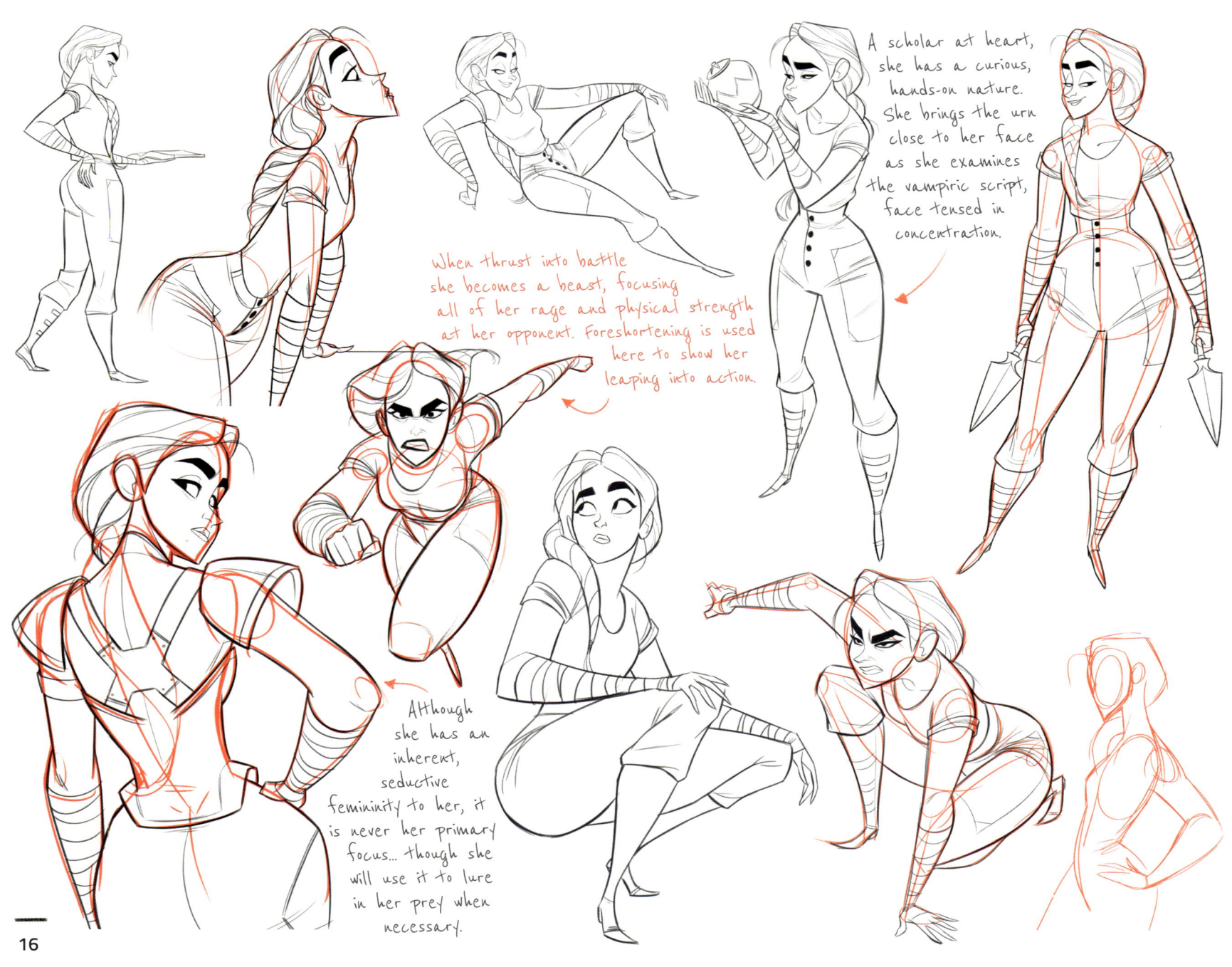

A scholar at heart, she has a curious, hands-on nature. She brings the urn close to her face as she examines the vampiric script, face tensed in concentration.

When thrust into battle she becomes a beast, focusing all of her rage and physical strength at her opponent. Foreshortening is used here to show her leaping into action.

Although she has an inherent, seductive femininity to her, it is never her primary focus... though she will use it to lure in her prey when necessary.

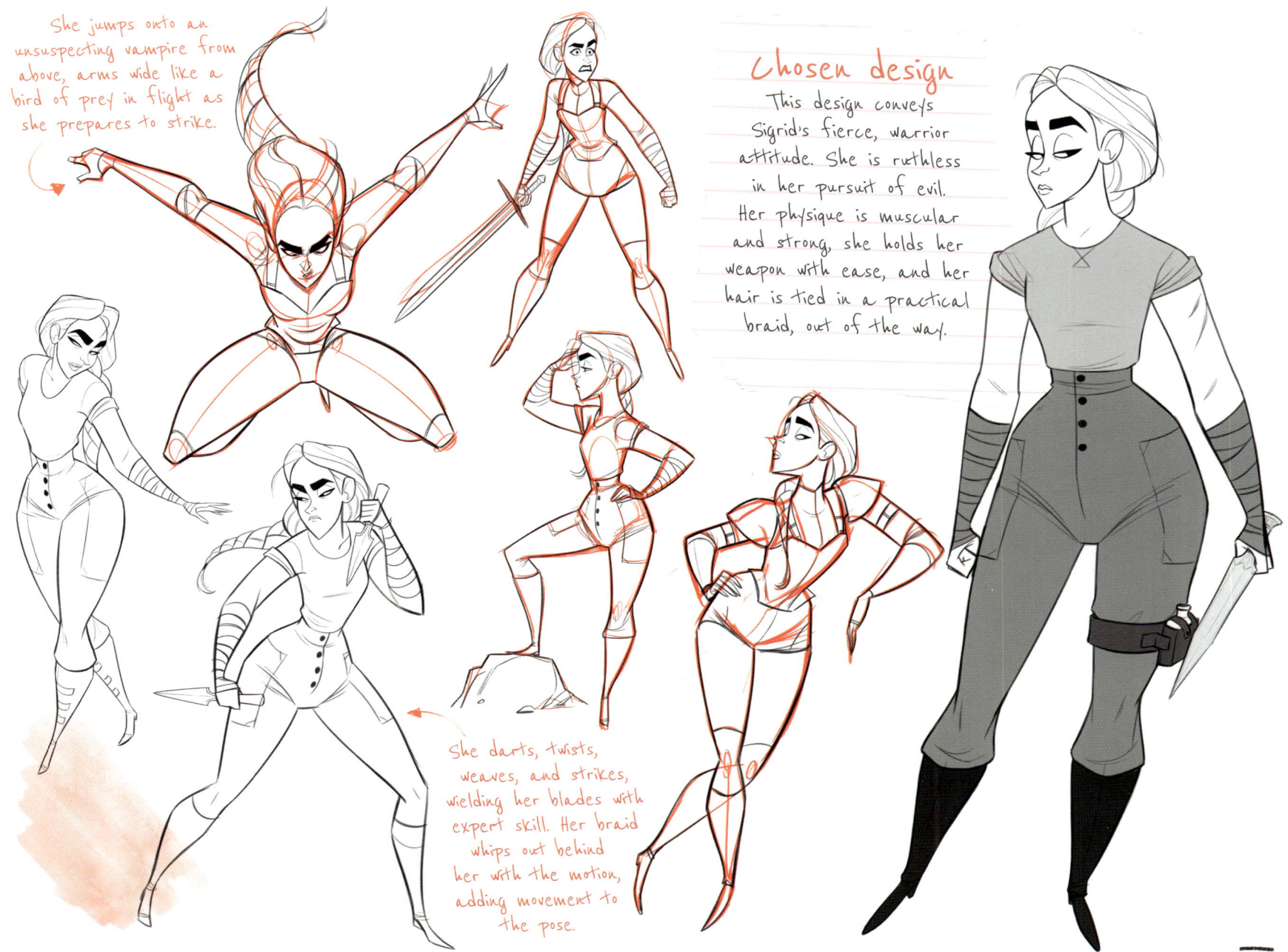

She jumps onto an unsuspecting vampire from above, arms wide like a bird of prey in flight as she prepares to strike.

Chosen design

This design conveys Sigrid's fierce, warrior attitude. She is ruthless in her pursuit of evil. Her physique is muscular and strong, she holds her weapon with ease, and her hair is tied in a practical braid, out of the way.

She darts, twists, weaves, and strikes, wielding her blades with expert skill. Her braid whips out behind her with the motion, adding movement to the pose.

Medieval Knight

THIS SKETCHBOOK BELONGS TO: Amagoia Agirre

This knight is fierce and courageous. Born into a small medieval township, Isolde's horse-riding skills and fearlessness in the face of danger were noticed by a passing noblewoman. She saw promise in the young girl and sponsored her training in secret. The only girl in a class full of boys, Isolde was teased and ridiculed, but this only made her more determined to triumph as top of the class. Highly skilled and disciplined in her training, she takes part in jousts and tournaments across the land, emerging victorious over those who once teased her. Not forgetting her roots, she secretly distributes the prize money among the poor in her township.

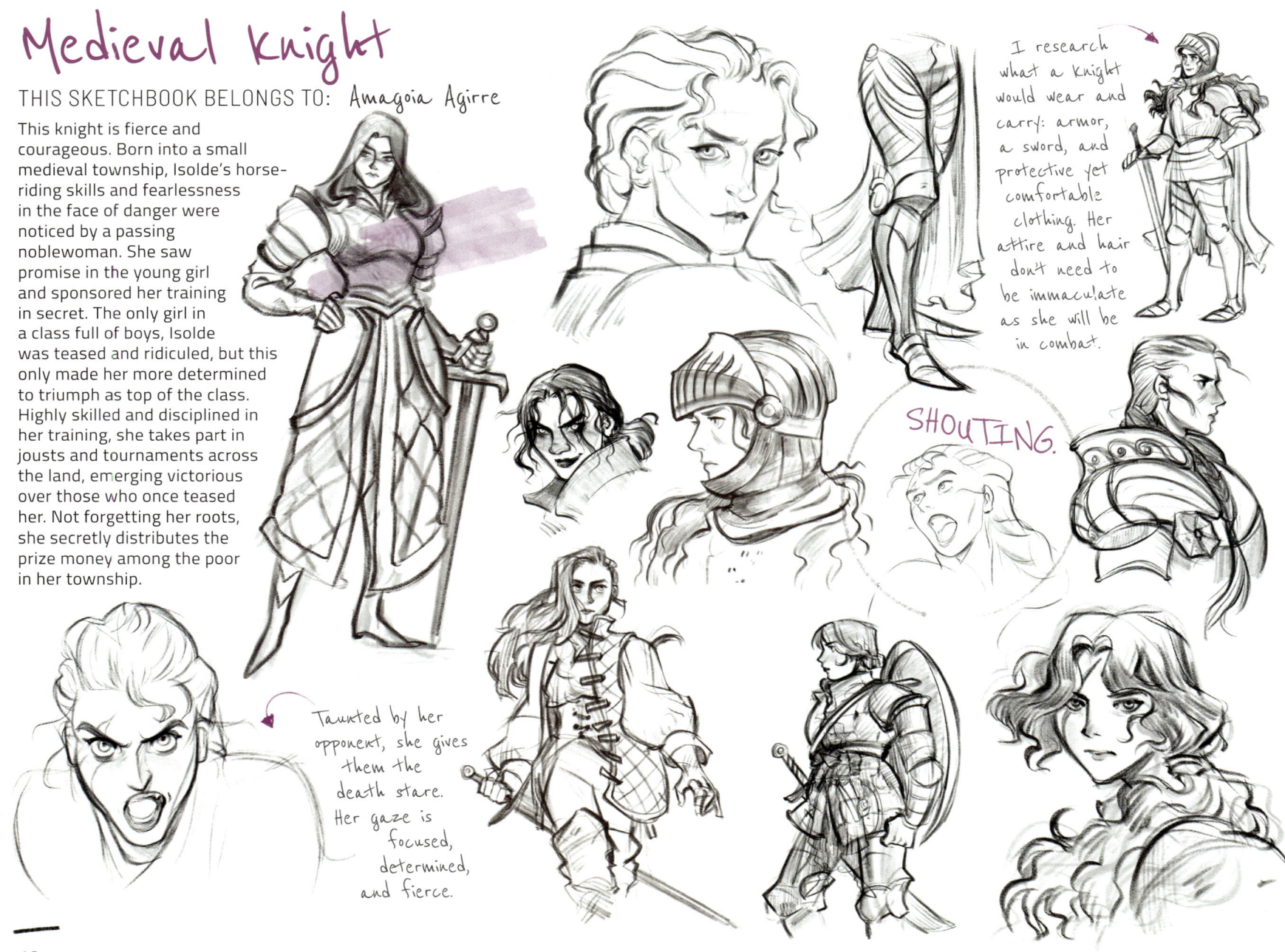

I research what a knight would wear and carry: armor, a sword, and protective yet comfortable clothing. Her attire and hair don't need to be immaculate as she will be in combat.

SHOUTING.

Taunted by her opponent, she gives them the death stare. Her gaze is focused, determined, and fierce.

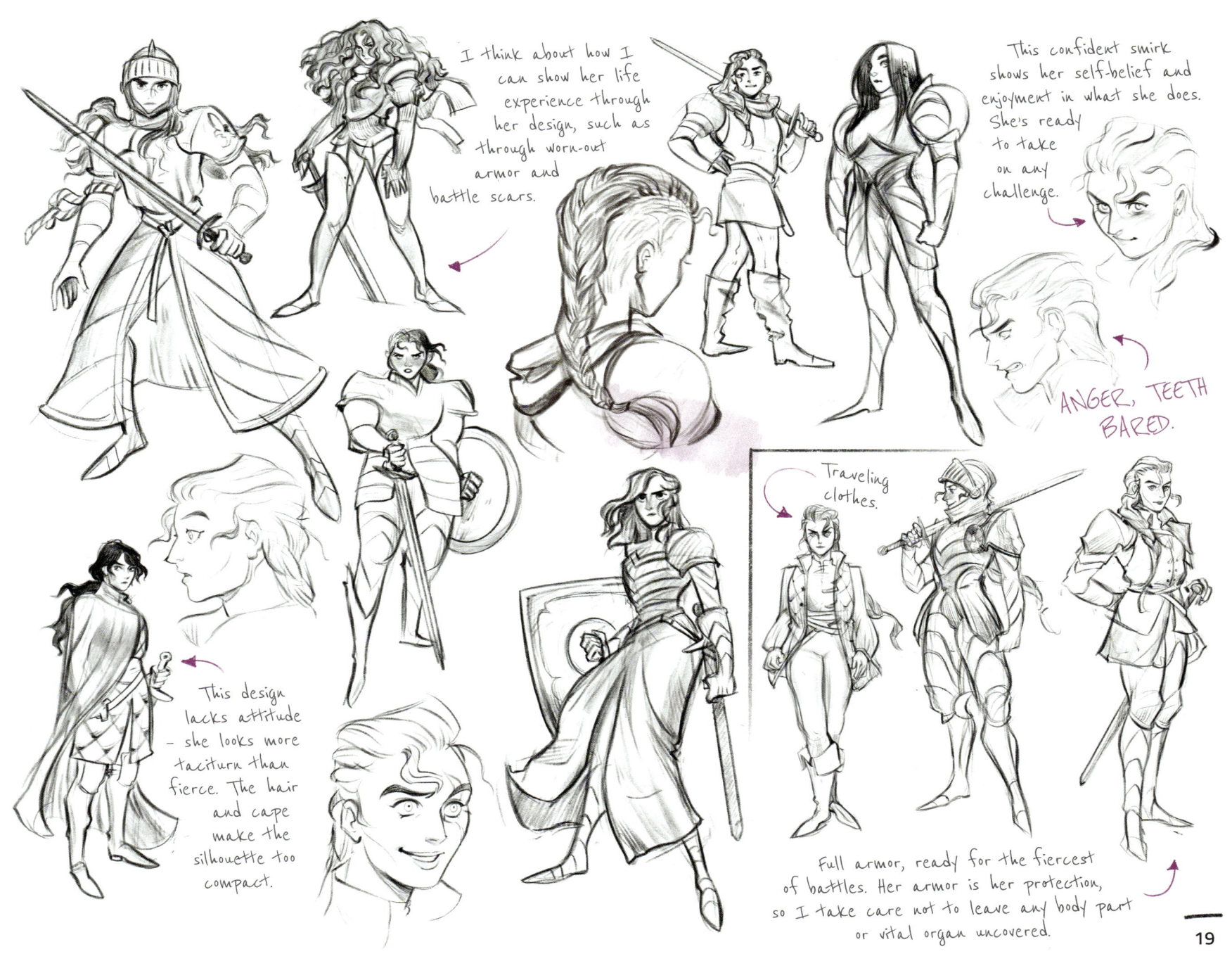

I think about how I can show her life experience through her design, such as through worn-out armor and battle scars.

This confident smirk shows her self-belief and enjoyment in what she does. She's ready to take on any challenge.

ANGER, TEETH BARED.

This design lacks attitude - she looks more taciturn than fierce. The hair and cape make the silhouette too compact.

Traveling clothes.

Full armor, ready for the fiercest of battles. Her armor is her protection, so I take care not to leave any body part or vital organ uncovered.

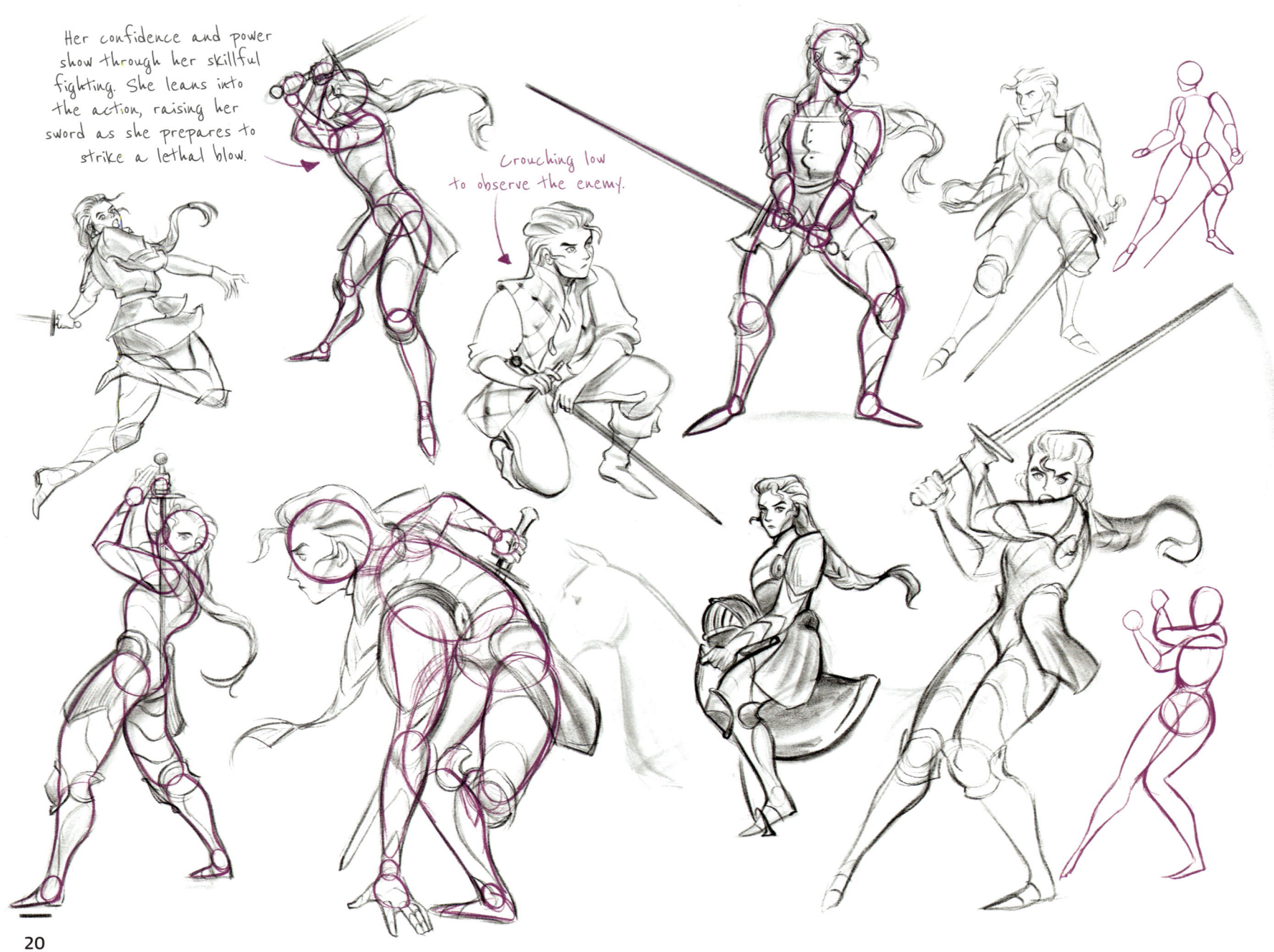

Her confidence and power show through her skillful fighting. She leans into the action, raising her sword as she prepares to strike a lethal blow.

Crouching low to observe the enemy.

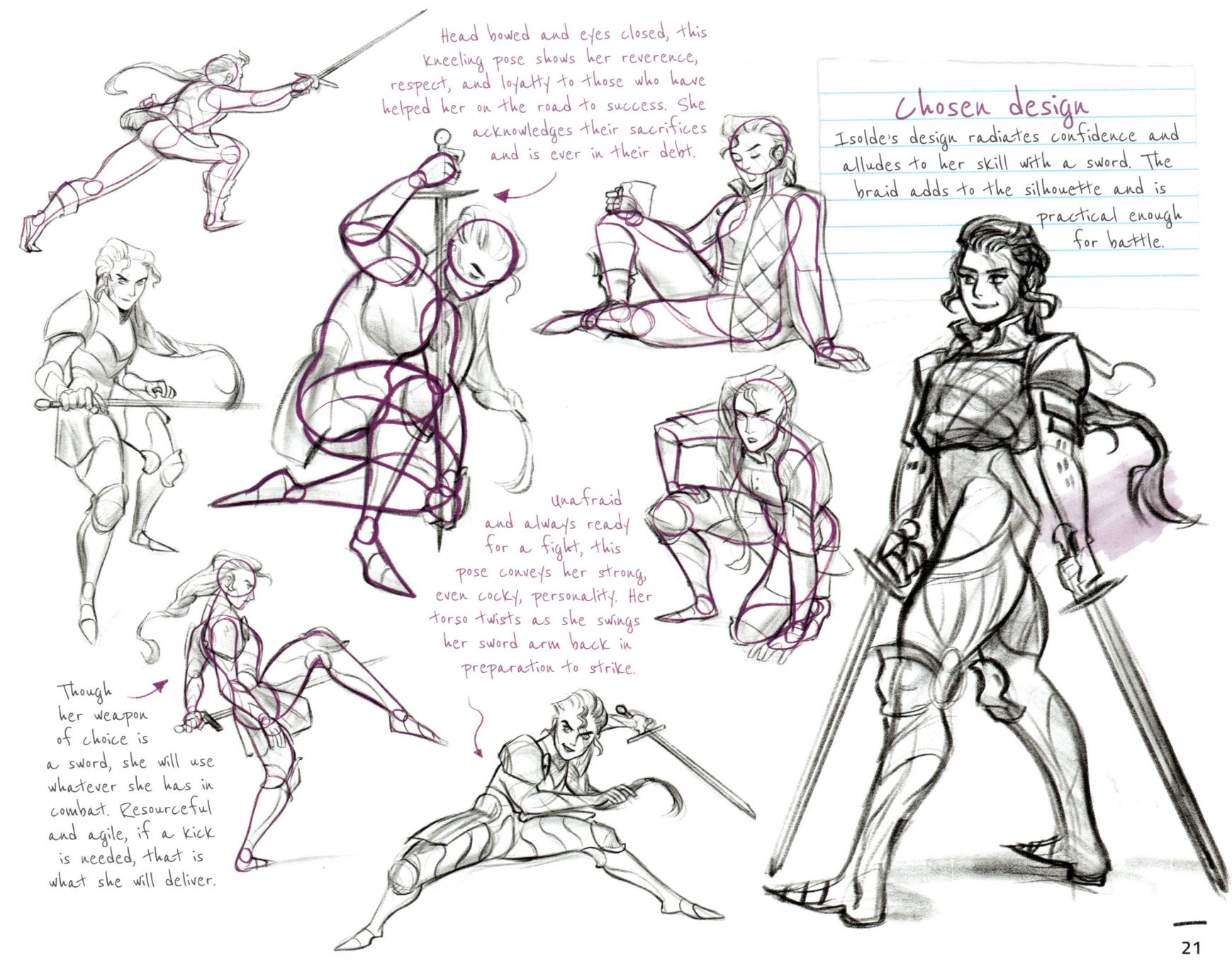

Head bowed and eyes closed, this kneeling pose shows her reverence, respect, and loyalty to those who have helped her on the road to success. She acknowledges their sacrifices and is ever in their debt.

Isolde's design radiates confidence and alludes to her skill with a sword. The braid adds to the silhouette and is practical enough for battle.

Unafraid and always ready for a fight, this pose conveys her strong, even cocky, personality. Her torso twists as she swings her sword arm back in preparation to strike.

Though her weapon of choice is a sword, she will use whatever she has in combat. Resourceful and agile, if a kick is needed, that is what she will deliver.

Fire superheroine

THIS SKETCHBOOK BELONGS TO: Ahmed Aldoori

Nara was chosen by higher beings to defend her corner of the galaxy. They gifted her with fiery powers, harnessing energy from the stars to allow her to shoot lethal red, blue, and black flames. She is of Moroccan descent, with long dark hair and an athletic build. Her superheroine outfit is recognizable by its fiery flame design. Willingly carrying her burden, she stands up for what she believes in, not what others want her to submit to.

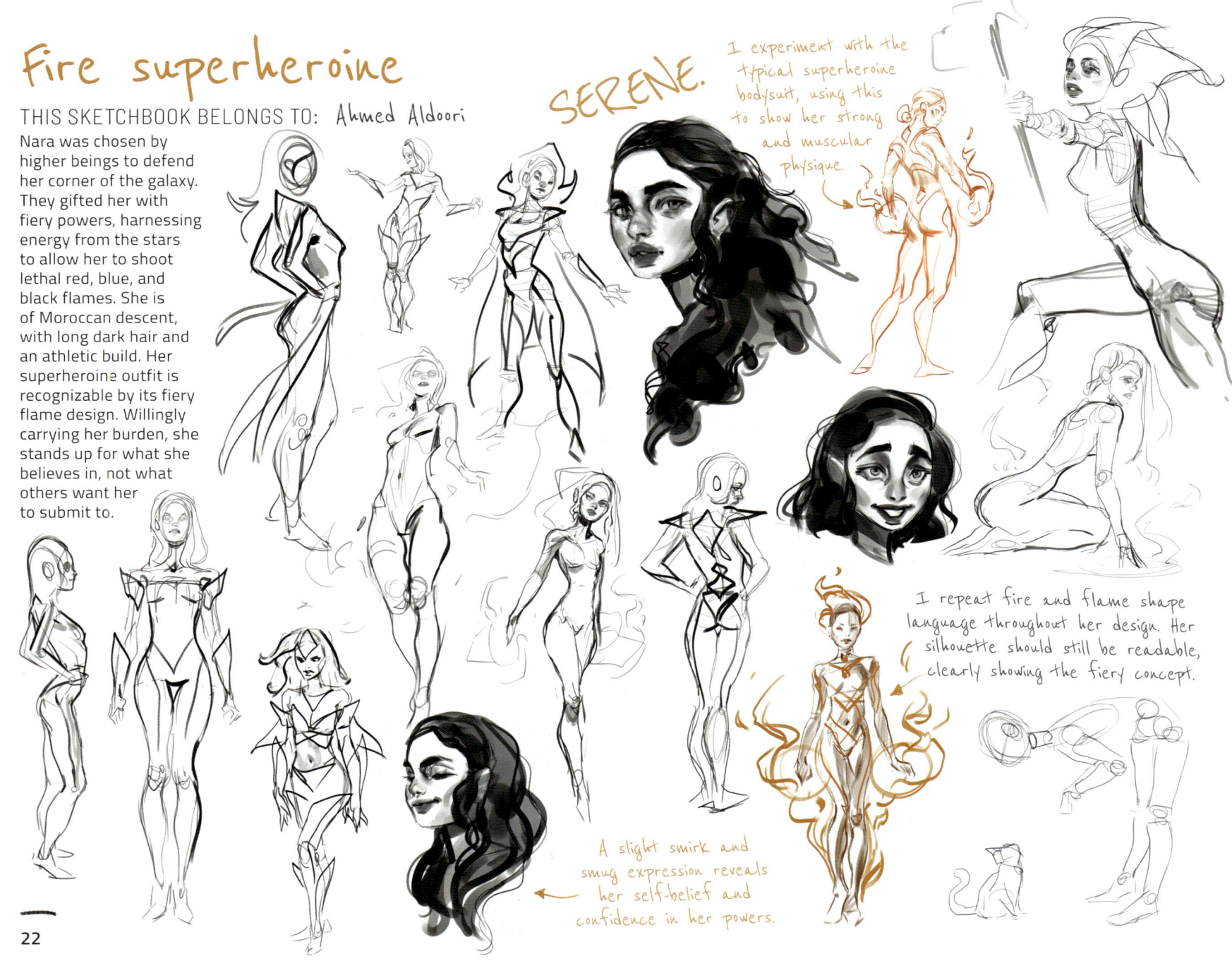

SERENE.

I experiment with the typical superheroine bodysuit, using this to show her strong and muscular physique.

I repeat fire and flame shape language throughout her design. Her silhouette should still be readable, clearly showing the fiery concept.

A slight smirk and smug expression reveals her self-belief and confidence in her powers.

22

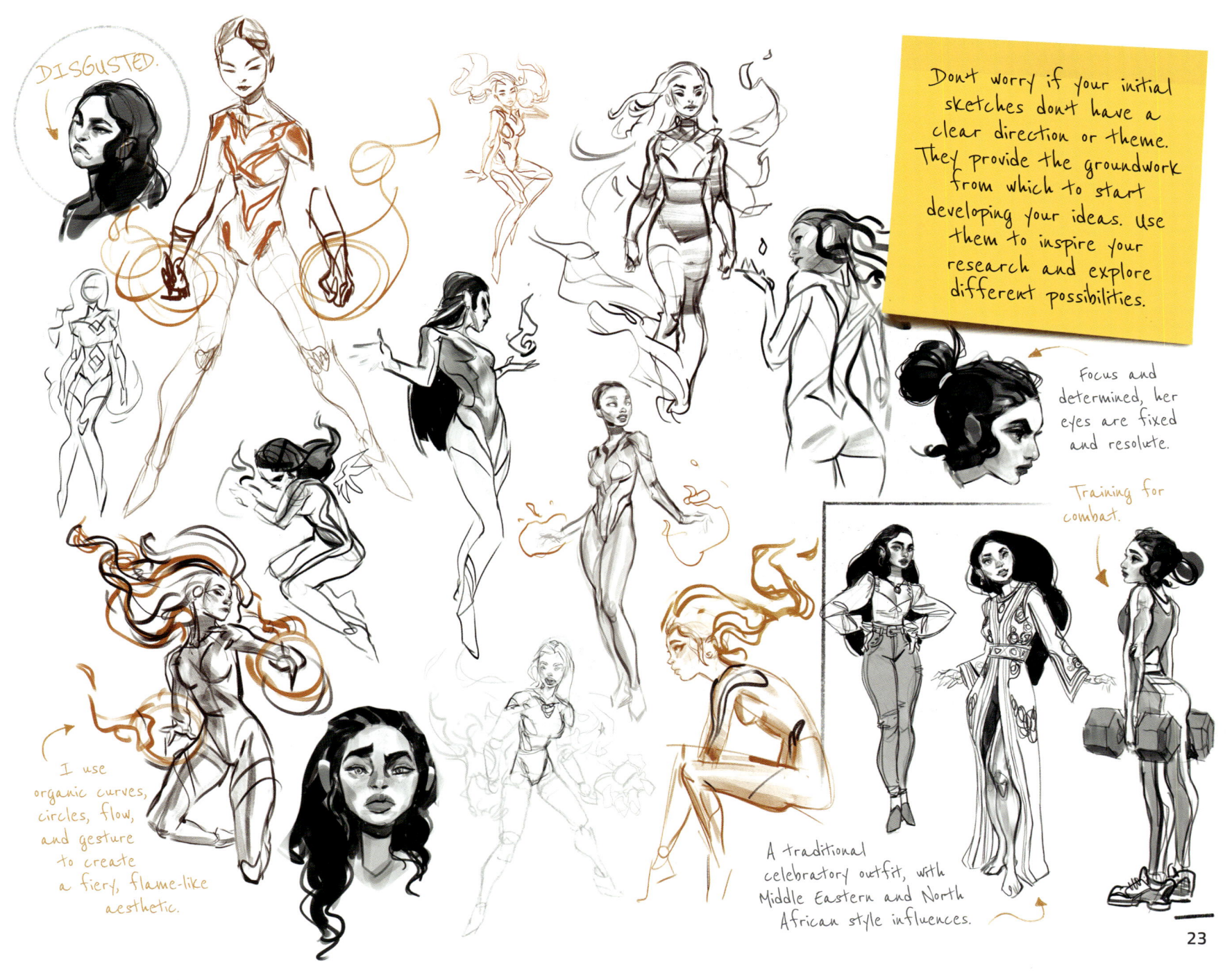

DISGUSTED.

Don't worry if your initial sketches don't have a clear direction or theme. They provide the groundwork from which to start developing your ideas. Use them to inspire your research and explore different possibilities.

Focus and determined, her eyes are fixed and resolute.

Training for combat.

I use organic curves, circles, flow, and gesture to create a fiery, flame-like aesthetic.

A traditional celebratory outfit, with Middle Eastern and North African style influences.

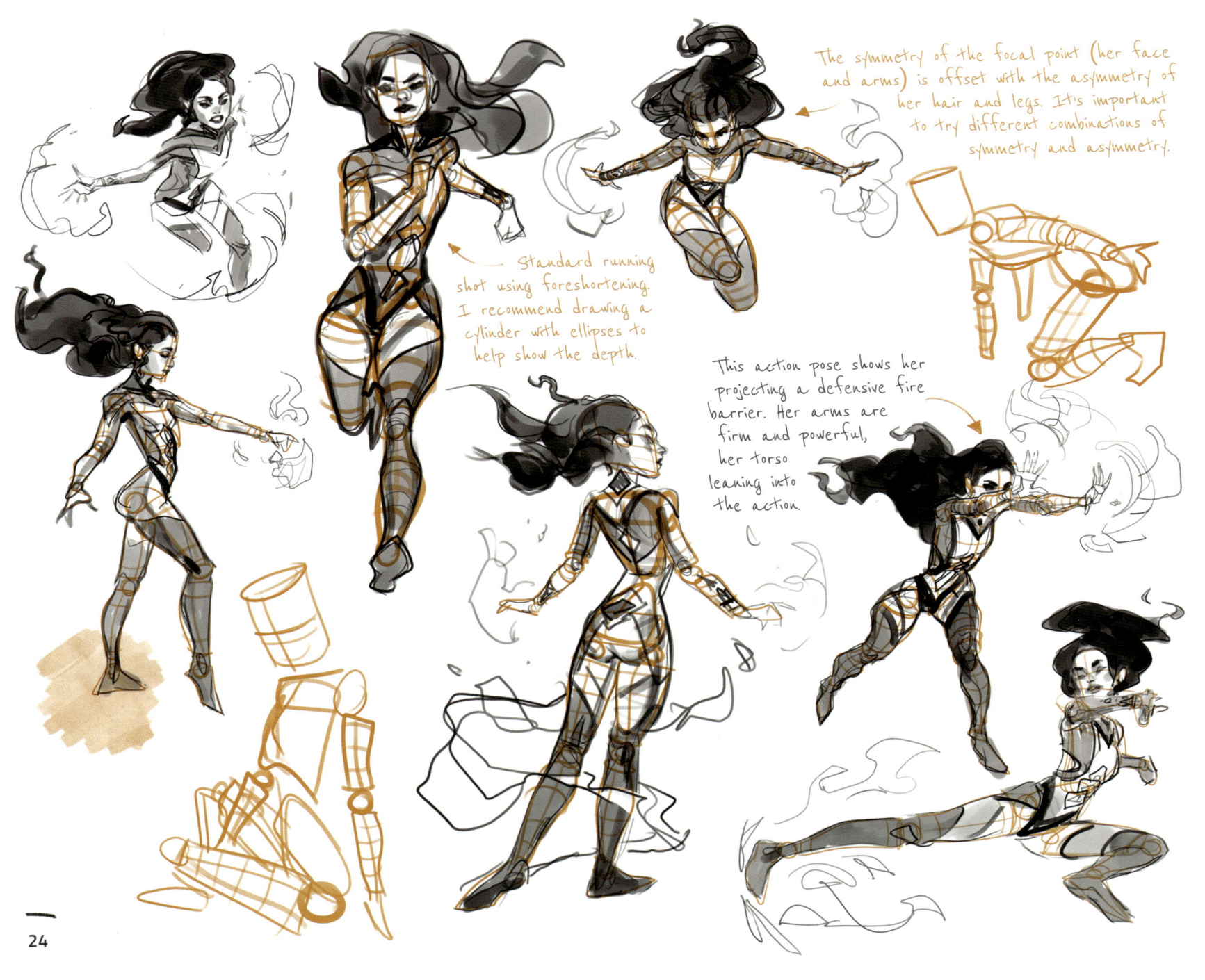

The symmetry of the focal point (her face and arms) is offset with the asymmetry of her hair and legs. It's important to try different combinations of symmetry and asymmetry.

Standard running shot using foreshortening. I recommend drawing a cylinder with ellipses to help show the depth.

This action pose shows her projecting a defensive fire barrier. Her arms are firm and powerful, her torso leaning into the action.

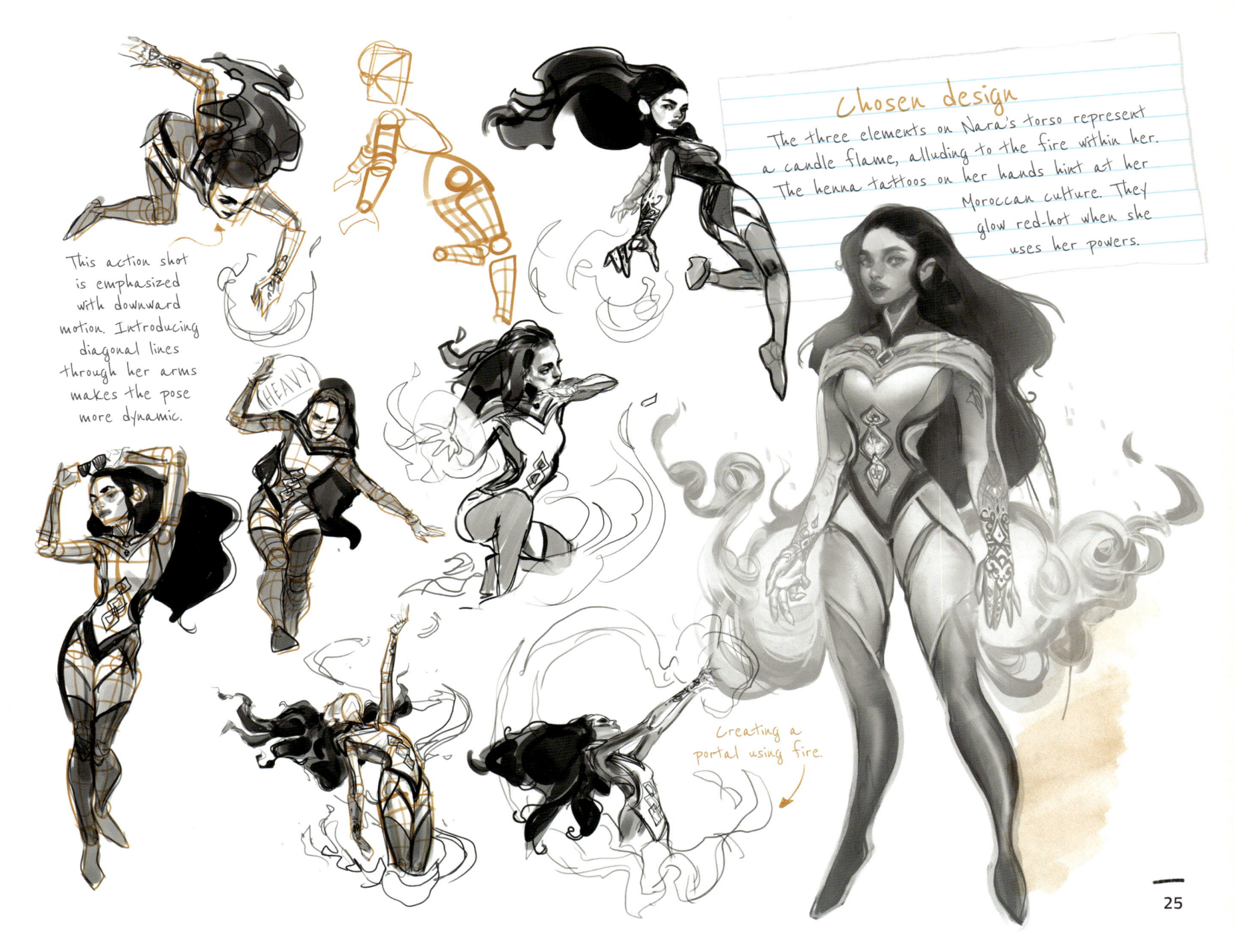

This action shot is emphasized with downward motion. Introducing diagonal lines through her arms makes the pose more dynamic.

HEAVY

The three elements on Nara's torso represent a candle flame, alluding to the fire within her. The henna tattoos on her hands hint at her Moroccan culture. They glow red-hot when she uses her powers.

Creating a portal using fire.

25

space medic

THIS SKETCHBOOK BELONGS TO: Dado "dadotronic" Almeida

The year is 2046 and the human race has begun space colonization. Forty-five-year-old Alice joins Expedition-Uno. She will be the field doctor for the colony, offering first aid and transporting critical patients back to the space station. While similar to earth, the chosen planet has a greater force of gravity, making it necessary for the crew to use exoskeleton robot devices to assist their work. The adventure begins when her robot device turns against her and she must overcome the weight of gravity and the tough decisions she will have to make to save humanity.

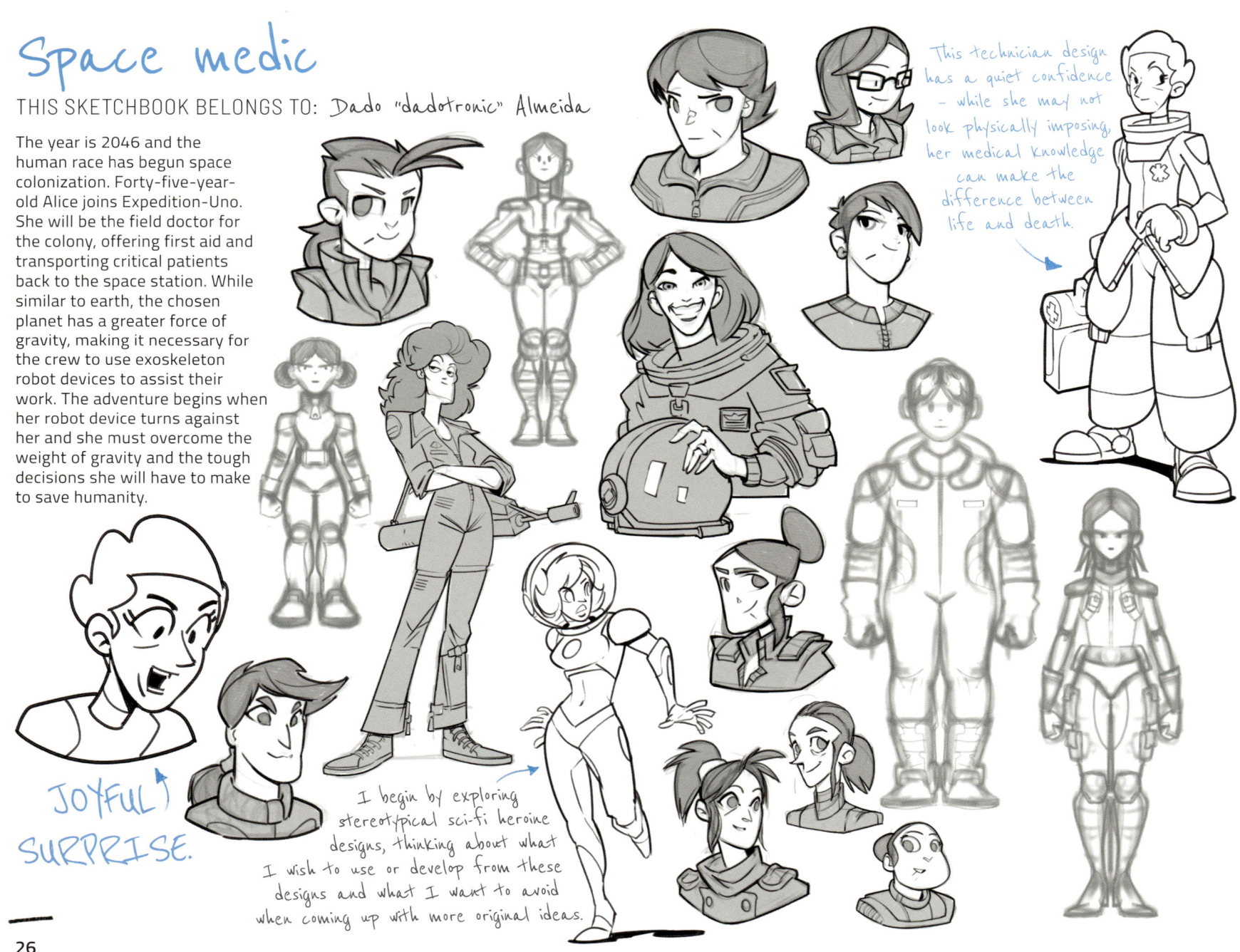

This technician design has a quiet confidence – while she may not look physically imposing, her medical knowledge can make the difference between life and death.

JOYFUL SURPRISE.

I begin by exploring stereotypical sci-fi heroine designs, thinking about what I wish to use or develop from these designs and what I want to avoid when coming up with more original ideas.

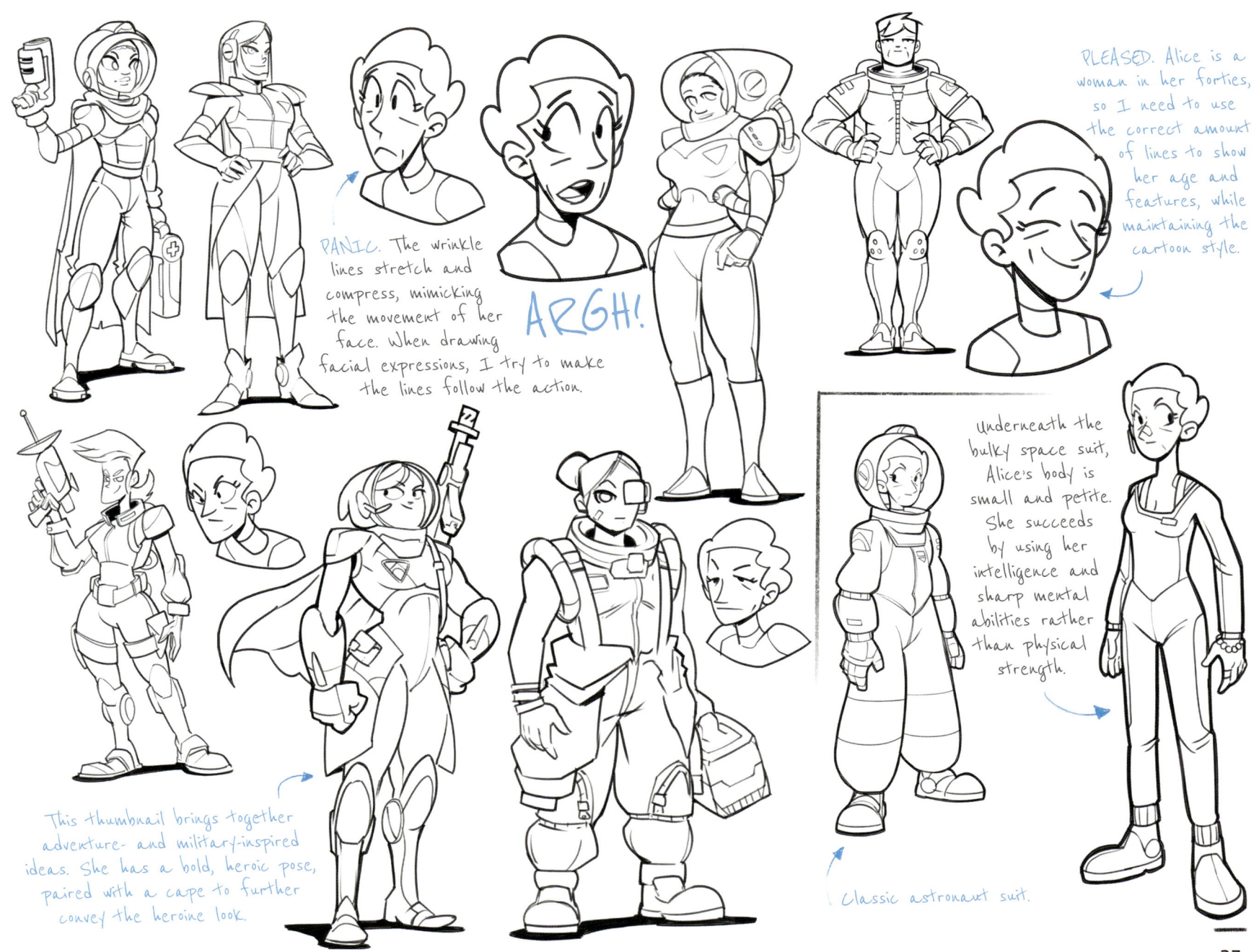

PANIC. The wrinkle lines stretch and compress, mimicking the movement of her face. When drawing facial expressions, I try to make the lines follow the action.

ARGH!

PLEASED. Alice is a woman in her forties, so I need to use the correct amount of lines to show her age and features, while maintaining the cartoon style.

This thumbnail brings together adventure- and military-inspired ideas. She has a bold, heroic pose, paired with a cape to further convey the heroine look.

underneath the bulky space suit, Alice's body is small and petite. She succeeds by using her intelligence and sharp mental abilities rather than physical strength.

Classic astronaut suit.

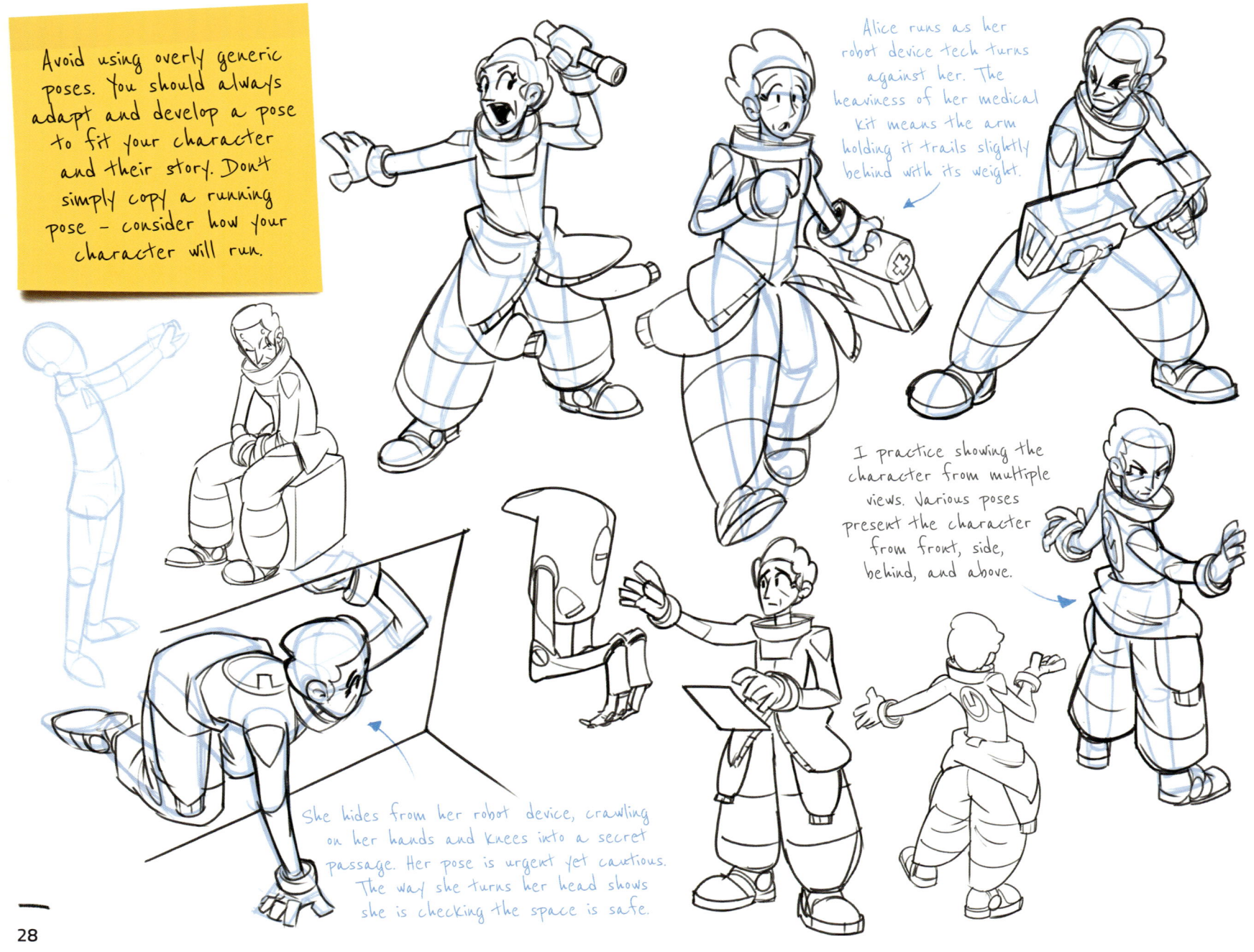

Avoid using overly generic poses. You should always adapt and develop a pose to fit your character and their story. Don't simply copy a running pose - consider how your character will run.

Alice runs as her robot device tech turns against her. The heaviness of her medical kit means the arm holding it trails slightly behind with its weight.

I practice showing the character from multiple views. Various poses present the character from front, side, behind, and above.

She hides from her robot device, crawling on her hands and knees into a secret passage. Her pose is urgent yet cautious. The way she turns her head shows she is checking the space is safe.

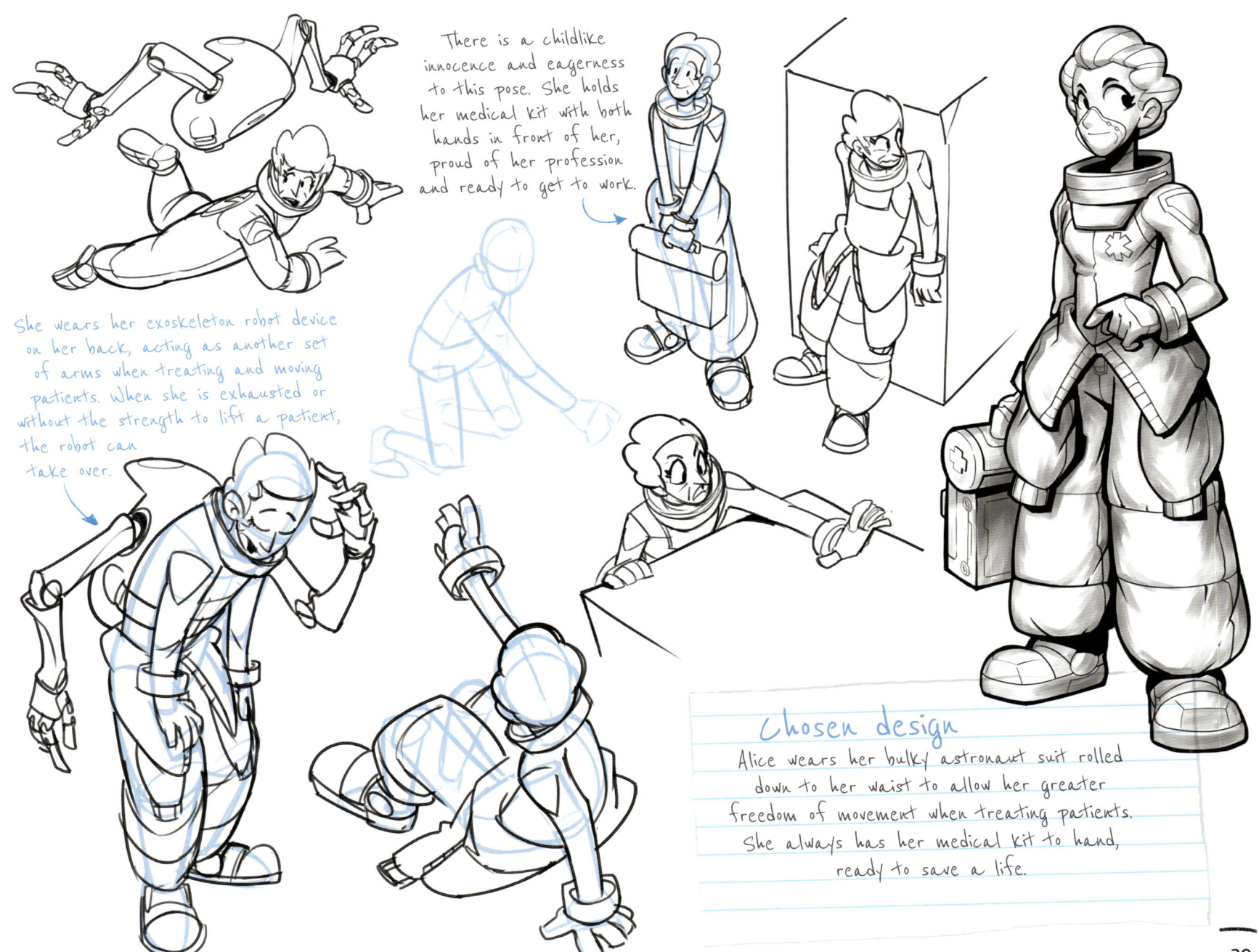

There is a childlike innocence and eagerness to this pose. She holds her medical kit with both hands in front of her, proud of her profession and ready to get to work.

She wears her exoskeleton robot device on her back, acting as another set of arms when treating and moving patients. When she is exhausted or without the strength to lift a patient, the robot can take over.

Chosen design

Alice wears her bulky astronaut suit rolled down to her waist to allow her greater freedom of movement when treating patients. She always has her medical kit to hand, ready to save a life.

Suffragette

THIS SKETCHBOOK BELONGS TO: Olga "Asu Rocks" Andriyenko

Athena is a suffragette from the early 1900s who ends up in the 21st century. She sees that women's fight for equal rights is not over and there's still work to be done. Brave, intelligent, and optimistic, she organizes protests as well as working full time. She wears early 20th century fashion and favors practical shoes (all the better for marching), clothing with pockets (to carry her pamphlets), and feminine accessories.

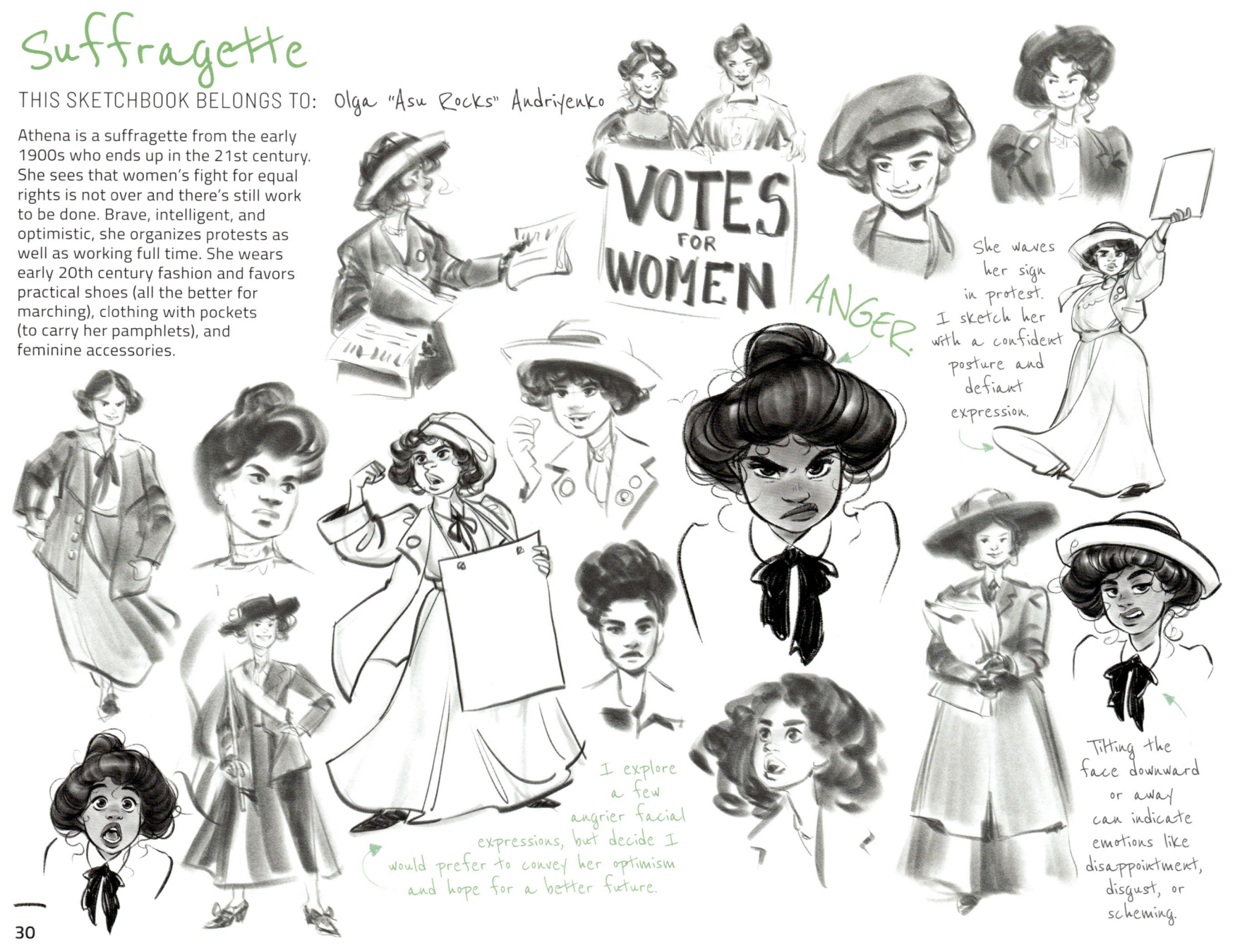

VOTES FOR WOMEN

ANGER.

She waves her sign in protest. I sketch her with a confident posture and defiant expression.

I explore a few angrier facial expressions, but decide I would prefer to convey her optimism and hope for a better future.

Tilting the face downward or away can indicate emotions like disappointment, disgust, or scheming.

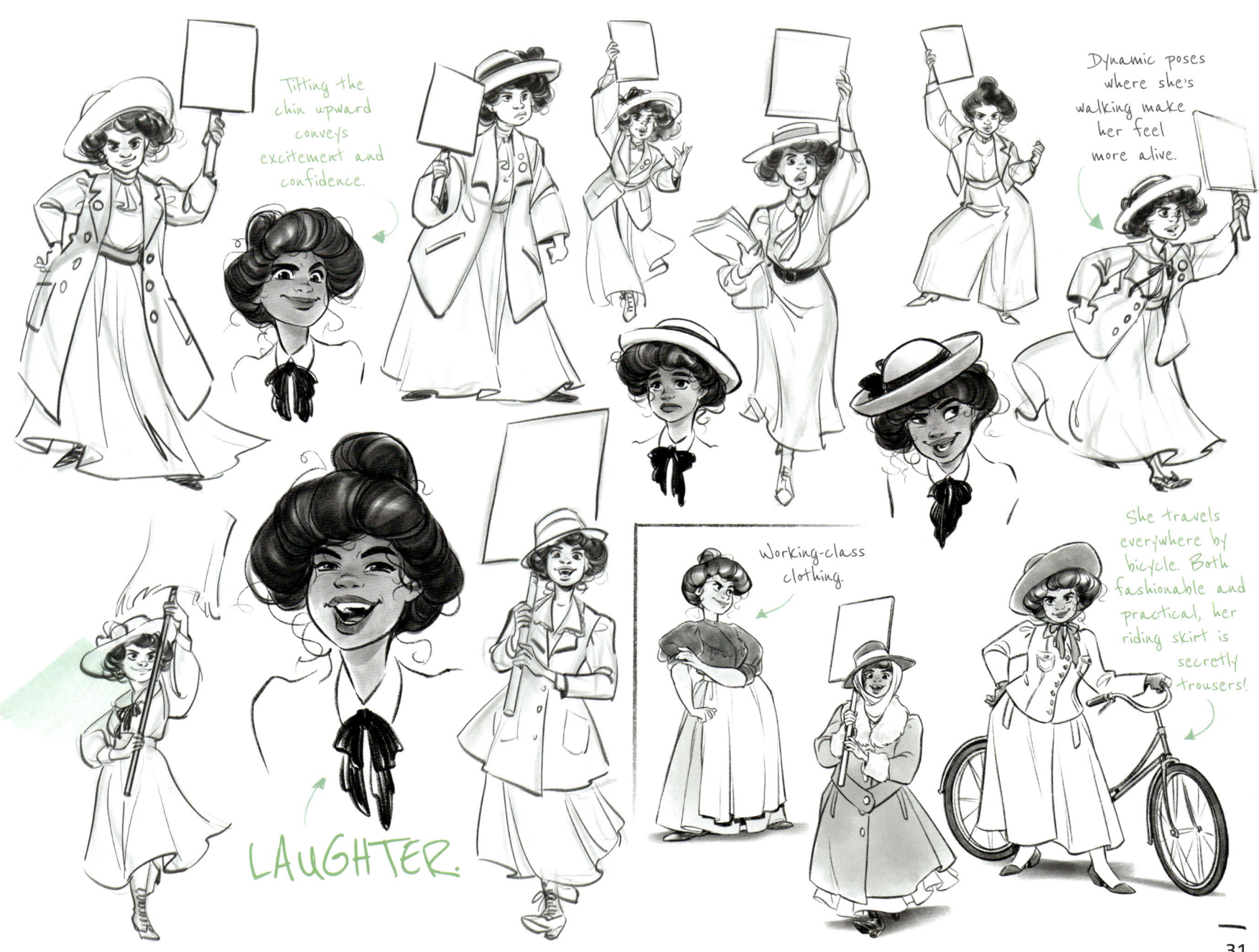

Tilting the chin upward conveys excitement and confidence.

Dynamic poses where she's walking make her feel more alive.

LAUGHTER.

She travels everywhere by bicycle. Both fashionable and practical, her riding skirt is secretly trousers!

Working-class clothing.

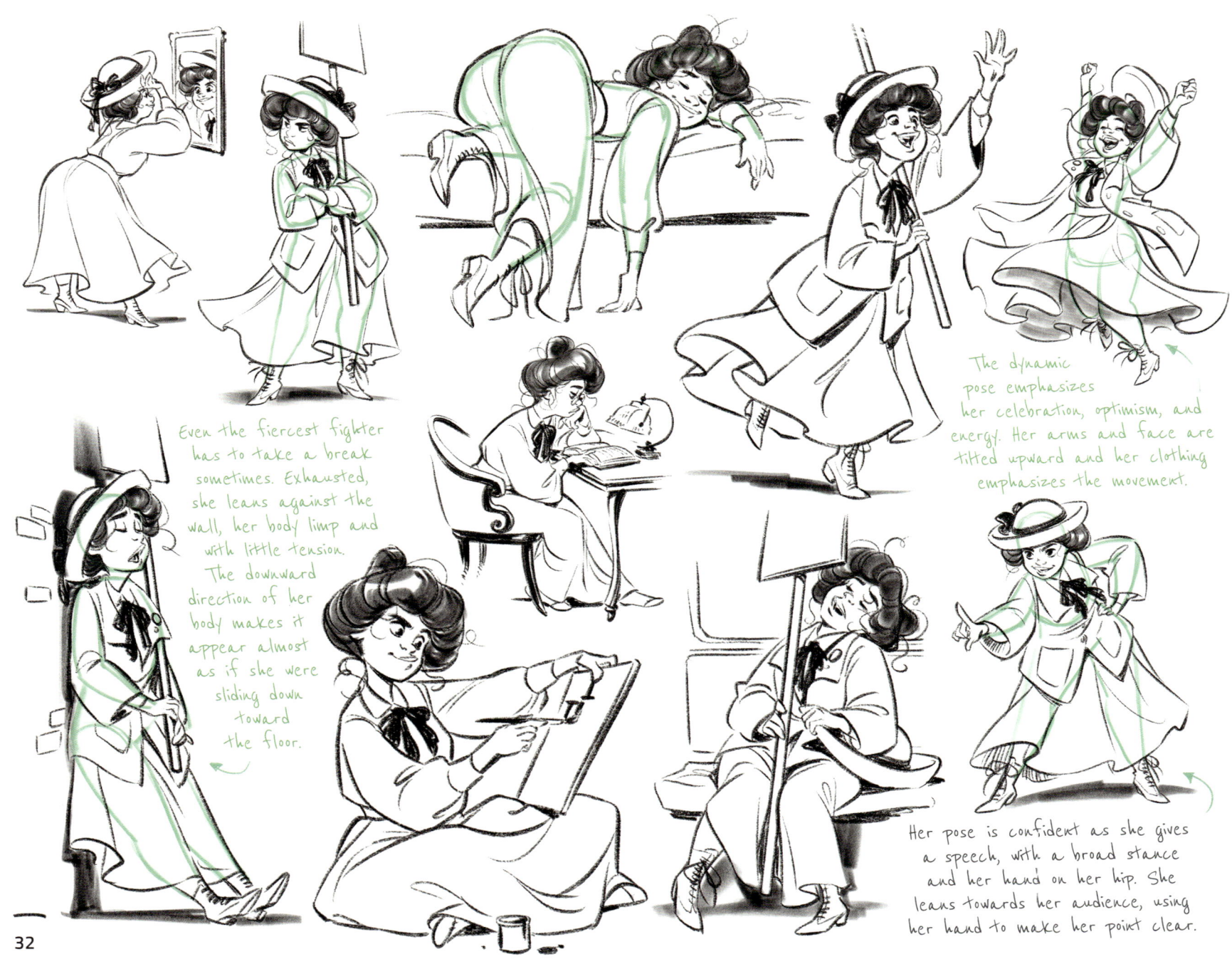

Even the fiercest fighter has to take a break sometimes. Exhausted, she leans against the wall, her body limp and with little tension. The downward direction of her body makes it appear almost as if she were sliding down toward the floor.

The dynamic pose emphasizes her celebration, optimism, and energy. Her arms and face are tilted upward and her clothing emphasizes the movement.

Her pose is confident as she gives a speech, with a broad stance and her hand on her hip. She leans towards her audience, using her hand to make her point clear.

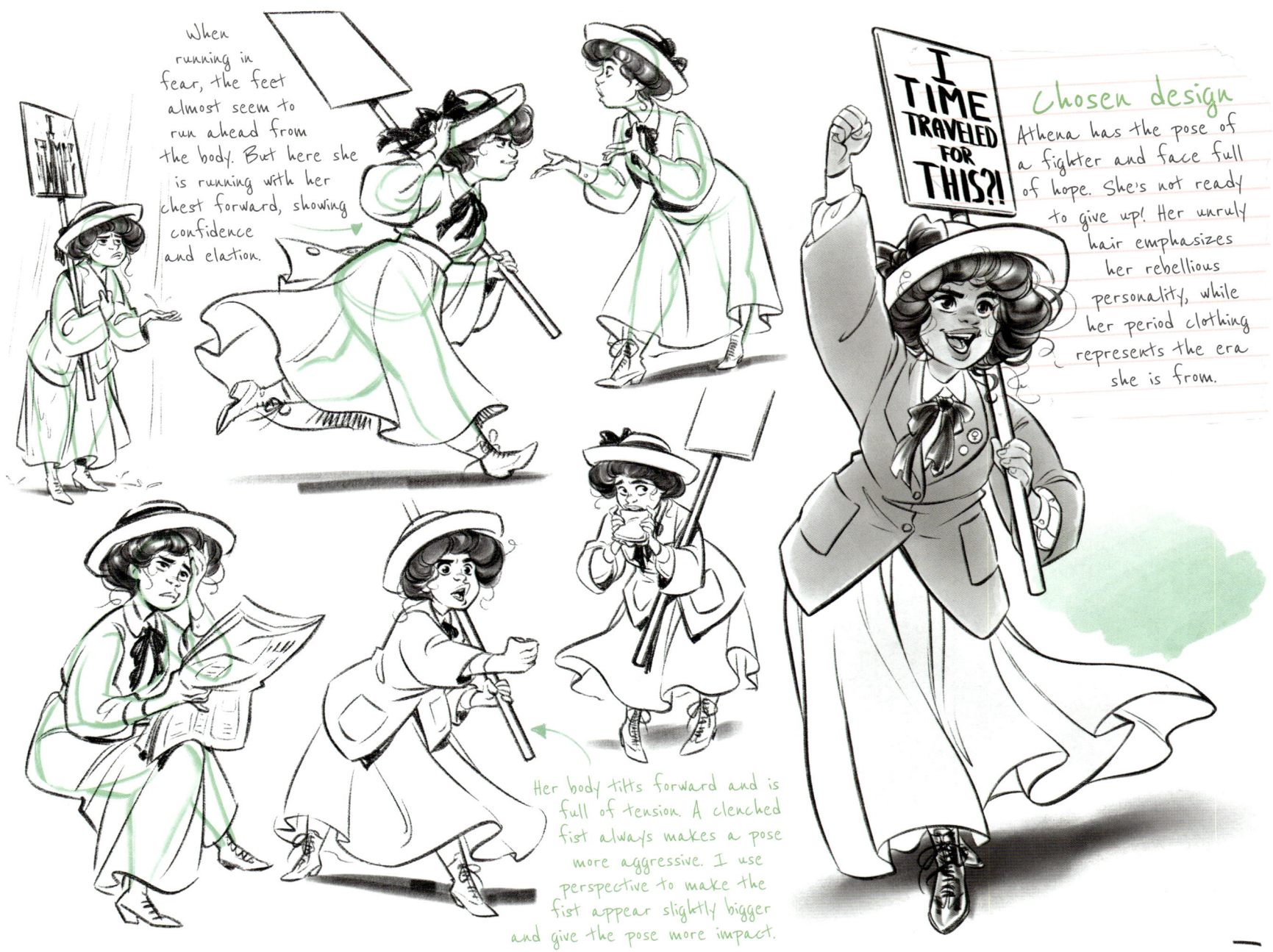

When running in fear, the feet almost seem to run ahead from the body. But here she is running with her chest forward, showing confidence and elation.

Chosen design

Athena has the pose of a fighter and face full of hope. She's not ready to give up! Her unruly hair emphasizes her rebellious personality, while her period clothing represents the era she is from.

I TIME TRAVELED FOR THIS?!

Her body tilts forward and is full of tension. A clenched fist always makes a pose more aggressive. I use perspective to make the fist appear slightly bigger and give the pose more impact.

Weather superheroine

THIS SKETCHBOOK BELONGS TO: Brett Bean

Black Ice is a superheroine with the ability to manipulate snow and ice. She starts to crystallize when driven to extreme anger, making her stronger in skill but weaker in body, with the risk of shattering. An ice-hockey player with a strong physique, she's able to handle most hits. Yet while her powers are icy, her heart is warm. Canadian and in her mid-twenties, she is confident, secure, and heroic.

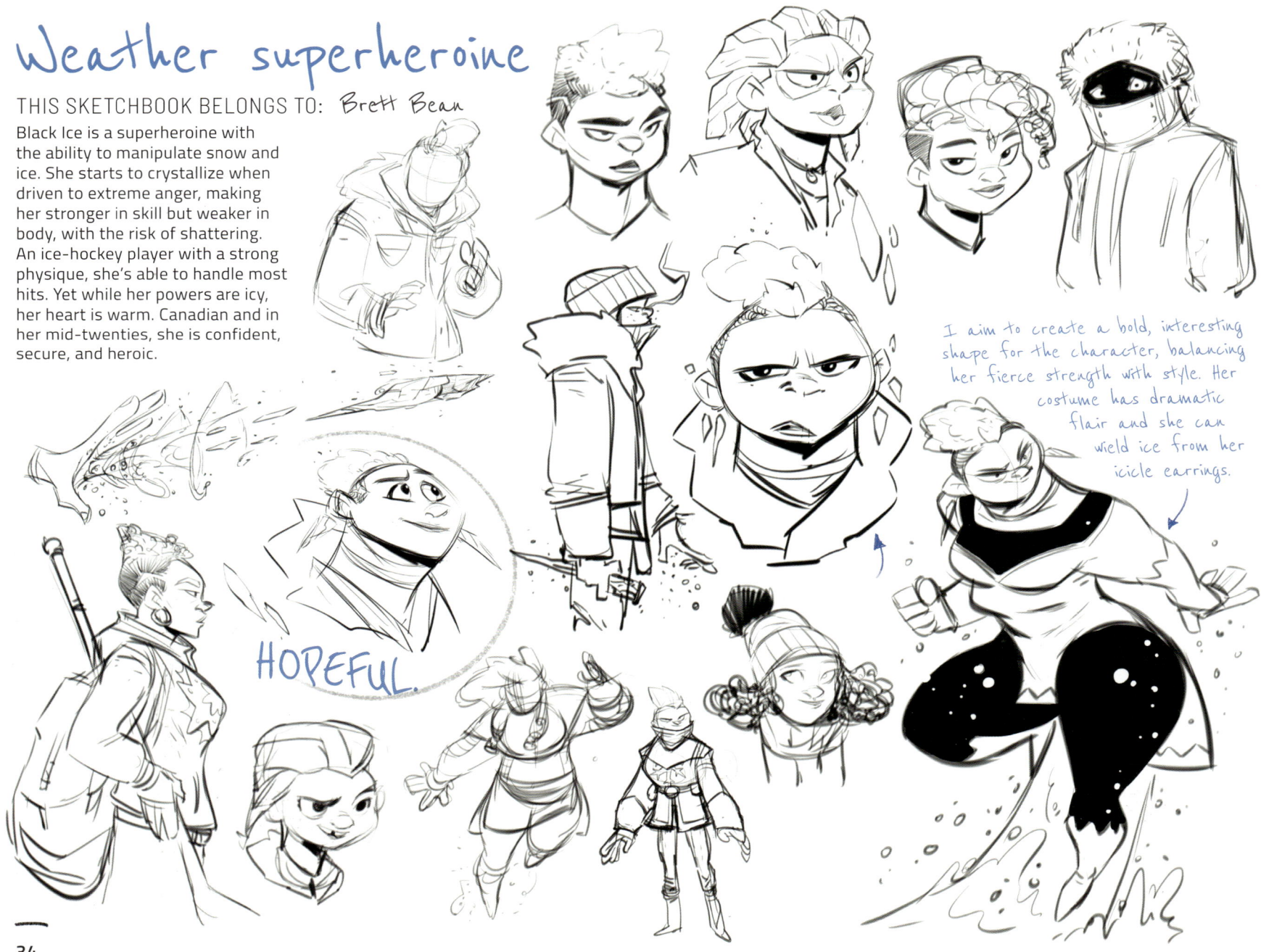

I aim to create a bold, interesting shape for the character, balancing her fierce strength with style. Her costume has dramatic flair and she can wield ice from her icicle earrings.

HOPEFUL.

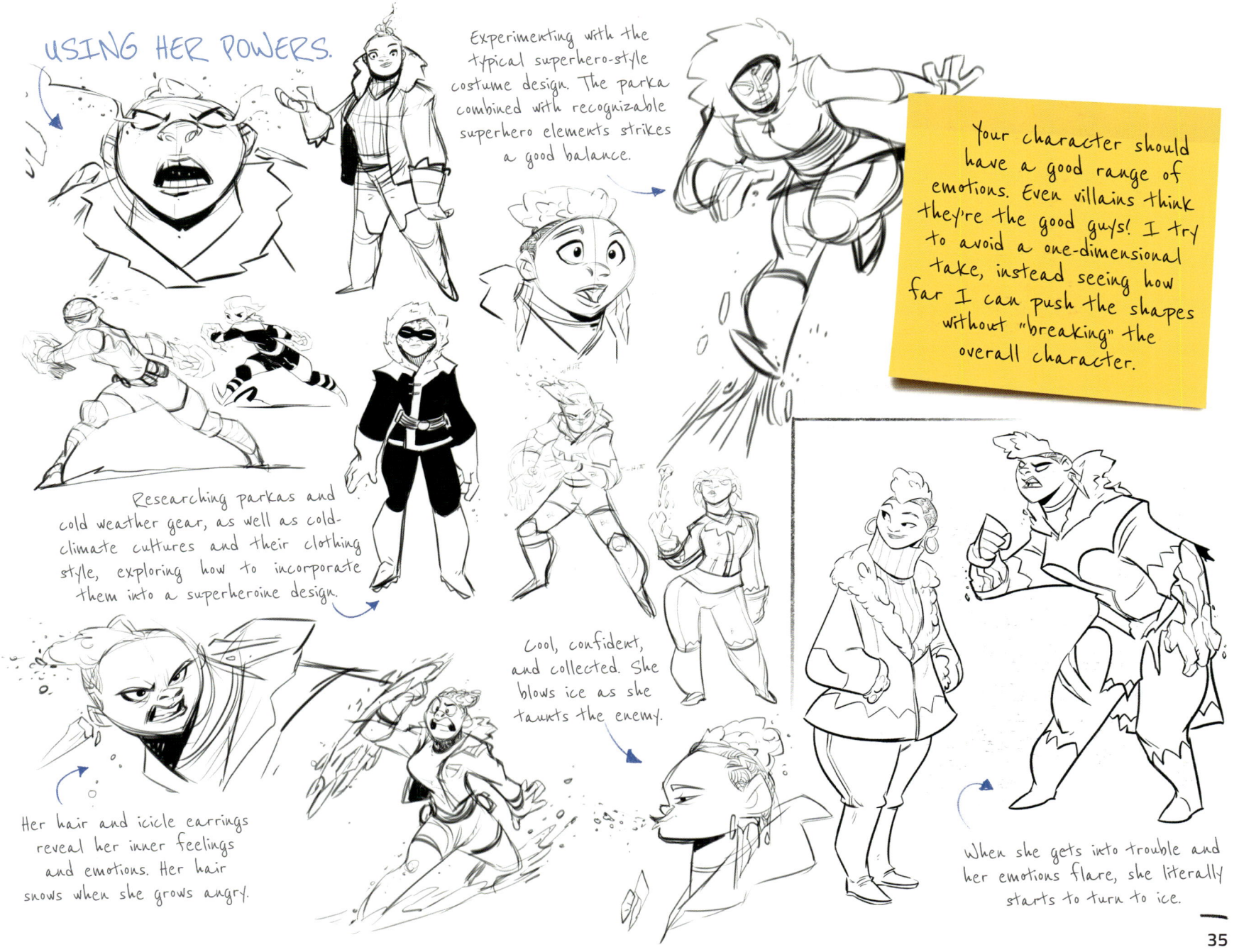

USING HER POWERS.

Experimenting with the typical superhero-style costume design. The parka combined with recognizable superhero elements strikes a good balance.

Your character should have a good range of emotions. Even villains think they're the good guys! I try to avoid a one-dimensional take, instead seeing how far I can push the shapes without "breaking" the overall character.

Researching parkas and cold weather gear, as well as cold-climate cultures and their clothing style, exploring how to incorporate them into a superheroine design.

Her hair and icicle earrings reveal her inner feelings and emotions. Her hair snows when she grows angry.

Cool, confident, and collected. She blows ice as she taunts the enemy.

When she gets into trouble and her emotions flare, she literally starts to turn to ice.

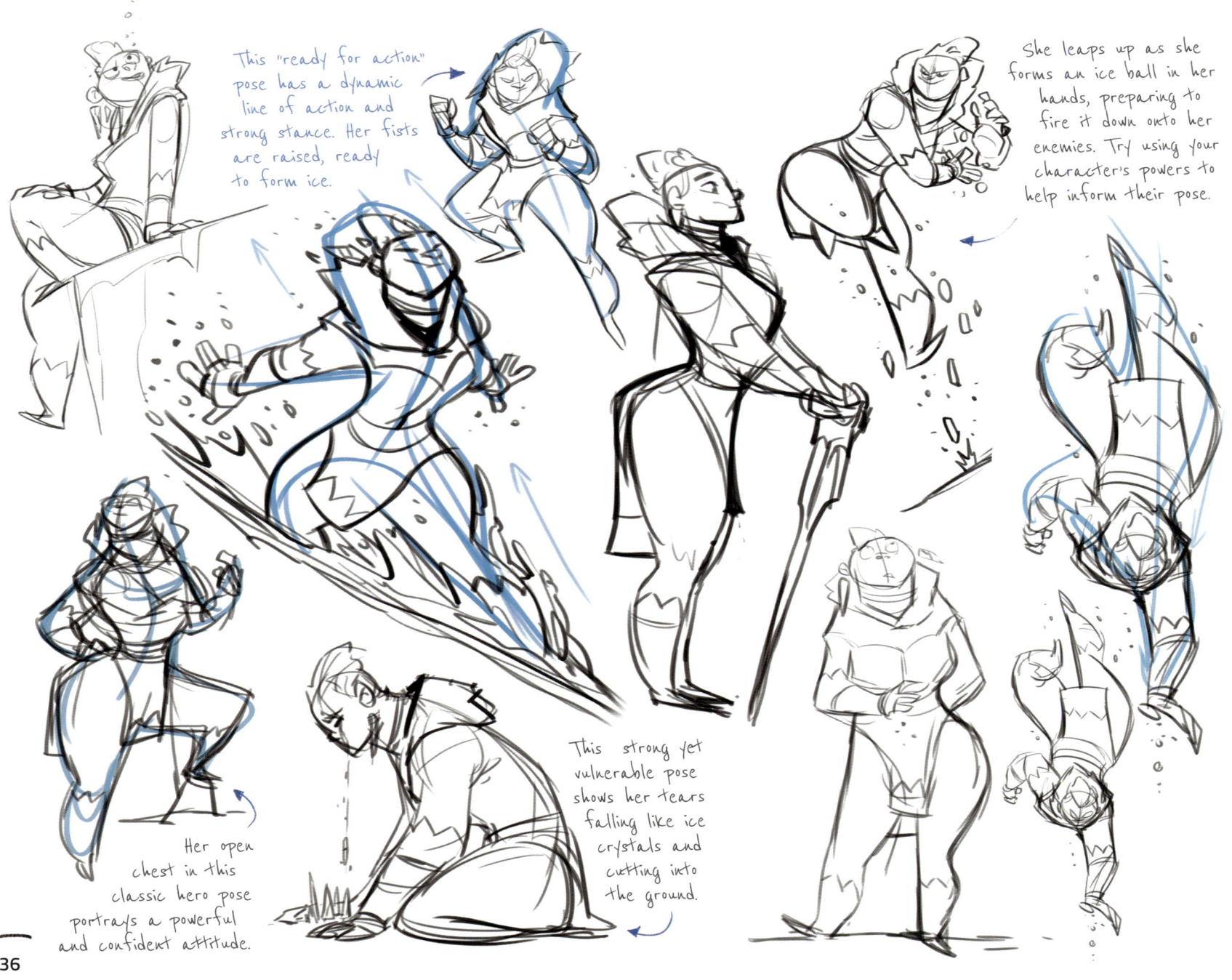

This "ready for action" pose has a dynamic line of action and strong stance. Her fists are raised, ready to form ice.

She leaps up as she forms an ice ball in her hands, preparing to fire it down onto her enemies. Try using your character's powers to help inform their pose.

Her open chest in this classic hero pose portrays a powerful and confident attitude.

This strong yet vulnerable pose shows her tears falling like ice crystals and cutting into the ground.

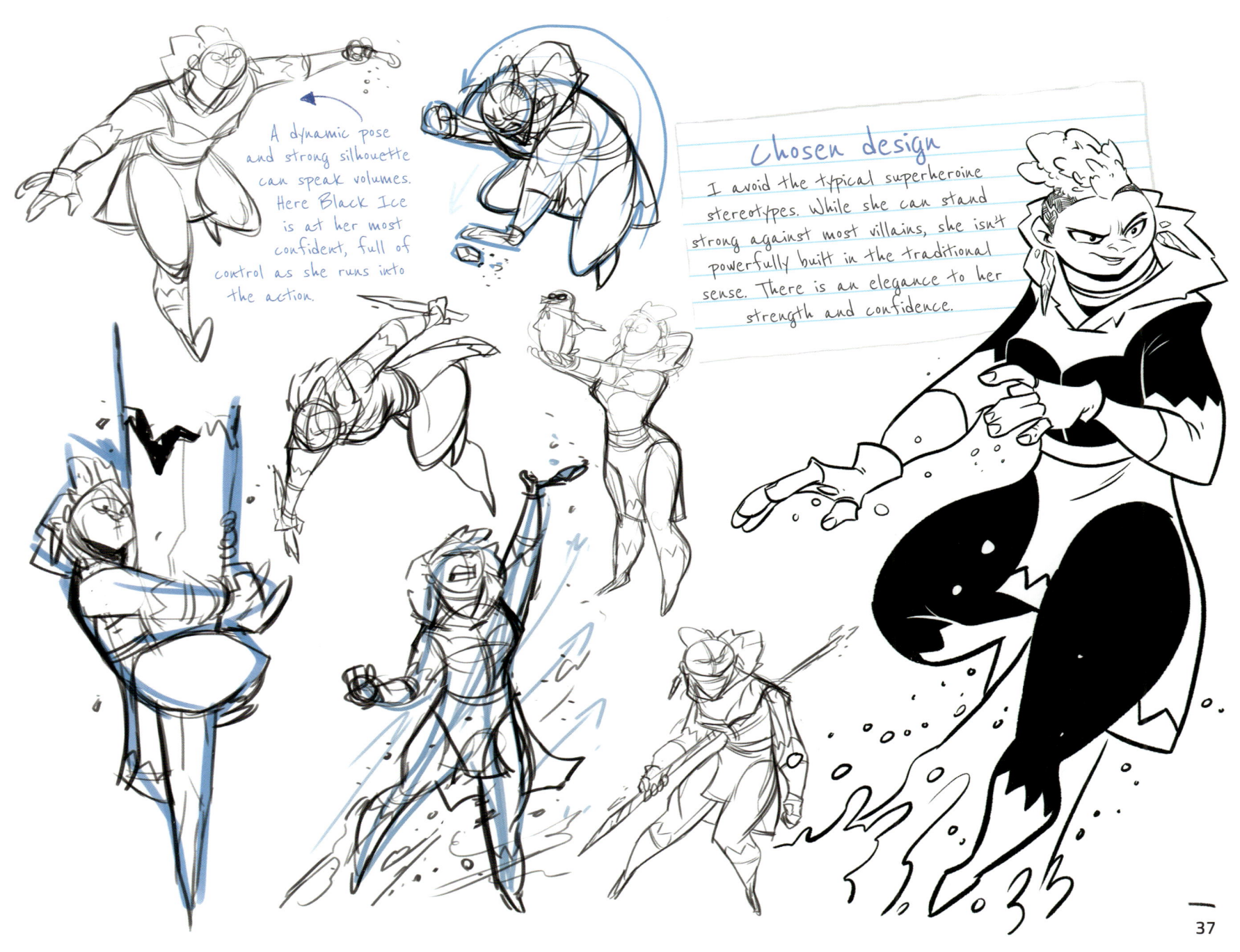

A dynamic pose and strong silhouette can speak volumes. Here Black Ice is at her most confident, full of control as she runs into the action.

Chosen design

I avoid the typical superheroine stereotypes. While she can stand strong against most villains, she isn't powerfully built in the traditional sense. There is an elegance to her strength and confidence.

Inventor

THIS SKETCHBOOK BELONGS TO: Allison Berg

This steampunk heroine is a quirky inventor who's passionate about learning, creating, and building. Though Ada may be young, her curious mind is bursting with ideas. With an odd sense of style and a somewhat eccentric nature, she can always be found with her trusty wrench and pockets full of tools. She lives in a bustling city during a time of technological revolution, explaining her drive to create and invent. She's not afraid to speak her mind and can often get swept up in her work.

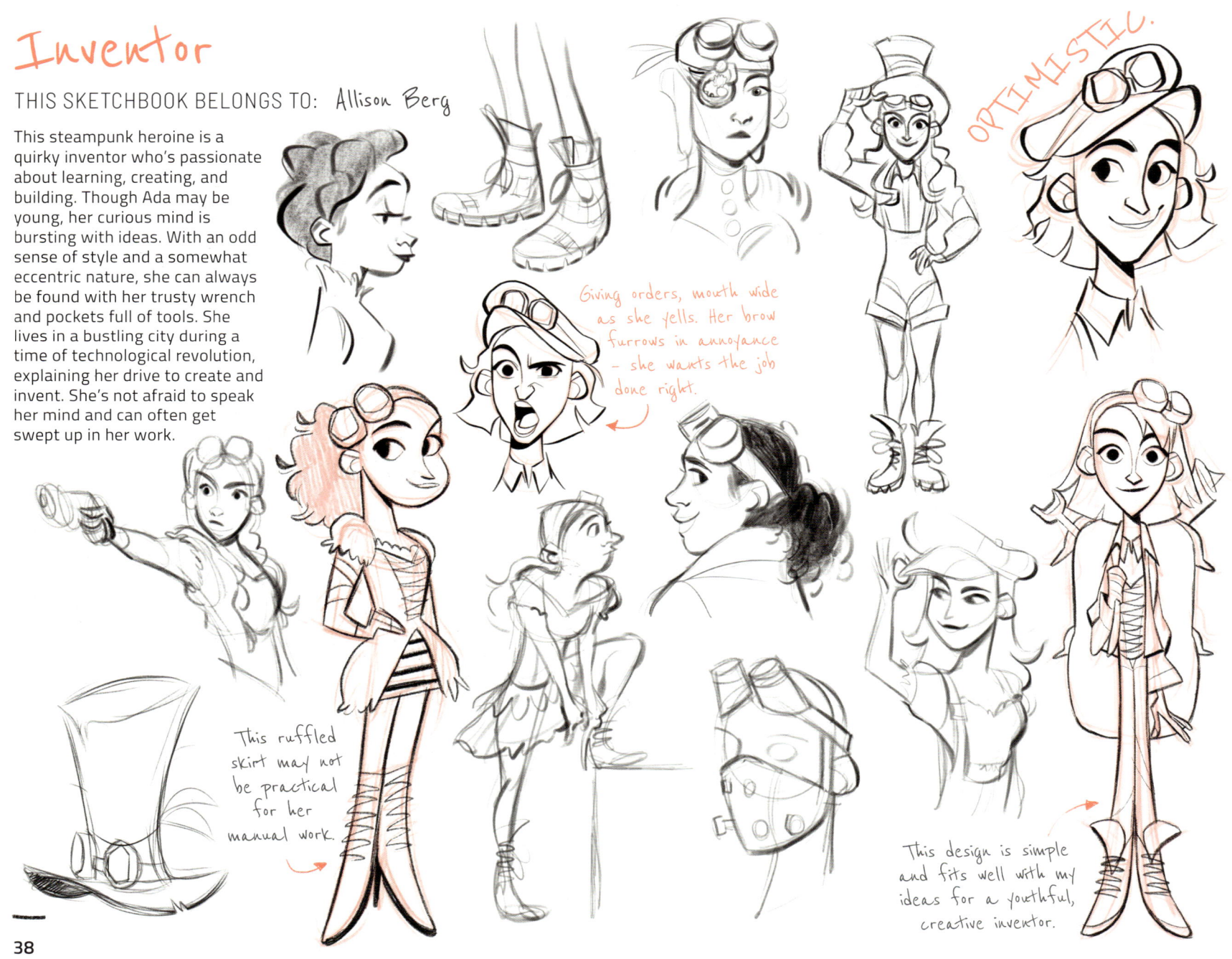

OPTIMISTIC.

Giving orders, mouth wide as she yells. Her brow furrows in annoyance — she wants the job done right.

This ruffled skirt may not be practical for her manual work.

This design is simple and fits well with my ideas for a youthful, creative inventor.

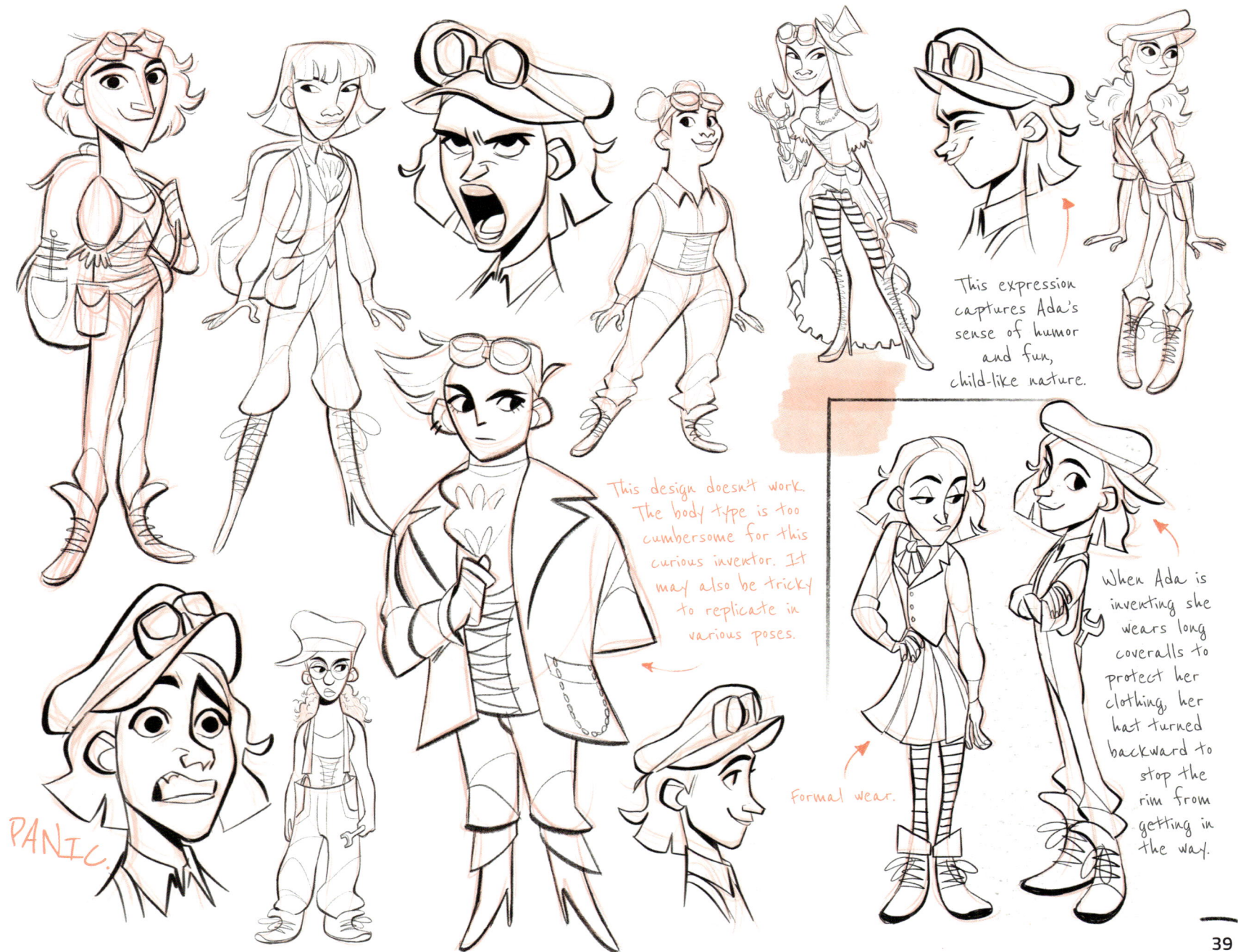

This expression captures Ada's sense of humor and fun, child-like nature.

This design doesn't work. The body type is too cumbersome for this curious inventor. It may also be tricky to replicate in various poses.

PANIC.

Formal wear.

When Ada is inventing she wears long coveralls to protect her clothing, her hat turned backward to stop the rim from getting in the way.

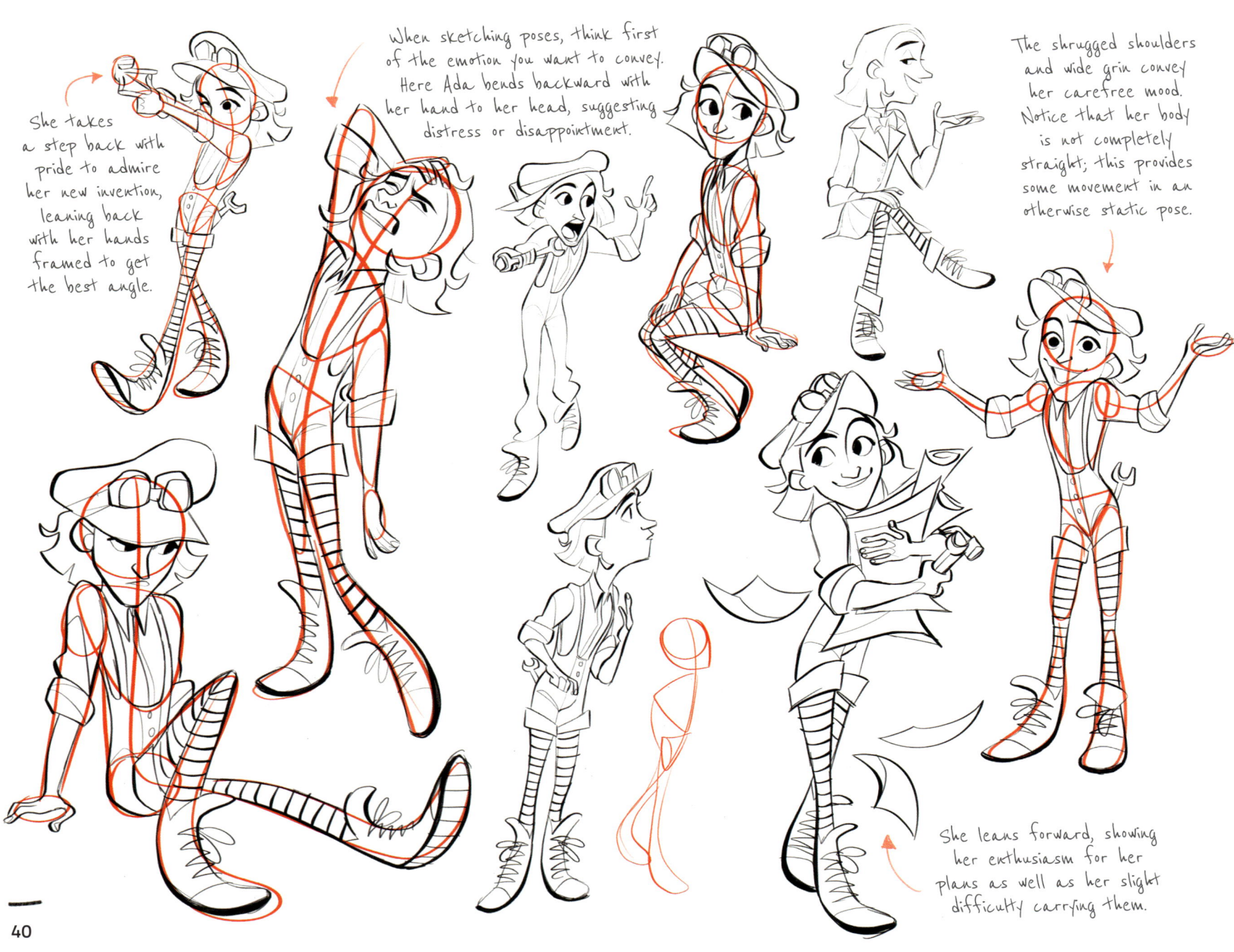

She takes a step back with pride to admire her new invention, leaning back with her hands framed to get the best angle.

When sketching poses, think first of the emotion you want to convey. Here Ada bends backward with her hand to her head, suggesting distress or disappointment.

The shrugged shoulders and wide grin convey her carefree mood. Notice that her body is not completely straight; this provides some movement in an otherwise static pose.

She leans forward, showing her enthusiasm for her plans as well as her slight difficulty carrying them.

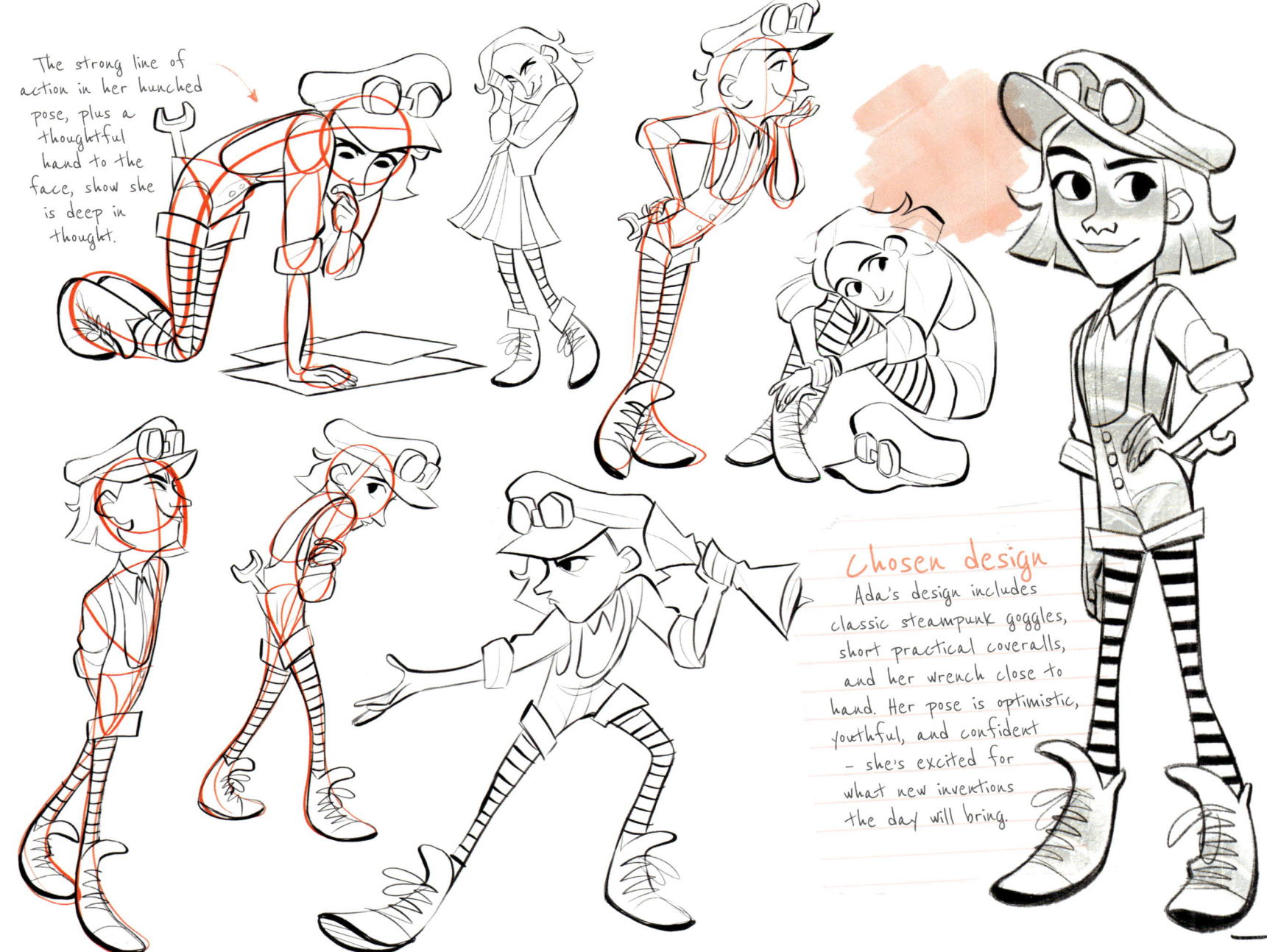

The strong line of action in her hunched pose, plus a thoughtful hand to the face, show she is deep in thought.

chosen design

Ada's design includes classic steampunk goggles, short practical coveralls, and her wrench close to hand. Her pose is optimistic, youthful, and confident – she's excited for what new inventions the day will bring.

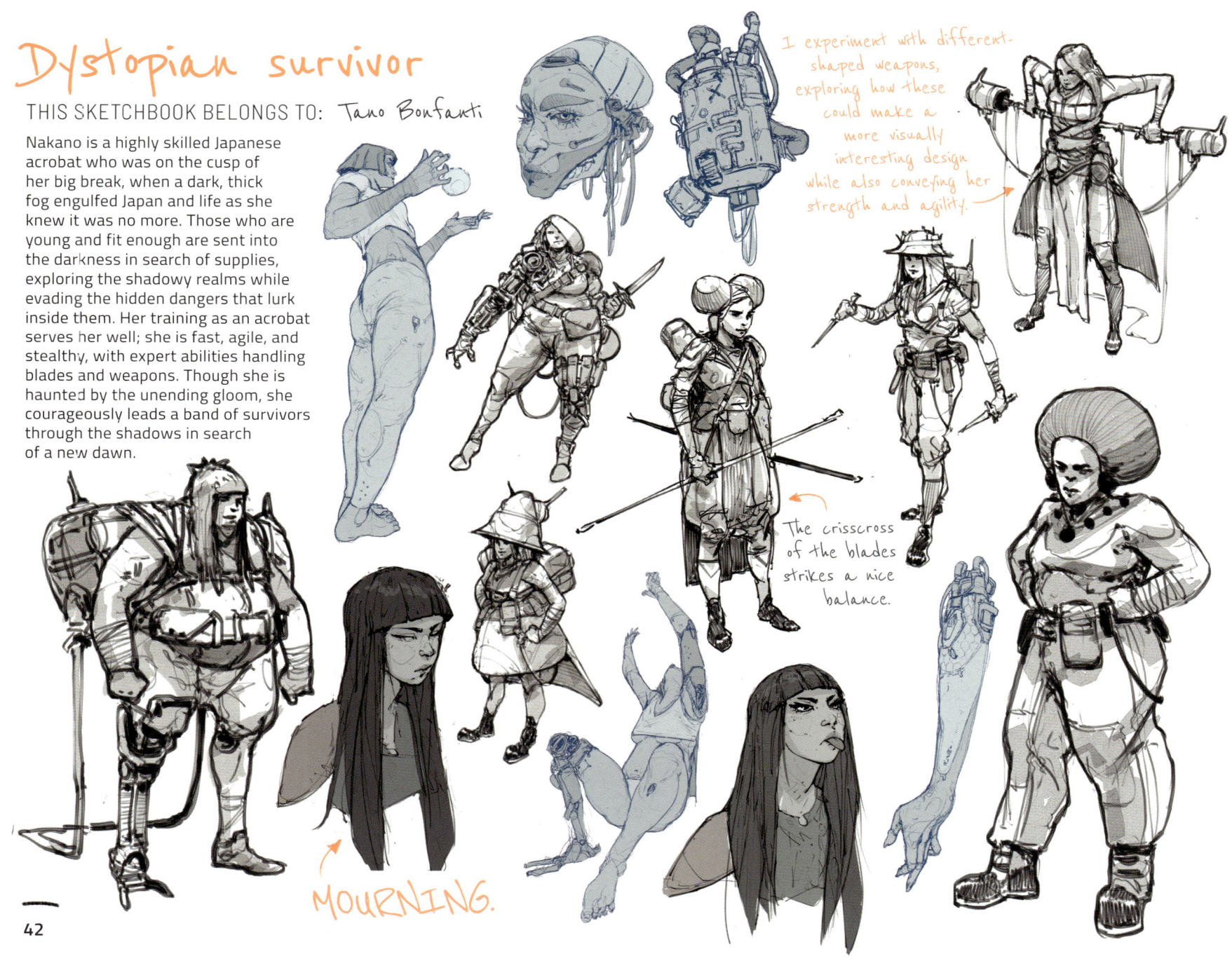

Dystopian survivor

THIS SKETCHBOOK BELONGS TO: Tano Bonfanti

Nakano is a highly skilled Japanese acrobat who was on the cusp of her big break, when a dark, thick fog engulfed Japan and life as she knew it was no more. Those who are young and fit enough are sent into the darkness in search of supplies, exploring the shadowy realms while evading the hidden dangers that lurk inside them. Her training as an acrobat serves her well; she is fast, agile, and stealthy, with expert abilities handling blades and weapons. Though she is haunted by the unending gloom, she courageously leads a band of survivors through the shadows in search of a new dawn.

I experiment with different-shaped weapons, exploring how these could make a more visually interesting design while also conveying her strength and agility.

The crisscross of the blades strikes a nice balance.

MOURNING.

42

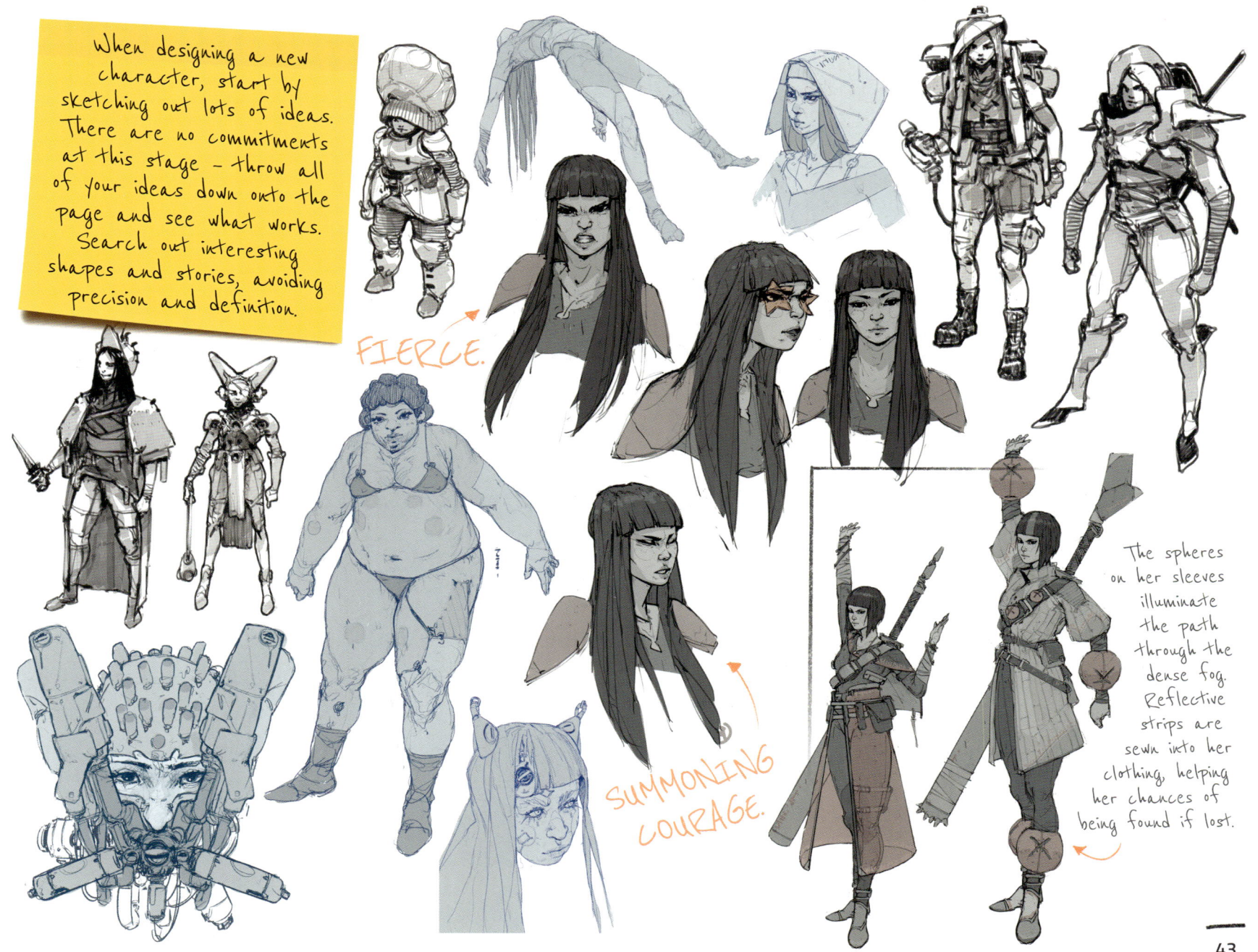

When designing a new character, start by sketching out lots of ideas. There are no commitments at this stage – throw all of your ideas down onto the page and see what works. Search out interesting shapes and stories, avoiding precision and definition.

FIERCE.

SUMMONING COURAGE.

The spheres on her sleeves illuminate the path through the dense fog. Reflective strips are sewn into her clothing, helping her chances of being found if lost.

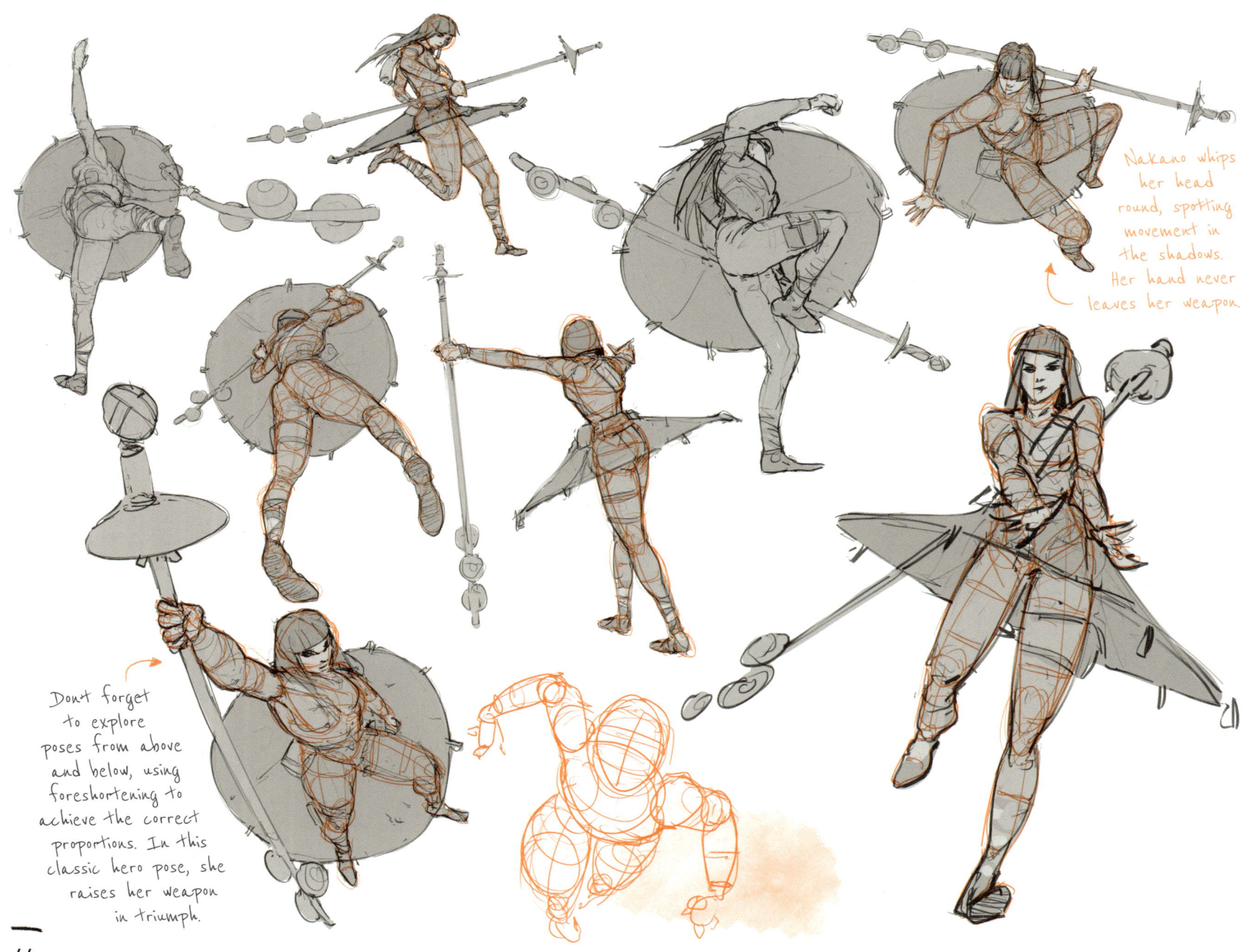

Nakano whips her head round, spotting movement in the shadows. Her hand never leaves her weapon.

Don't forget to explore poses from above and below, using foreshortening to achieve the correct proportions. In this classic hero pose, she raises her weapon in triumph.

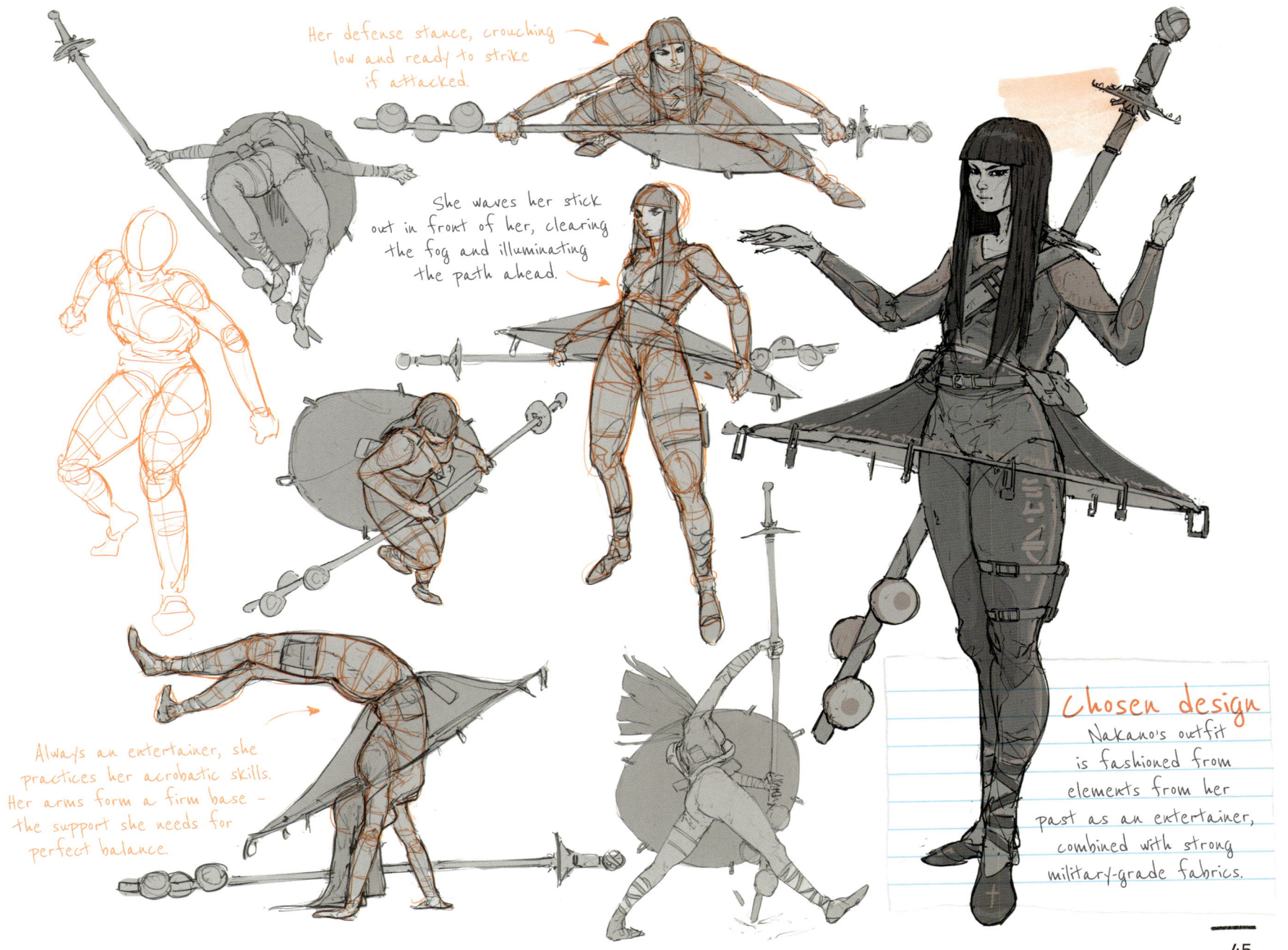

Her defense stance, crouching low and ready to strike if attacked.

She waves her stick out in front of her, clearing the fog and illuminating the path ahead.

Always an entertainer, she practices her acrobatic skills. Her arms form a firm base - the support she needs for perfect balance.

Chosen design

Nakano's outfit is fashioned from elements from her past as an entertainer, combined with strong military-grade fabrics.

Psychic superheroine

THIS SKETCHBOOK BELONGS TO: Laura Braga

Echo is a royal superheroine living in a futuristic, apocalyptic land. She has a good soul and fights for the rights of her people. Though she is strong and is skilled in martial arts, her main power is her psychic abilities, which allow her to get inside people's minds, move objects, and create energy with the power of thought. She is pregnant and her priority is the safety of her child, so she spends most of her time protected in her palace. She communicates with the other heroes and heroines in the land, giving them directions.

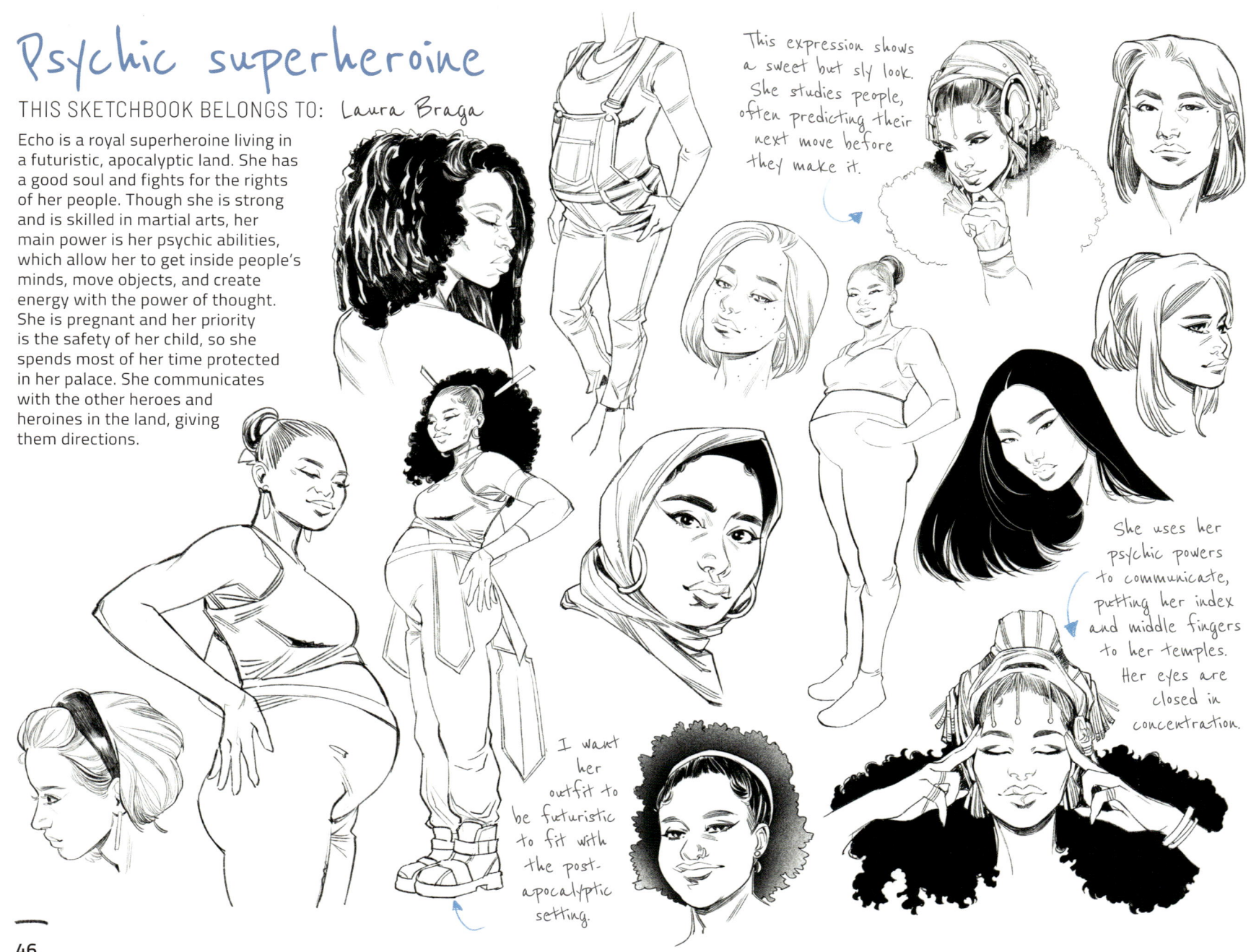

This expression shows a sweet but sly look. She studies people, often predicting their next move before they make it.

She uses her psychic powers to communicate, putting her index and middle fingers to her temples. Her eyes are closed in concentration.

I want her outfit to be futuristic to fit with the post-apocalyptic setting.

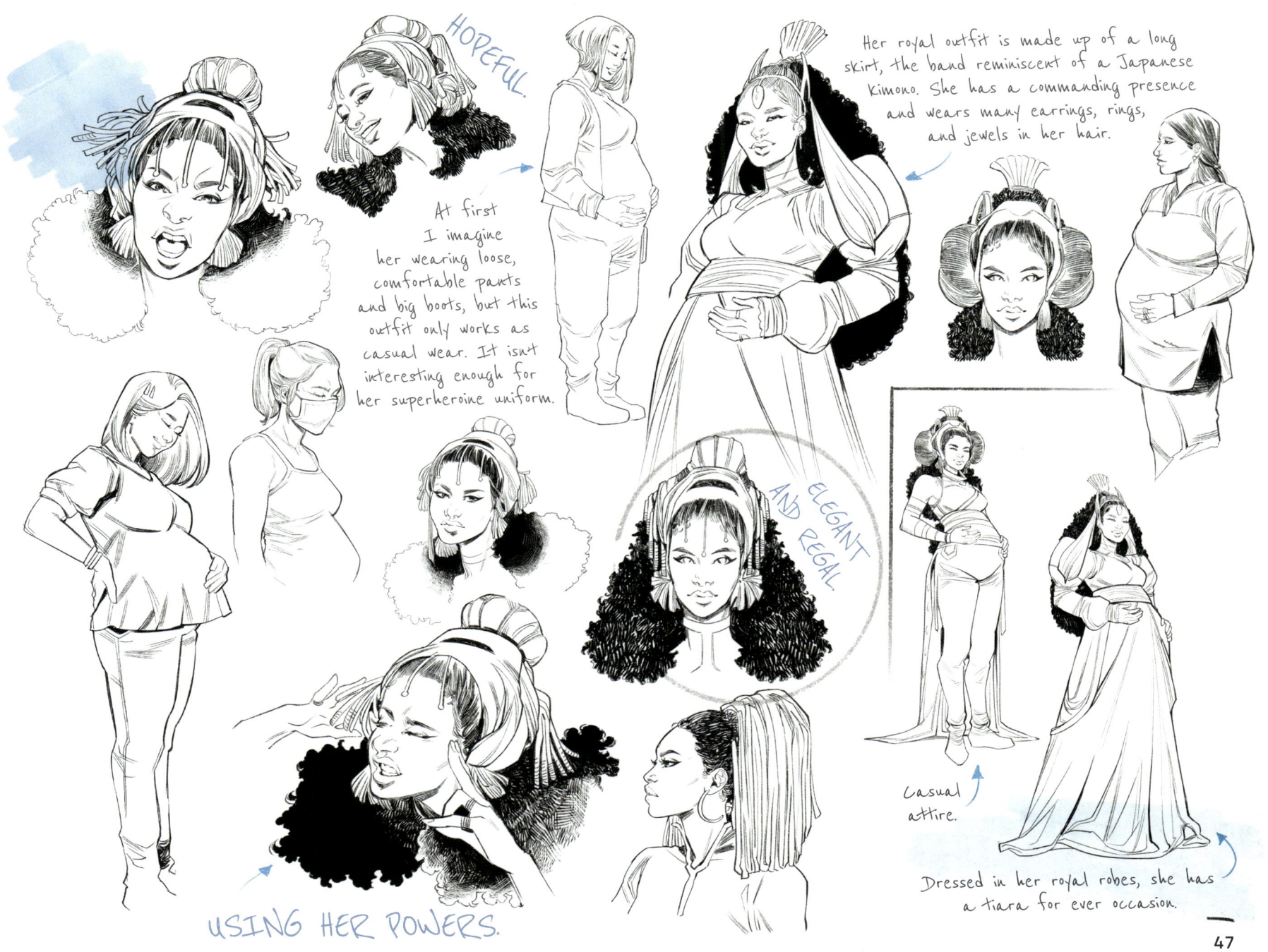

HOPEFUL.

Her royal outfit is made up of a long skirt, the band reminiscent of a Japanese kimono. She has a commanding presence and wears many earrings, rings, and jewels in her hair.

At first I imagine her wearing loose, comfortable pants and big boots, but this outfit only works as casual wear. It isn't interesting enough for her superheroine uniform.

ELEGANT AND REGAL.

Casual attire.

Dressed in her royal robes, she has a tiara for ever occasion.

USING HER POWERS.

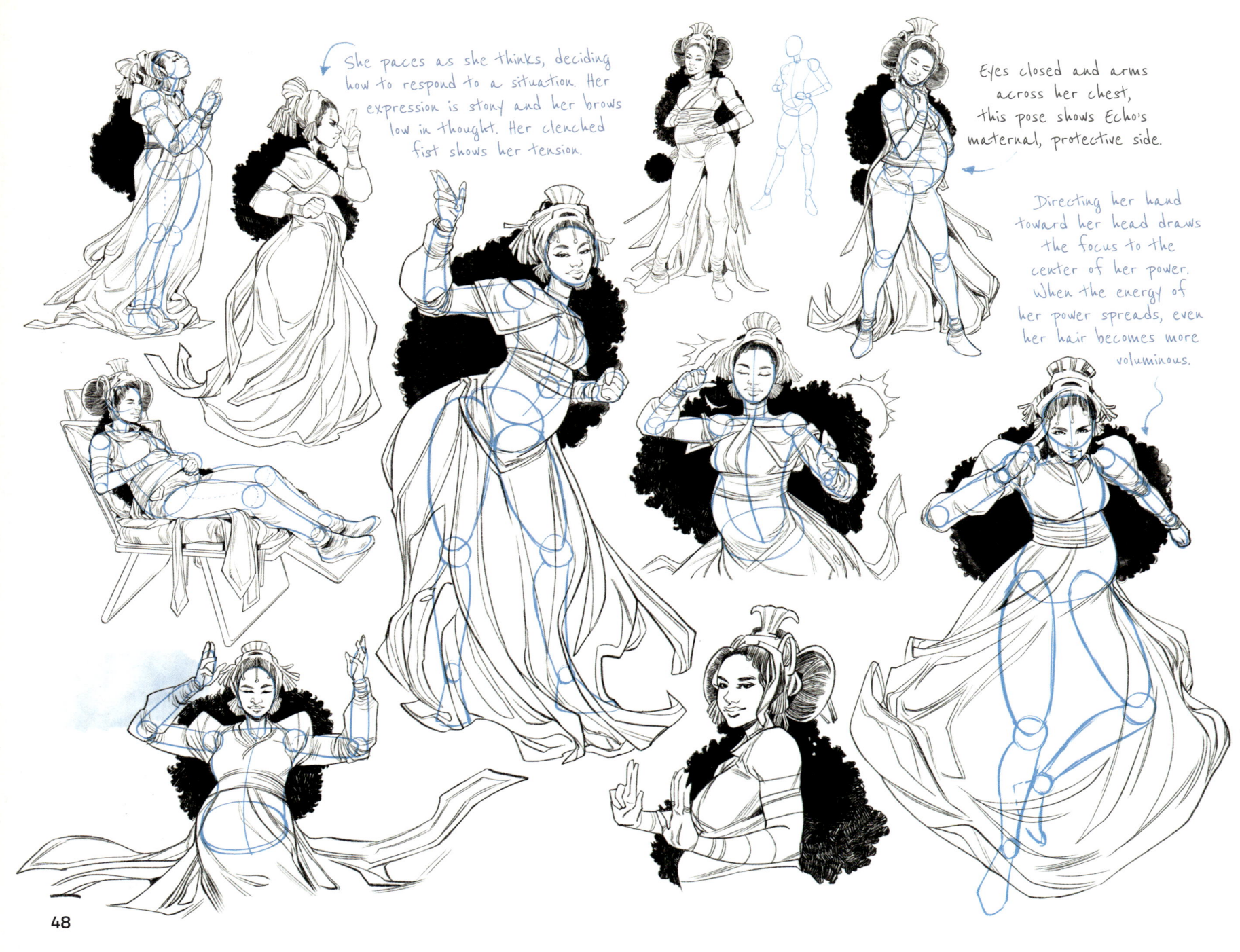

She paces as she thinks, deciding how to respond to a situation. Her expression is stony and her brows low in thought. Her clenched fist shows her tension.

Eyes closed and arms across her chest, this pose shows Echo's maternal, protective side.

Directing her hand toward her head draws the focus to the center of her power. When the energy of her power spreads, even her hair becomes more voluminous.

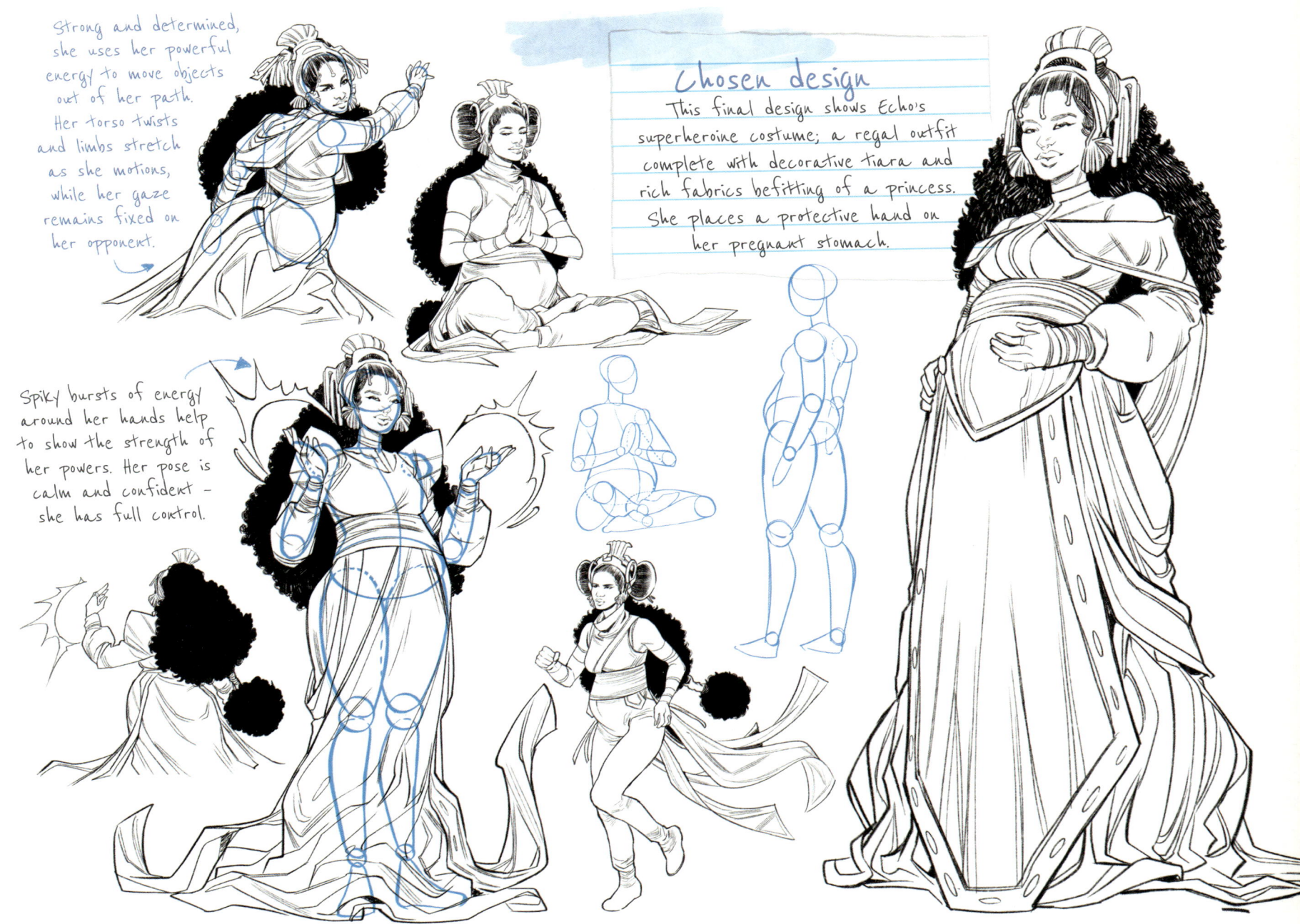

Strong and determined, she uses her powerful energy to move objects out of her path. Her torso twists and limbs stretch as she motions, while her gaze remains fixed on her opponent.

Chosen design

This final design shows Echo's superheroine costume; a regal outfit complete with decorative tiara and rich fabrics befitting of a princess. She places a protective hand on her pregnant stomach.

Spiky bursts of energy around her hands help to show the strength of her powers. Her pose is calm and confident – she has full control.

49

Animal superheroine

THIS SKETCHBOOK BELONGS TO: Devon Bragg

Simms is an independent woman, part-time vet, and ranch owner. Her powers were gifted to her by the previous hero of the Pegasus line, cementing her destiny to become a superheroine. She's a veteran superheroine, guardian, and is often looked to as a leader. She fights for those who can't protect themselves and to bring about justice. With a muscular body made up of strong angles, Simms stands at six feet tall and has thick, graying braids that run down her back, decorated with gold and silver metals.

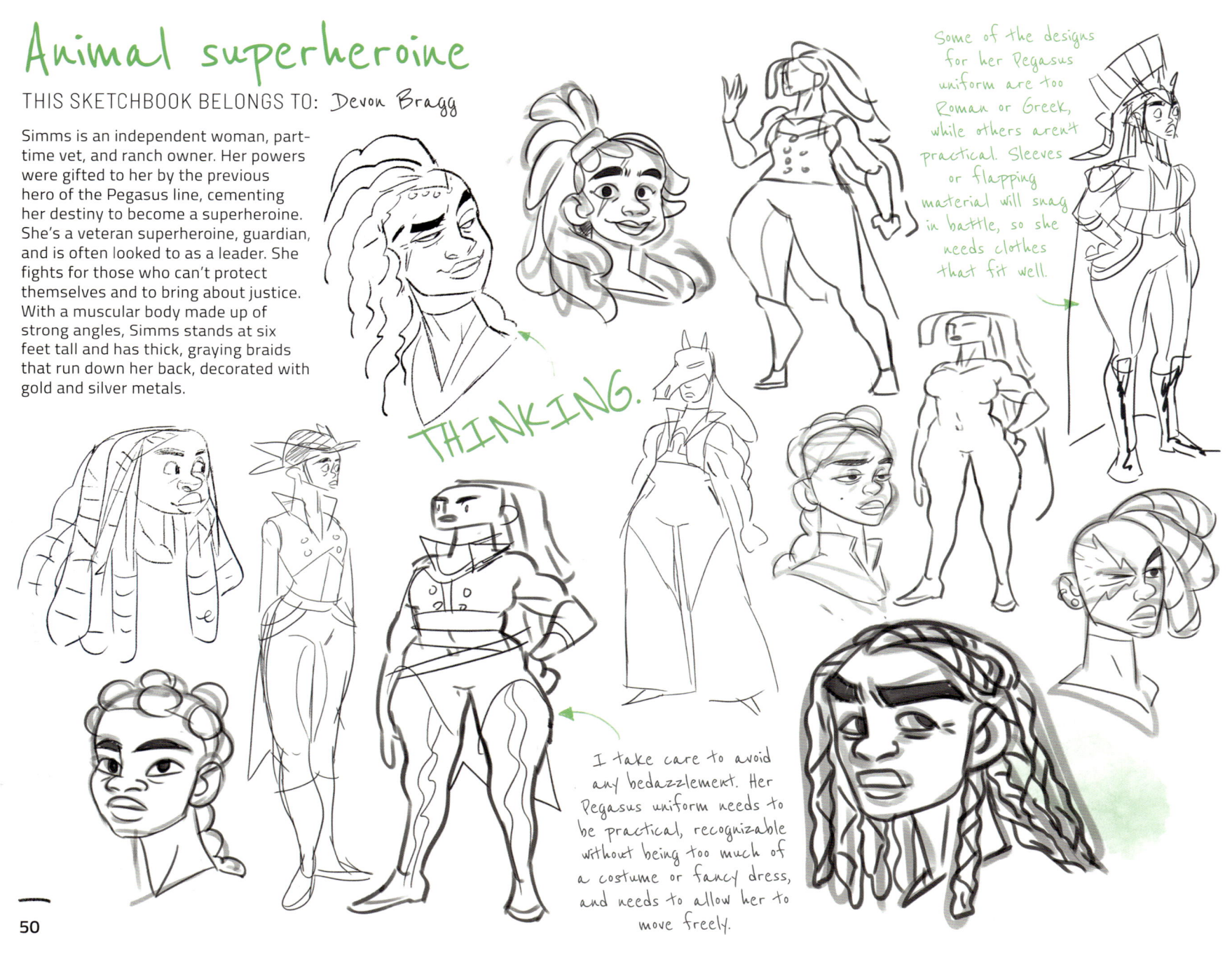

THINKING.

Some of the designs for her Pegasus uniform are too Roman or Greek, while others aren't practical. Sleeves or flapping material will snag in battle, so she needs clothes that fit well.

I take care to avoid any bedazzlement. Her Pegasus uniform needs to be practical, recognizable without being too much of a costume or fancy dress, and needs to allow her to move freely.

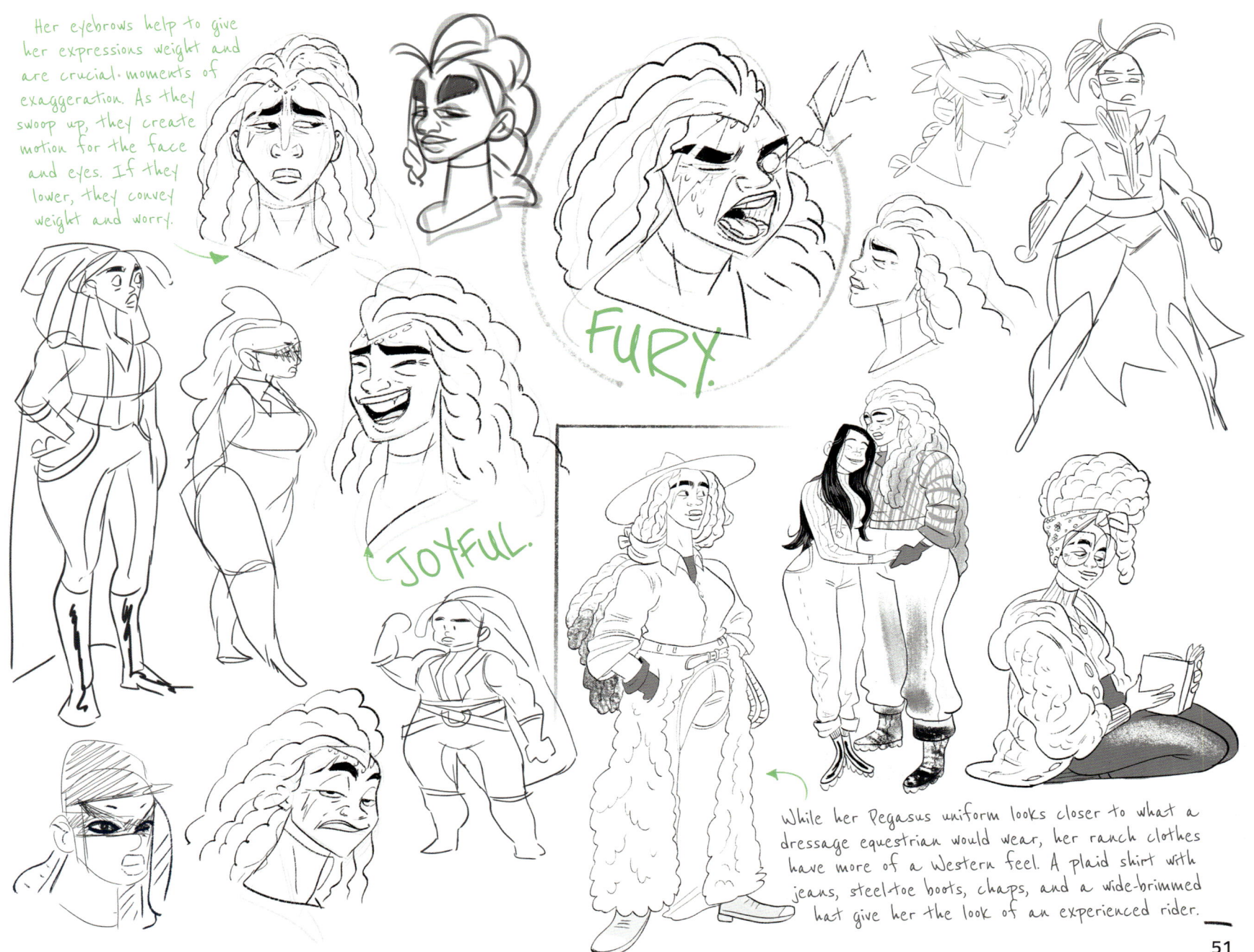

Her eyebrows help to give her expressions weight and are crucial moments of exaggeration. As they swoop up, they create motion for the face and eyes. If they lower, they convey weight and worry.

FURY.

JOYFUL.

While her Pegasus uniform looks closer to what a dressage equestrian would wear, her ranch clothes have more of a Western feel. A plaid shirt with jeans, steel-toe boots, chaps, and a wide-brimmed hat give her the look of an experienced rider.

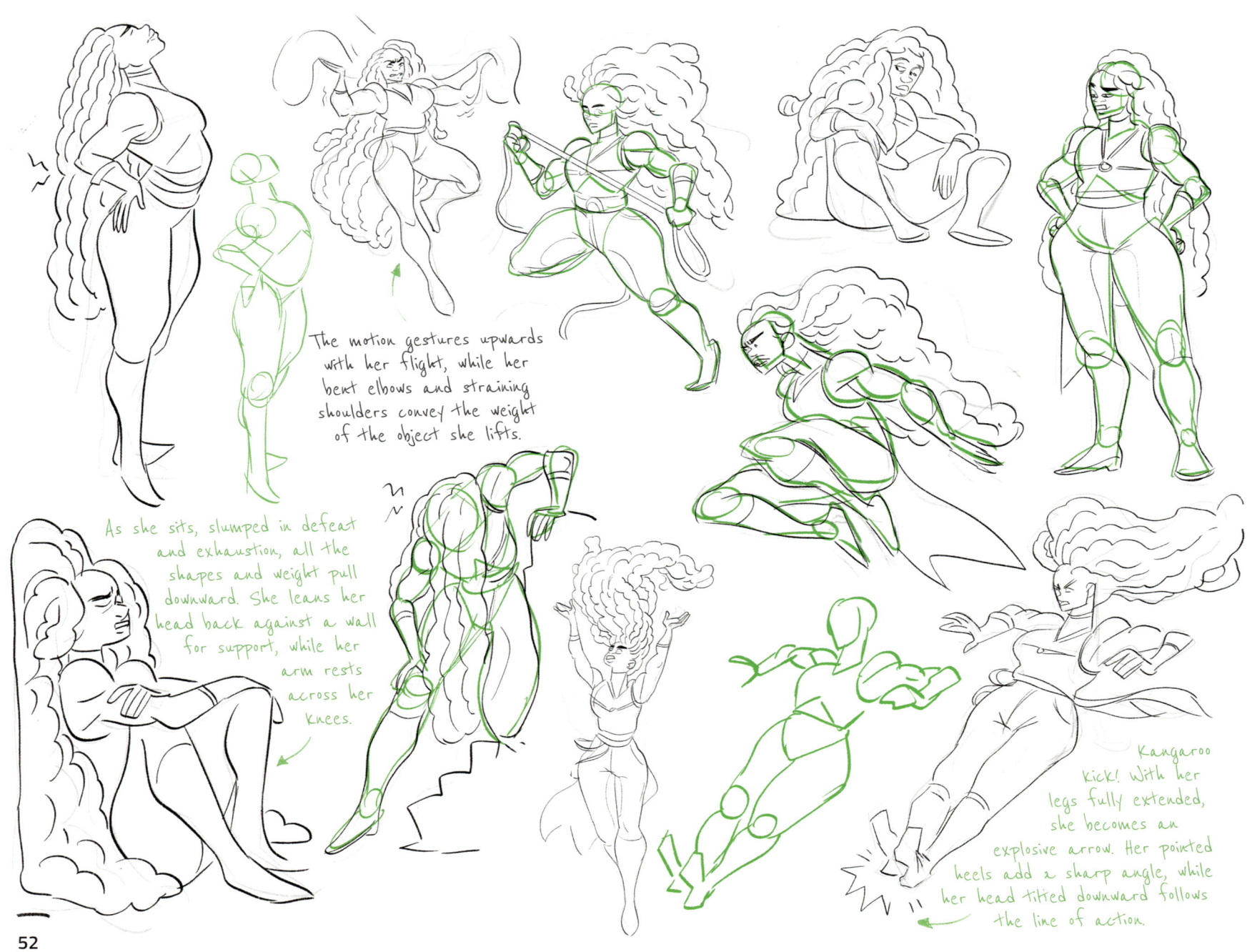

The motion gestures upwards with her flight, while her bent elbows and straining shoulders convey the weight of the object she lifts.

As she sits, slumped in defeat and exhaustion, all the shapes and weight pull downward. She leans her head back against a wall for support, while her arm rests across her knees.

Kangaroo kick! With her legs fully extended, she becomes an explosive arrow. Her pointed heels add a sharp angle, while her head tilted downward follows the line of action.

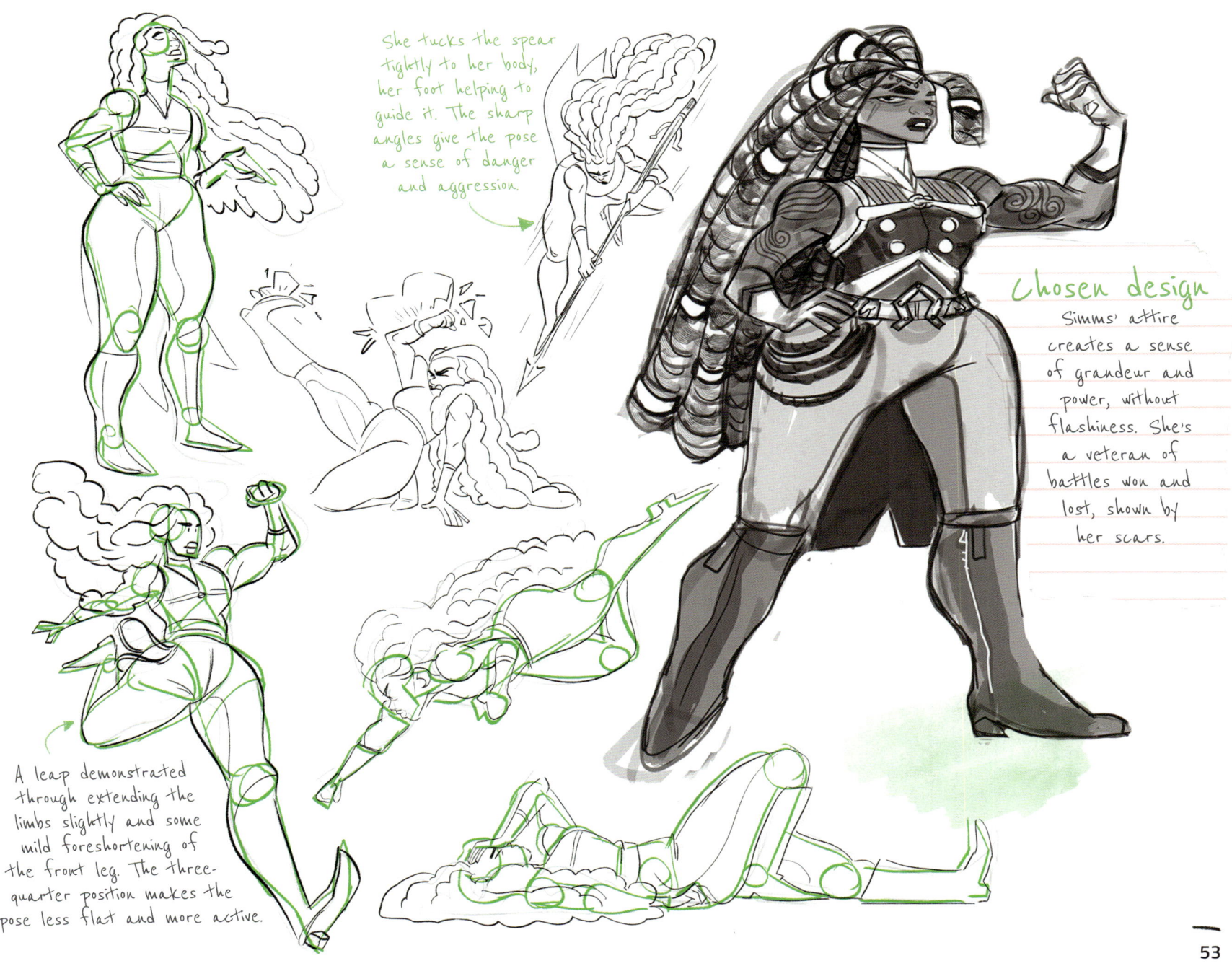

She tucks the spear tightly to her body, her foot helping to guide it. The sharp angles give the pose a sense of danger and aggression.

Chosen design

Simms' attire creates a sense of grandeur and power, without flashiness. She's a veteran of battles won and lost, shown by her scars.

A leap demonstrated through extending the limbs slightly and some mild foreshortening of the front leg. The three-quarter position makes the pose less flat and more active.

Witch

THIS SKETCHBOOK BELONGS TO: Eva Cabrera

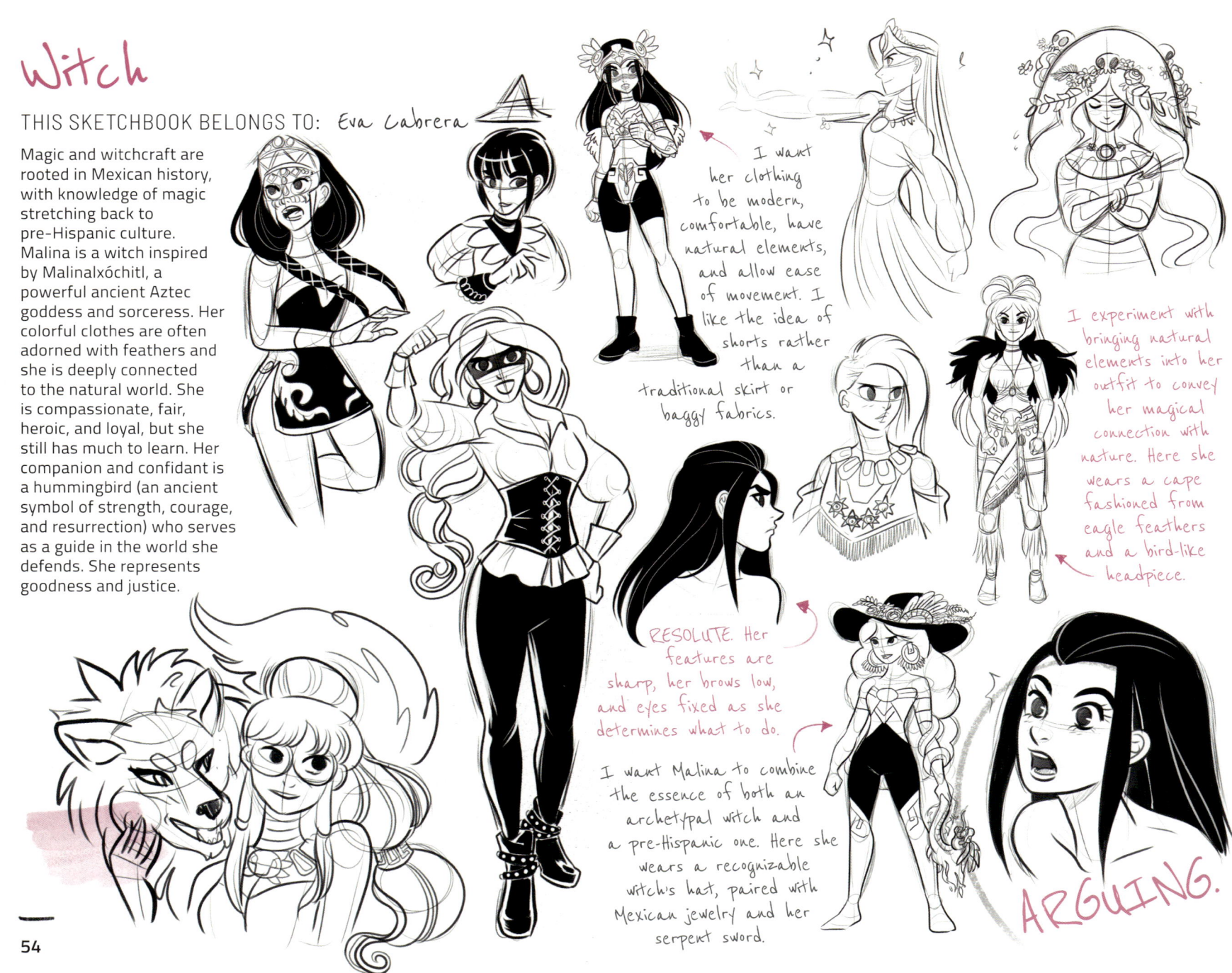

Magic and witchcraft are rooted in Mexican history, with knowledge of magic stretching back to pre-Hispanic culture. Malina is a witch inspired by Malinalxóchitl, a powerful ancient Aztec goddess and sorceress. Her colorful clothes are often adorned with feathers and she is deeply connected to the natural world. She is compassionate, fair, heroic, and loyal, but she still has much to learn. Her companion and confidant is a hummingbird (an ancient symbol of strength, courage, and resurrection) who serves as a guide in the world she defends. She represents goodness and justice.

I want her clothing to be modern, comfortable, have natural elements, and allow ease of movement. I like the idea of shorts rather than a traditional skirt or baggy fabrics.

I experiment with bringing natural elements into her outfit to convey her magical connection with nature. Here she wears a cape fashioned from eagle feathers and a bird-like headpiece.

RESOLUTE. Her features are sharp, her brows low, and eyes fixed as she determines what to do.

I want Malina to combine the essence of both an archetypal witch and a pre-Hispanic one. Here she wears a recognizable witch's hat, paired with Mexican jewelry and her serpent sword.

ARGUING.

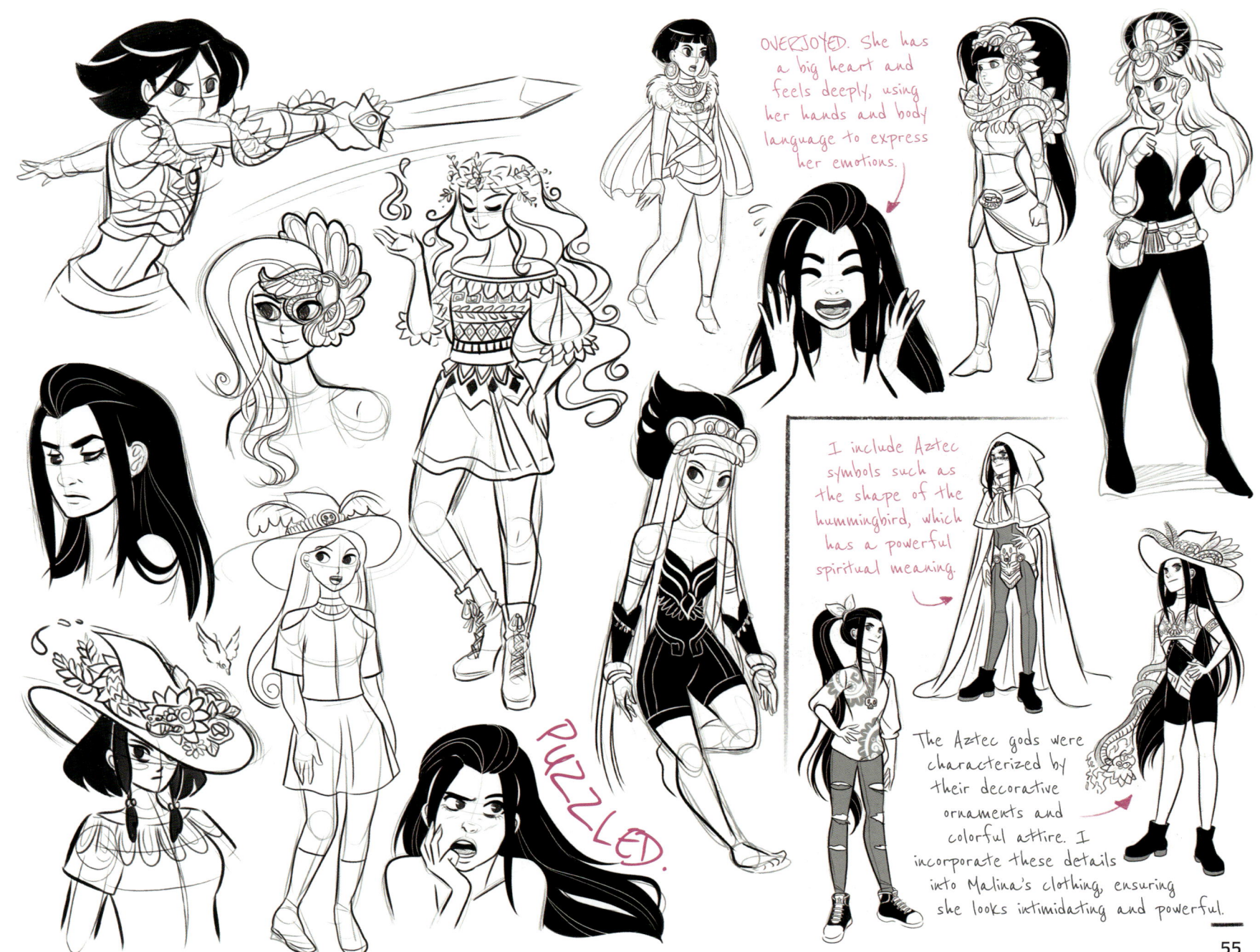

OVERJOYED. She has a big heart and feels deeply, using her hands and body language to express her emotions.

I include Aztec symbols such as the shape of the hummingbird, which has a powerful spiritual meaning.

PUZZLED.

The Aztec gods were characterized by their decorative ornaments and colorful attire. I incorporate these details into Malina's clothing, ensuring she looks intimidating and powerful.

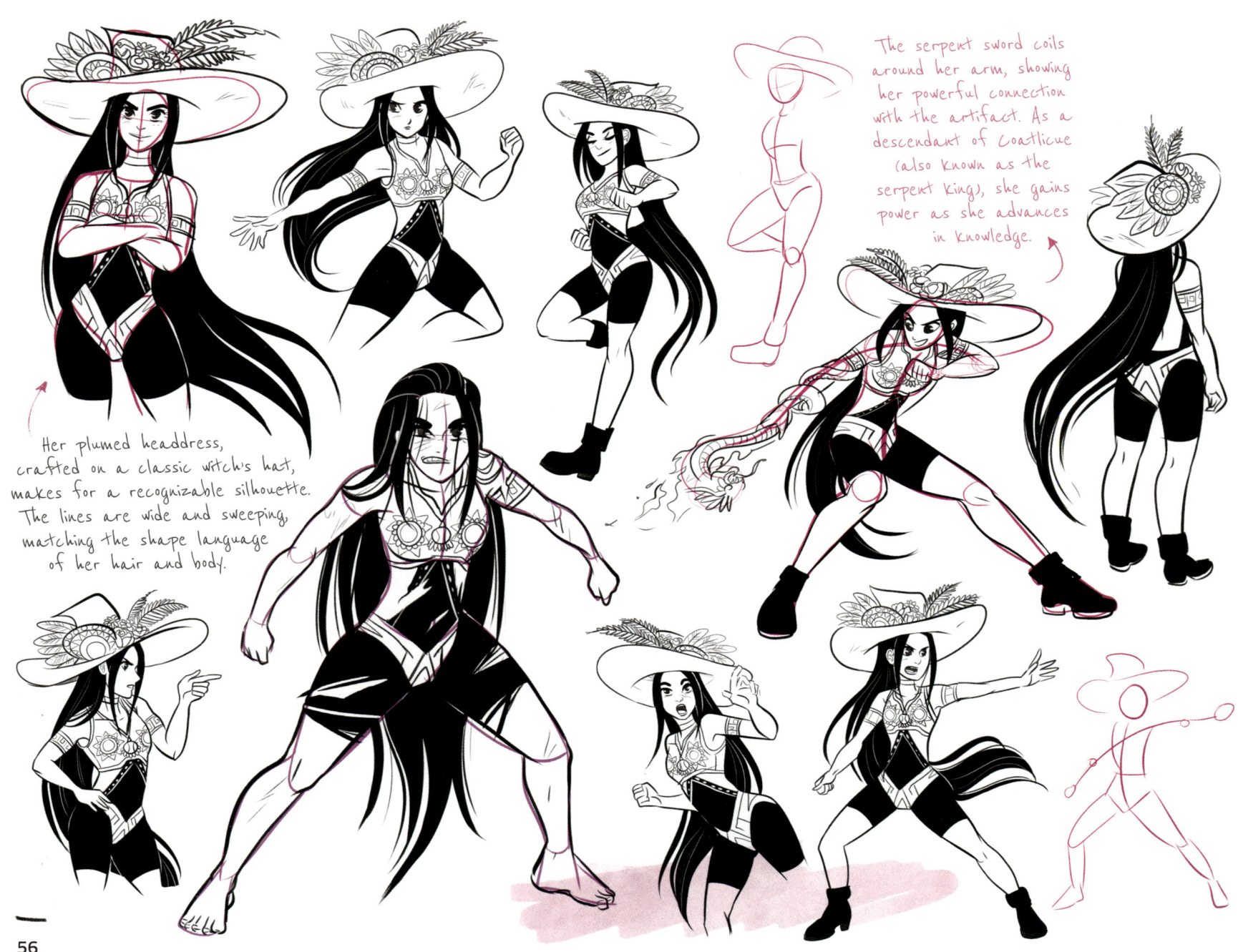

The serpent sword coils around her arm, showing her powerful connection with the artifact. As a descendant of Coatlicue (also known as the serpent king), she gains power as she advances in knowledge.

Her plumed headdress, crafted on a classic witch's hat, makes for a recognizable silhouette. The lines are wide and sweeping, matching the shape language of her hair and body.

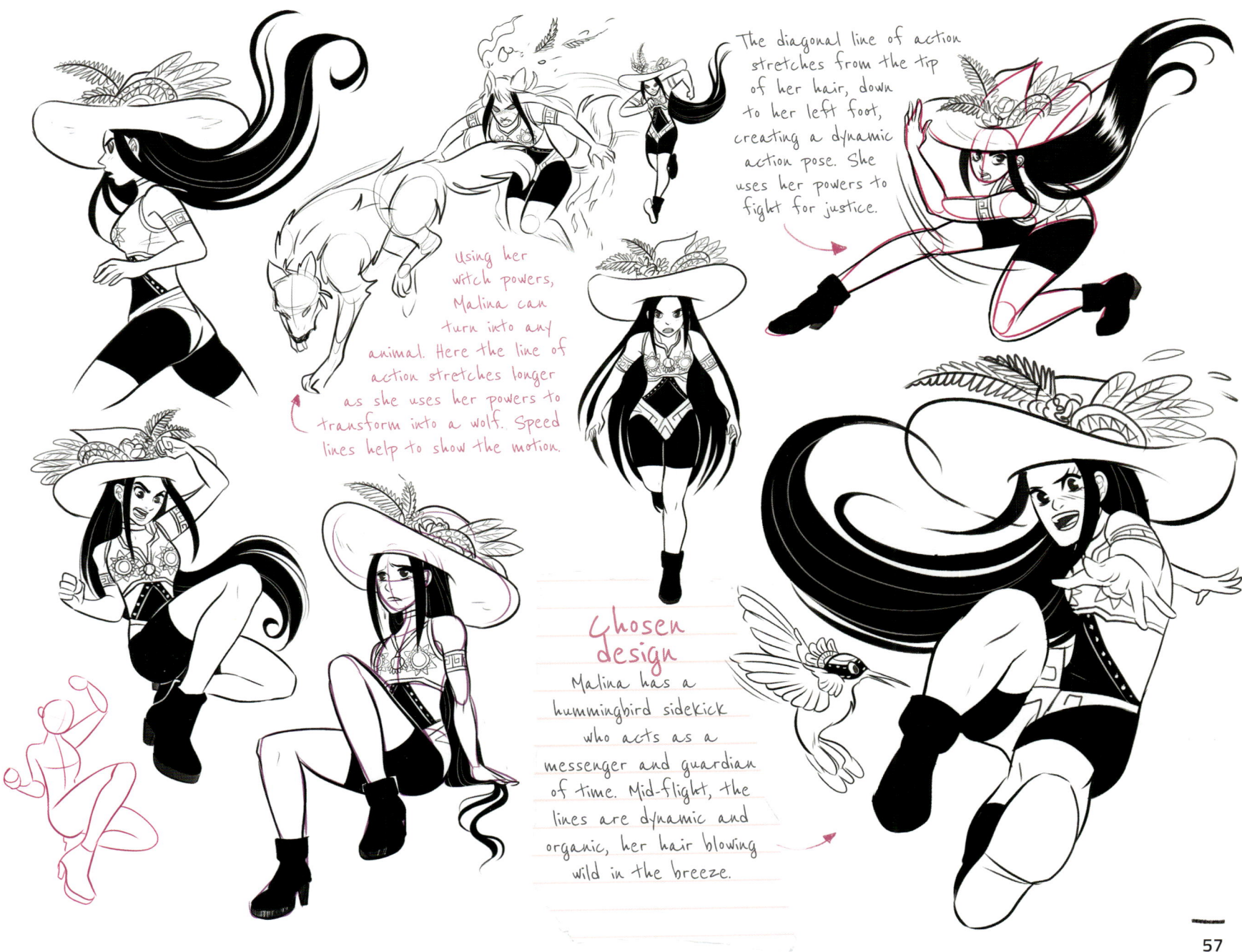

The diagonal line of action stretches from the tip of her hair, down to her left foot, creating a dynamic action pose. She uses her powers to fight for justice.

Using her witch powers, Malina can turn into any animal. Here the line of action stretches longer as she uses her powers to transform into a wolf. Speed lines help to show the motion.

Chosen design

Malina has a hummingbird sidekick who acts as a messenger and guardian of time. Mid-flight, the lines are dynamic and organic, her hair blowing wild in the breeze.

Dancer

THIS SKETCHBOOK BELONGS TO: Laura Catrinella

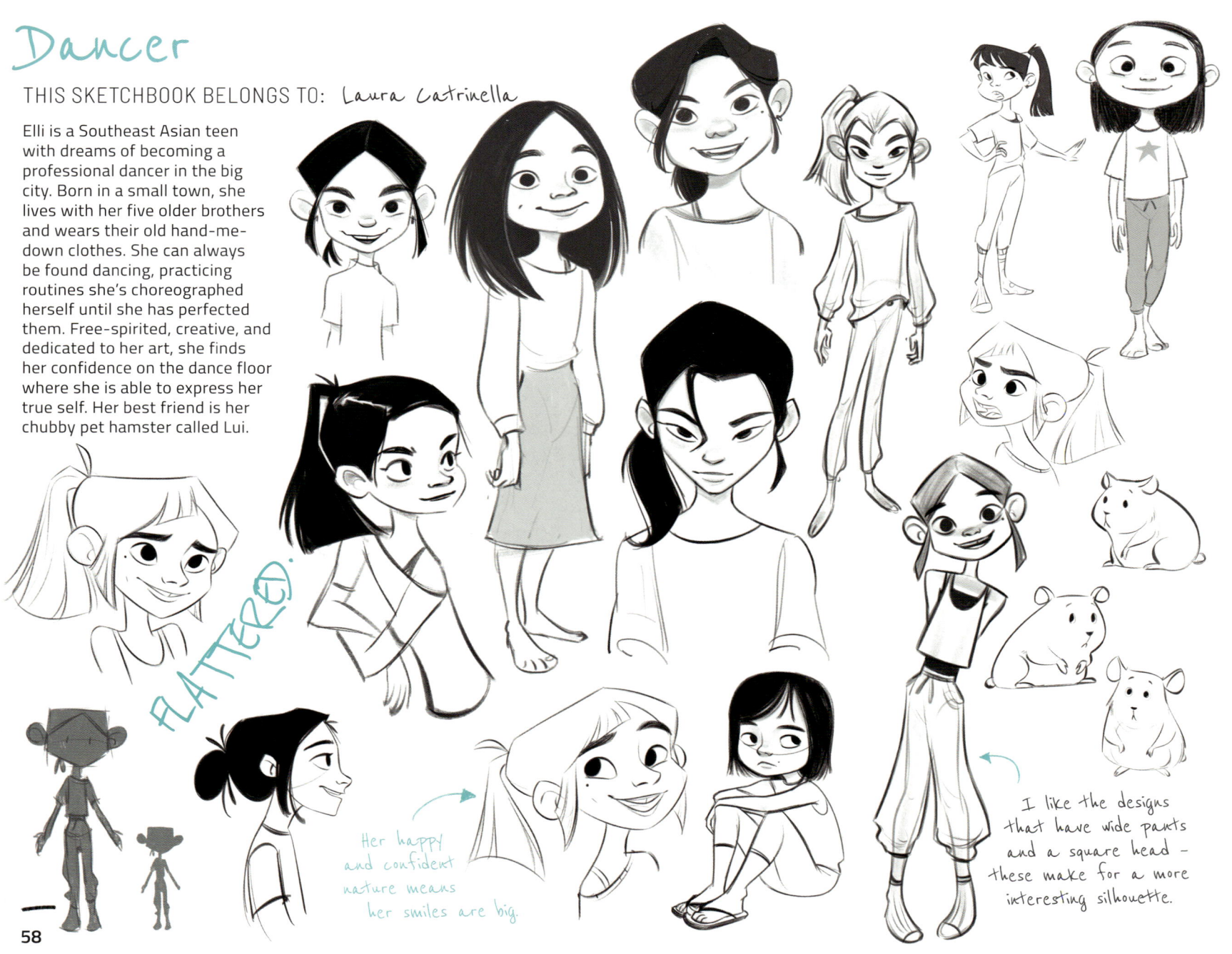

Elli is a Southeast Asian teen with dreams of becoming a professional dancer in the big city. Born in a small town, she lives with her five older brothers and wears their old hand-me-down clothes. She can always be found dancing, practicing routines she's choreographed herself until she has perfected them. Free-spirited, creative, and dedicated to her art, she finds her confidence on the dance floor where she is able to express her true self. Her best friend is her chubby pet hamster called Lui.

FLATTERED.

Her happy and confident nature means her smiles are big.

I like the designs that have wide pants and a square head – these make for a more interesting silhouette.

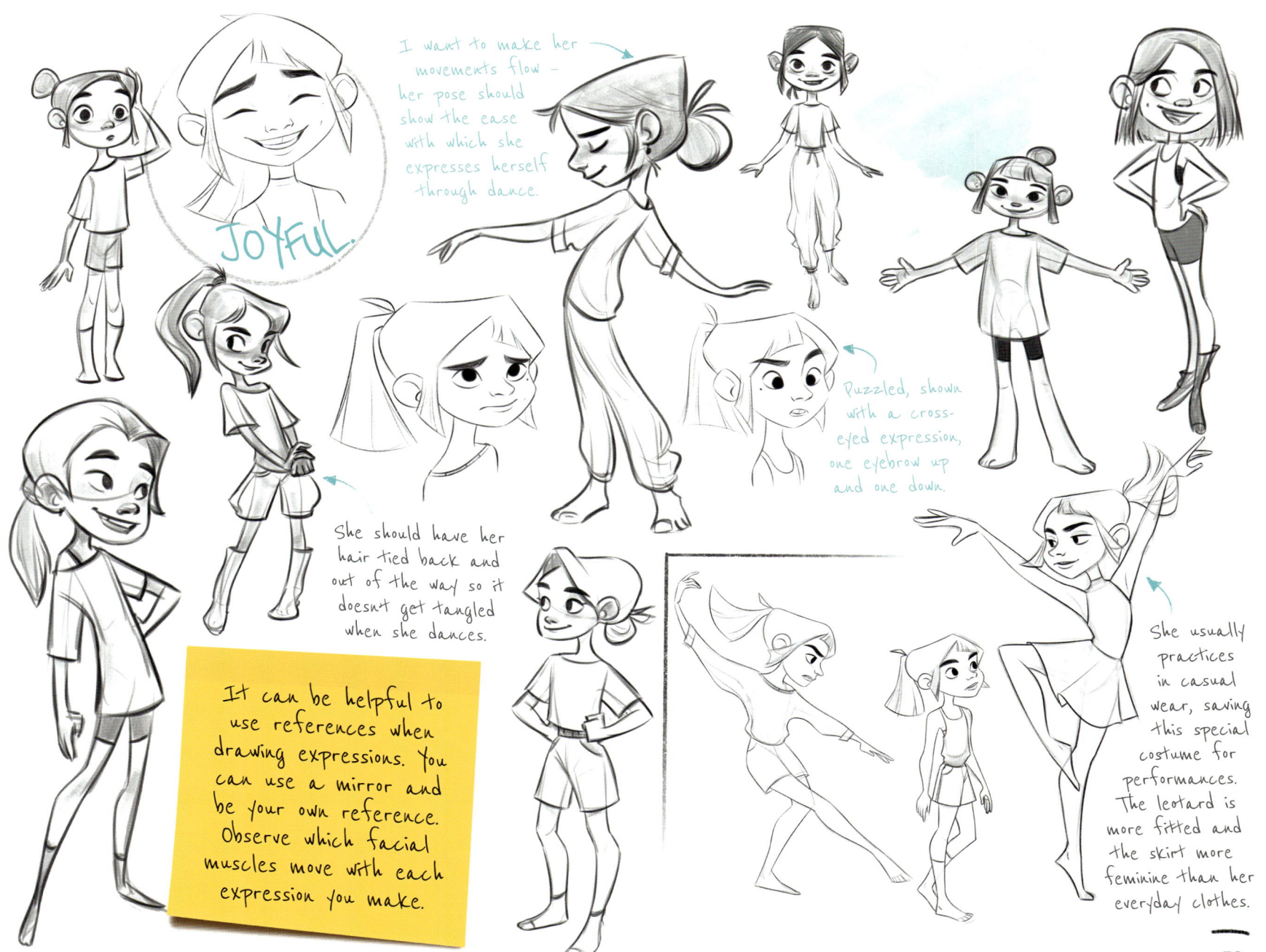

I want to make her movements flow — her pose should show the ease with which she expresses herself through dance.

JOYFUL.

Puzzled, shown with a cross-eyed expression, one eyebrow up and one down.

She should have her hair tied back and out of the way so it doesn't get tangled when she dances.

It can be helpful to use references when drawing expressions. You can use a mirror and be your own reference. Observe which facial muscles move with each expression you make.

She usually practices in casual wear, saving this special costume for performances. The leotard is more fitted and the skirt more feminine than her everyday clothes.

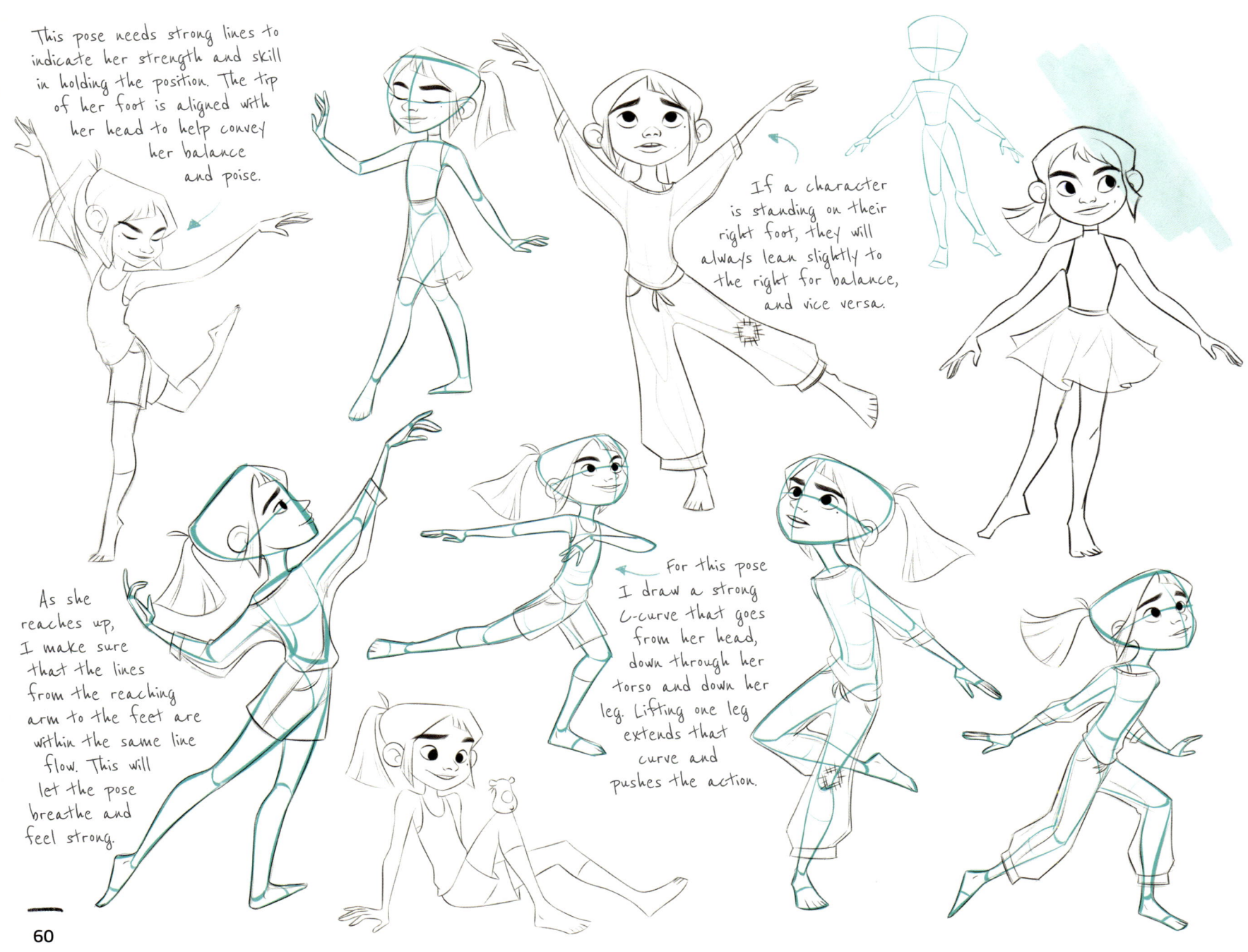

This pose needs strong lines to indicate her strength and skill in holding the position. The tip of her foot is aligned with her head to help convey her balance and poise.

If a character is standing on their right foot, they will always lean slightly to the right for balance, and vice versa.

As she reaches up, I make sure that the lines from the reaching arm to the feet are within the same line flow. This will let the pose breathe and feel strong.

For this pose I draw a strong C-curve that goes from her head, down through her torso and down her leg. Lifting one leg extends that curve and pushes the action.

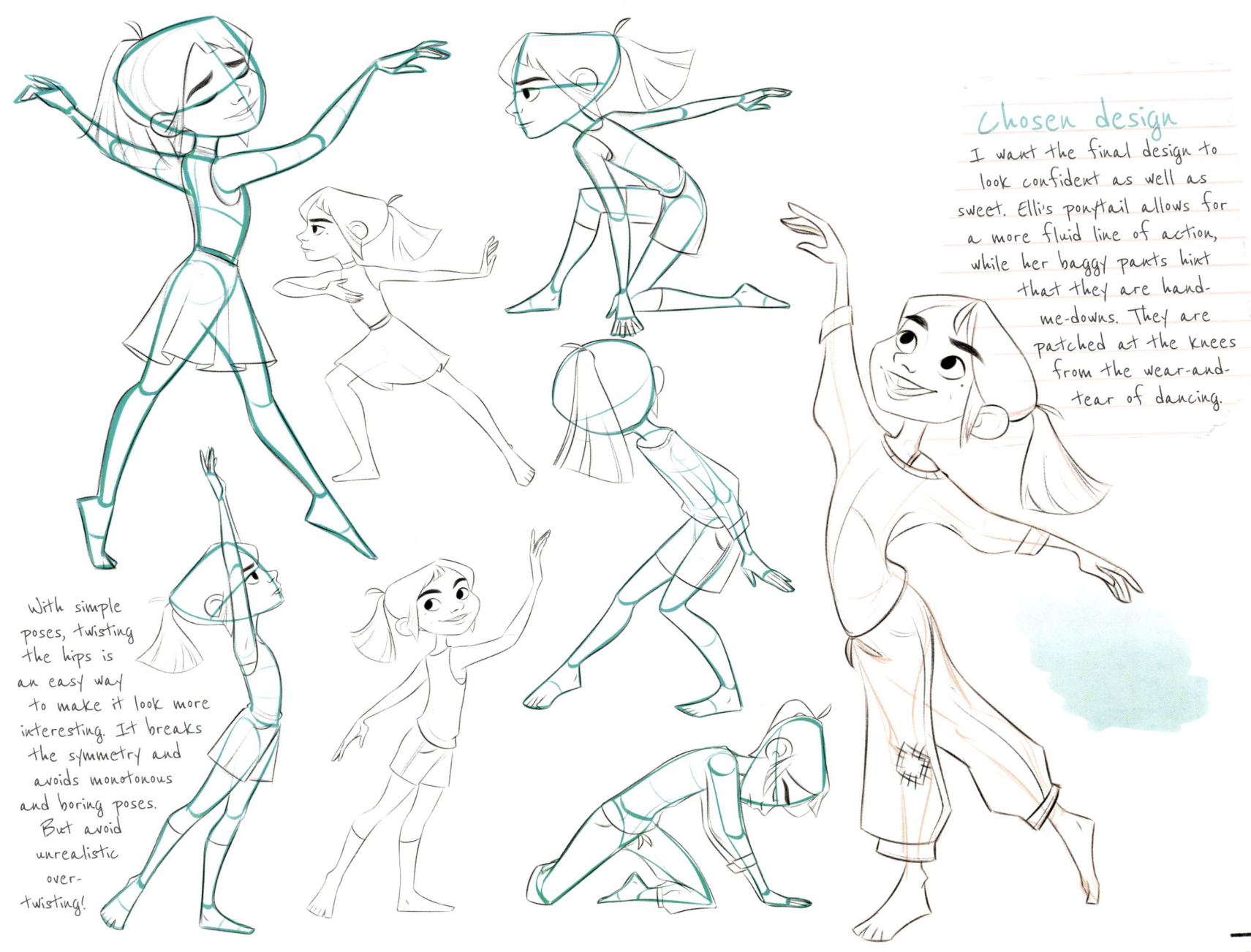

Chosen design

I want the final design to look confident as well as sweet. Elli's ponytail allows for a more fluid line of action, while her baggy pants hint that they are hand-me-downs. They are patched at the knees from the wear-and-tear of dancing.

With simple poses, twisting the hips is an easy way to make it look more interesting. It breaks the symmetry and avoids monotonous and boring poses. But avoid unrealistic over-twisting!

61

Bird superheroine

THIS SKETCHBOOK BELONGS TO: Thomas Chamberlain - Keen

Talon is an owl superheroine who strikes an interesting departure from the typical muscular superhero archetype. Owls are excellent hunters thanks to their exceptional eyesight and stealthy flight, attributes which lend themselves to a heroine geared toward search and rescue rather than fierce combat. This stealth focus carries into her personality – Talon is wise, has a mild temperament, and likes to keep to herself.

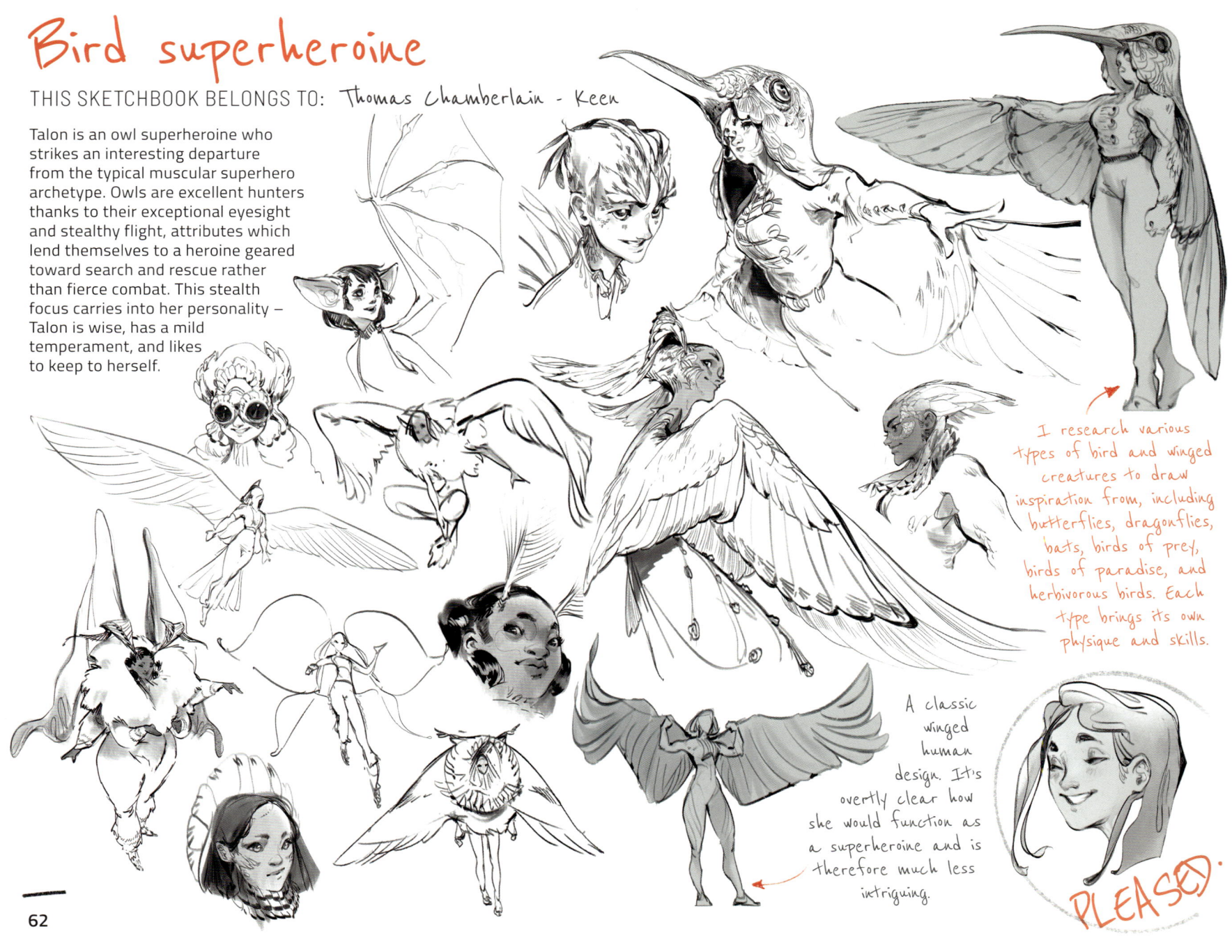

I research various types of bird and winged creatures to draw inspiration from, including butterflies, dragonflies, bats, birds of prey, birds of paradise, and herbivorous birds. Each type brings its own physique and skills.

A classic winged human design. It's overtly clear how she would function as a superheroine and is therefore much less intriguing.

PLEASE.

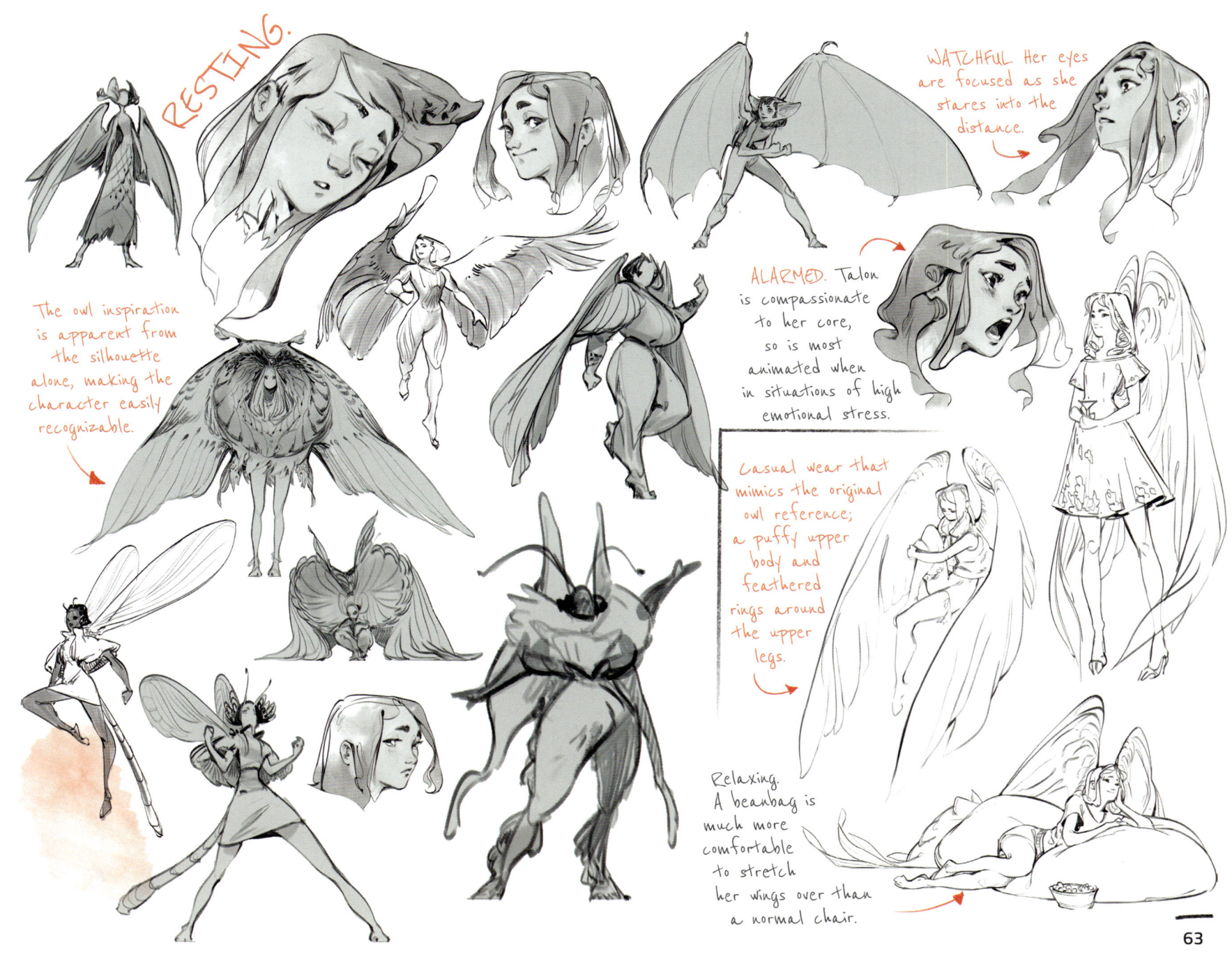

RESTING.

The owl inspiration is apparent from the silhouette alone, making the character easily recognizable.

WATCHFUL. Her eyes are focused as she stares into the distance.

ALARMED. Talon is compassionate to her core, so is most animated when in situations of high emotional stress.

Casual wear that mimics the original owl reference; a puffy upper body and feathered rings around the upper legs.

Relaxing. A beanbag is much more comfortable to stretch her wings over than a normal chair.

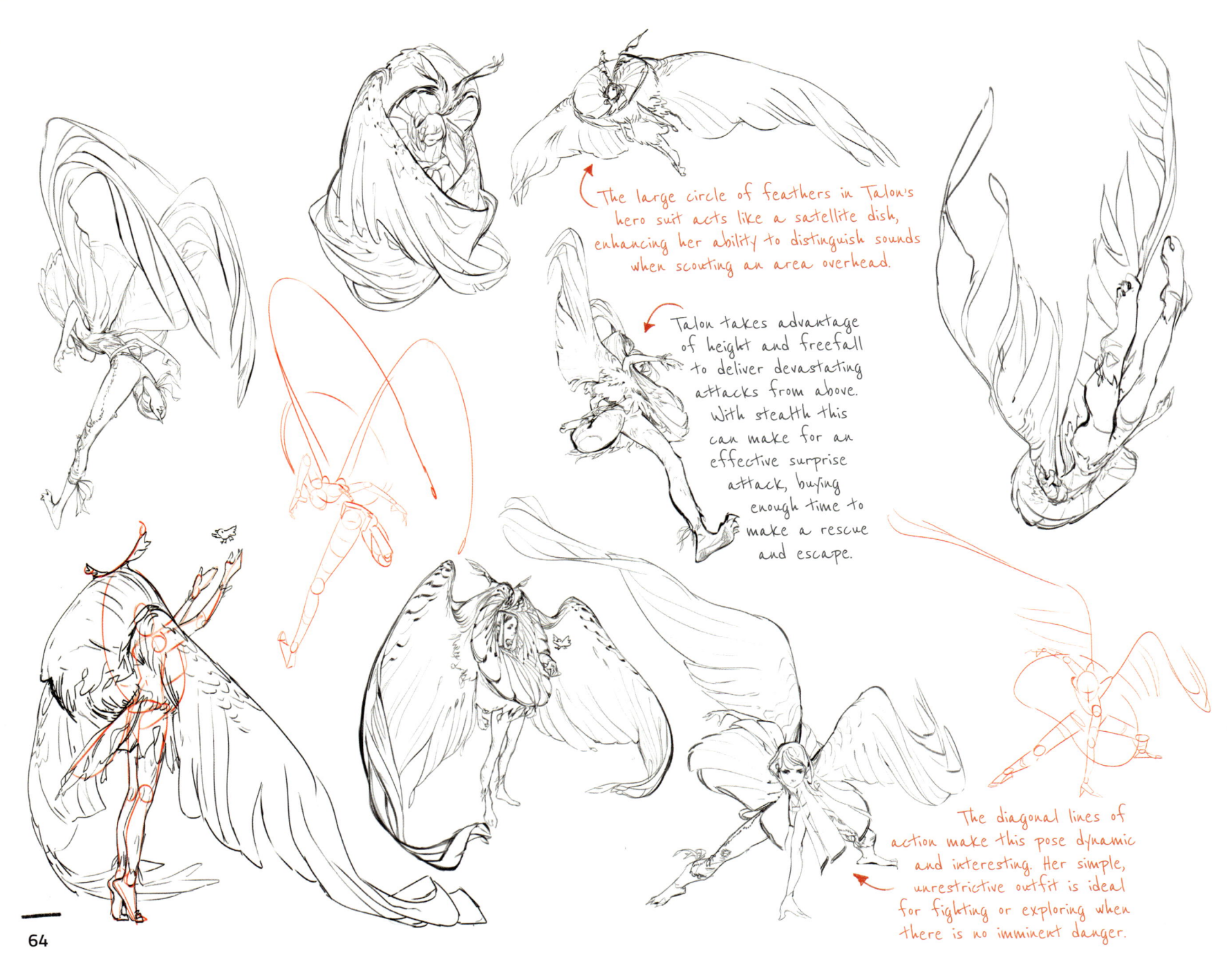

The large circle of feathers in Talon's hero suit acts like a satellite dish, enhancing her ability to distinguish sounds when scouting an area overhead.

Talon takes advantage of height and freefall to deliver devastating attacks from above. With stealth this can make for an effective surprise attack, buying enough time to make a rescue and escape.

The diagonal lines of action make this pose dynamic and interesting. Her simple, unrestrictive outfit is ideal for fighting or exploring when there is no imminent danger.

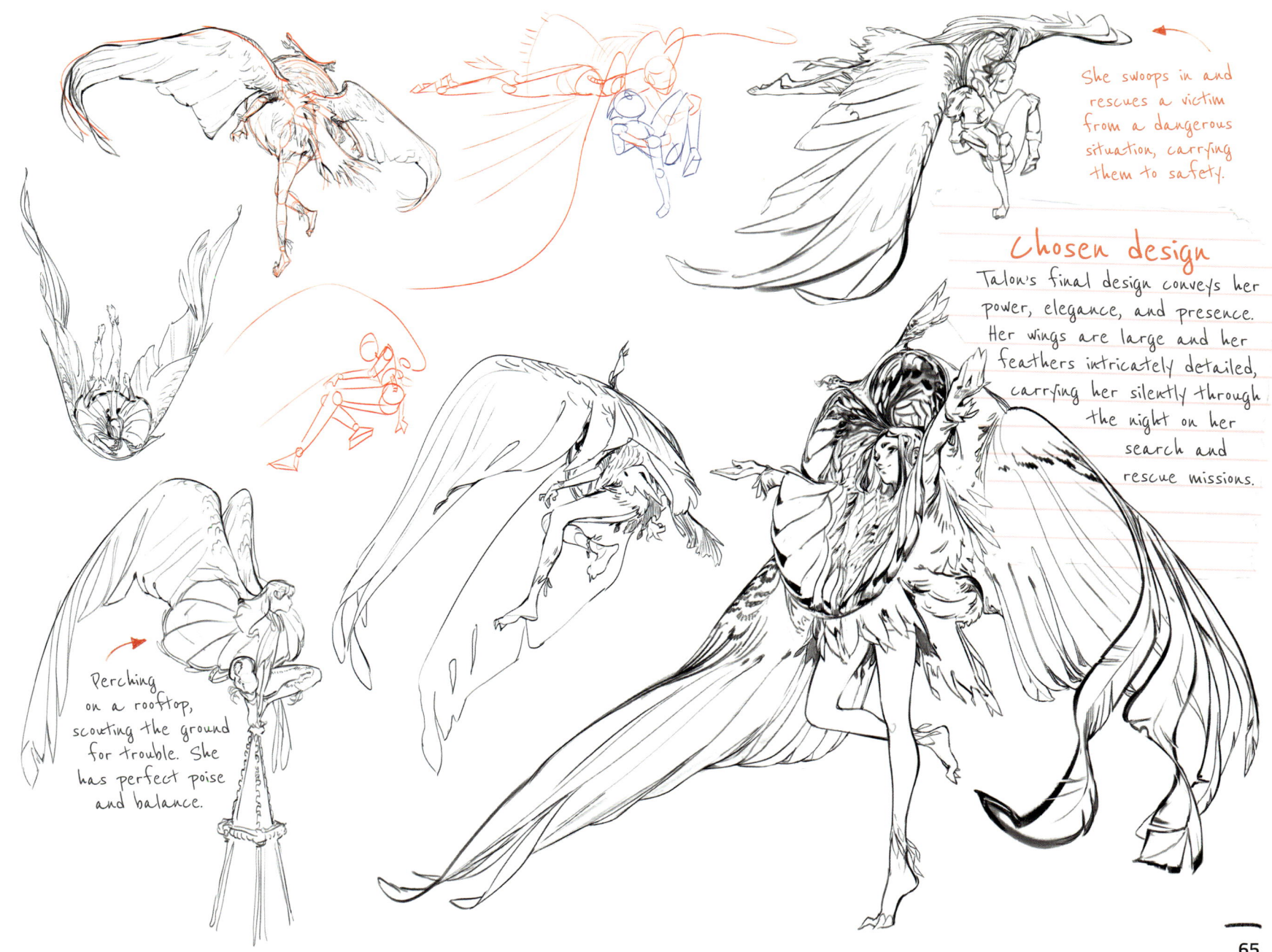

She swoops in and rescues a victim from a dangerous situation, carrying them to safety.

Chosen design

Talon's final design conveys her power, elegance, and presence. Her wings are large and her feathers intricately detailed, carrying her silently through the night on her search and rescue missions.

Perching on a rooftop, scouting the ground for trouble. She has perfect poise and balance.

Stuntwoman

THIS SKETCHBOOK BELONGS TO: Sandro Cleuzo

Lenna is a courageous and highly skilled stuntwoman who works at various movie studios in Hollywood. Born into a Hispanic family, she has dark hair, big brown eyes, and is in her late twenties. She is confident, fit, and active, with a love of sports with an element of danger. Lenna travels to work on her motorbike, relishing the feeling of the wind in her hair.

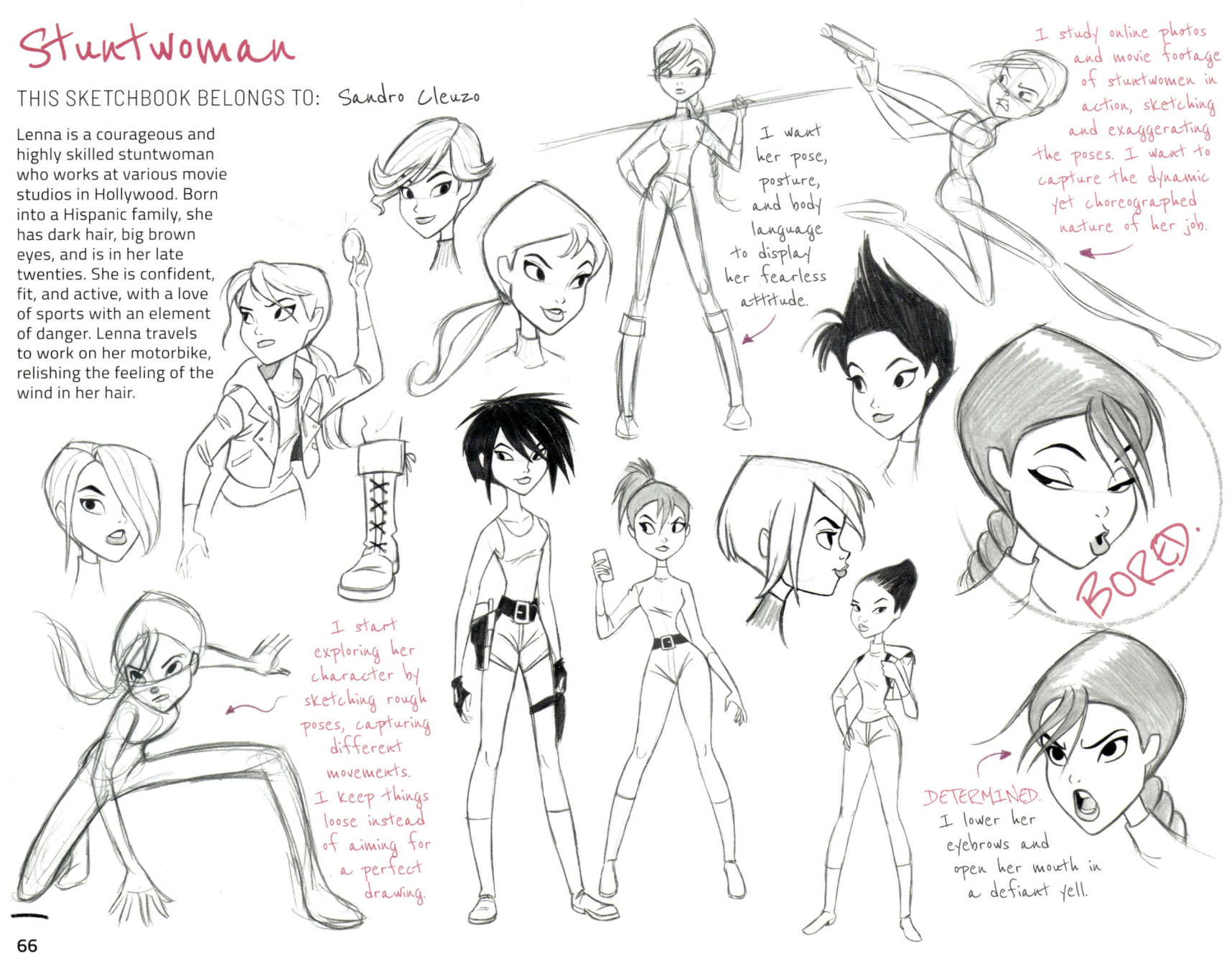

I want her pose, posture, and body language to display her fearless attitude.

I study online photos and movie footage of stuntwomen in action, sketching and exaggerating the poses. I want to capture the dynamic yet choreographed nature of her job.

I start exploring her character by sketching rough poses, capturing different movements. I keep things loose instead of aiming for a perfect drawing.

BORED.

DETERMINED. I lower her eyebrows and open her mouth in a defiant yell.

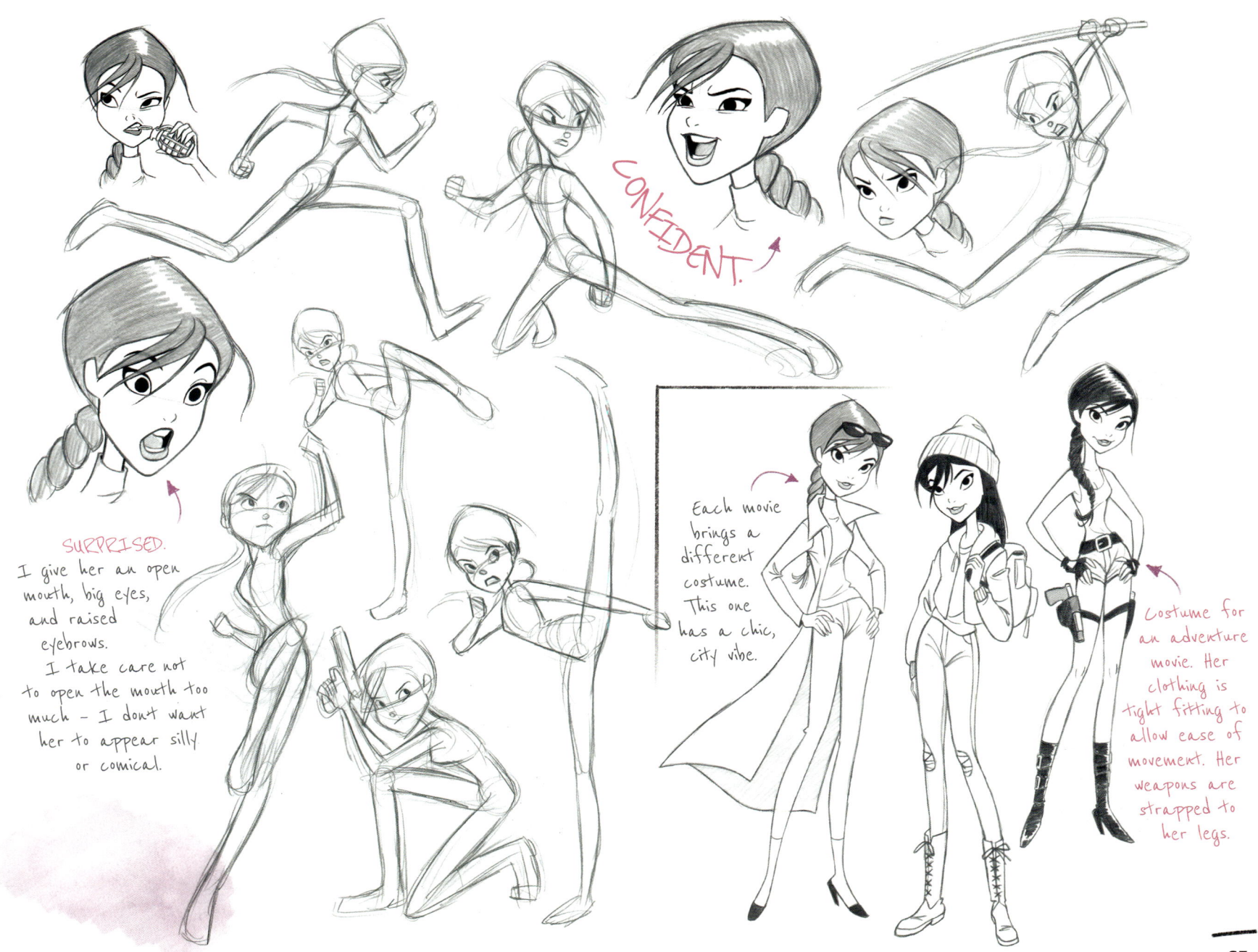

CONFIDENT.

SURPRISED.
I give her an open mouth, big eyes, and raised eyebrows.
I take care not to open the mouth too much – I don't want her to appear silly or comical.

Each movie brings a different costume. This one has a chic, city vibe.

Costume for an adventure movie. Her clothing is tight fitting to allow ease of movement. Her weapons are strapped to her legs.

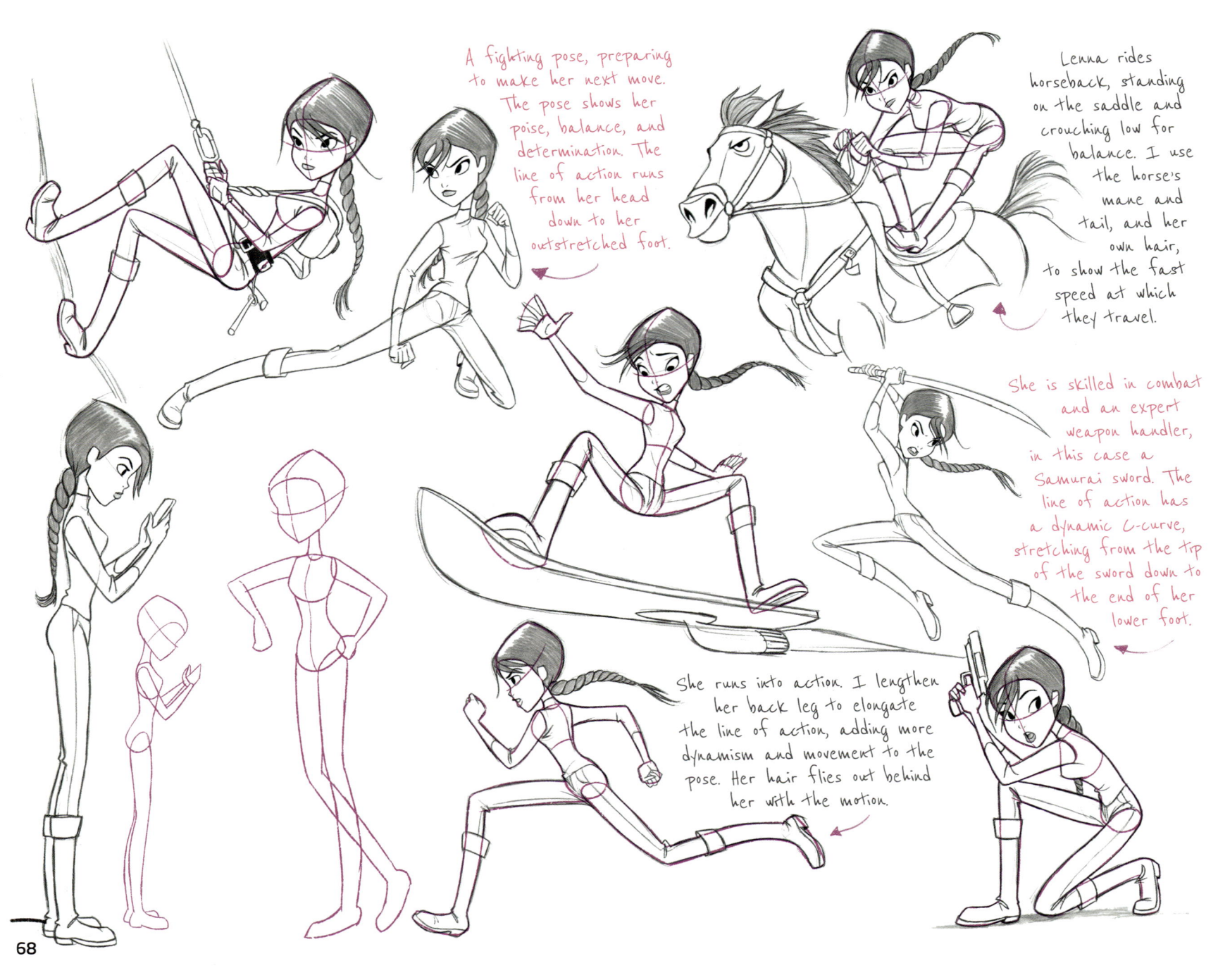

A fighting pose, preparing to make her next move. The pose shows her poise, balance, and determination. The line of action runs from her head down to her outstretched foot.

Lenna rides horseback, standing on the saddle and crouching low for balance. I use the horse's mane and tail, and her own hair, to show the fast speed at which they travel.

She is skilled in combat and an expert weapon handler, in this case a Samurai sword. The line of action has a dynamic C-curve, stretching from the tip of the sword down to the end of her lower foot.

She runs into action. I lengthen her back leg to elongate the line of action, adding more dynamism and movement to the pose. Her hair flies out behind her with the motion.

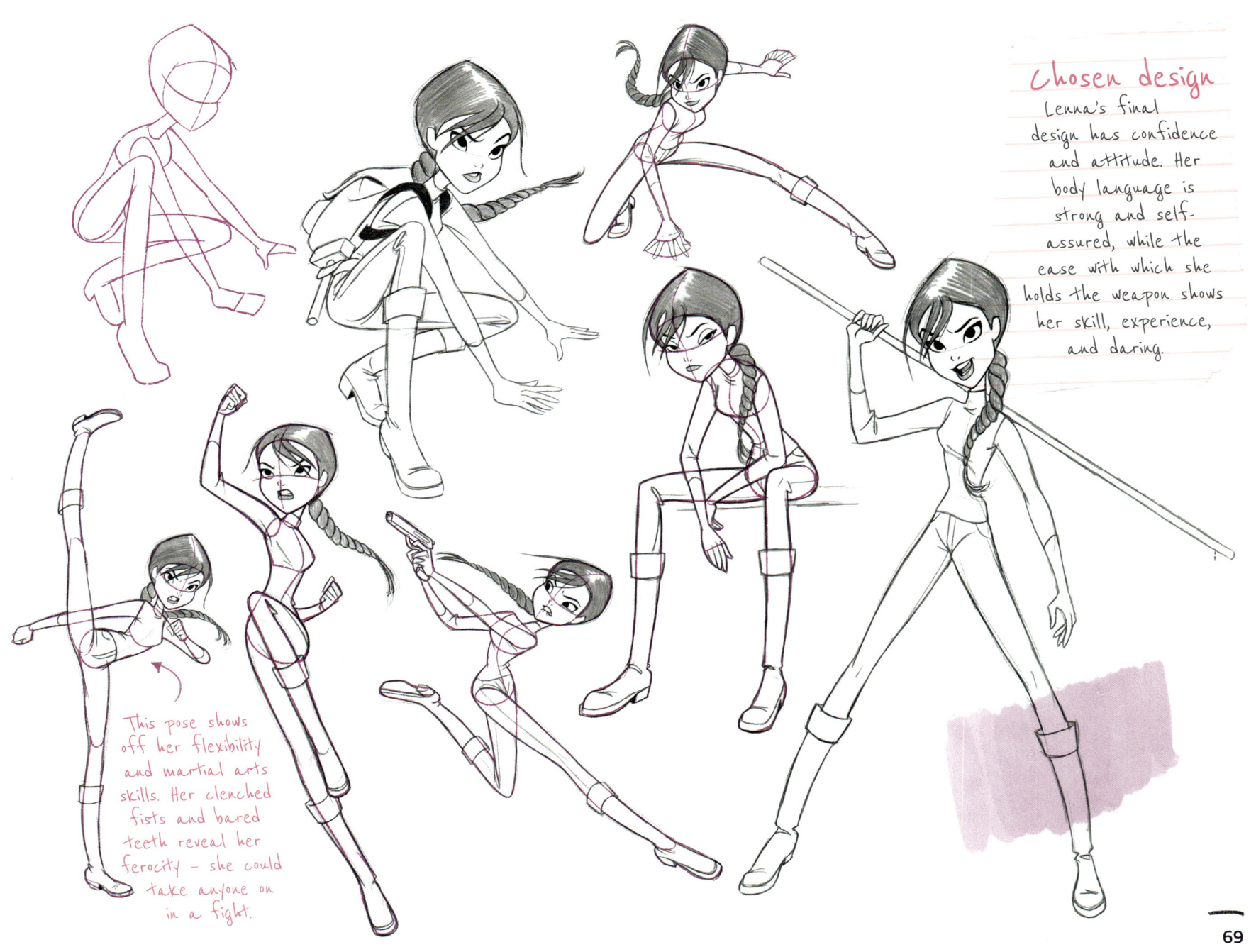

Chosen design

Lenna's final design has confidence and attitude. Her body language is strong and self-assured, while the ease with which she holds the weapon shows her skill, experience, and daring.

This pose shows off her flexibility and martial arts skills. Her clenched fists and bared teeth reveal her ferocity — she could take anyone on in a fight.

Sea pixie

THIS SKETCHBOOK BELONGS TO: Sarah Conradsen

This jellyfish pixie is a feisty free spirit who loves exploring the ocean. Kaia is a small, inquisitive, happy-go-lucky character with a fiery temper when provoked. Her legs are covered with scales and fins, and though her natural color is a semi-translucent blue-green, she changes to a pink and orange when angry. One day a plastic bag collides with her. Initially she doesn't know what it is, but as more and more plastic surrounds her, she takes it upon herself to go on a quest and fight the intruder who's disturbed her paradise.

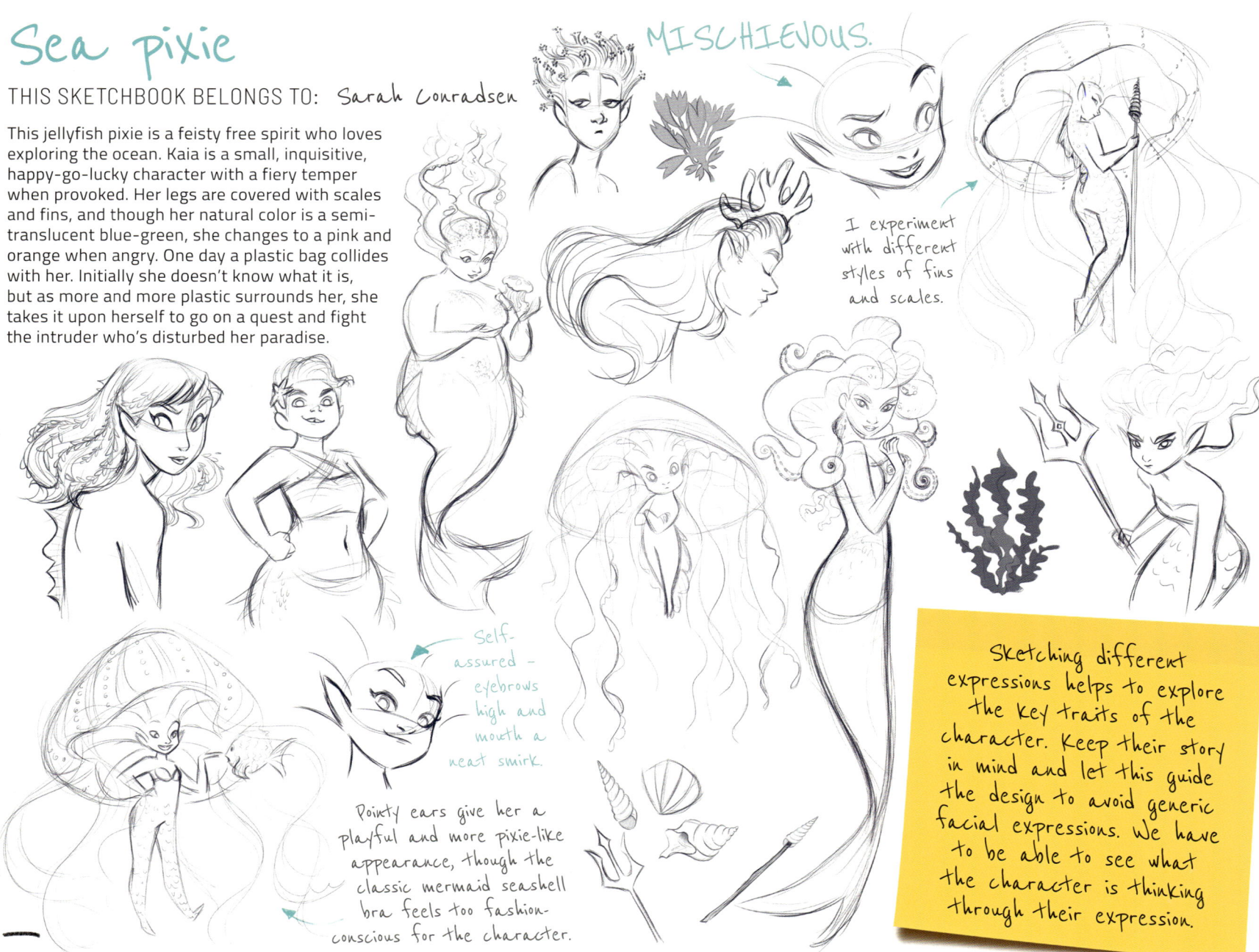

MISCHIEVOUS.

I experiment with different styles of fins and scales.

Self-assured – eyebrows high and mouth a neat smirk.

Pointy ears give her a playful and more pixie-like appearance, though the classic mermaid seashell bra feels too fashion-conscious for the character.

Sketching different expressions helps to explore the key traits of the character. Keep their story in mind and let this guide the design to avoid generic facial expressions. We have to be able to see what the character is thinking through their expression.

70

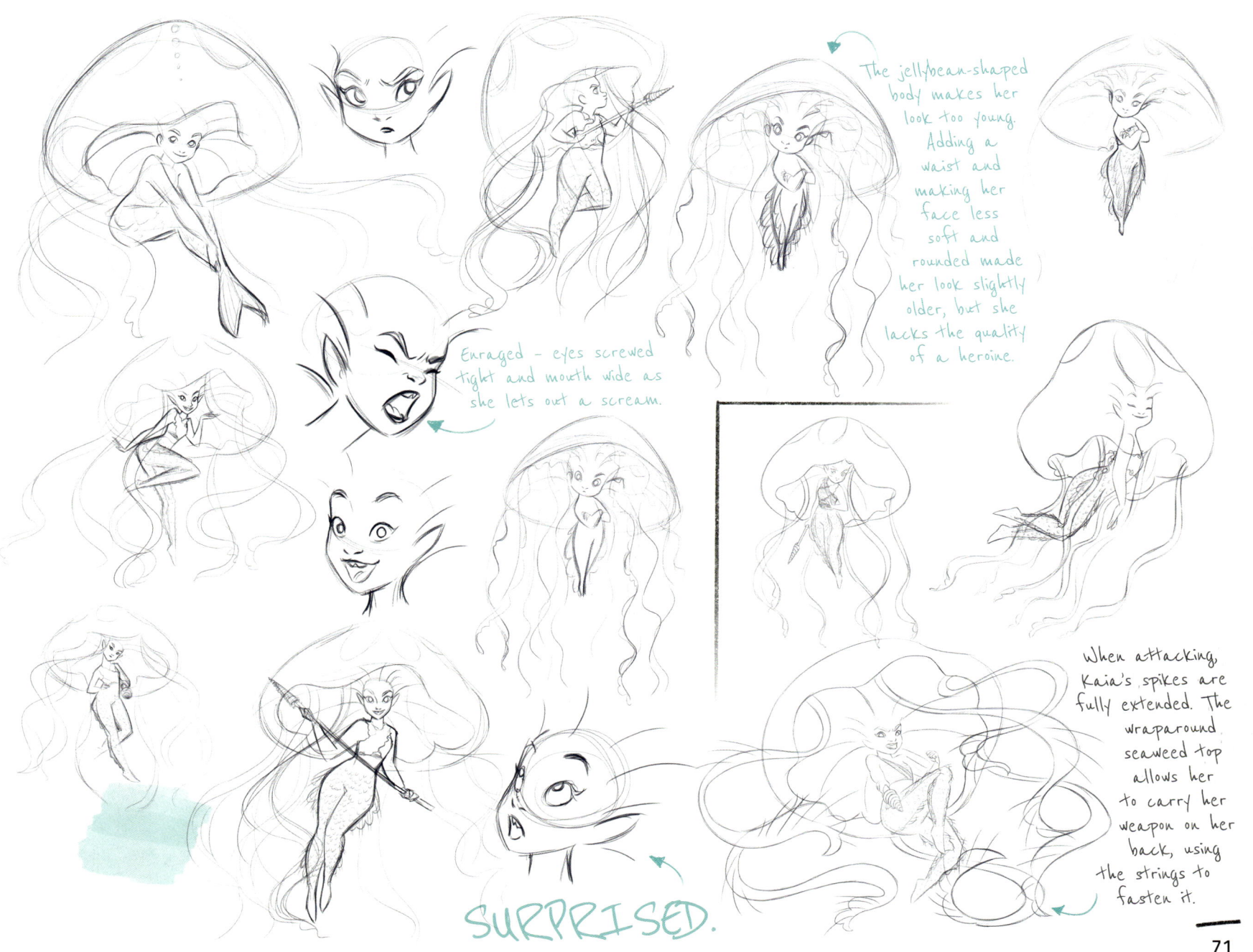

The jellybean-shaped body makes her look too young. Adding a waist and making her face less soft and rounded made her look slightly older, but she lacks the quality of a heroine.

Enraged - eyes screwed tight and mouth wide as she lets out a scream.

When attacking, Kaia's spikes are fully extended. The wraparound seaweed top allows her to carry her weapon on her back, using the strings to fasten it.

SURPRISED.

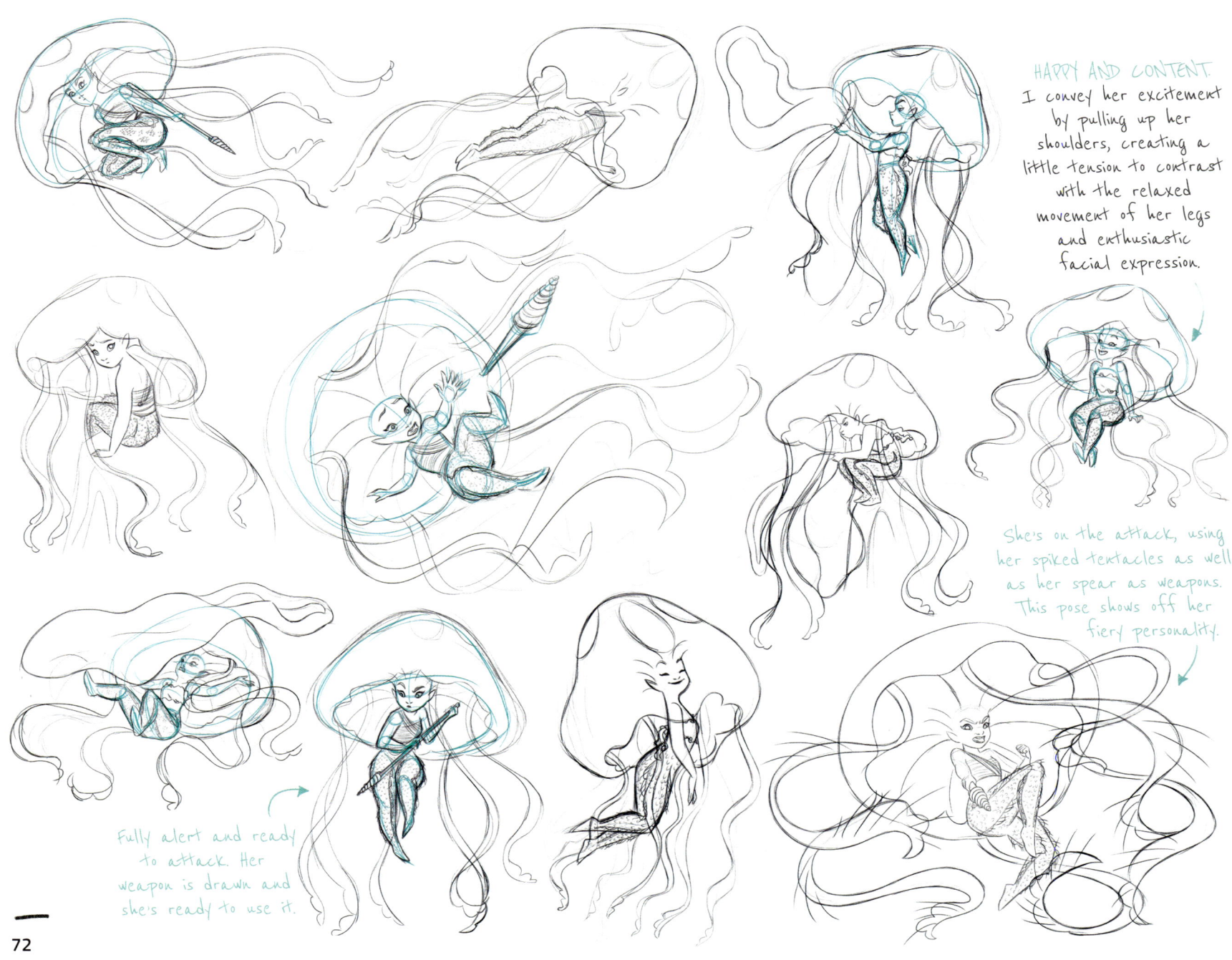

HAPPY AND CONTENT.
I convey her excitement
by pulling up her
shoulders, creating a
little tension to contrast
with the relaxed
movement of her legs
and enthusiastic
facial expression.

She's on the attack, using
her spiked tentacles as well
as her spear as weapons.
This pose shows off her
fiery personality.

Fully alert and ready
to attack. Her
weapon is drawn and
she's ready to use it.

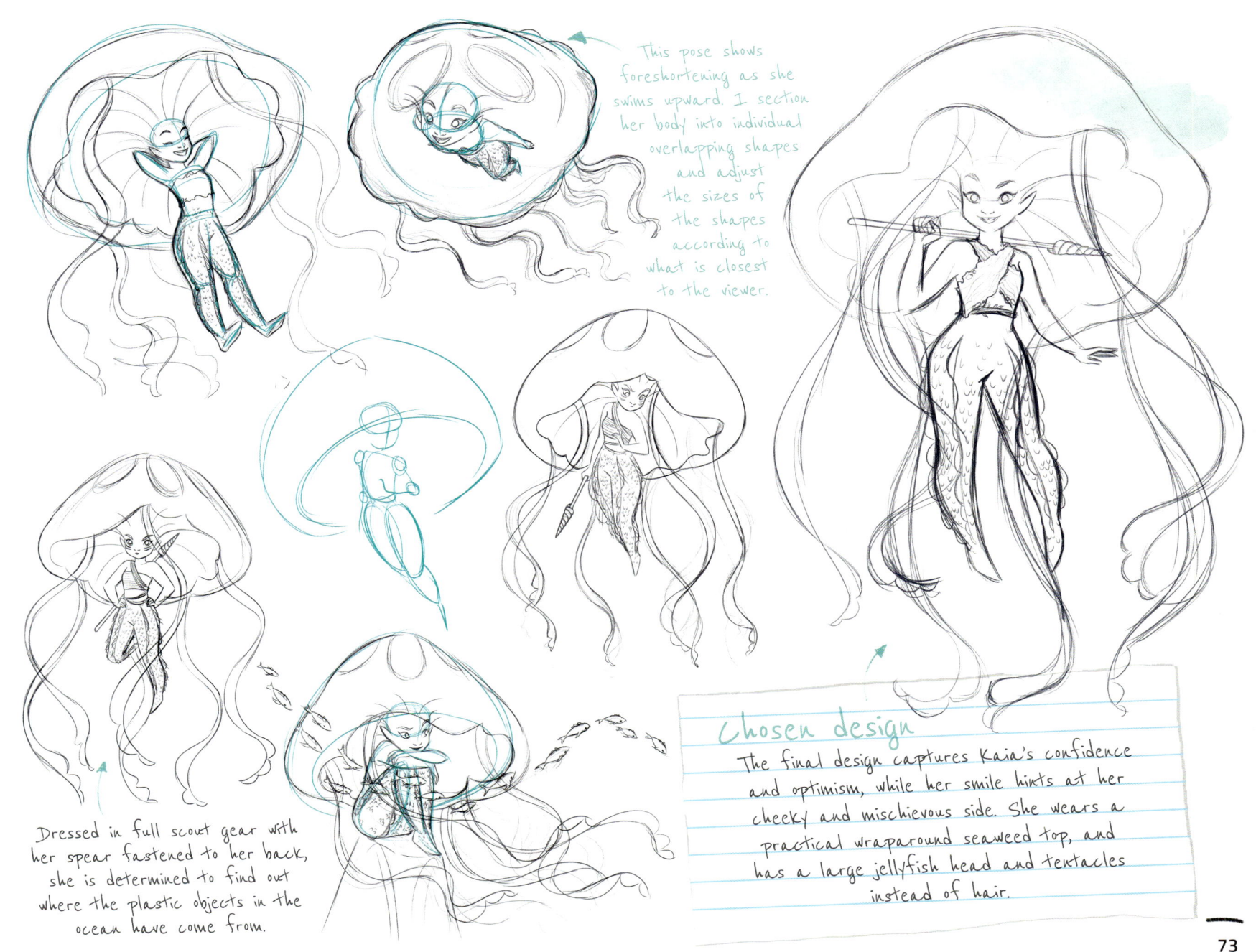

This pose shows foreshortening as she swims upward. I section her body into individual overlapping shapes and adjust the sizes of the shapes according to what is closest to the viewer.

Dressed in full scout gear with her spear fastened to her back, she is determined to find out where the plastic objects in the ocean have come from.

Chosen design

The final design captures Kaia's confidence and optimism, while her smile hints at her cheeky and mischievous side. She wears a practical wraparound seaweed top, and has a large jellyfish head and tentacles instead of hair.

Forest imp

THIS SKETCHBOOK BELONGS TO: Russell Del Socorro

Iris is a mischievous forest imp. She is a gatherer, traveler, and free spirit. Born from an ancient race or deity, she lives in the forest and is deeply connected to nature, and is wary of the modern world. She has magical plant powers, can fly, and uses natural elements like leaves and seed pods as weapons to protect herself.

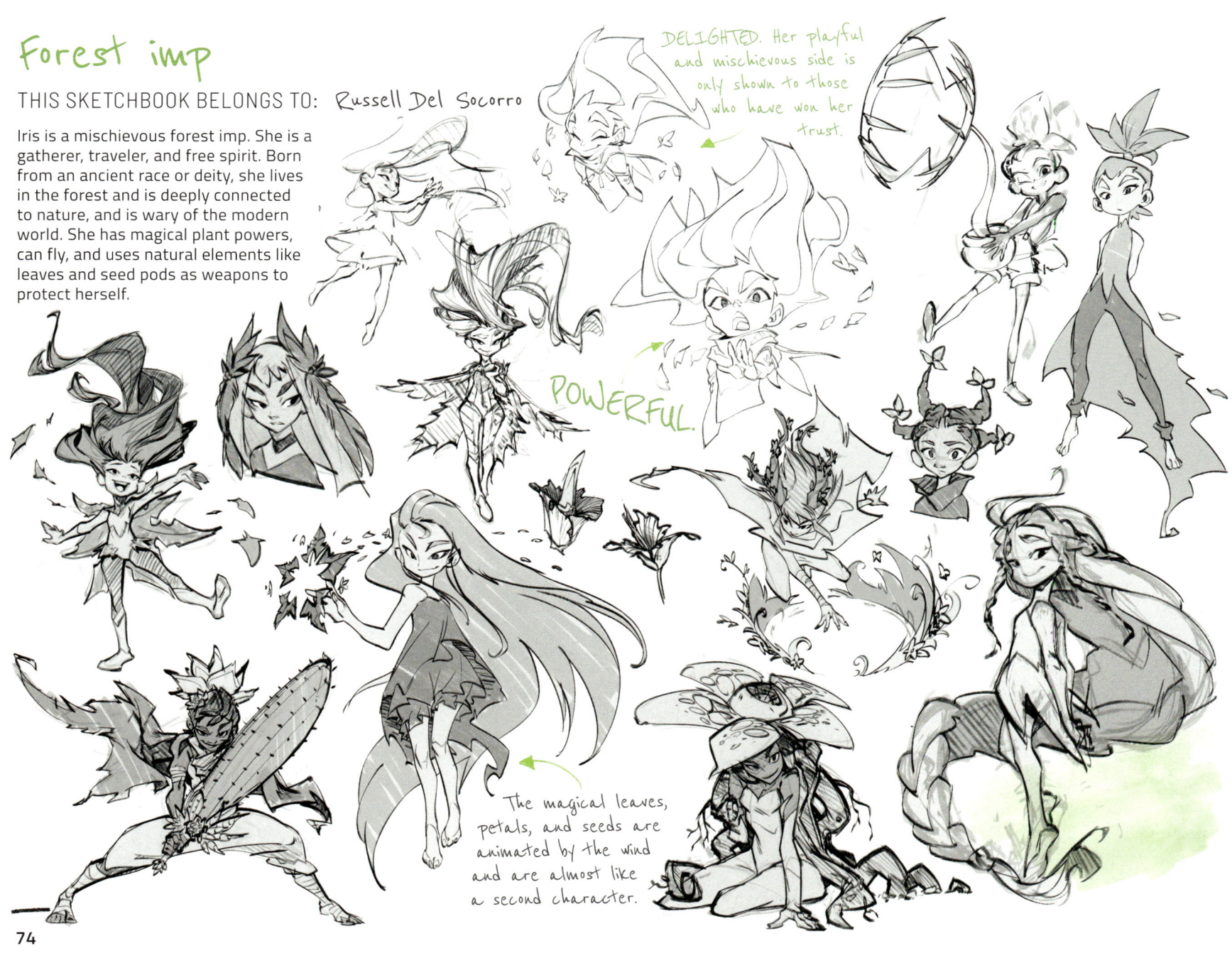

DELIGHTED. Her playful and mischievous side is only shown to those who have won her trust.

POWERFUL.

The magical leaves, petals, and seeds are animated by the wind and are almost like a second character.

74

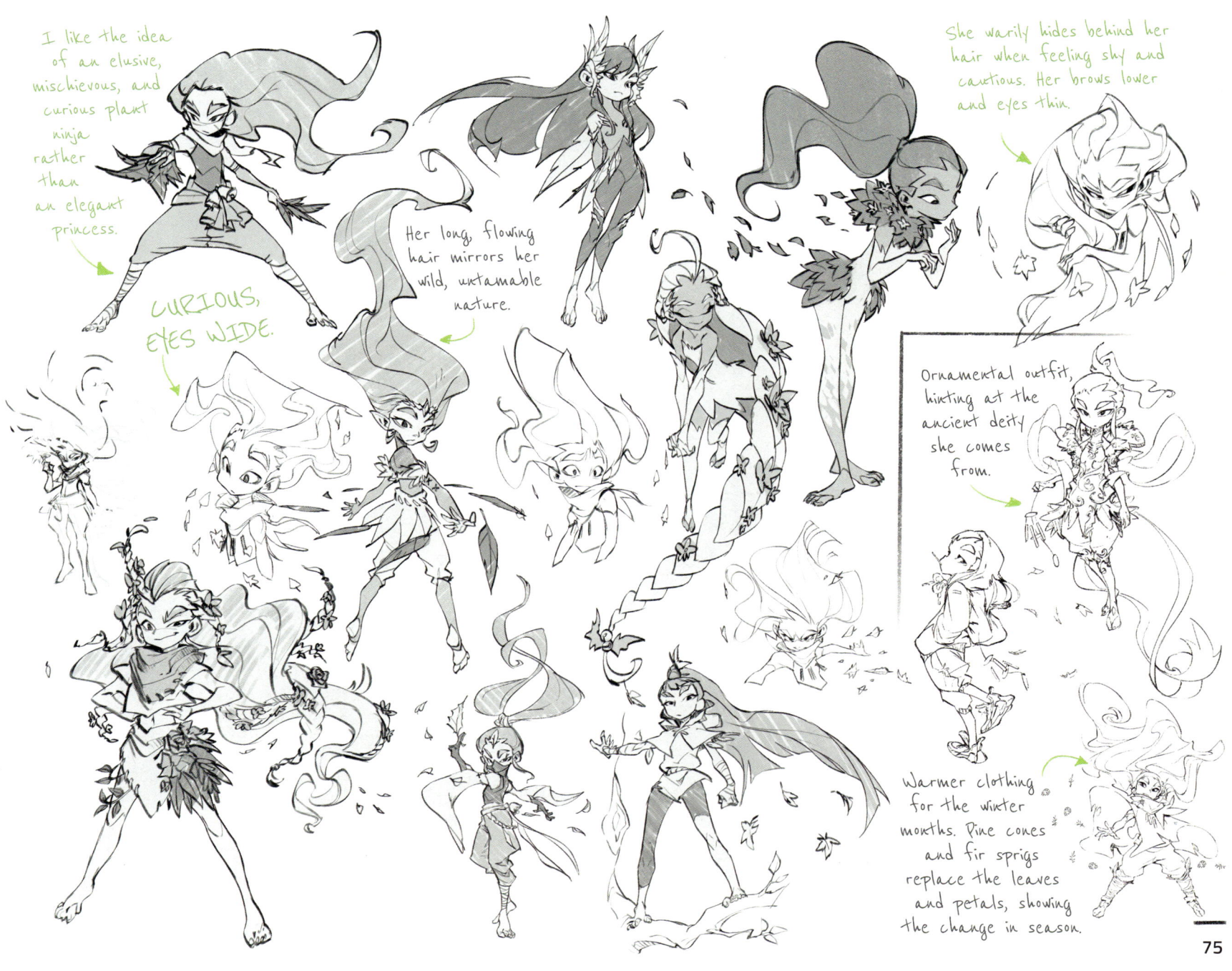

I like the idea of an elusive, mischievous, and curious plant ninja rather than an elegant princess.

She warily hides behind her hair when feeling shy and cautious. Her brows lower and eyes thin.

Her long, flowing hair mirrors her wild, untamable nature.

CURIOUS, EYES WIDE.

Ornamental outfit, hinting at the ancient deity she comes from.

Warmer clothing for the winter months. Pine cones and fir sprigs replace the leaves and petals, showing the change in season.

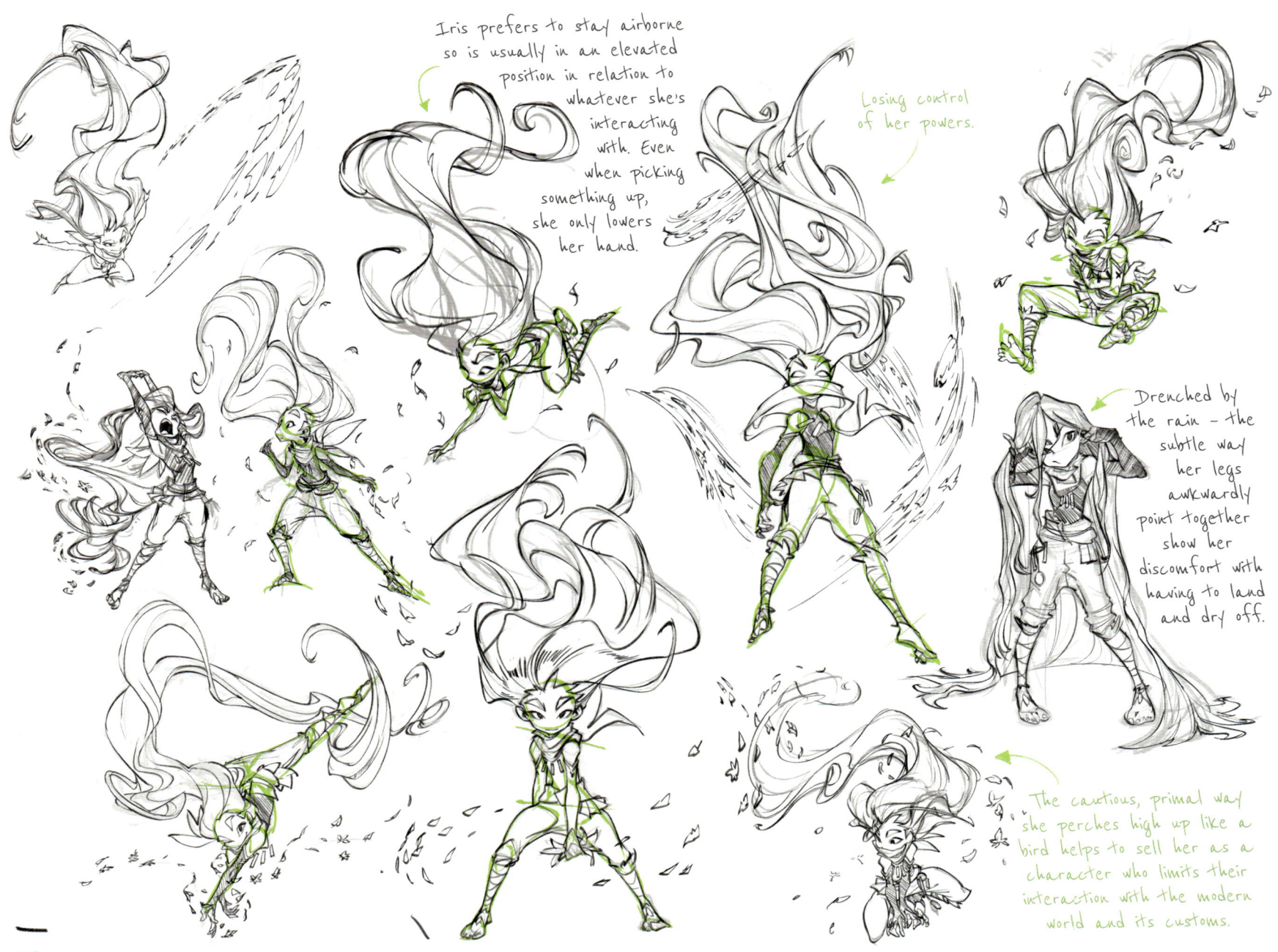

Iris prefers to stay airborne so is usually in an elevated position in relation to whatever she's interacting with. Even when picking something up, she only lowers her hand.

Losing control of her powers.

Drenched by the rain – the subtle way her legs awkwardly point together show her discomfort with having to land and dry off.

The cautious, primal way she perches high up like a bird helps to sell her as a character who limits their interaction with the modern world and its customs.

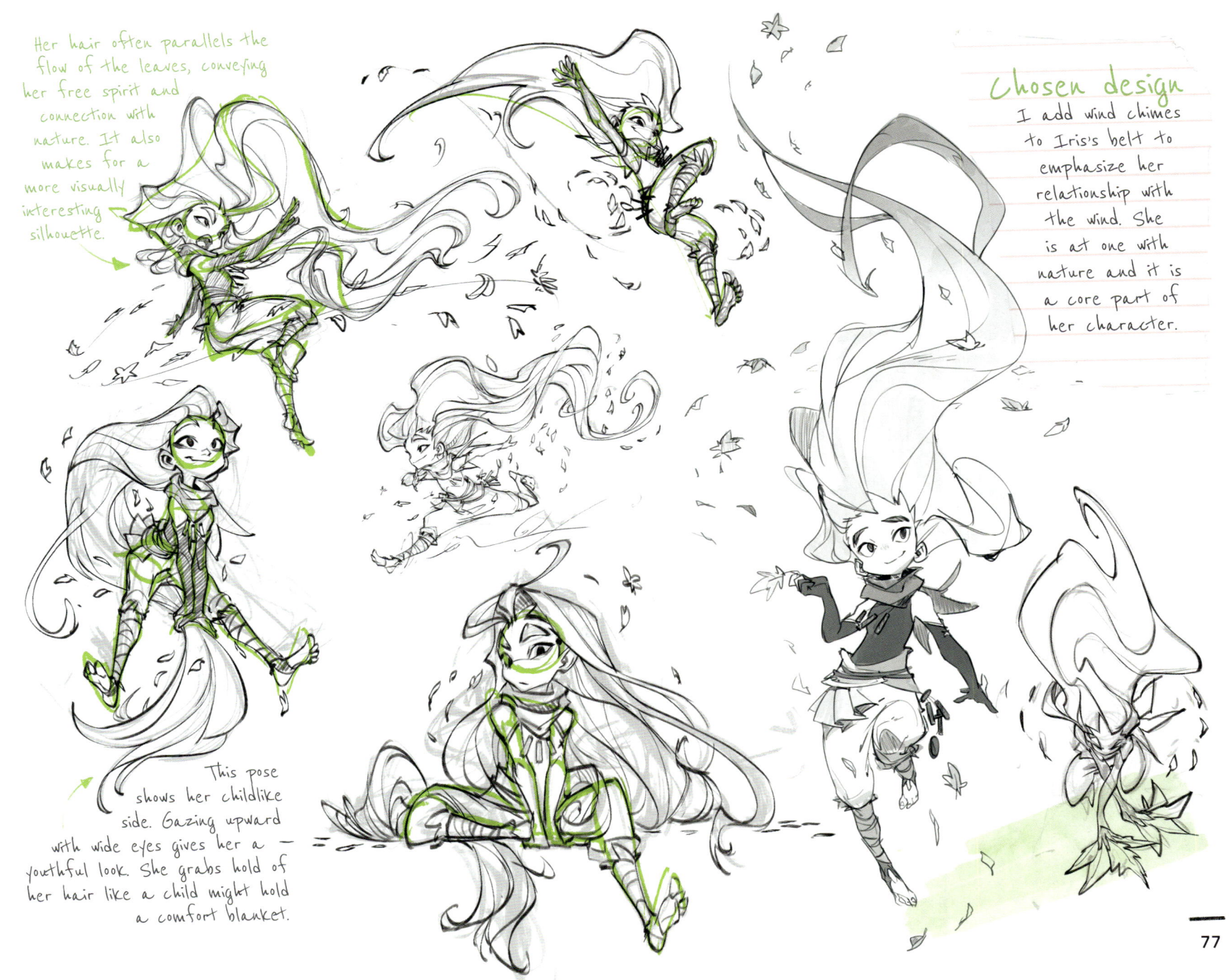

Her hair often parallels the flow of the leaves, conveying her free spirit and connection with nature. It also makes for a more visually interesting silhouette.

I add wind chimes to Iris's belt to emphasize her relationship with the wind. She is at one with nature and it is a core part of her character.

This pose shows her childlike side. Gazing upward with wide eyes gives her a youthful look. She grabs hold of her hair like a child might hold a comfort blanket.

Animal superheroine

THIS SKETCHBOOK BELONGS TO: Magdalina Dianova

Wesley is a teenage girl from Brooklyn, New York. A rebel by nature and a bit of a tomboy, she never bothers to brush her hair and survives on a diet of fast food. Though she attends school by day, she emerges at twilight to skulk around the neighborhood as a raccoon-themed superheroine. Cunning, sly, and highly intelligent, she is a skilled fighter and has astute sensory awareness. She's also curious, easygoing, and fun, with a weird habit of rooting through the trash on the hunt for an interesting find.

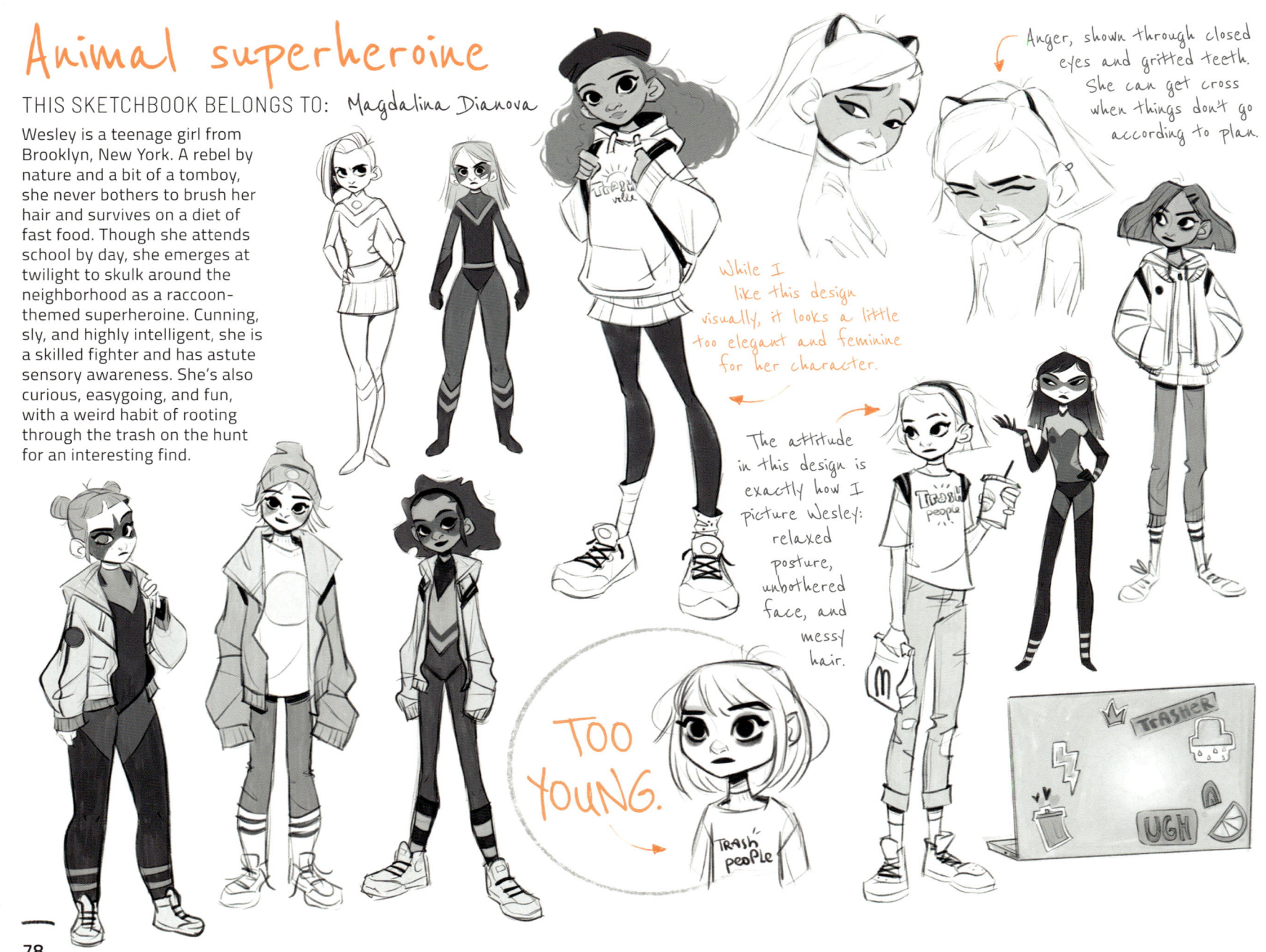

Anger, shown through closed eyes and gritted teeth. She can get cross when things don't go according to plan.

While I like this design visually, it looks a little too elegant and feminine for her character.

The attitude in this design is exactly how I picture Wesley: relaxed posture, unbothered face, and messy hair.

TOO YOUNG.

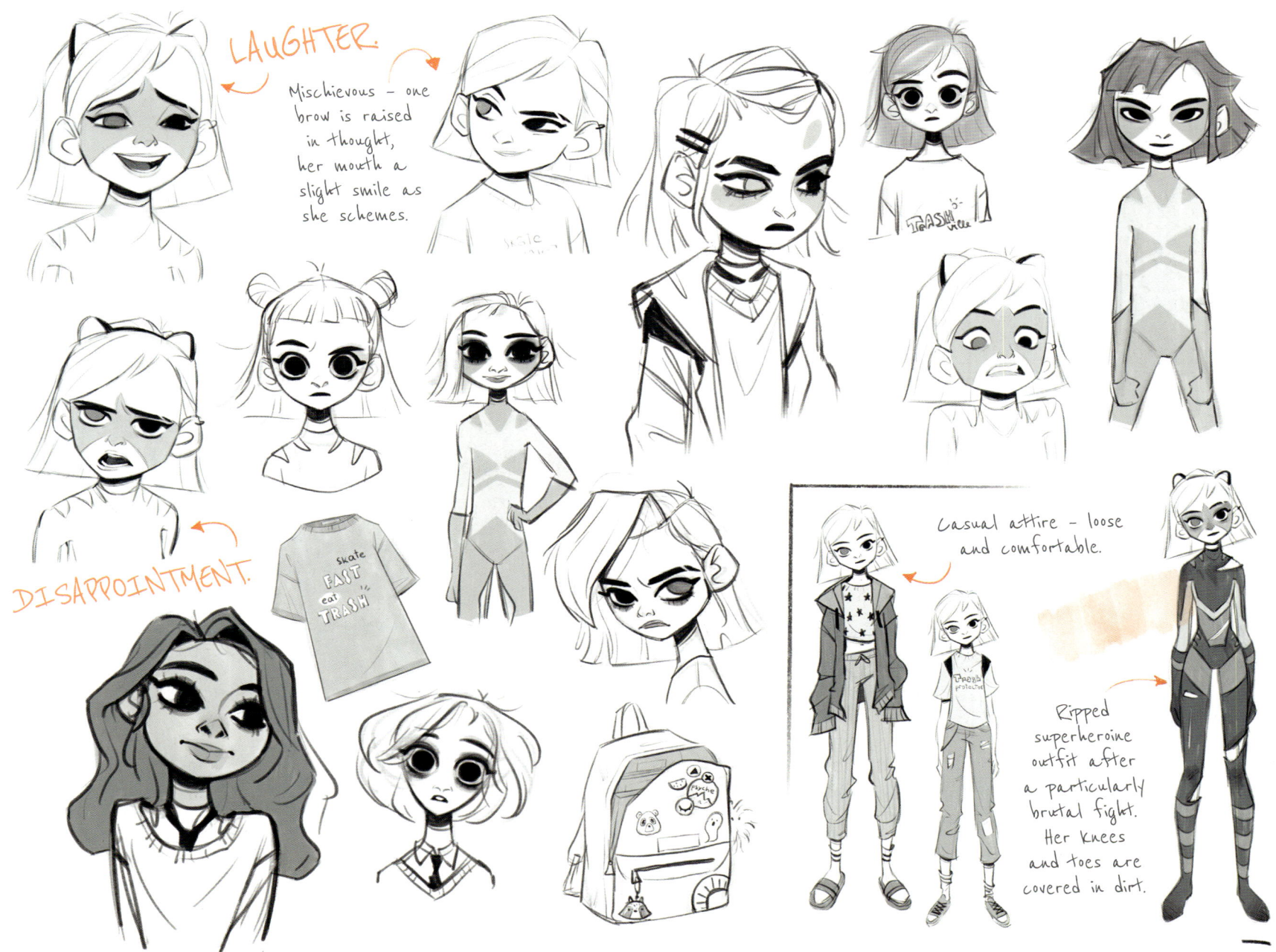

LAUGHTER.

Mischievous - one brow is raised in thought, her mouth a slight smile as she schemes.

DISAPPOINTMENT.

Casual attire - loose and comfortable.

Ripped superheroine outfit after a particularly brutal fight. Her knees and toes are covered in dirt.

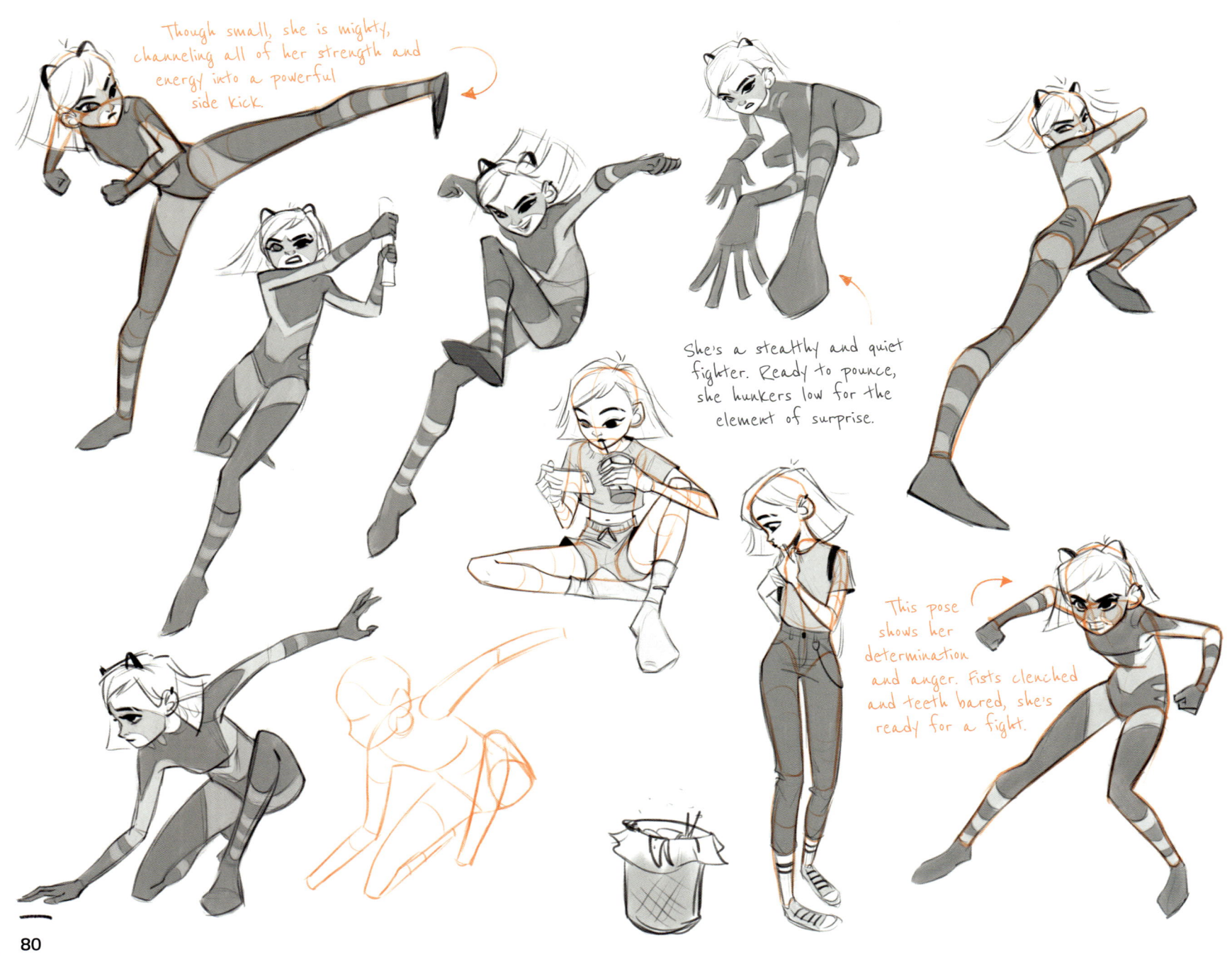

Though small, she is mighty, channeling all of her strength and energy into a powerful side kick.

She's a stealthy and quiet fighter. Ready to pounce, she hunkers low for the element of surprise.

This pose shows her determination and anger. Fists clenched and teeth bared, she's ready for a fight.

80

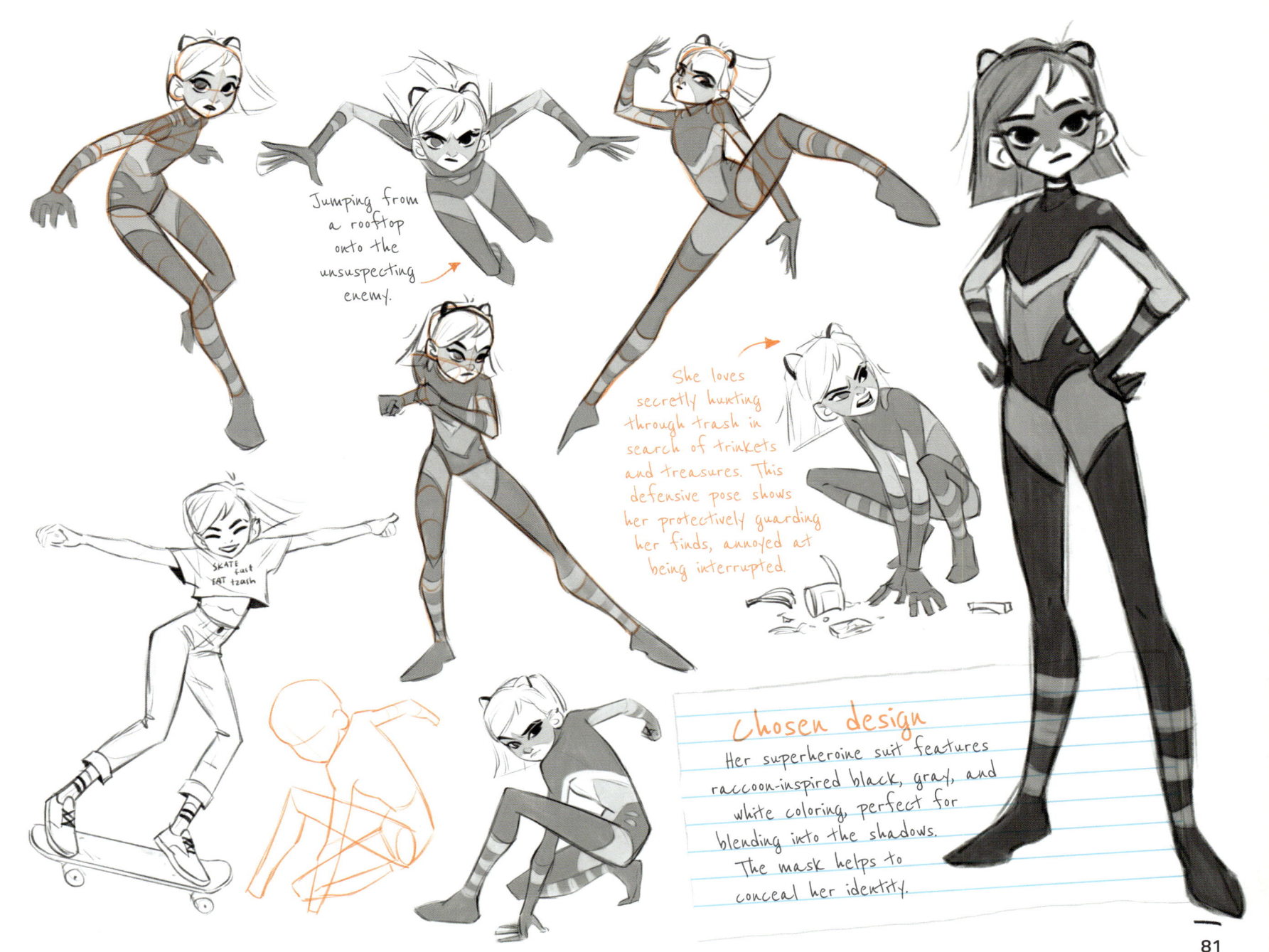

Jumping from a rooftop onto the unsuspecting enemy.

She loves secretly hunting through trash in search of trinkets and treasures. This defensive pose shows her protectively guarding her finds, annoyed at being interrupted.

SKATE fast
EAT trash

Chosen design
Her superheroine suit features raccoon-inspired black, gray, and white coloring, perfect for blending into the shadows. The mask helps to conceal her identity.

Teen superheroine

THIS SKETCHBOOK BELONGS TO: Jackie Droujko

Many know Darya as the quiet, introverted star of the school swim team... but she's also a strong, confident water-bending teen superheroine! Cool and collected, she has a casual superheroine costume, almost like she could have put it together herself over her swimming uniform. Avoiding the sexy superheroine cliché, she has a youthful appearance and strong swimmer legs that fit with her petite frame.

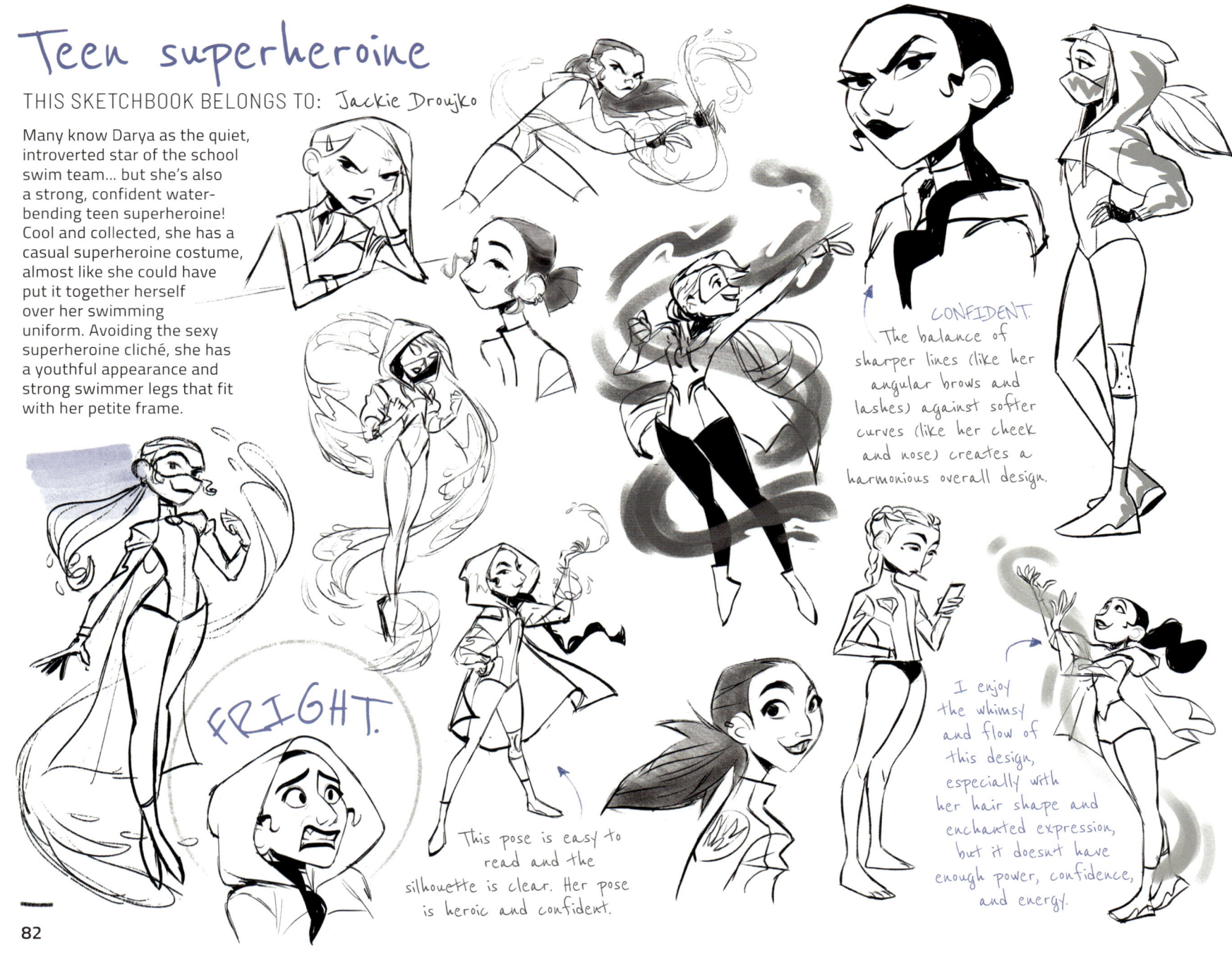

CONFIDENT.
The balance of sharper lines (like her angular brows and lashes) against softer curves (like her cheek and nose) creates a harmonious overall design.

FRIGHT.

This pose is easy to read and the silhouette is clear. Her pose is heroic and confident.

I enjoy the whimsy and flow of this design, especially with her hair shape and enchanted expression, but it doesn't have enough power, confidence, and energy.

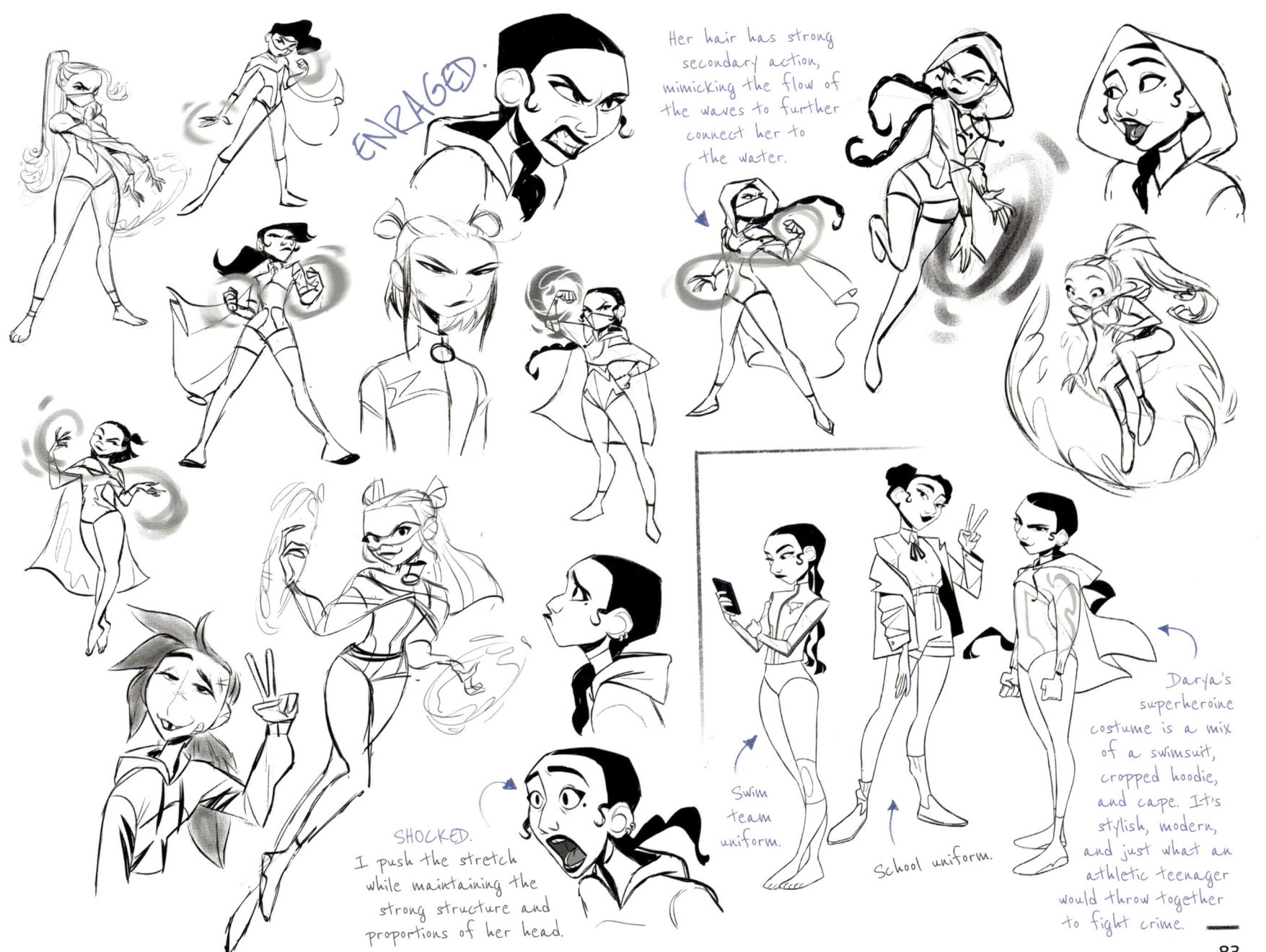

ENRAGED.

Her hair has strong secondary action, mimicking the flow of the waves to further connect her to the water.

SHOCKED.
I push the stretch while maintaining the strong structure and proportions of her head.

Swim team uniform.

School uniform.

Darya's superheroine costume is a mix of a swimsuit, cropped hoodie, and cape. It's stylish, modern, and just what an athletic teenager would throw together to fight crime.

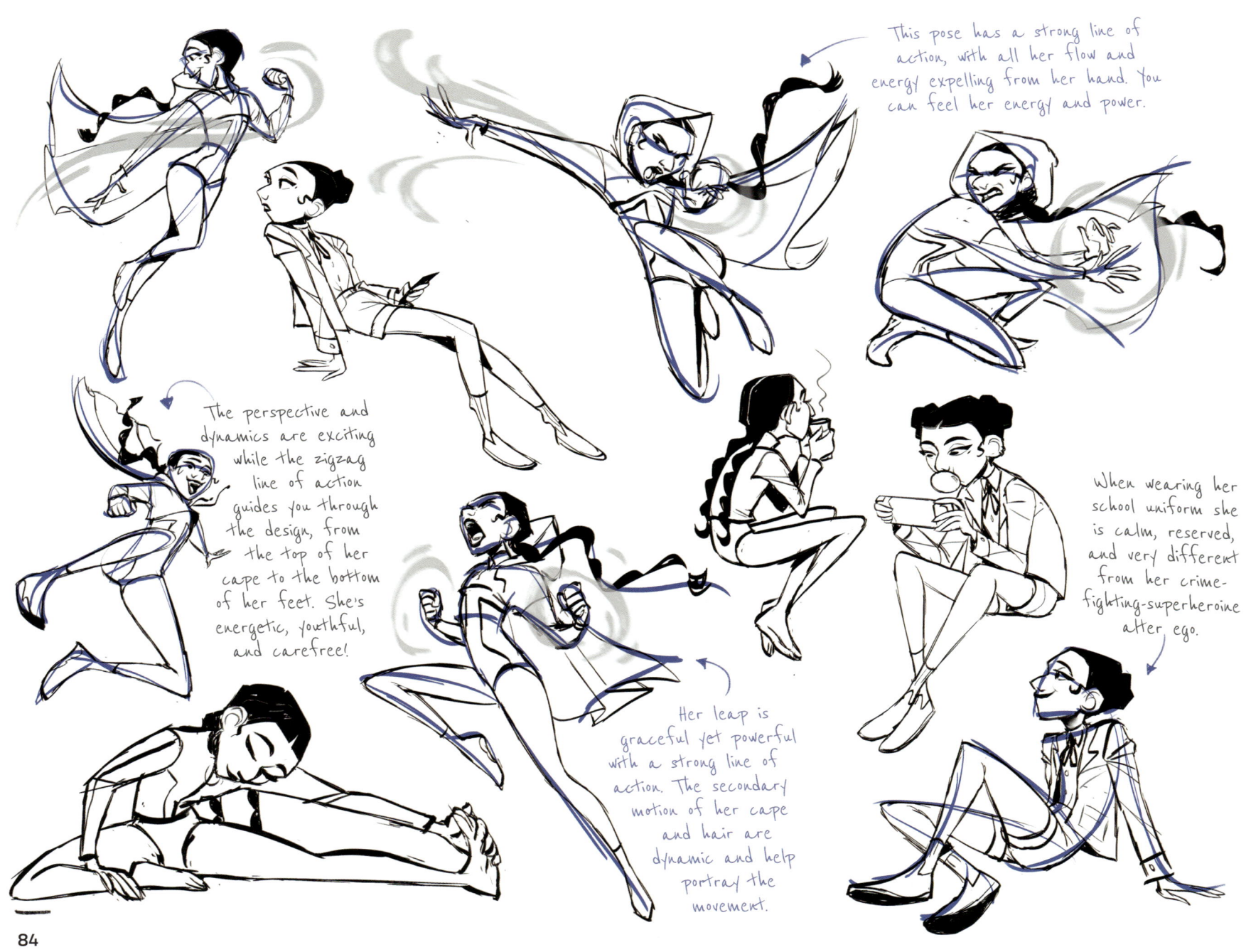

This pose has a strong line of action, with all her flow and energy expelling from her hand. You can feel her energy and power.

The perspective and dynamics are exciting while the zigzag line of action guides you through the design, from the top of her cape to the bottom of her feet. She's energetic, youthful, and carefree!

Her leap is graceful yet powerful with a strong line of action. The secondary motion of her cape and hair are dynamic and help portray the movement.

When wearing her school uniform she is calm, reserved, and very different from her crime-fighting-superheroine alter ego.

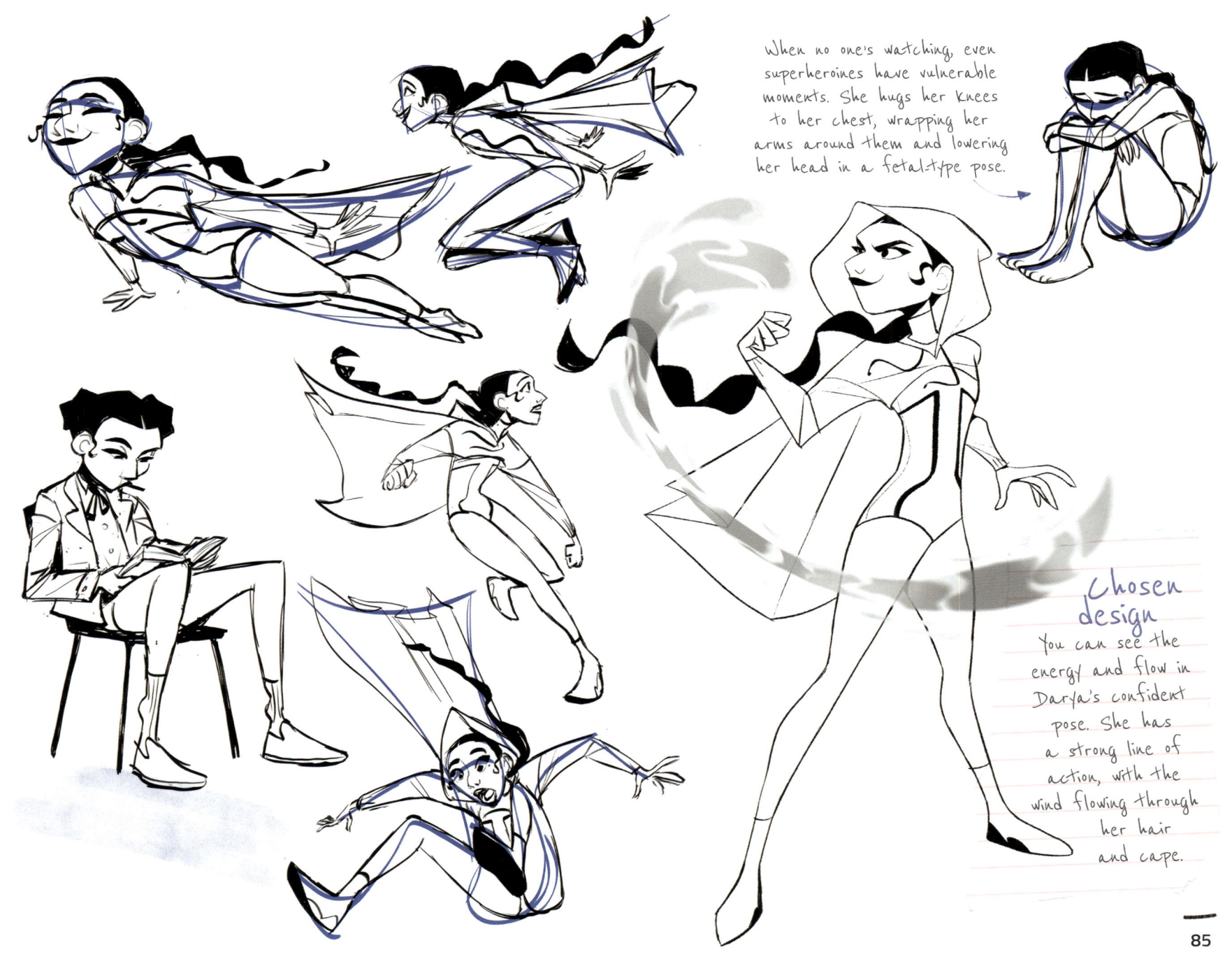

When no one's watching, even superheroines have vulnerable moments. She hugs her knees to her chest, wrapping her arms around them and lowering her head in a fetal-type pose.

Chosen design
You can see the energy and flow in Darya's confident pose. She has a strong line of action, with the wind flowing through her hair and cape.

Ancient Egyptian warrior

THIS SKETCHBOOK BELONGS TO: Marta García Navarro "MARGANA"

Stubborn and a little proud, Sekhmet is an Ancient Egyptian heroine from a wealthy, noble family close to the pharaoh. Though she was raised to be a courtier and marry well, she's set against a marriage of convenience and wants to become a warrior. Training in secret, she is lethal with a spear and defends the village people from the pharaoh's abusive soldiers. Graceful yet fierce, she is taller than most women and hates attending superficial parties for Egypt's nobility.

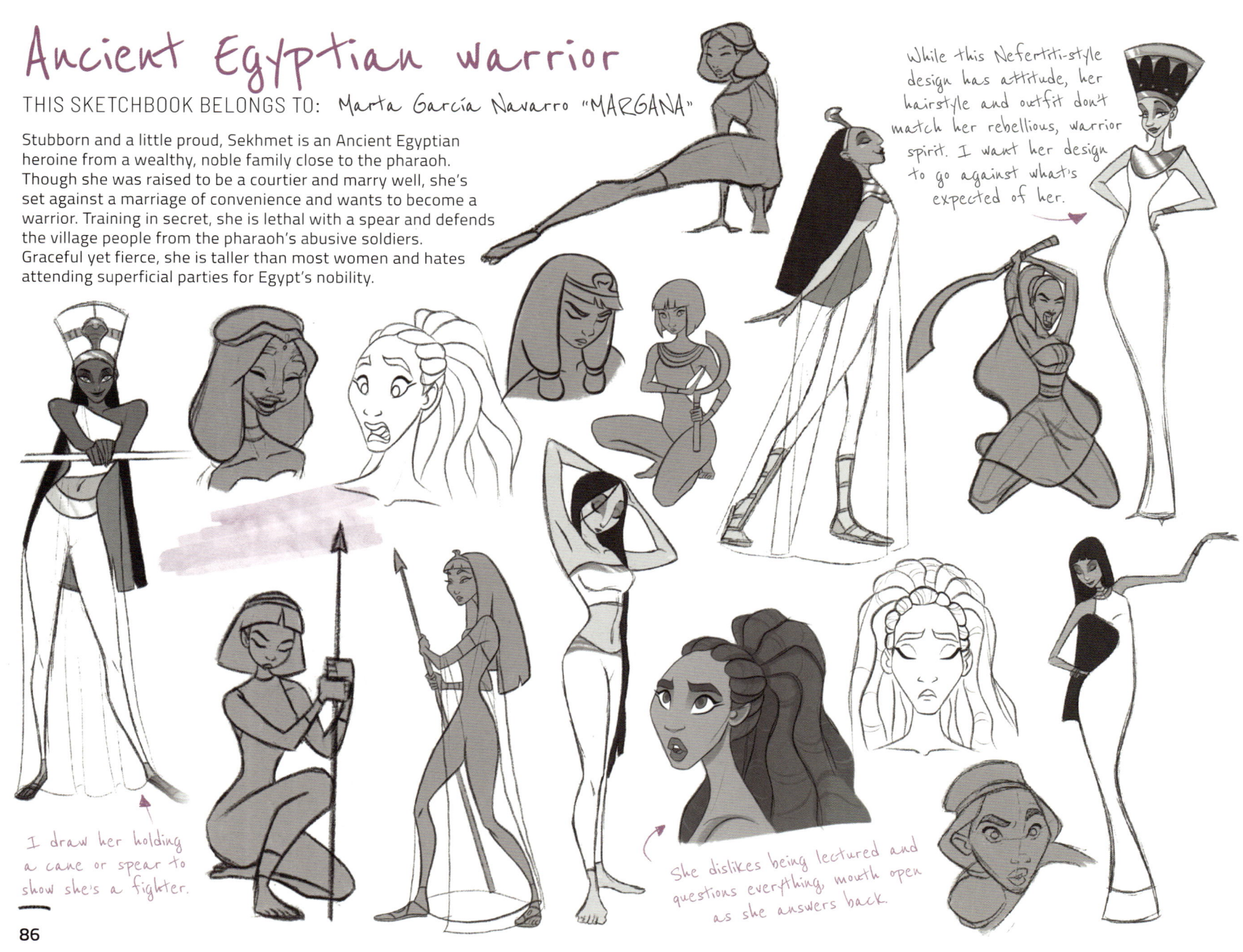

While this Nefertiti-style design has attitude, her hairstyle and outfit don't match her rebellious, warrior spirit. I want her design to go against what's expected of her.

I draw her holding a cane or spear to show she's a fighter.

She dislikes being lectured and questions everything, mouth open as she answers back.

86

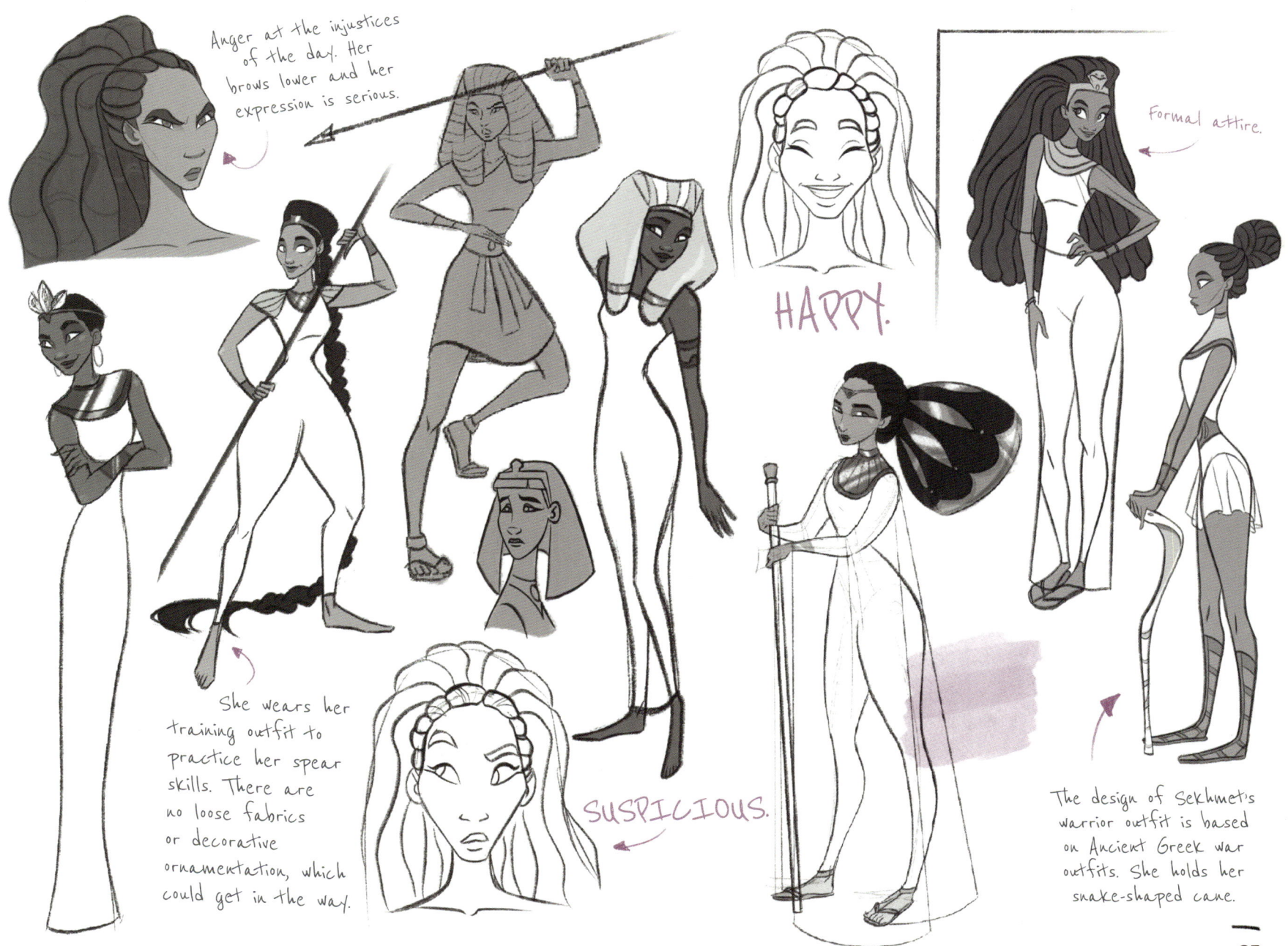

Anger at the injustices of the day. Her brows lower and her expression is serious.

Formal attire.

HAPPY.

She wears her training outfit to practice her spear skills. There are no loose fabrics or decorative ornamentation, which could get in the way.

SUSPICIOUS.

The design of Sekhmet's warrior outfit is based on Ancient Greek war outfits. She holds her snake-shaped cane.

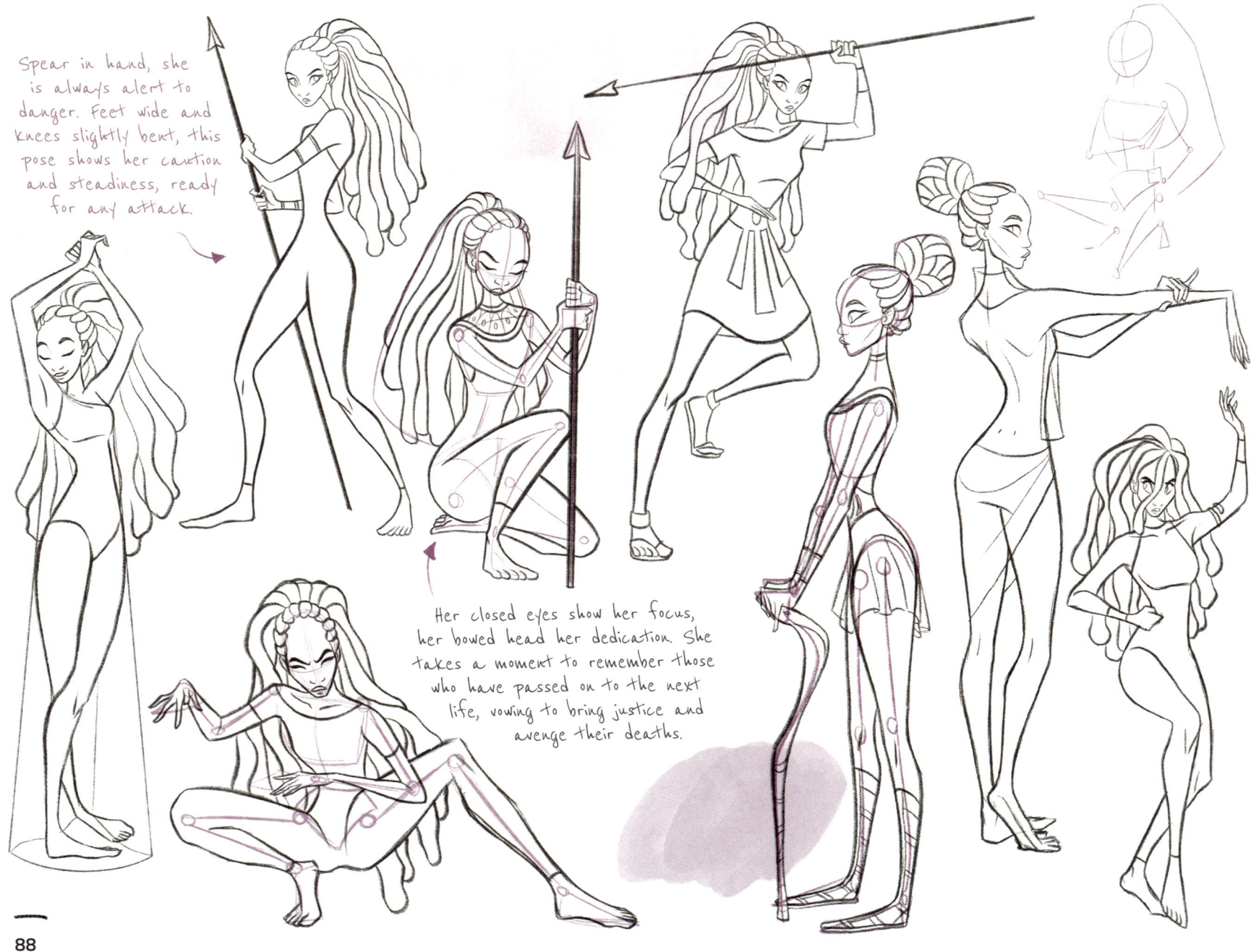

Spear in hand, she is always alert to danger. Feet wide and knees slightly bent, this pose shows her caution and steadiness, ready for any attack.

Her closed eyes show her focus, her bowed head her dedication. She takes a moment to remember those who have passed on to the next life, vowing to bring justice and avenge their deaths.

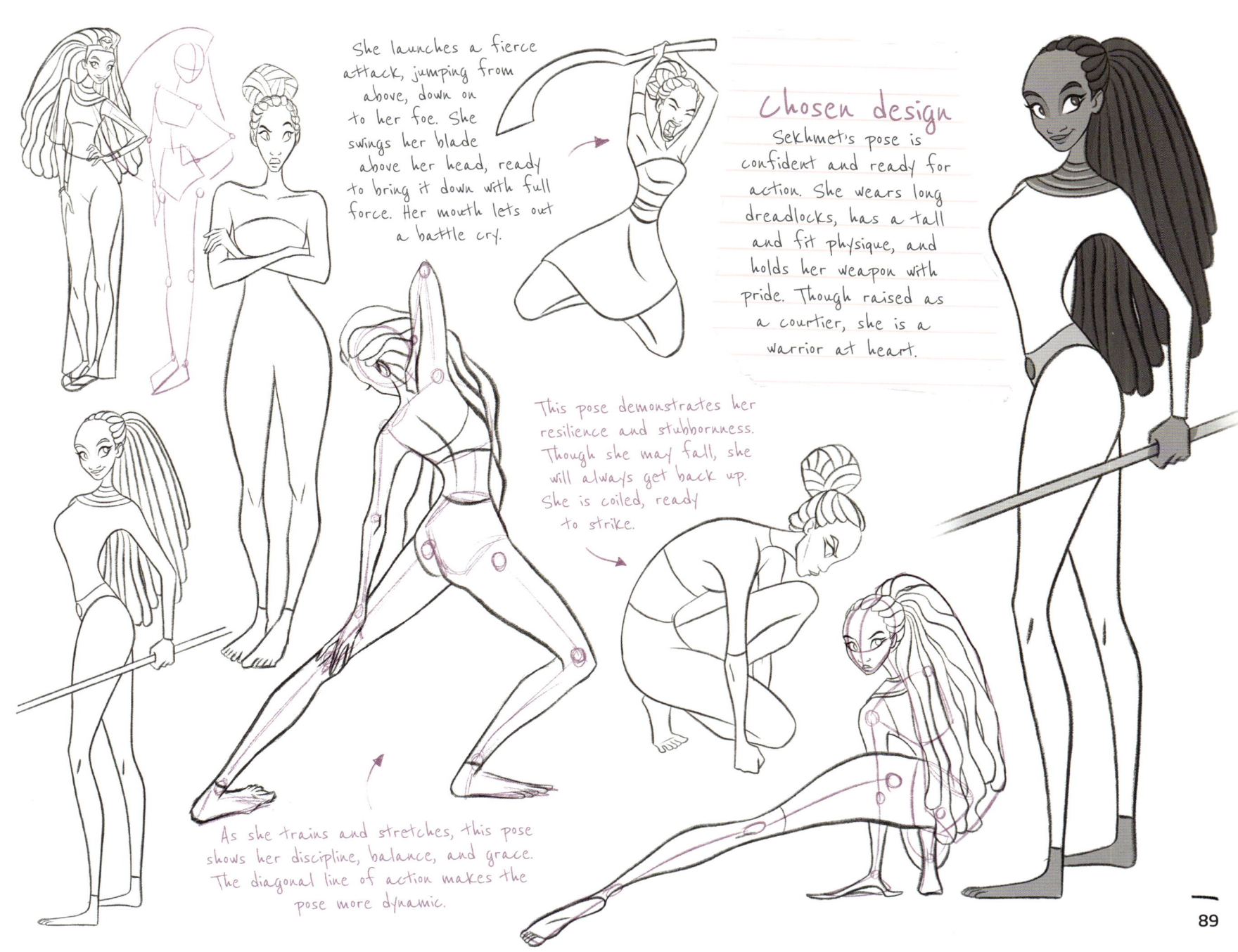

She launches a fierce attack, jumping from above, down on to her foe. She swings her blade above her head, ready to bring it down with full force. Her mouth lets out a battle cry.

Chosen design

Sekhmet's pose is confident and ready for action. She wears long dreadlocks, has a tall and fit physique, and holds her weapon with pride. Though raised as a courtier, she is a warrior at heart.

This pose demonstrates her resilience and stubbornness. Though she may fall, she will always get back up. She is coiled, ready to strike.

As she trains and stretches, this pose shows her discipline, balance, and grace. The diagonal line of action makes the pose more dynamic.

89

Samurai

Senshi is a sword-fighting samurai who grew up in a matriarchal society of strong, resilient women. Though there is no established hierarchy, it is a traditional culture and there is respect for the elderly and those who have gone before them. They work hard in the field by day, but are also experienced warriors, defending their region from those who would wish them harm. From a young age she has been taught not to be afraid of warfare or death, but to face the harshness of life head-on. Fierce, skilled, and brave, she lives and survives by the sword.

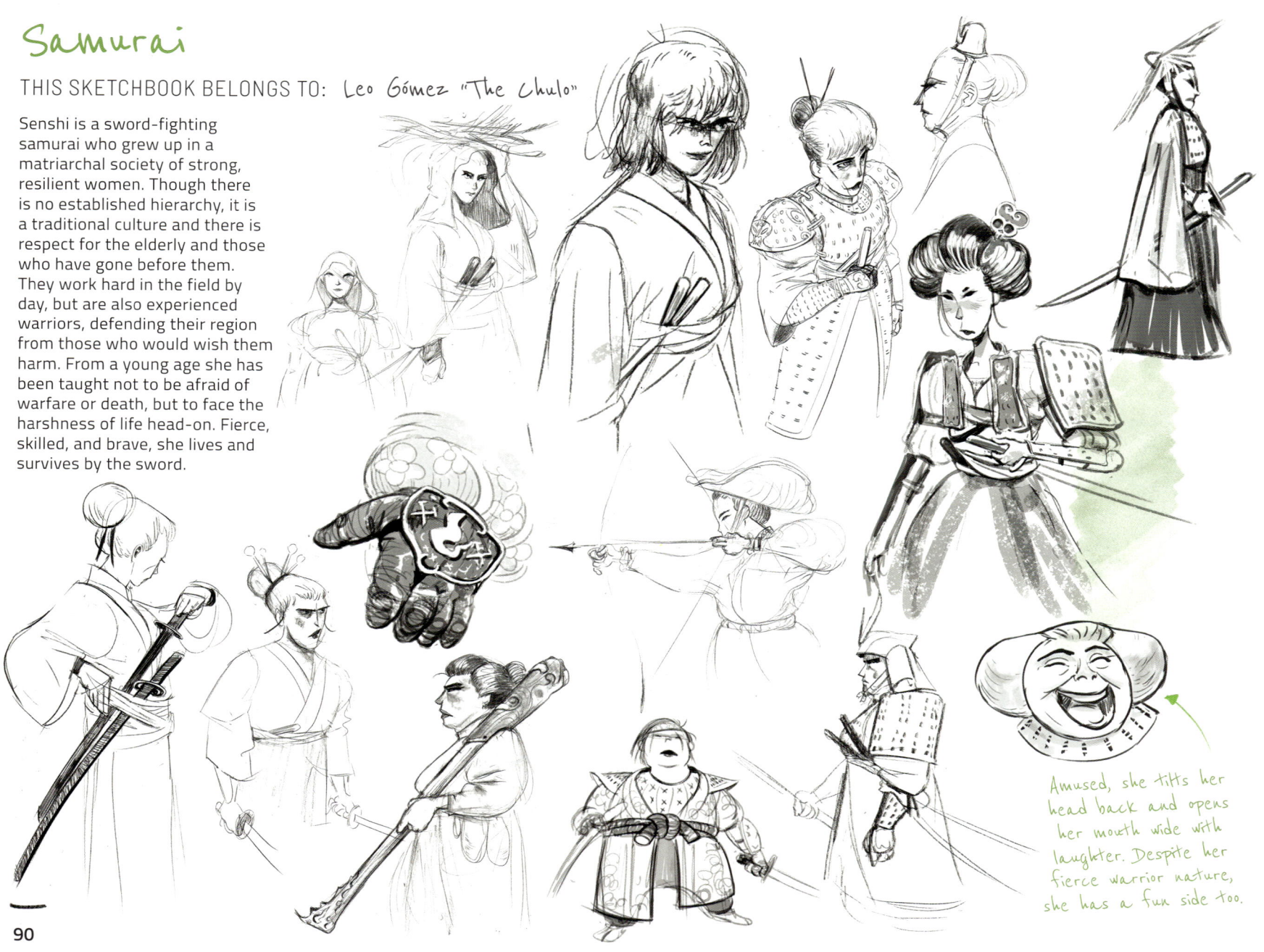

Amused, she tilts her head back and opens her mouth wide with laughter. Despite her fierce warrior nature, she has a fun side too.

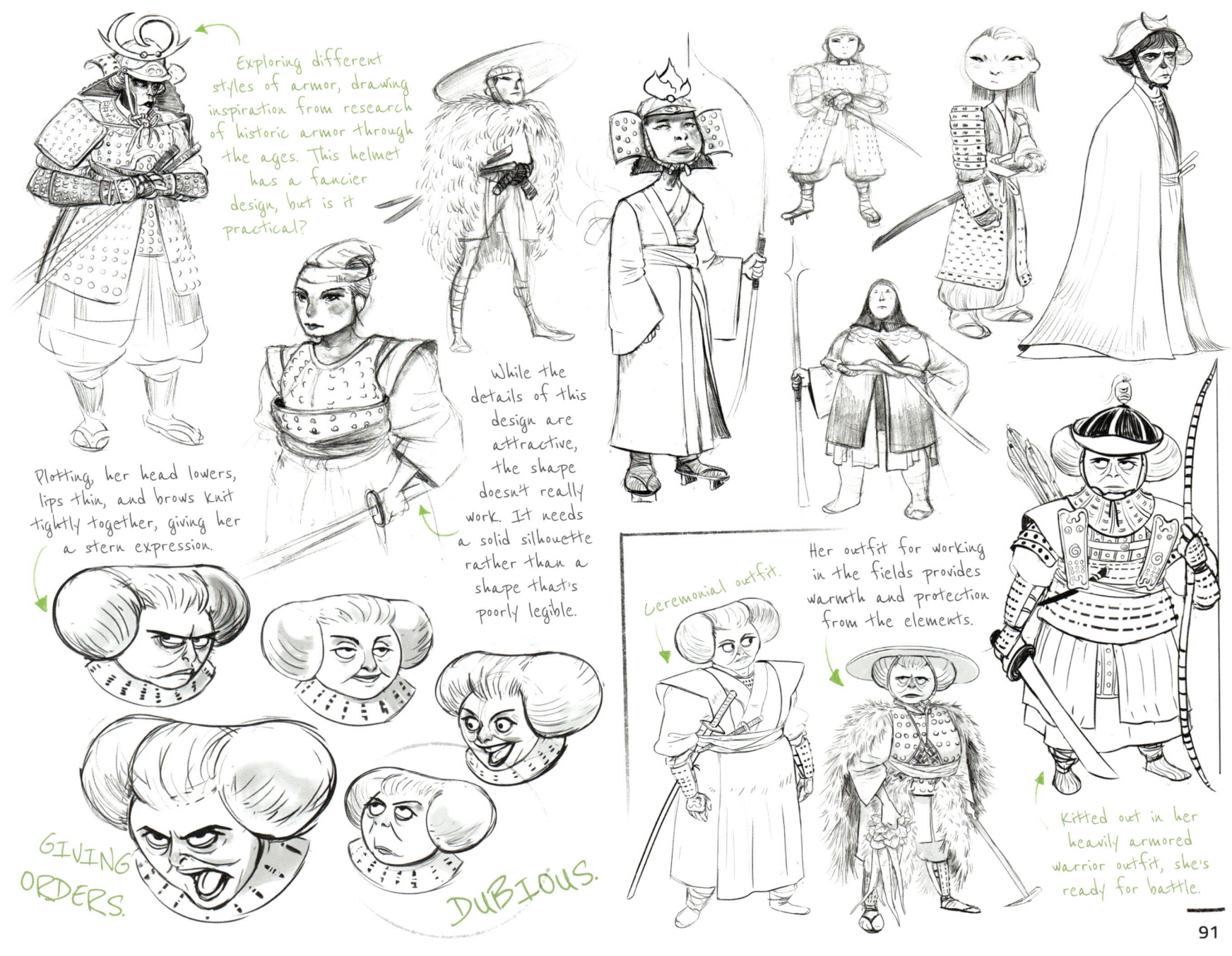

Exploring different styles of armor, drawing inspiration from research of historic armor through the ages. This helmet has a fancier design, but is it practical?

Plotting, her head lowers, lips thin, and brows knit tightly together, giving her a stern expression.

While the details of this design are attractive, the shape doesn't really work. It needs a solid silhouette rather than a shape that's poorly legible.

GIVING ORDERS.

DUBIOUS.

Ceremonial outfit.

Her outfit for working in the fields provides warmth and protection from the elements.

Kitted out in her heavily armored warrior outfit, she's ready for battle.

91

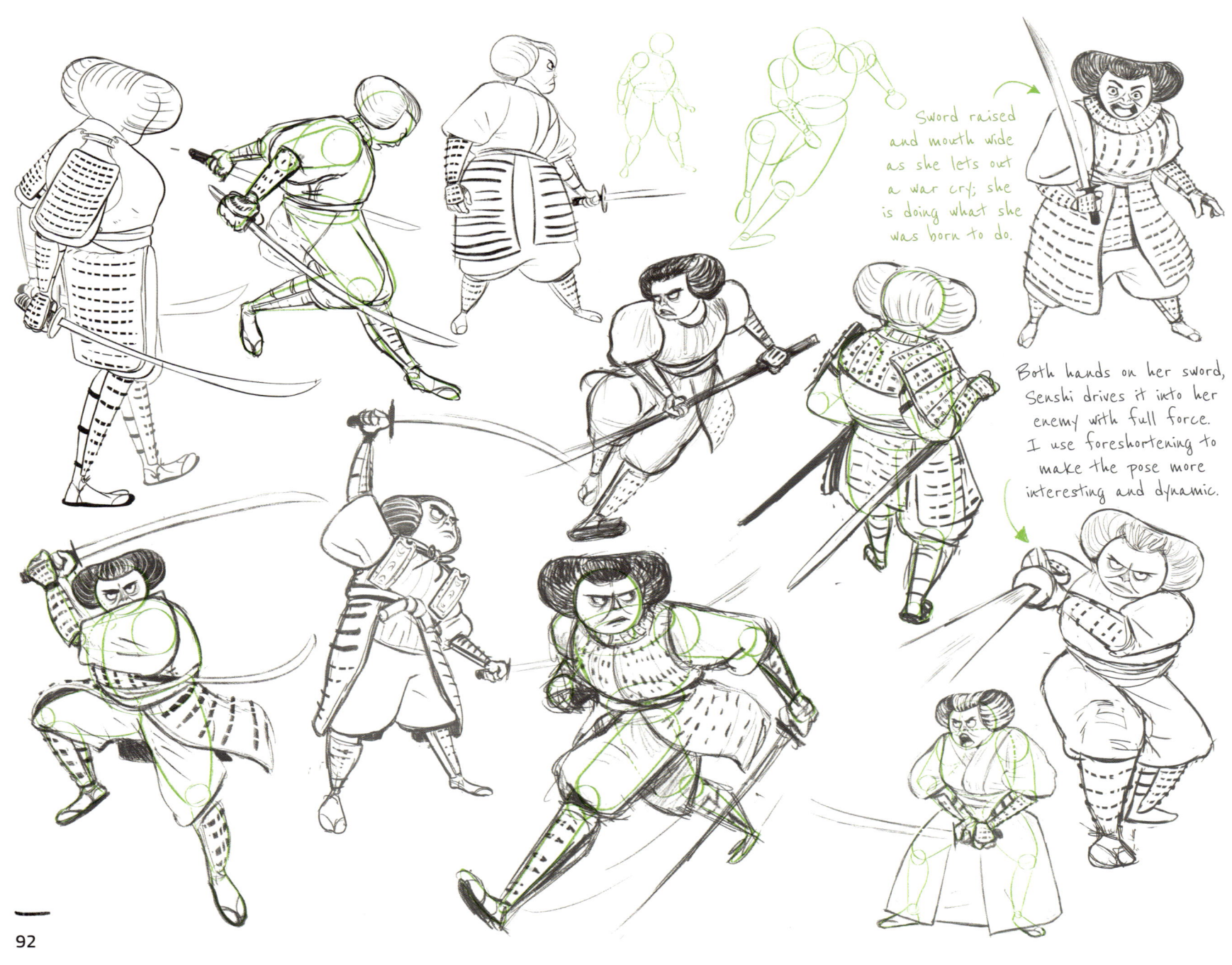

Sword raised and mouth wide as she lets out a war cry; she is doing what she was born to do.

Both hands on her sword, Senshi drives it into her enemy with full force. I use foreshortening to make the pose more interesting and dynamic.

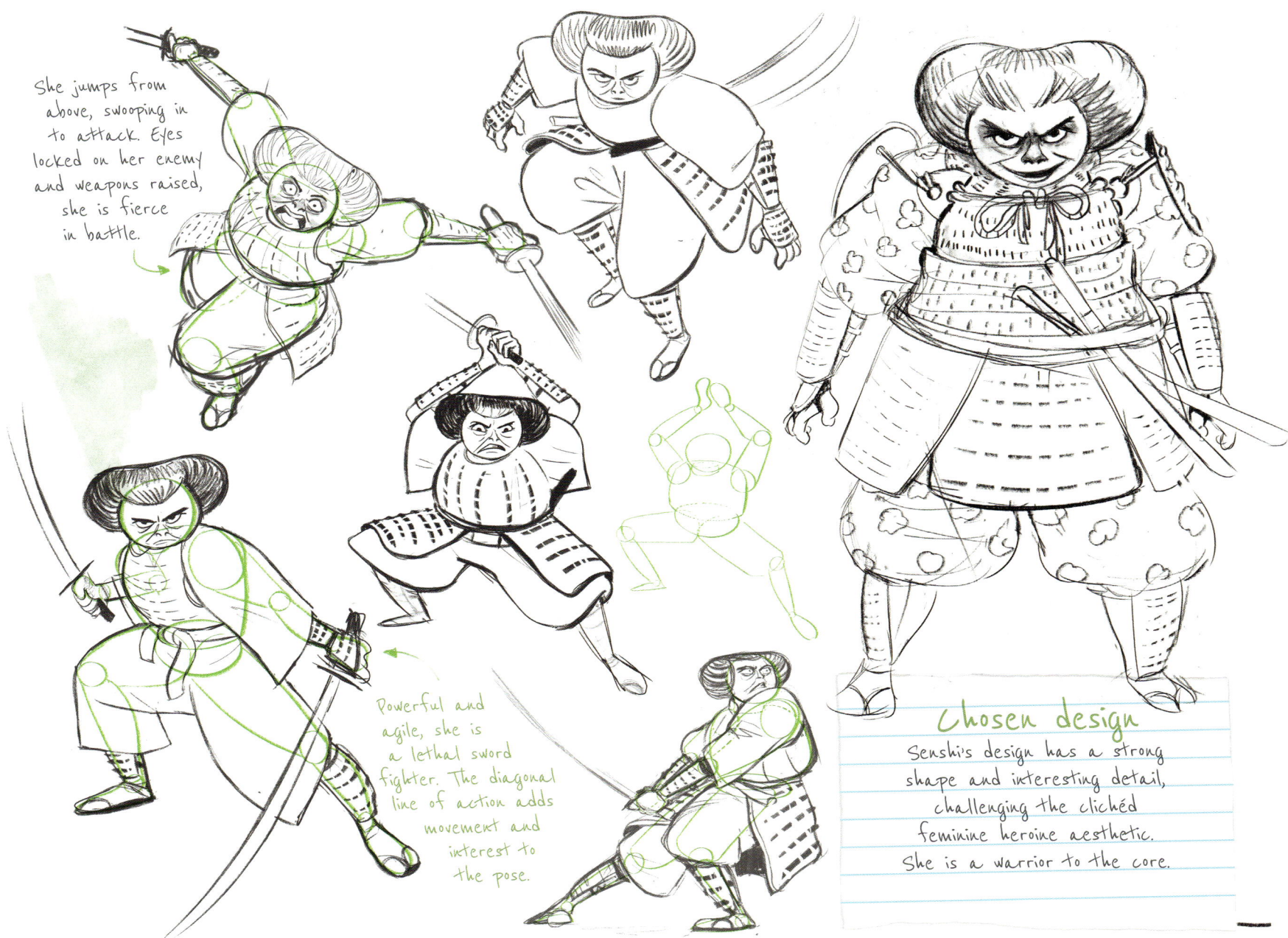

She jumps from above, swooping in to attack. Eyes locked on her enemy and weapons raised, she is fierce in battle.

Powerful and agile, she is a lethal sword fighter. The diagonal line of action adds movement and interest to the pose.

Chosen design

Senshi's design has a strong shape and interesting detail, challenging the clichéd feminine heroine aesthetic. She is a warrior to the core.

Persian princess

THIS SKETCHBOOK BELONGS TO: Taraneh Karimi

Princess Fatemeh Khanum "Esmat al-Dowleh" was a princess in 19th Persia, now modern-day Iran. Though living in a religious, patriarchal society, her father trusted her with the responsibility of serving as the host for all the female foreign guests to the court. Confident, brave, and with a sense of agency, she wasn't afraid to take risks and went against tradition when she learned to play the piano and became a photographer. Typical of the beauty standards of the day, she had long curly hair, a plus-size figure, uni-brow, and faint mustache.

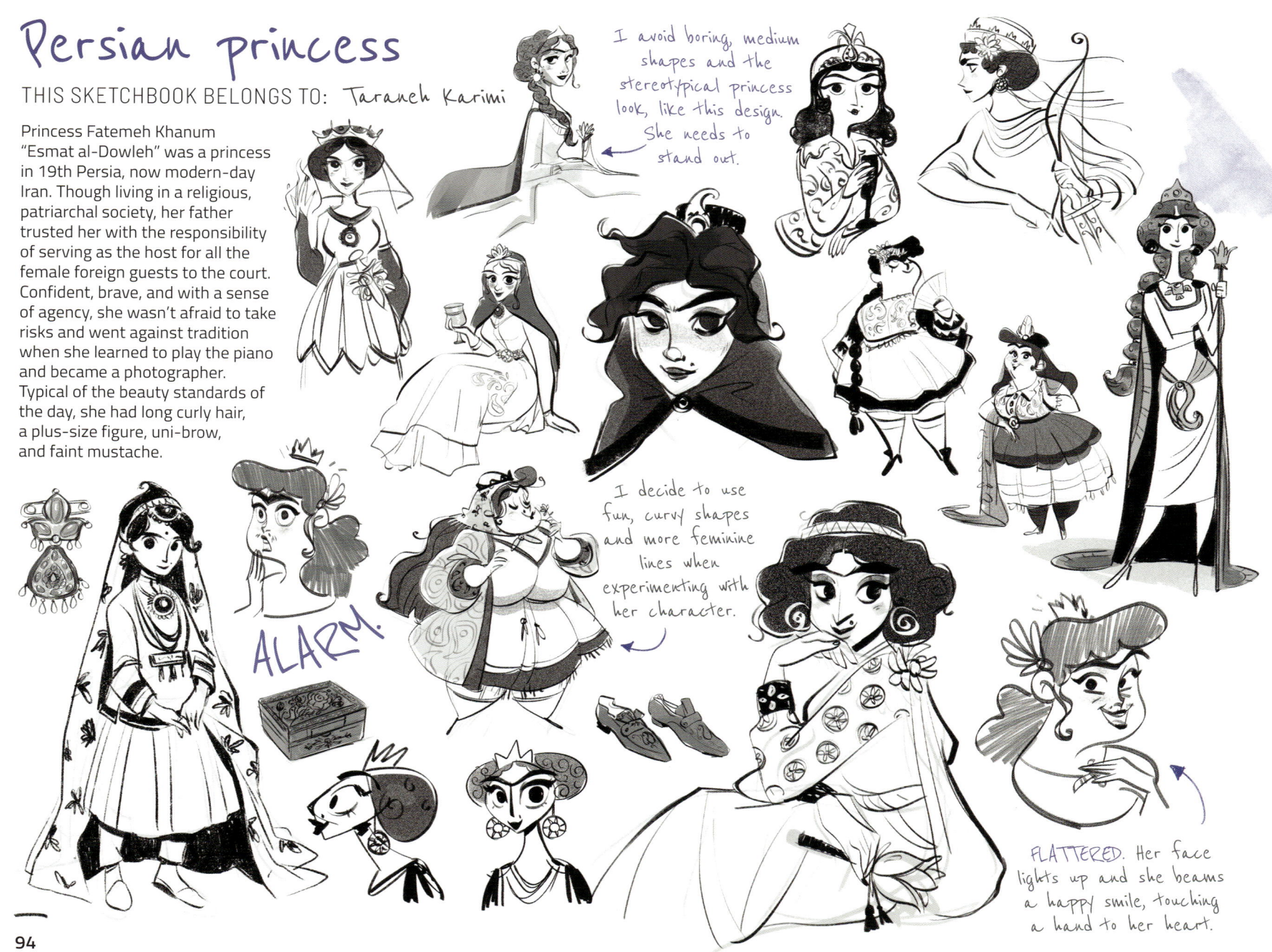

I avoid boring, medium shapes and the stereotypical princess look, like this design. She needs to stand out.

I decide to use fun, curvy shapes and more feminine lines when experimenting with her character.

ALARM.

FLATTERED. Her face lights up and she beams a happy smile, touching a hand to her heart.

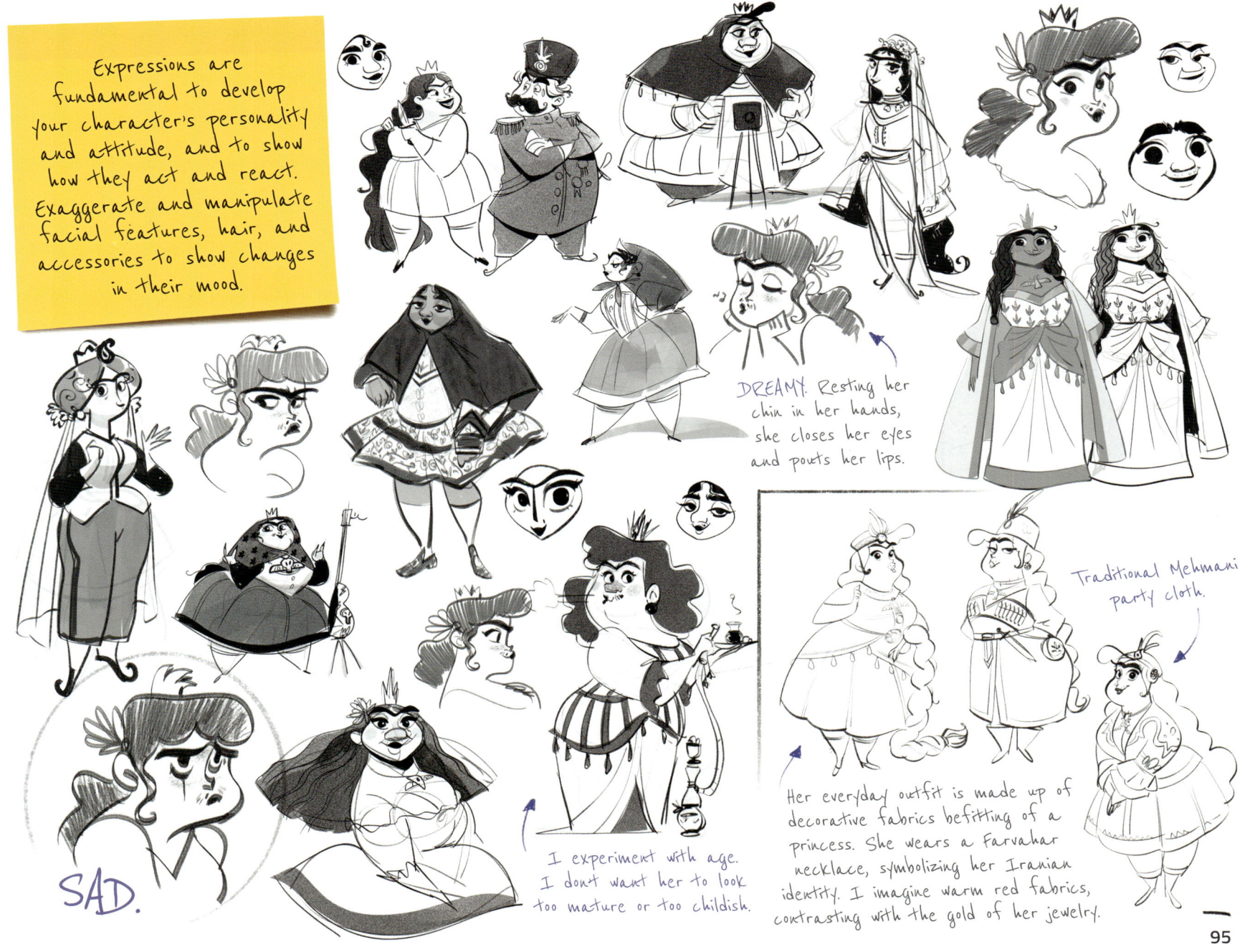

Expressions are fundamental to develop your character's personality and attitude, and to show how they act and react. Exaggerate and manipulate facial features, hair, and accessories to show changes in their mood.

DREAMY. Resting her chin in her hands, she closes her eyes and pouts her lips.

Traditional Mehmani party cloth.

SAD.

I experiment with age. I don't want her to look too mature or too childish.

Her everyday outfit is made up of decorative fabrics befitting of a princess. She wears a Farvahar necklace, symbolizing her Iranian identity. I imagine warm red fabrics, contrasting with the gold of her jewelry.

95

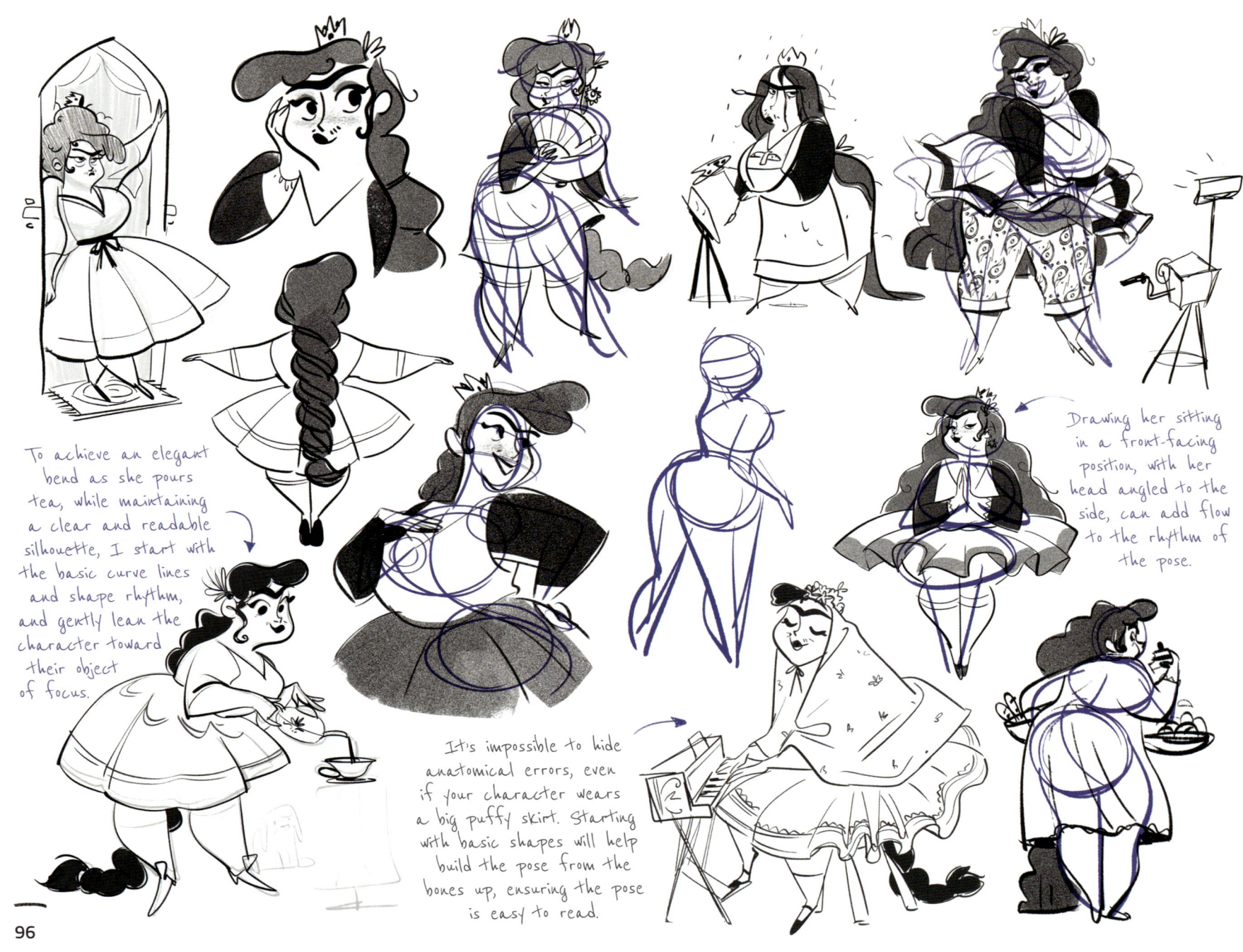

To achieve an elegant bend as she pours tea, while maintaining a clear and readable silhouette, I start with the basic curve lines and shape rhythm, and gently lean the character toward their object of focus.

It's impossible to hide anatomical errors, even if your character wears a big puffy skirt. Starting with basic shapes will help build the pose from the bones up, ensuring the pose is easy to read.

Drawing her sitting in a front-facing position, with her head angled to the side, can add flow to the rhythm of the pose.

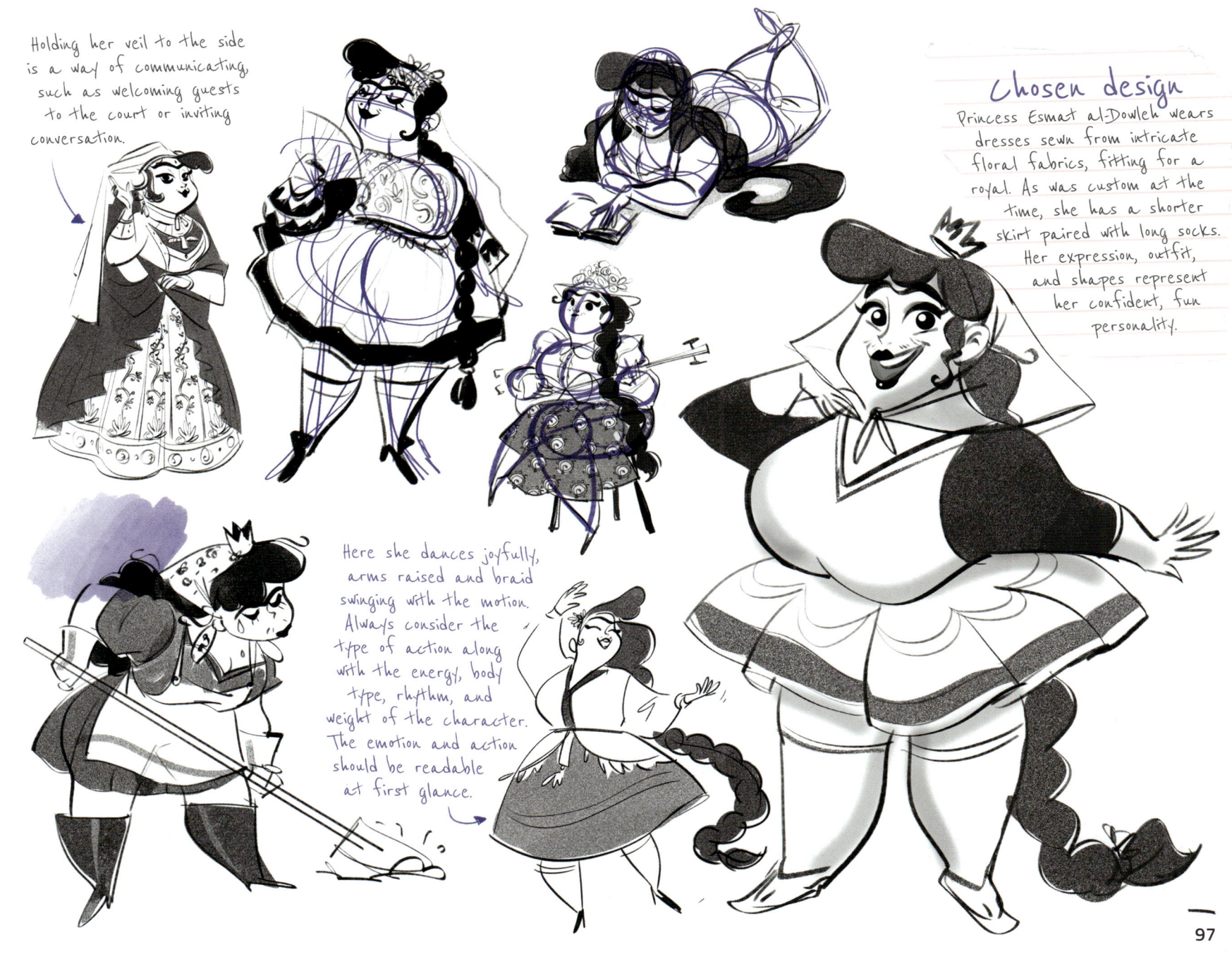

Holding her veil to the side is a way of communicating, such as welcoming guests to the court or inviting conversation.

Chosen design

Princess Esmat al-Dowleh wears dresses sewn from intricate floral fabrics, fitting for a royal. As was custom at the time, she has a shorter skirt paired with long socks. Her expression, outfit, and shapes represent her confident, fun personality.

Here she dances joyfully, arms raised and braid swinging with the motion. Always consider the type of action along with the energy, body type, rhythm, and weight of the character. The emotion and action should be readable at first glance.

97

Ancient Greek goddess

THIS SKETCHBOOK BELONGS TO: Margaux Kindhauser

Hecate is an ancient Greek goddess, often associated with night, death, spirits, and witchcraft. She is ambiguous and mysterious, sometimes perceived as evil, but also considered a healer, motherly figure, and a symbol of sorority. Hecate is often depicted carrying a torch, knife, and the keys to hell. She is tall and elegant, but her costumes and accessories reveal her more feral side. Other elements depict her softer, maternal personality. She is also known for being wise and ready to help when women face injustice.

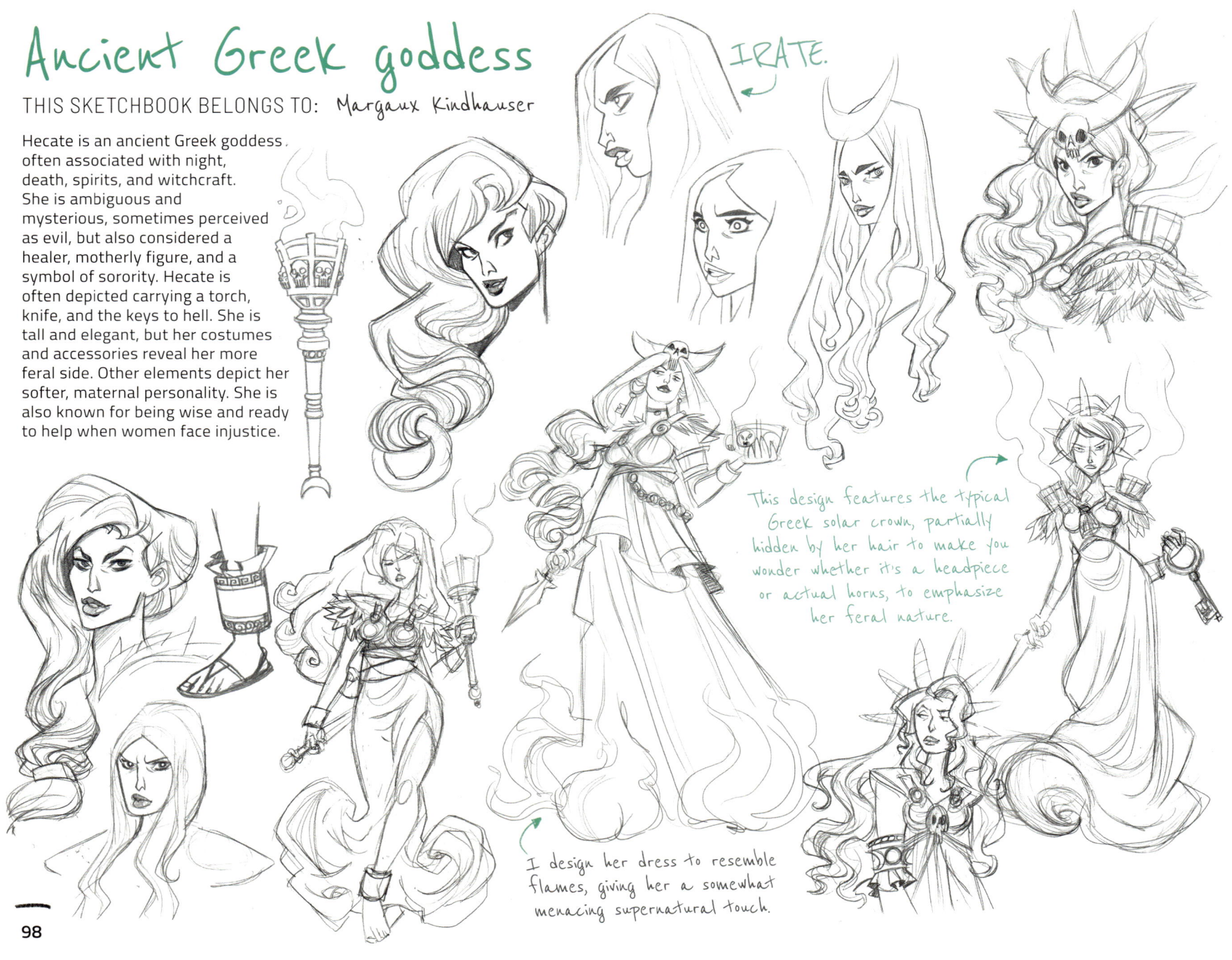

IRATE.

This design features the typical Greek solar crown, partially hidden by her hair to make you wonder whether it's a headpiece or actual horns, to emphasize her feral nature.

I design her dress to resemble flames, giving her a somewhat menacing supernatural touch.

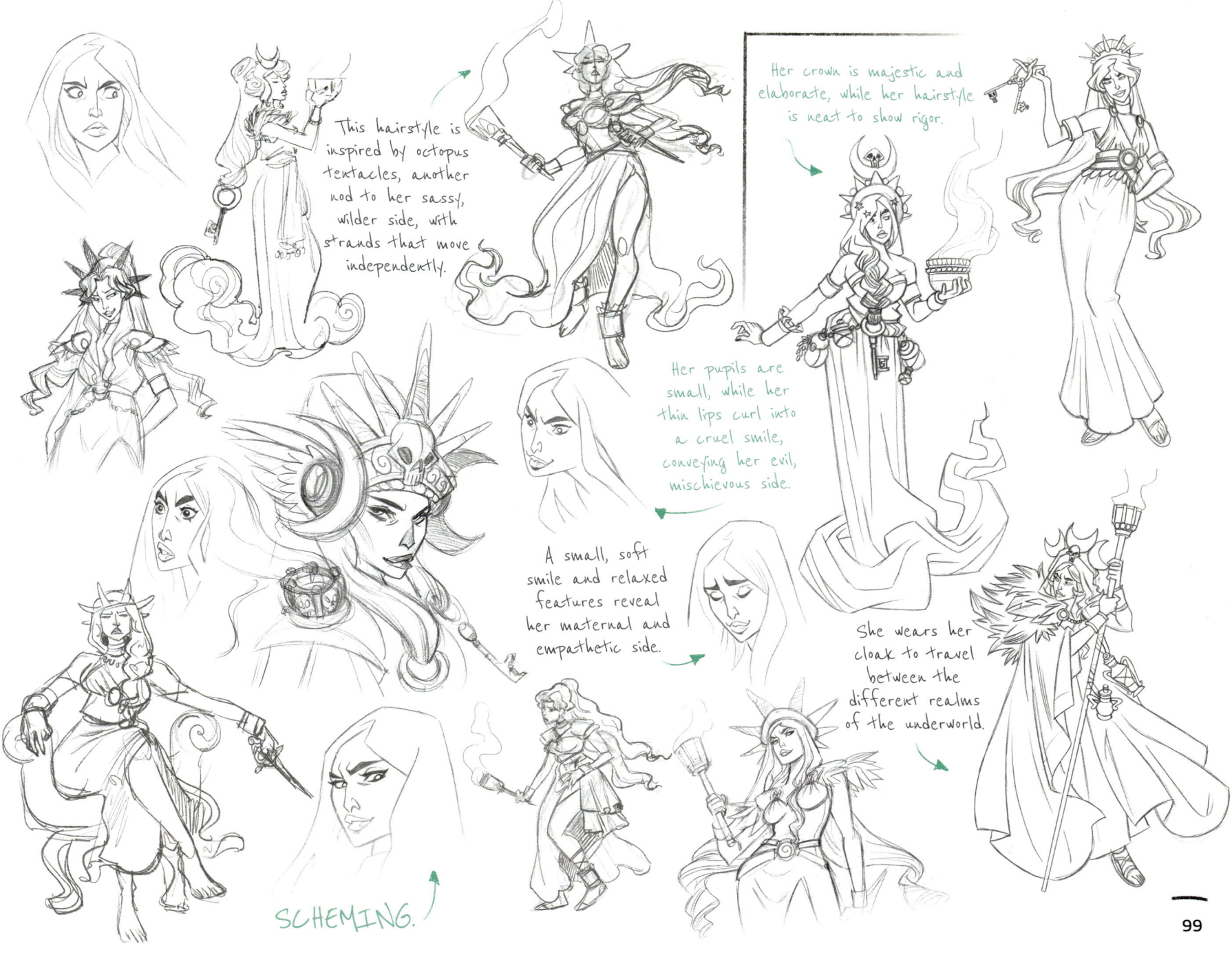

This hairstyle is inspired by octopus tentacles, another nod to her sassy, wilder side, with strands that move independently.

Her crown is majestic and elaborate, while her hairstyle is neat to show rigor.

Her pupils are small, while her thin lips curl into a cruel smile, conveying her evil, mischievous side.

A small, soft smile and relaxed features reveal her maternal and empathetic side.

She wears her cloak to travel between the different realms of the underworld.

SCHEMING.

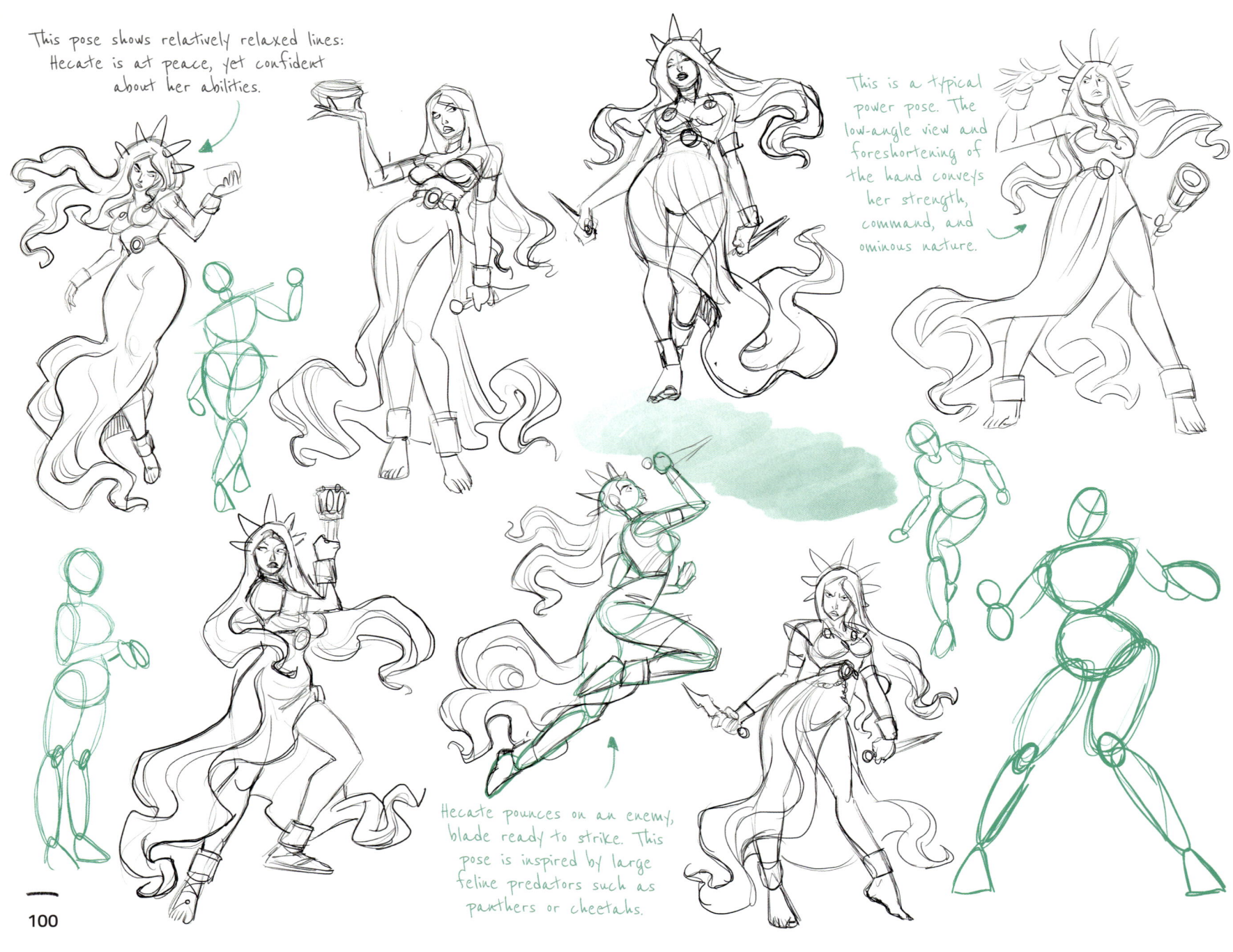

This pose shows relatively relaxed lines: Hecate is at peace, yet confident about her abilities.

This is a typical power pose. The low-angle view and foreshortening of the hand conveys her strength, command, and ominous nature.

Hecate pounces on an enemy, blade ready to strike. This pose is inspired by large feline predators such as panthers or cheetahs.

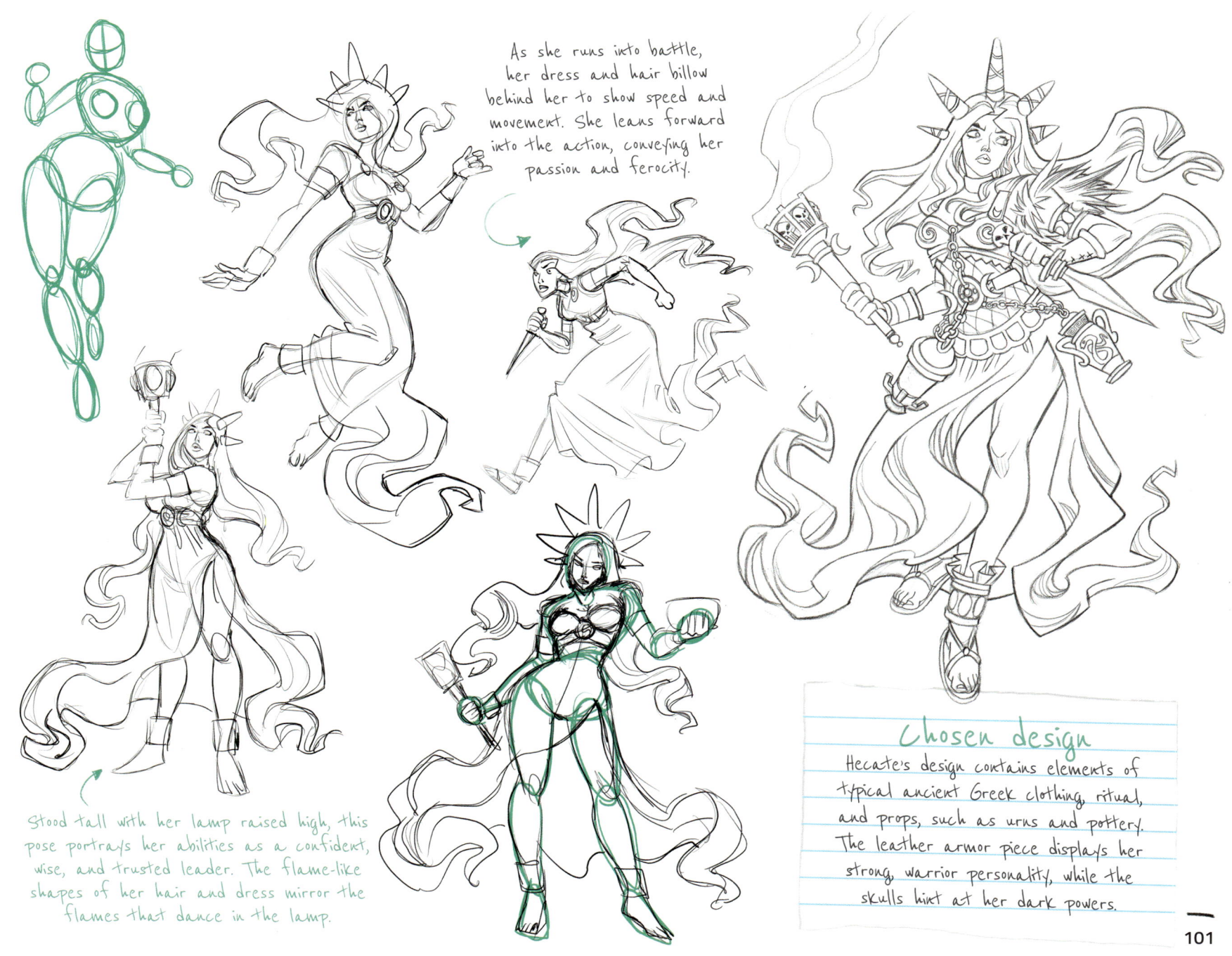

As she runs into battle, her dress and hair billow behind her to show speed and movement. She leans forward into the action, conveying her passion and ferocity.

Stood tall with her lamp raised high, this pose portrays her abilities as a confident, wise, and trusted leader. The flame-like shapes of her hair and dress mirror the flames that dance in the lamp.

Chosen design

Hecate's design contains elements of typical ancient Greek clothing, ritual, and props, such as urns and pottery. The leather armor piece displays her strong, warrior personality, while the skulls hint at her dark powers.

Archaeologist

THIS SKETCHBOOK BELONGS TO: Lisanne Koeteeuw

Mkali is an archaeologist, treasure hunter, and adventurer who travels the world in search of rare gems and lost artifacts. Inquisitive, intelligent, and daring, she isn't afraid to take risks in her pursuit of scientific knowledge. Whether exploring crypts or abseiling into volcanoes, she wears practical outdoor clothing and climbing gear to enable her to scale rocks and crawl into caves and tombs.

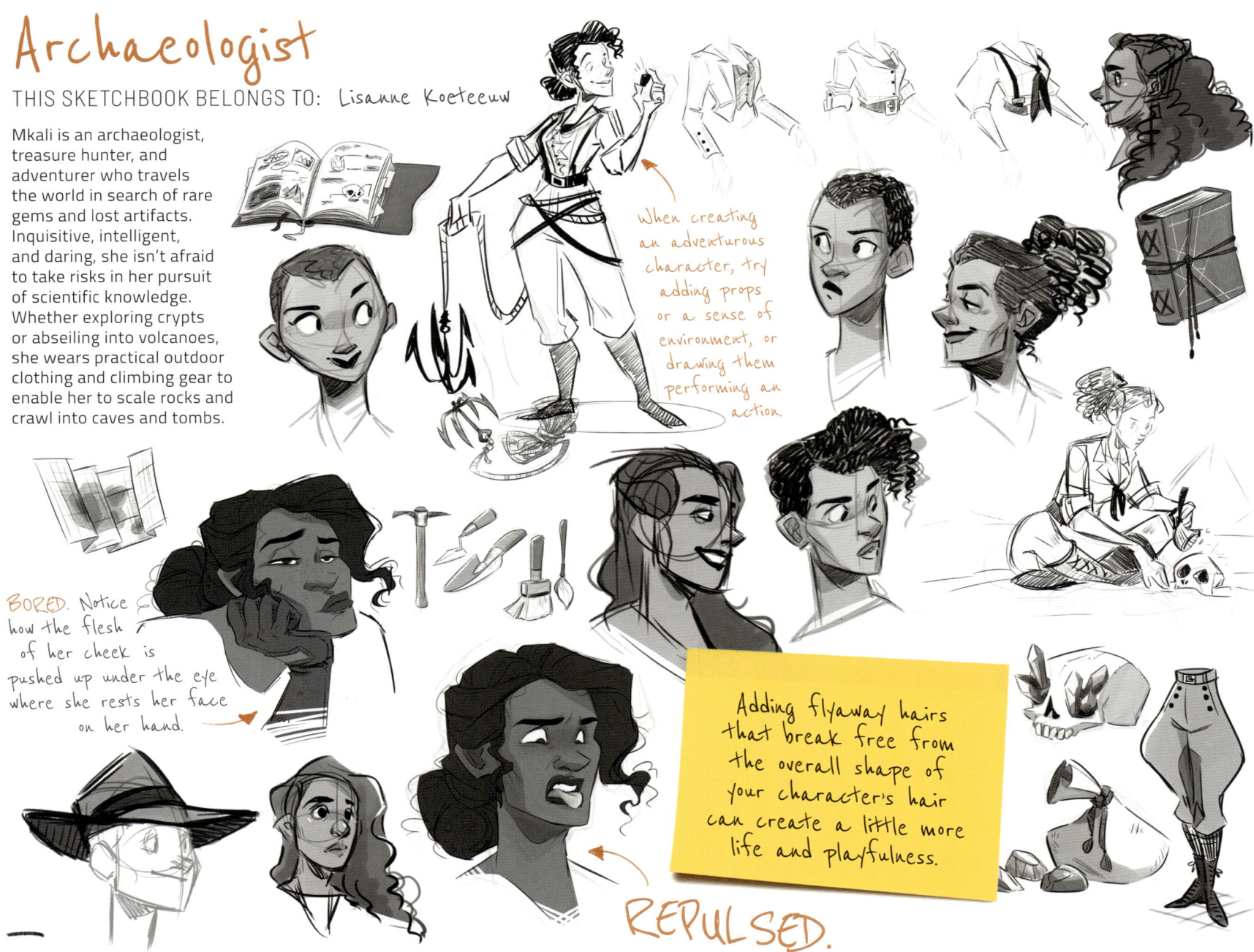

When creating an adventurous character, try adding props or a sense of environment, or drawing them performing an action.

BORED. Notice how the flesh of her cheek is pushed up under the eye where she rests her face on her hand.

Adding flyaway hairs that break free from the overall shape of your character's hair can create a little more life and playfulness.

REPULSED.

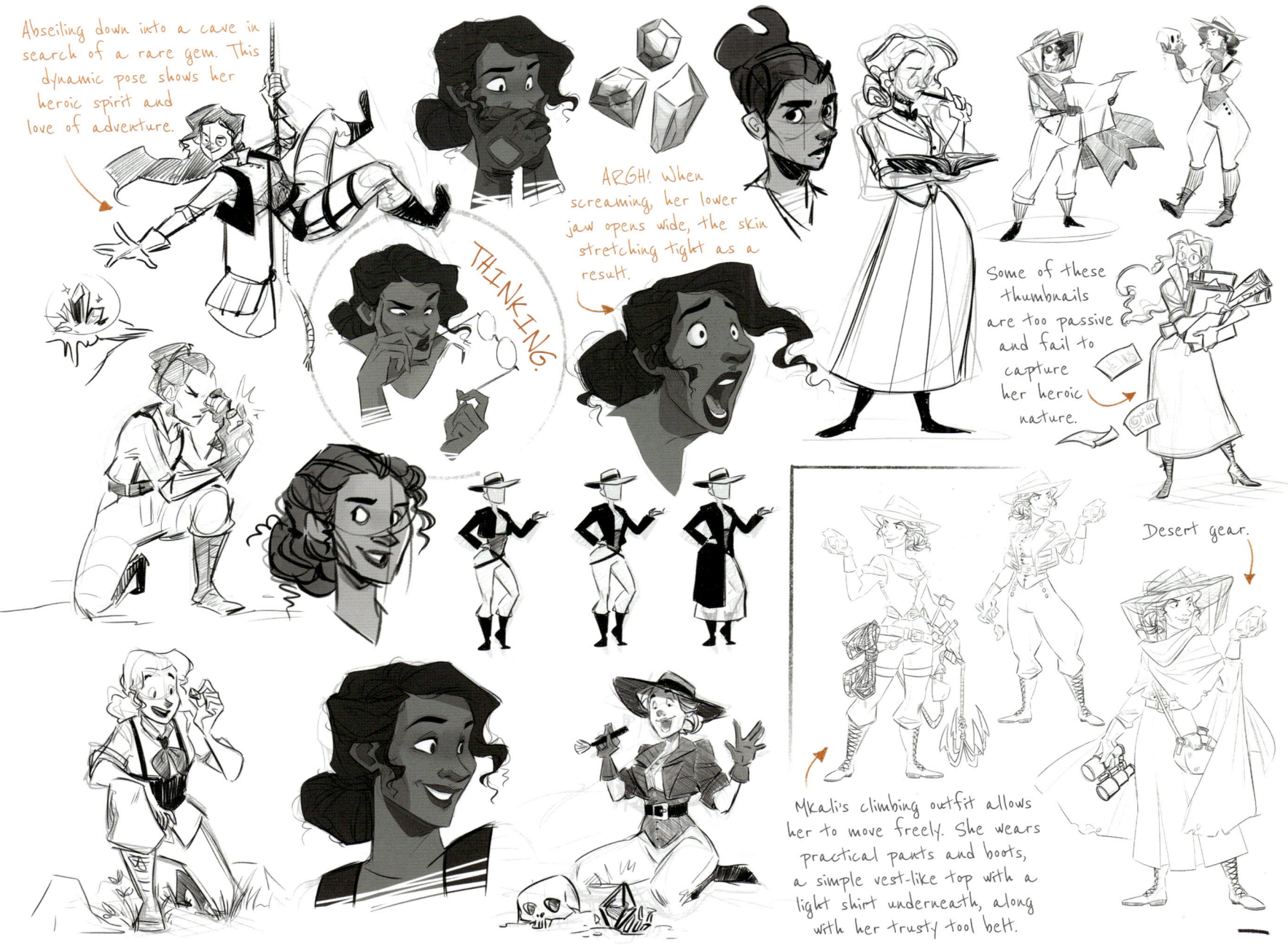

Abseiling down into a cave in search of a rare gem. This dynamic pose shows her heroic spirit and love of adventure.

ARGH! When screaming, her lower jaw opens wide, the skin stretching tight as a result.

THINKING.

Some of these thumbnails are too passive and fail to capture her heroic nature.

Desert gear.

Mkali's climbing outfit allows her to move freely. She wears practical pants and boots, a simple vest-like top with a light shirt underneath, along with her trusty tool belt.

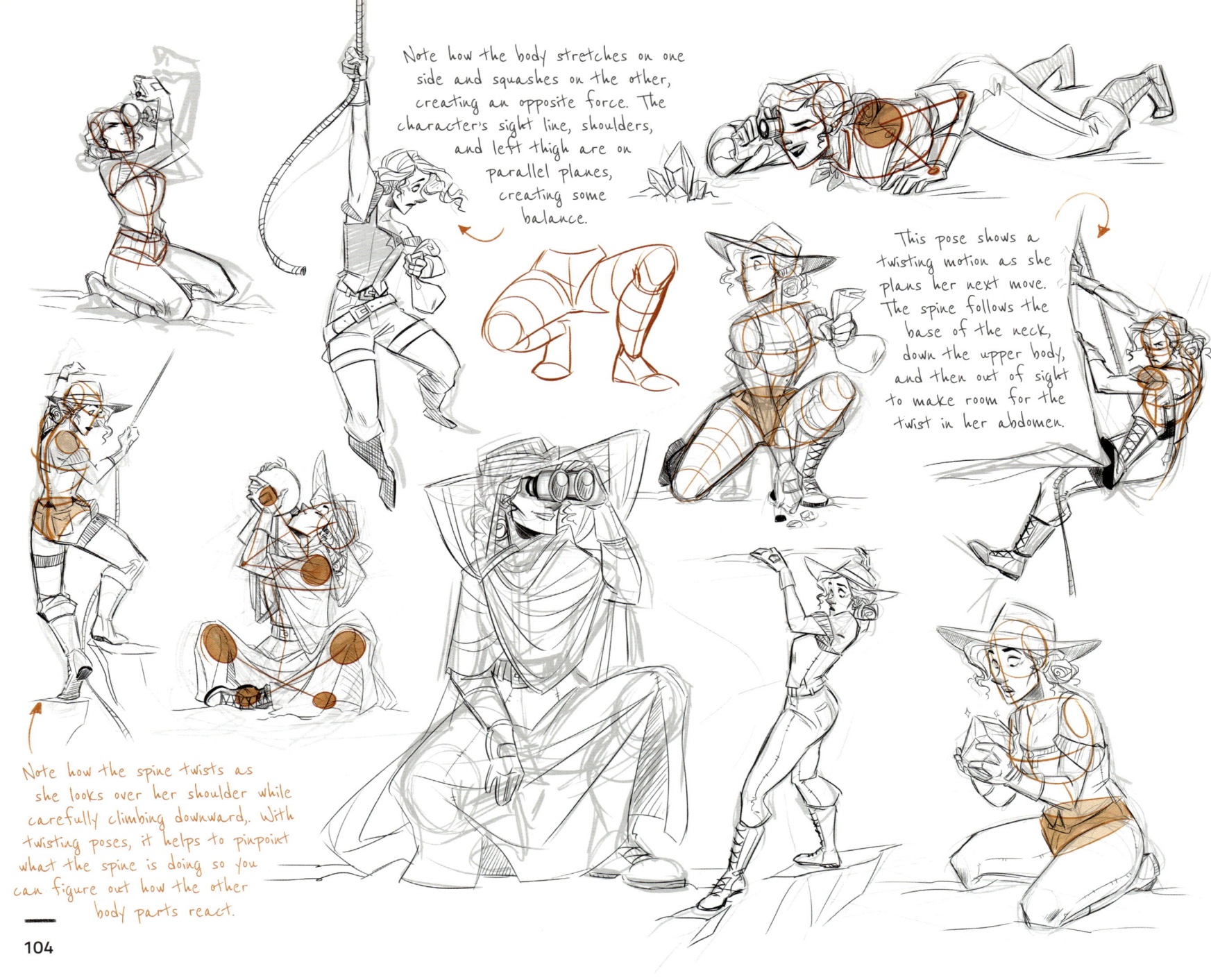

Note how the body stretches on one side and squashes on the other, creating an opposite force. The character's sight line, shoulders, and left thigh are on parallel planes, creating some balance.

This pose shows a twisting motion as she plans her next move. The spine follows the base of the neck, down the upper body, and then out of sight to make room for the twist in her abdomen.

Note how the spine twists as she looks over her shoulder while carefully climbing downward,. With twisting poses, it helps to pinpoint what the spine is doing so you can figure out how the other body parts react.

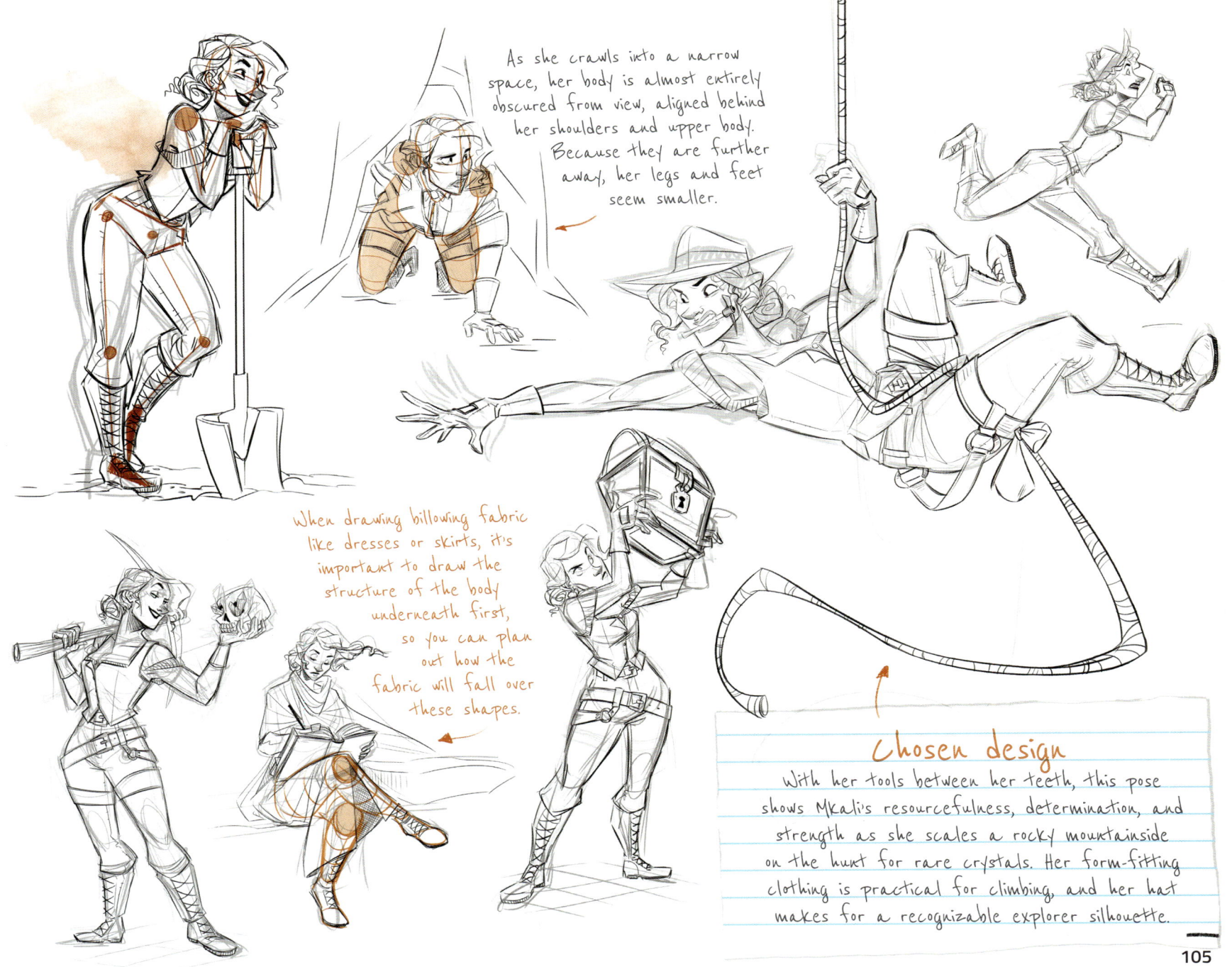

As she crawls into a narrow space, her body is almost entirely obscured from view, aligned behind her shoulders and upper body. Because they are further away, her legs and feet seem smaller.

When drawing billowing fabric like dresses or skirts, it's important to draw the structure of the body underneath first, so you can plan out how the fabric will fall over these shapes.

Chosen design

With her tools between her teeth, this pose shows Mkali's resourcefulness, determination, and strength as she scales a rocky mountainside on the hunt for rare crystals. Her form-fitting clothing is practical for climbing, and her hat makes for a recognizable explorer silhouette.

Super-stretchy superheroine

THIS SKETCHBOOK BELONGS TO: Cassey Kuo

Scatter-Shot is an Asian-American superheroine on the verge of retirement. Though she feels the years of burden weighing her down, she still believes in fighting for a brighter future. Strong, determined, and resilient, she has stretch superpowers thanks to engineered hydrogel that reinforces her limbs and absorbs shock upon impact. The gel can form into rubber bands that she uses to slingshot herself, or objects, in combat. It forms the cushion in her shoes and can transform into skates to increase her speed and mobility. It also serves to gather more friction, which allows her body to stretch even more. An aging core member to a network of superheroes across America, she spends her time training the younger heroes and heroines.

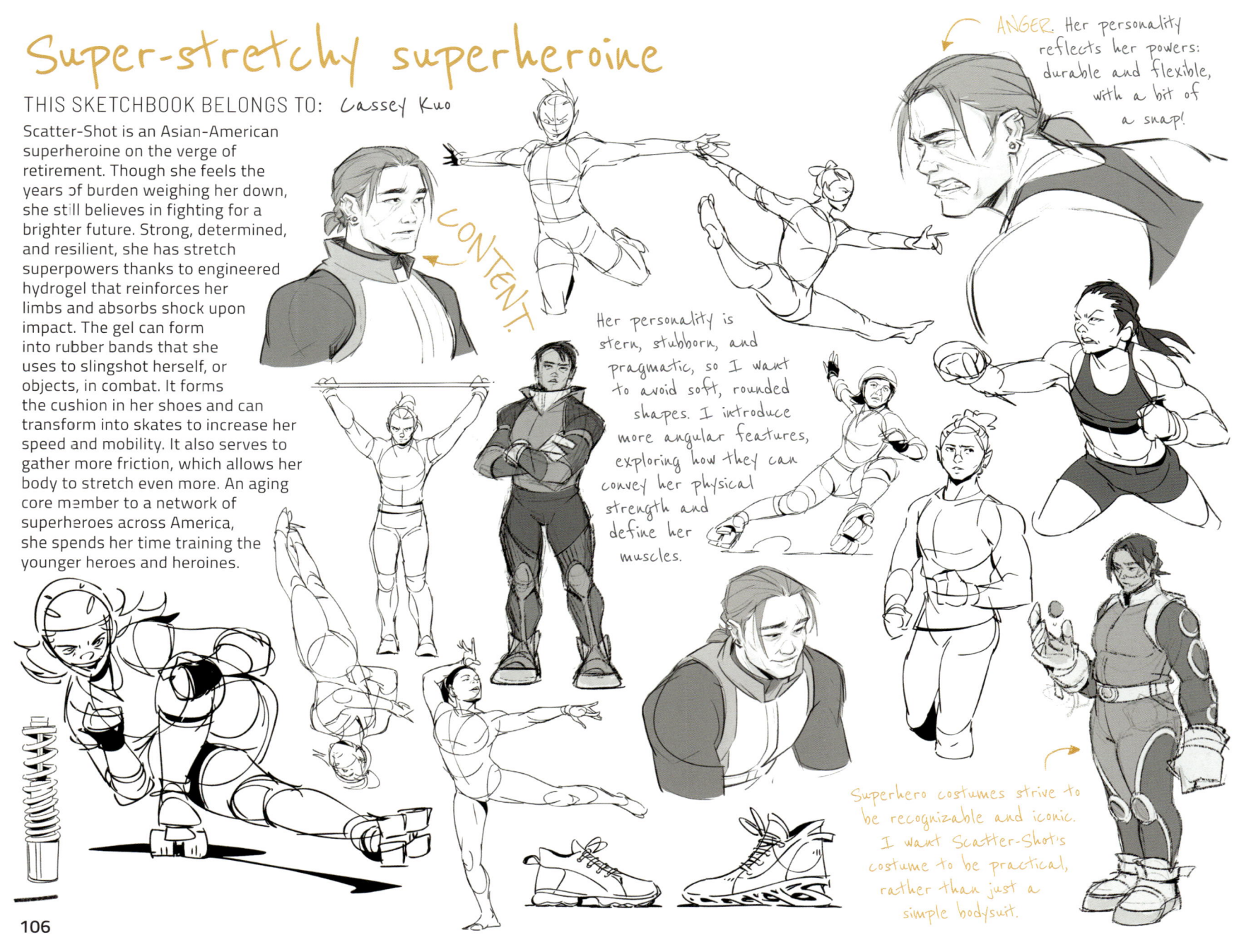

CONTENT.

ANGER. Her personality reflects her powers: durable and flexible, with a bit of a snap!

Her personality is stern, stubborn, and pragmatic, so I want to avoid soft, rounded shapes. I introduce more angular features, exploring how they can convey her physical strength and define her muscles.

Superhero costumes strive to be recognizable and iconic. I want Scatter-Shot's costume to be practical, rather than just a simple bodysuit.

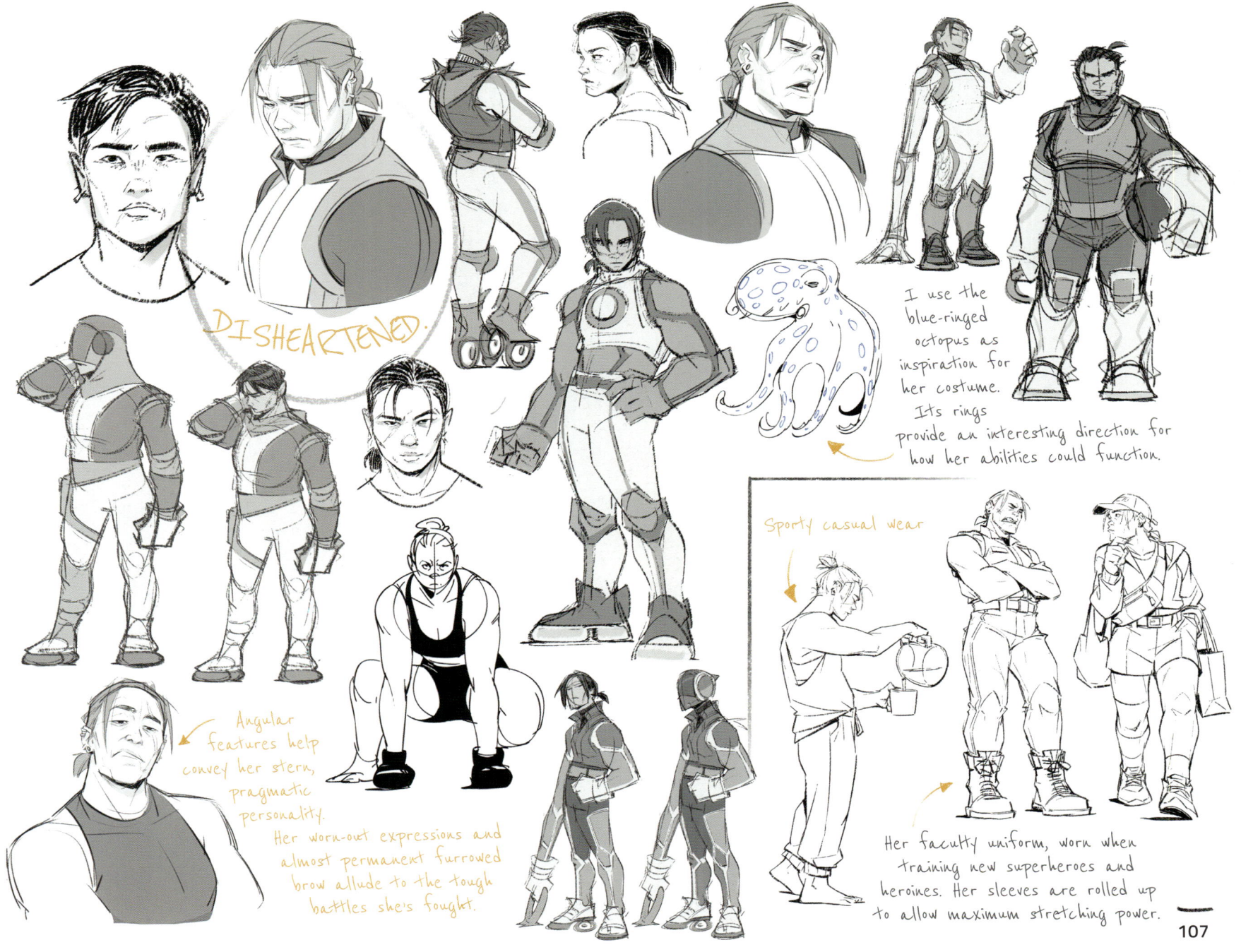

DISHEARTENED.

I use the blue-ringed octopus as inspiration for her costume. Its rings provide an interesting direction for how her abilities could function.

Sporty casual wear

Angular features help convey her stern, pragmatic personality.
Her worn-out expressions and almost permanent furrowed brow allude to the tough battles she's fought.

Her faculty uniform, worn when training new superheroes and heroines. Her sleeves are rolled up to allow maximum stretching power.

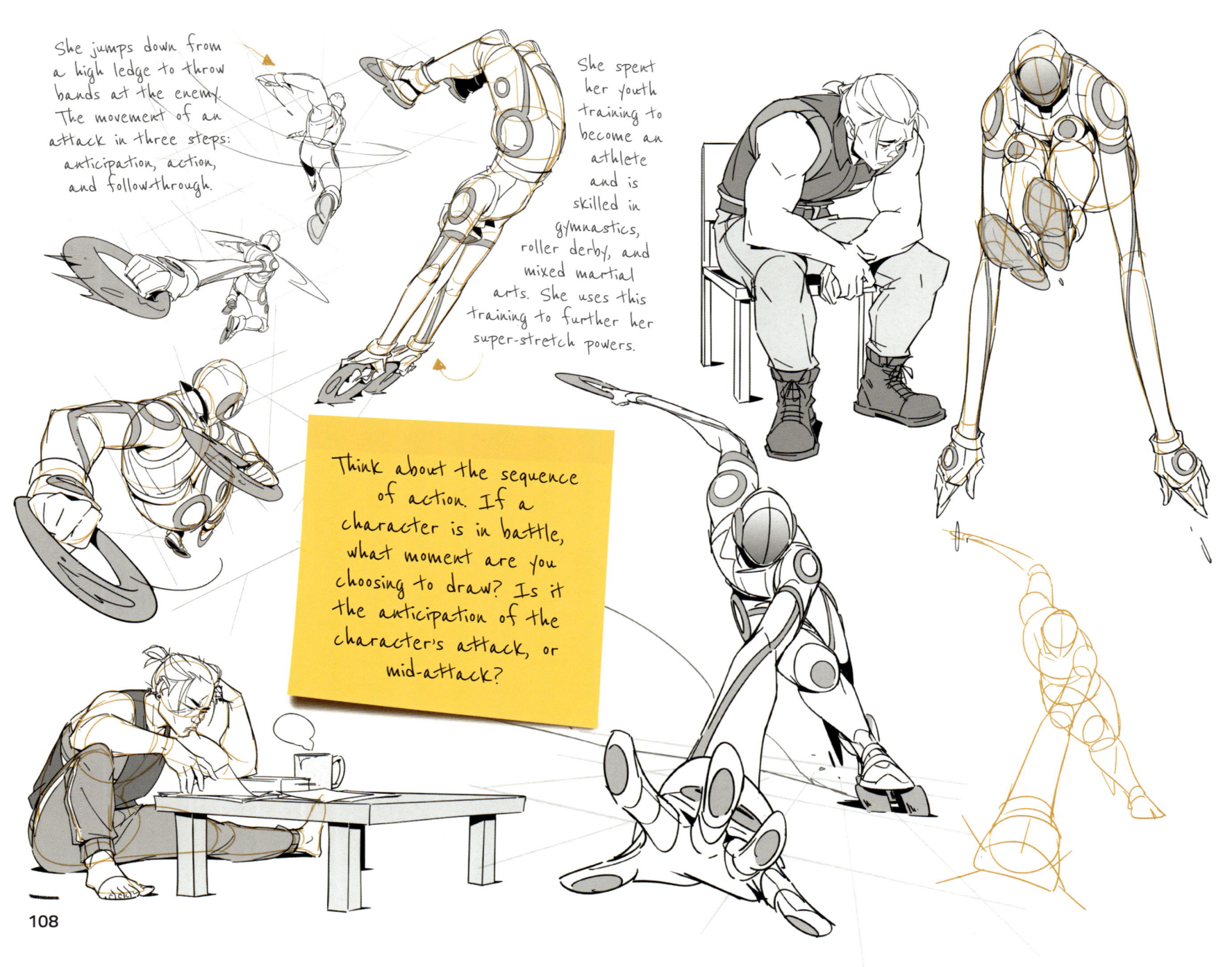

She jumps down from a high ledge to throw bands at the enemy. The movement of an attack in three steps: anticipation, action, and follow-through.

She spent her youth training to become an athlete and is skilled in gymnastics, roller derby, and mixed martial arts. She uses this training to further her super-stretch powers.

Think about the sequence of action. If a character is in battle, what moment are you choosing to draw? Is it the anticipation of the character's attack, or mid-attack?

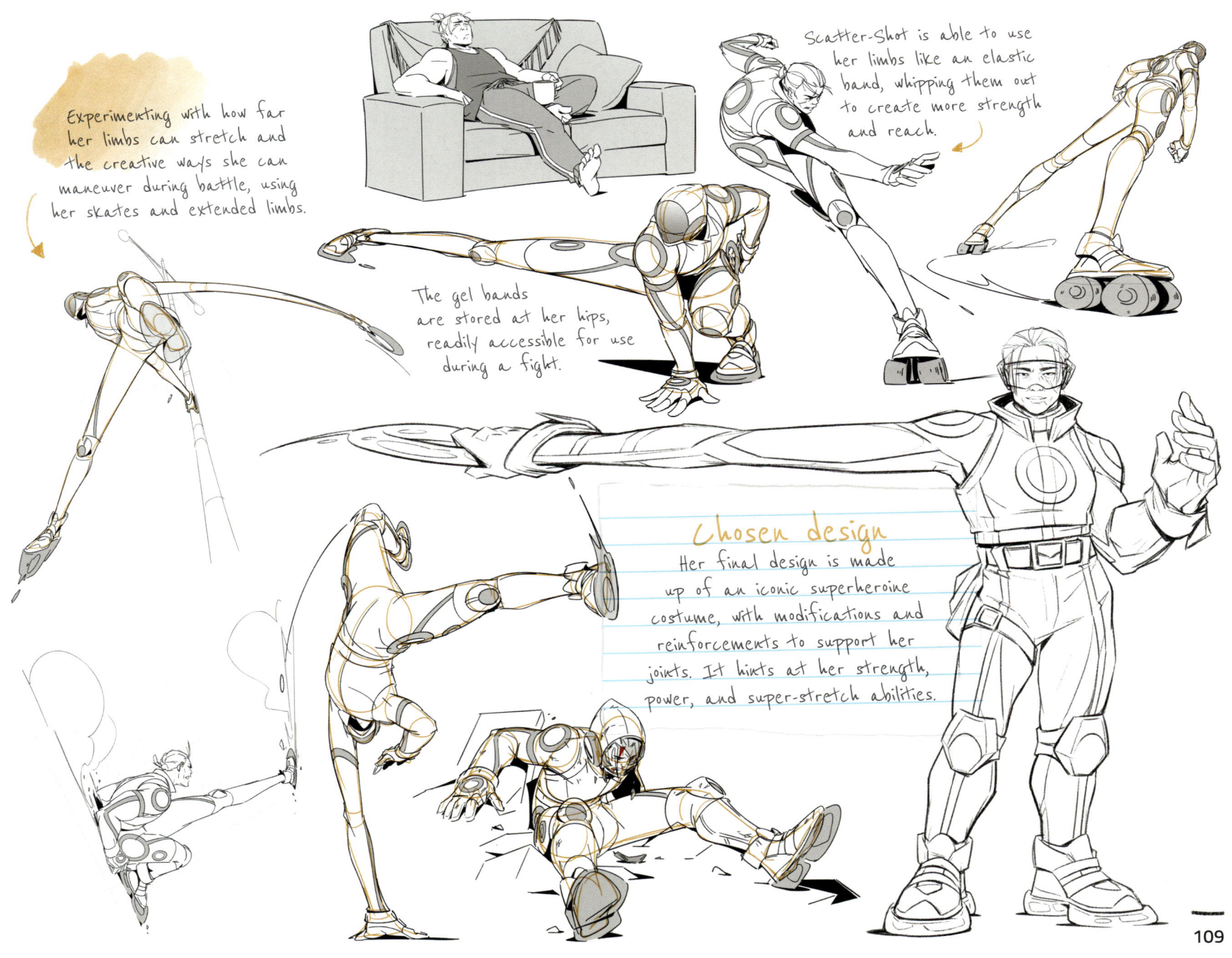

Experimenting with how far her limbs can stretch and the creative ways she can maneuver during battle, using her skates and extended limbs.

Scatter-Shot is able to use her limbs like an elastic band, whipping them out to create more strength and reach.

The gel bands are stored at her hips, readily accessible for use during a fight.

Chosen design

Her final design is made up of an iconic superheroine costume, with modifications and reinforcements to support her joints. It hints at her strength, power, and super-stretch abilities.

Aeronaut

THIS SKETCHBOOK BELONGS TO: Jordi Lafebre

Zippora is a talented aeronautical engineer and pilot. She has the intelligence and practical skill required for operating complex machinery and software, as well as the calmness, coordination, and physical ability required to fly planes. Though her young age means she is not as strong or experienced as the older pilots, it also means she has a fresh, innovative, and freestyle way of approaching the job. Intuitive, brave, clever, and passionate, she loves being in the air.

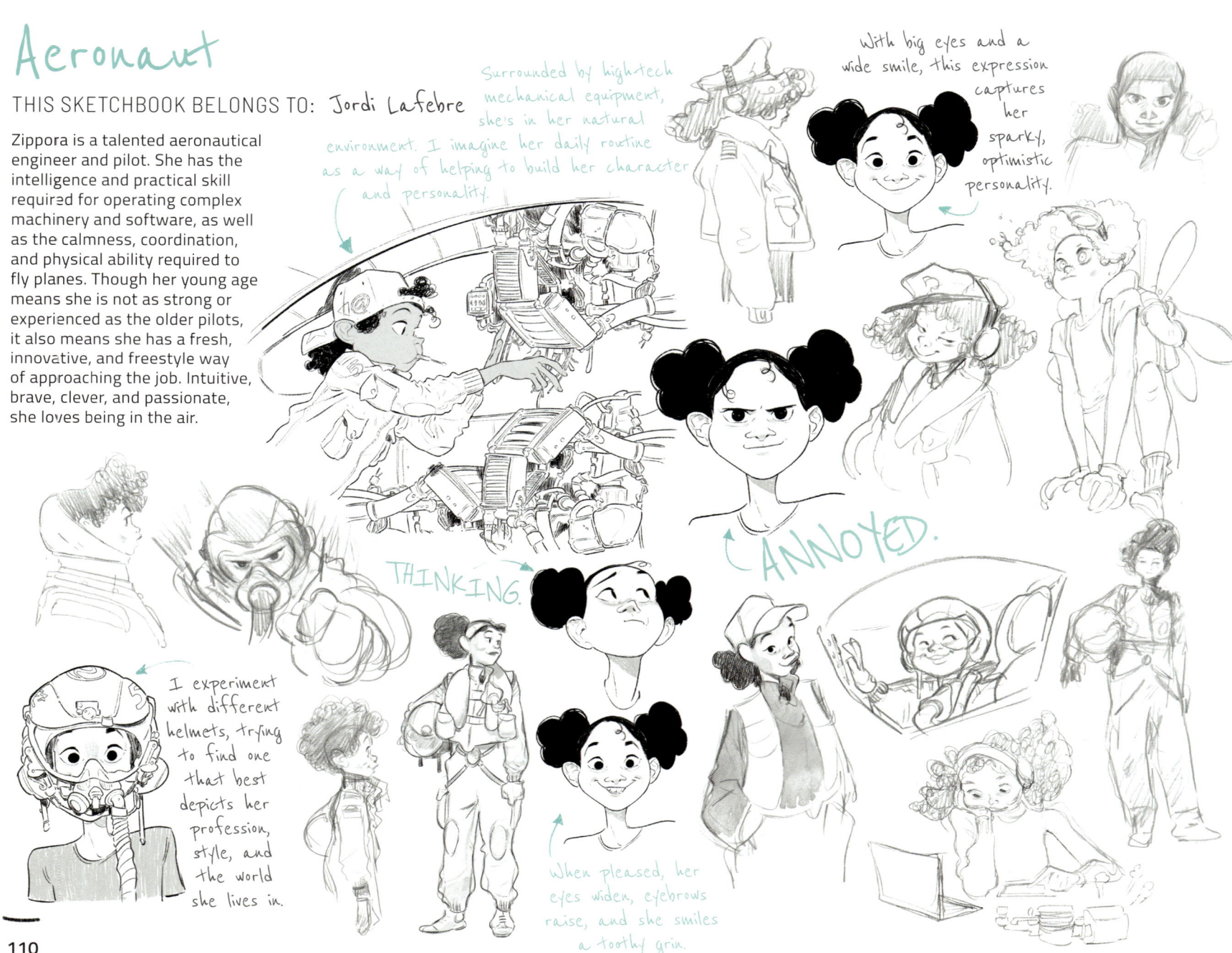

Surrounded by high-tech mechanical equipment, she's in her natural environment. I imagine her daily routine as a way of helping to build her character and personality.

With big eyes and a wide smile, this expression captures her sparky, optimistic personality.

THINKING.

ANNOYED.

I experiment with different helmets, trying to find one that best depicts her profession, style, and the world she lives in.

When pleased, her eyes widen, eyebrows raise, and she smiles a toothy grin.

110

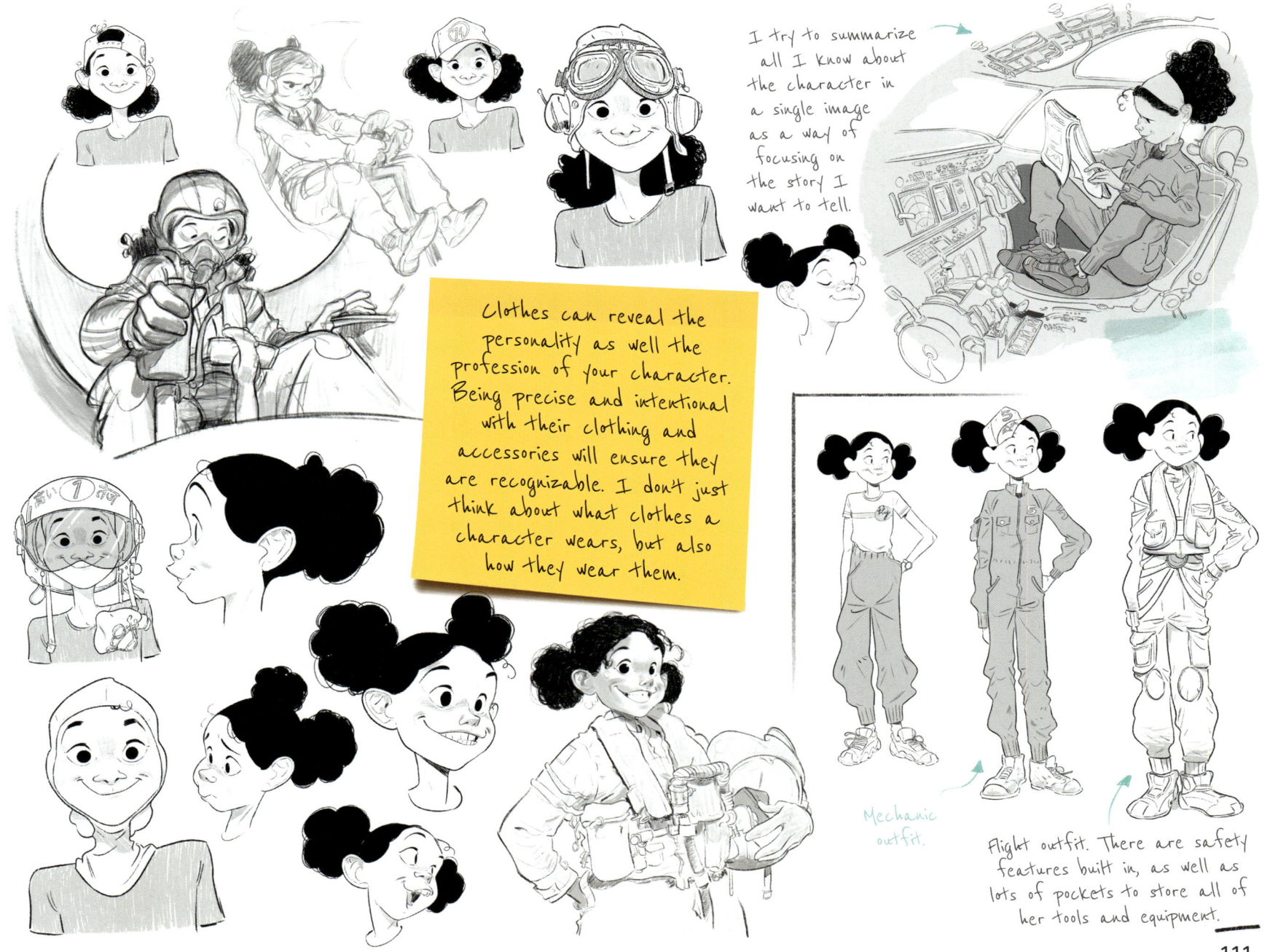

I try to summarize all I know about the character in a single image as a way of focusing on the story I want to tell.

Clothes can reveal the personality as well the profession of your character. Being precise and intentional with their clothing and accessories will ensure they are recognizable. I don't just think about what clothes a character wears, but also how they wear them.

Mechanic outfit.

Flight outfit. There are safety features built in, as well as lots of pockets to store all of her tools and equipment.

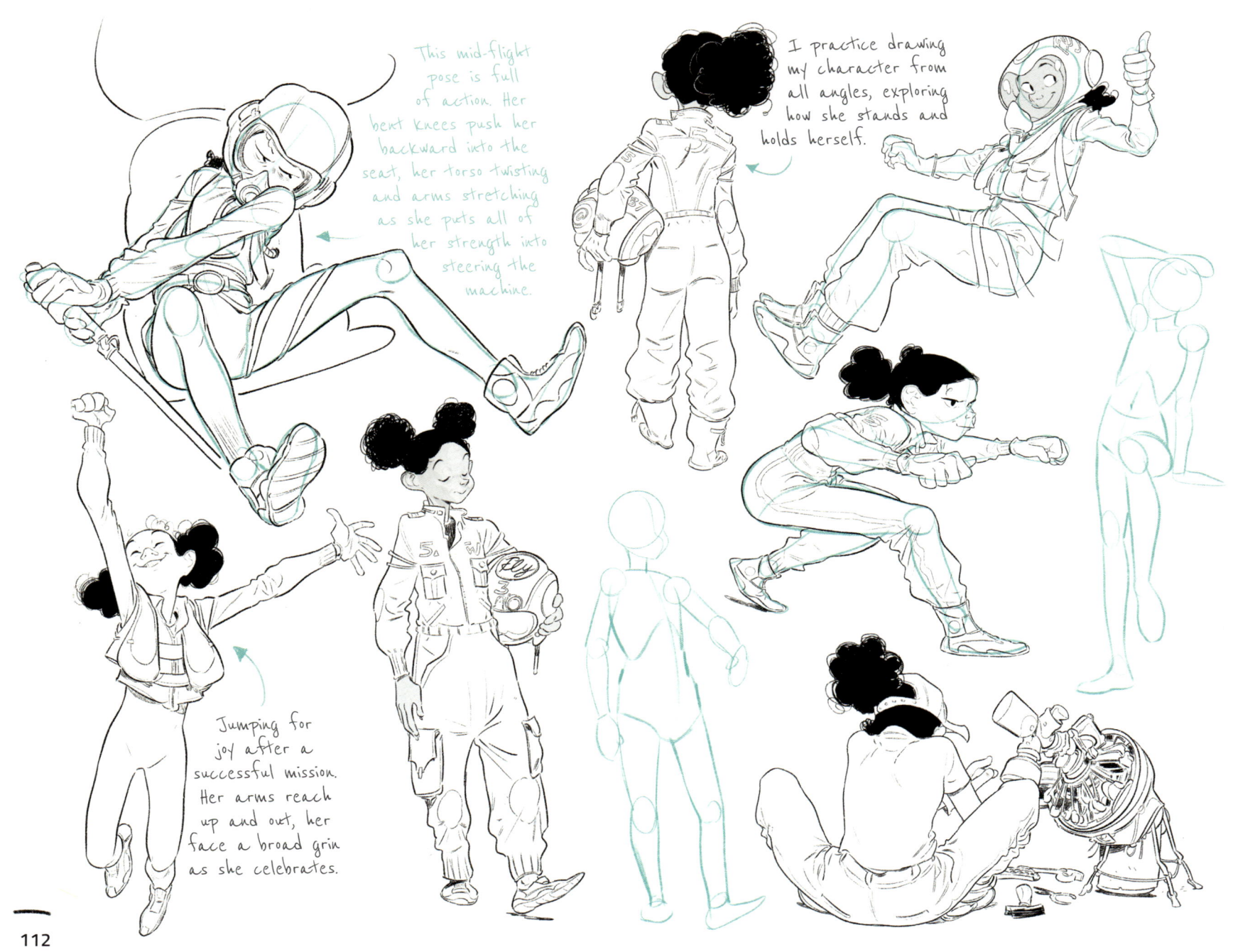

This mid-flight pose is full of action. Her bent knees push her backward into the seat, her torso twisting and arms stretching as she puts all of her strength into steering the machine.

I practice drawing my character from all angles, exploring how she stands and holds herself.

Jumping for joy after a successful mission. Her arms reach up and out, her face a broad grin as she celebrates.

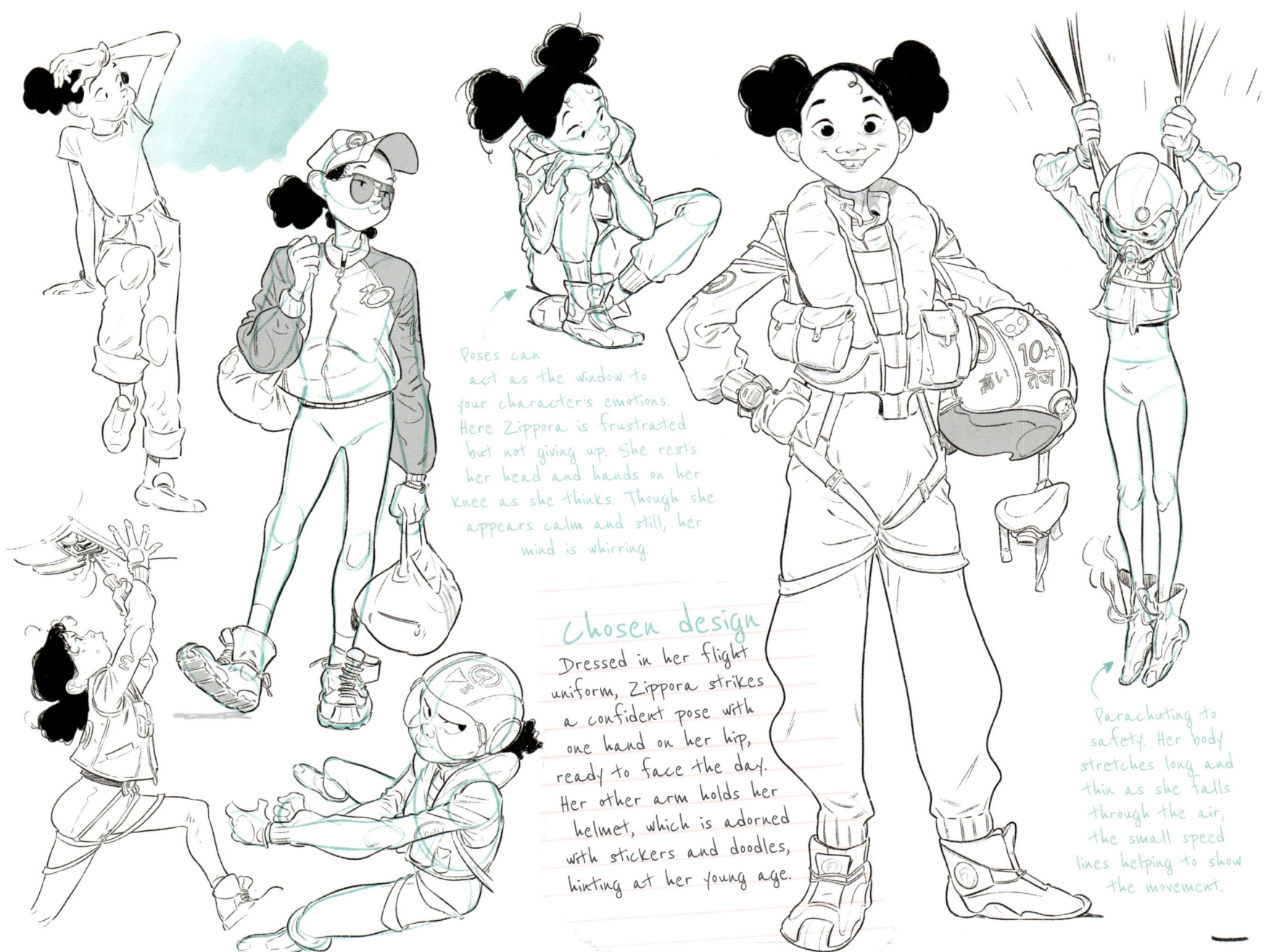

Poses can act as the window to your character's emotions. Here Zippora is frustrated but not giving up. She rests her head and hands on her knee as she thinks. Though she appears calm and still, her mind is whirring.

Chosen design

Dressed in her flight uniform, Zippora strikes a confident pose with one hand on her hip, ready to face the day. Her other arm holds her helmet, which is adorned with stickers and doodles, hinting at her young age.

Parachuting to safety. Her body stretches long and thin as she falls through the air, the small speed lines helping to show the movement.

Mermaid

THIS SKETCHBOOK BELONGS TO: Jacquelin de Leon

Nerida is a young mermaid who lives in a faraway, underwater world where the ocean has covered the planet save for a few islands. She was born into an ancient mermaid clan who live beneath a giant kelp forest alongside sea otters and porpoises. Curious and intrepid, she longs to explore the open seas. One day she discovers a ship's anchor and climbs aboard, befriending the pirate crew. She enjoys sneaking off to join their seafaring adventures when they're passing through her stretch of ocean.

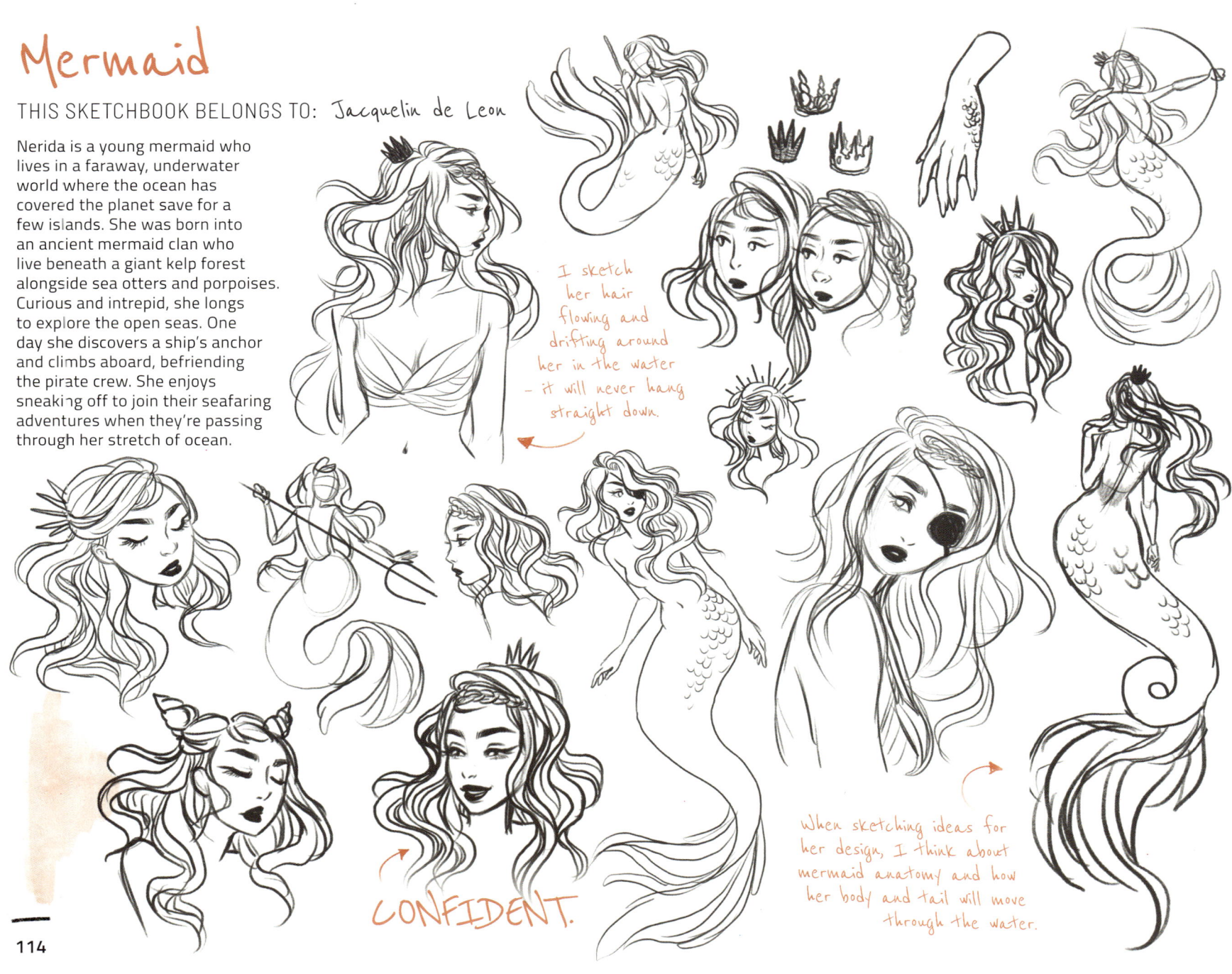

I sketch her hair flowing and drifting around her in the water – it will never hang straight down.

CONFIDENT.

When sketching ideas for her design, I think about mermaid anatomy and how her body and tail will move through the water.

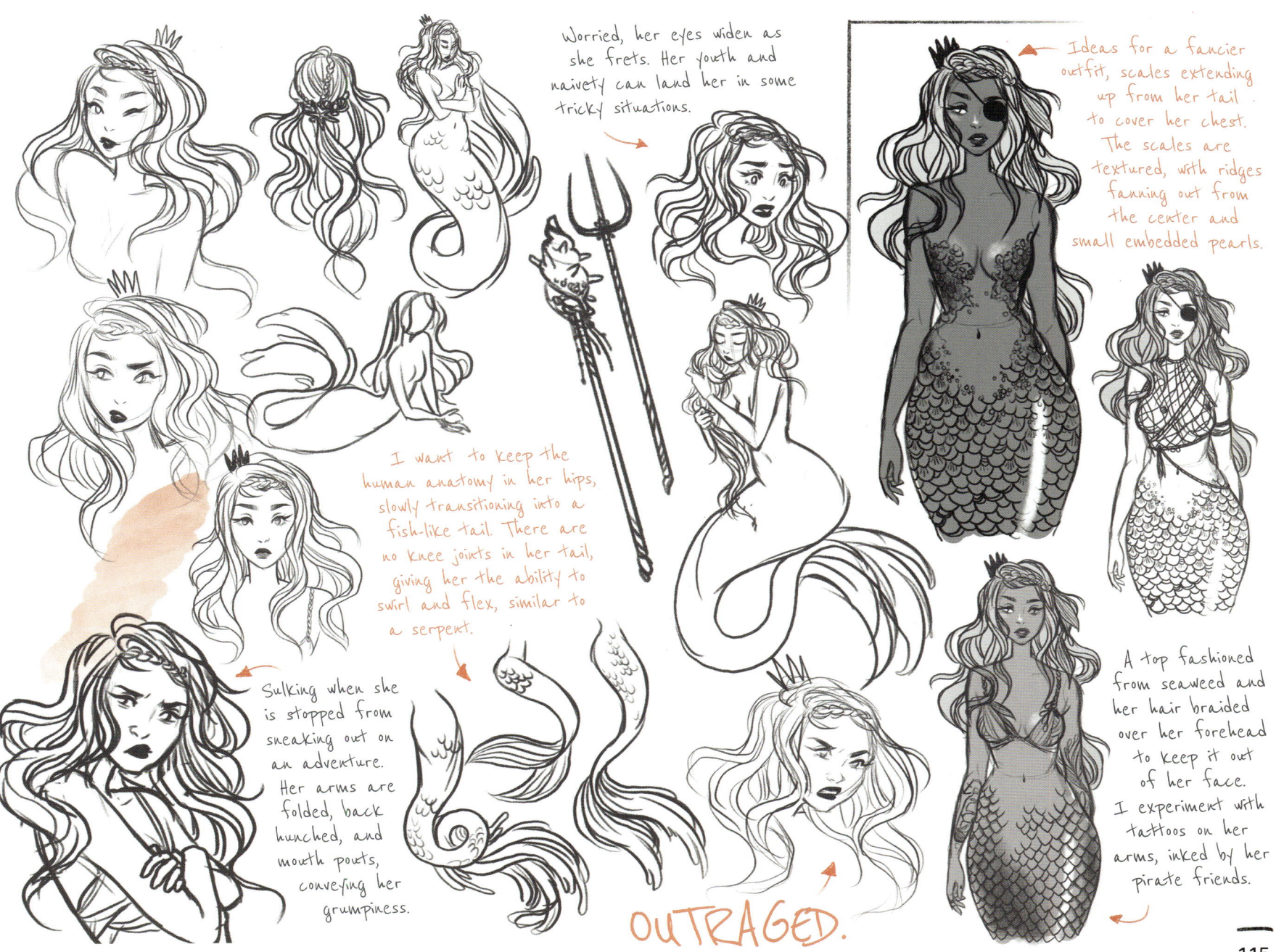

Worried, her eyes widen as she frets. Her youth and naivety can land her in some tricky situations.

Ideas for a fancier outfit, scales extending up from her tail to cover her chest. The scales are textured, with ridges fanning out from the center and small embedded pearls.

I want to keep the human anatomy in her hips, slowly transitioning into a fish-like tail. There are no knee joints in her tail, giving her the ability to swirl and flex, similar to a serpent.

Sulking when she is stopped from sneaking out on an adventure. Her arms are folded, back hunched, and mouth pouts, conveying her grumpiness.

OUTRAGED.

A top fashioned from seaweed and her hair braided over her forehead to keep it out of her face. I experiment with tattoos on her arms, inked by her pirate friends.

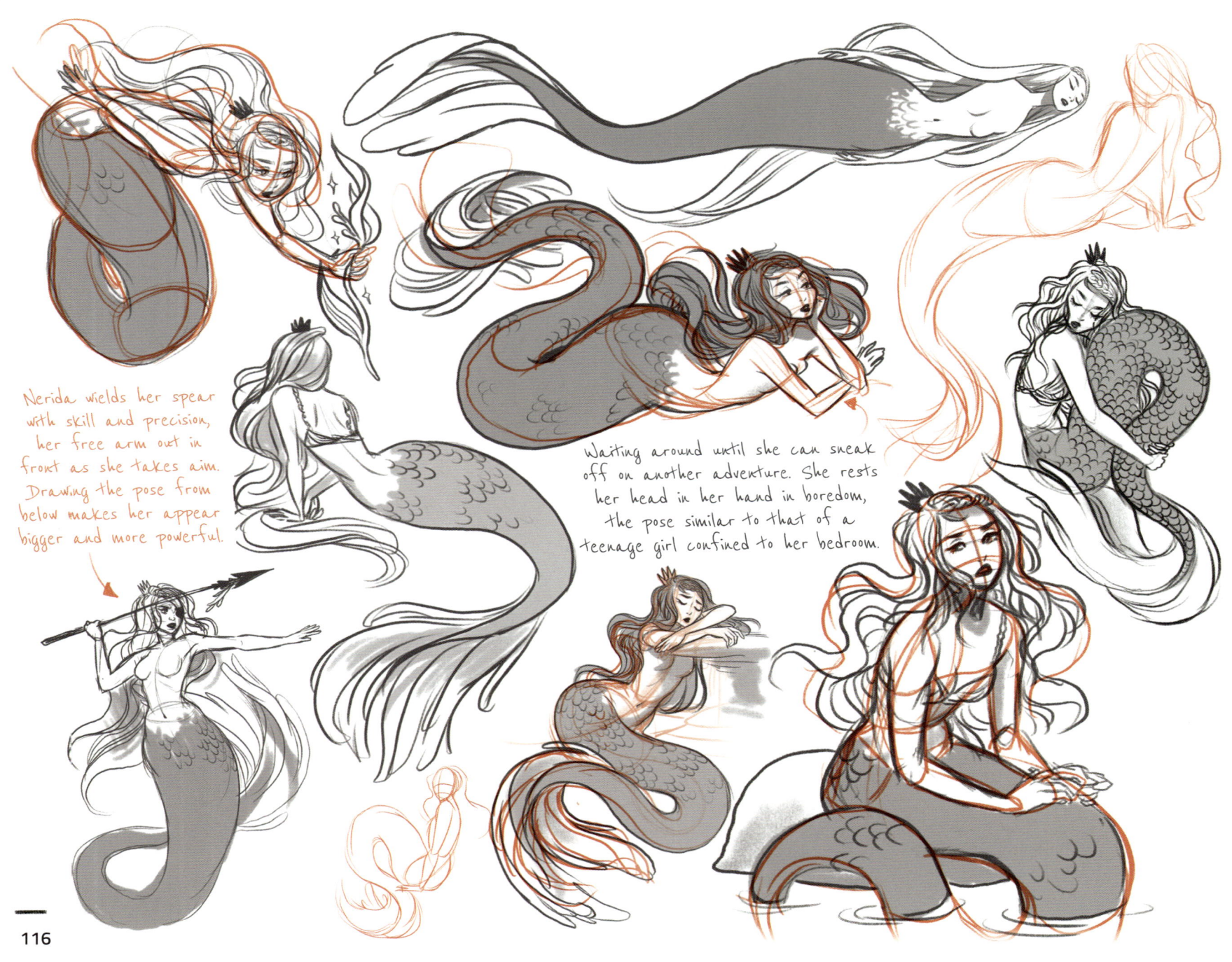

Nerida wields her spear with skill and precision, her free arm out in front as she takes aim. Drawing the pose from below makes her appear bigger and more powerful.

Waiting around until she can sneak off on another adventure. She rests her head in her hand in boredom, the pose similar to that of a teenage girl confined to her bedroom.

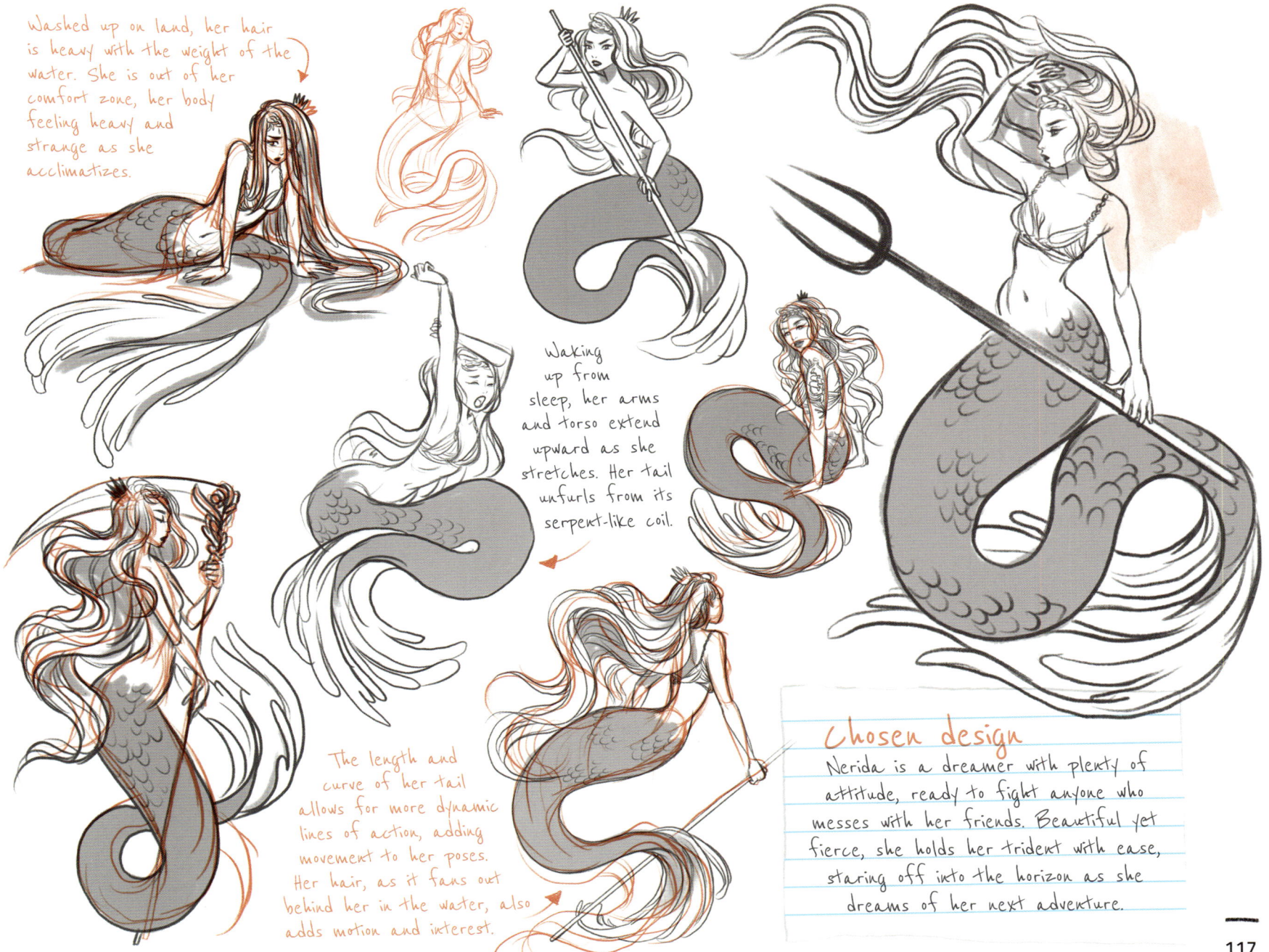

Washed up on land, her hair is heavy with the weight of the water. She is out of her comfort zone, her body feeling heavy and strange as she acclimatizes.

Waking up from sleep, her arms and torso extend upward as she stretches. Her tail unfurls from its serpent-like coil.

The length and curve of her tail allows for more dynamic lines of action, adding movement to her poses. Her hair, as it fans out behind her in the water, also adds motion and interest.

Chosen design

Nerida is a dreamer with plenty of attitude, ready to fight anyone who messes with her friends. Beautiful yet fierce, she holds her trident with ease, staring off into the horizon as she dreams of her next adventure.

117

Plant superheroine

The year is 2250, four years after a global event altered the DNA of numerous people. Thistle is an escaped test subject, now part of the Gaian Alliance – a small rebel force and rescue team who escaped the vast testing complexes that experiment on the affected people. Her supernatural abilities allow her to grow plants to enormous sizes and produce flora from her skin, but extreme anger or adrenaline can cause her to lose control and sprout thorns and vines. The heart rate nodes on her bodysuit light up and beep to warn her to regain control. She is determined, protective, and empathetic.

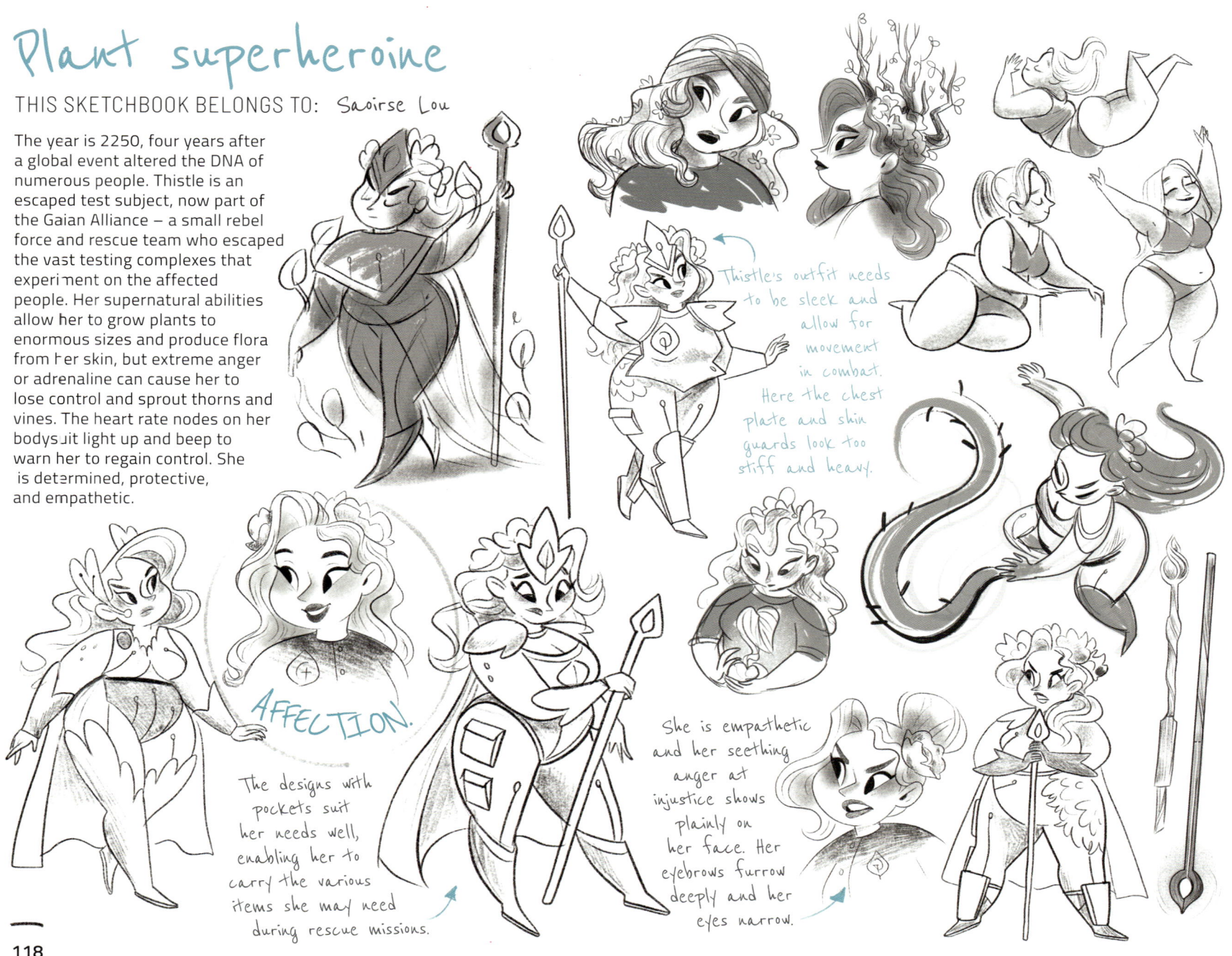

Thistle's outfit needs to be sleek and allow for movement in combat. Here the chest plate and shin guards look too stiff and heavy.

AFFECTION.

The designs with pockets suit her needs well, enabling her to carry the various items she may need during rescue missions.

She is empathetic and her seething anger at injustice shows plainly on her face. Her eyebrows furrow deeply and her eyes narrow.

118

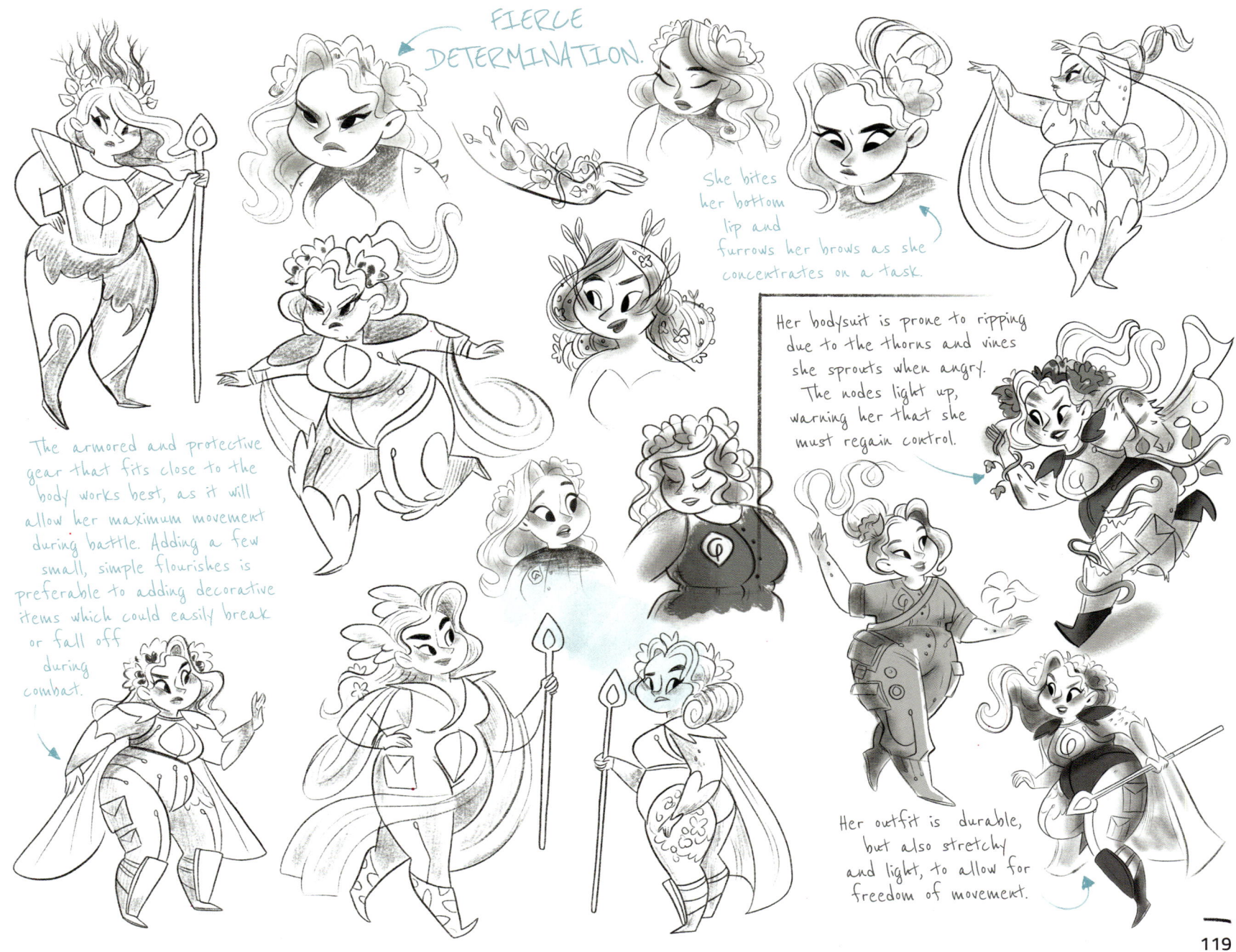

FIERCE DETERMINATION.

She bites her bottom lip and furrows her brows as she concentrates on a task.

Her bodysuit is prone to ripping due to the thorns and vines she sprouts when angry. The nodes light up, warning her that she must regain control.

The armored and protective gear that fits close to the body works best, as it will allow her maximum movement during battle. Adding a few small, simple flourishes is preferable to adding decorative items which could easily break or fall off during combat.

Her outfit is durable, but also stretchy and light, to allow for freedom of movement.

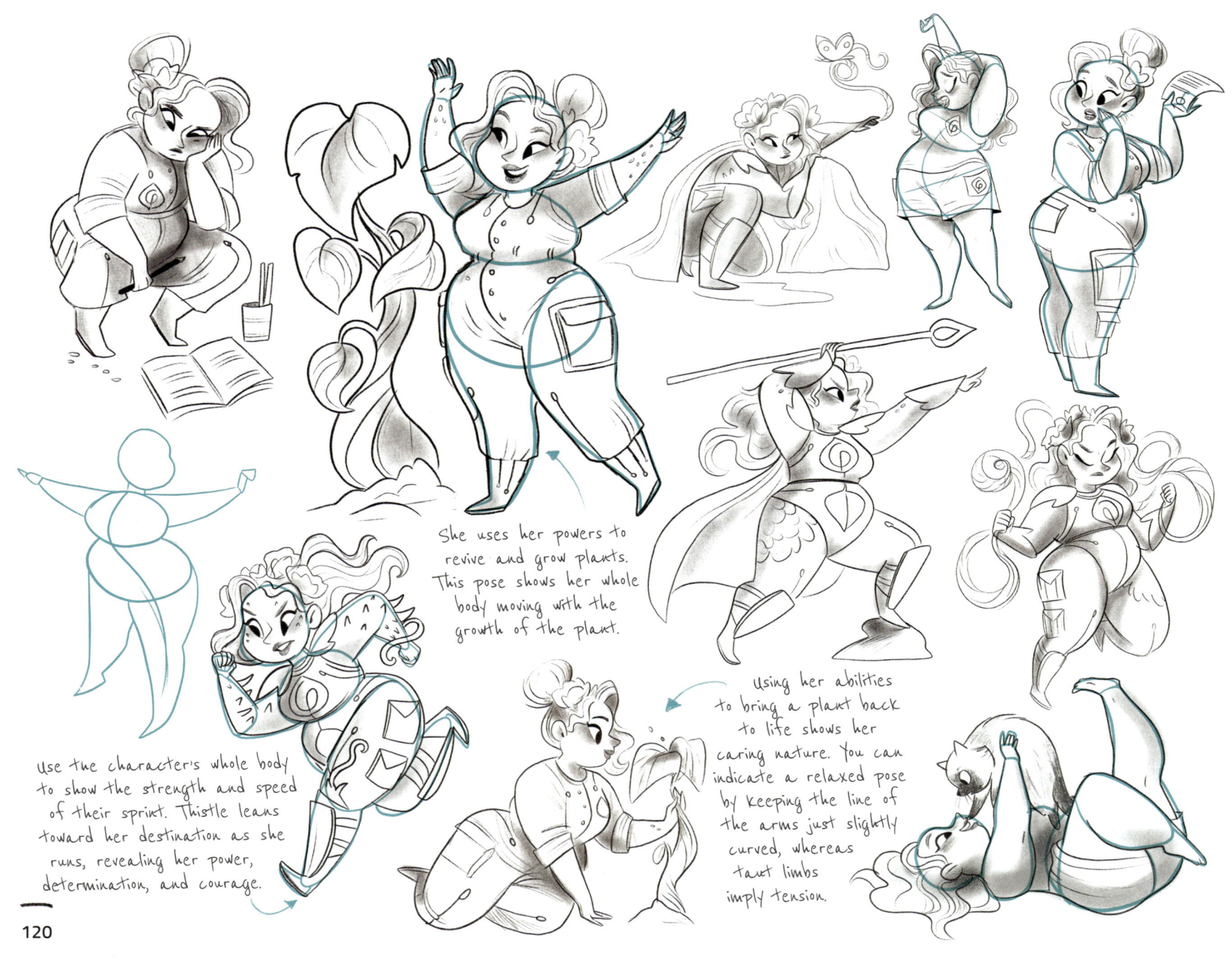

She uses her powers to revive and grow plants. This pose shows her whole body moving with the growth of the plant.

Use the character's whole body to show the strength and speed of their sprint. Thistle leans toward her destination as she runs, revealing her power, determination, and courage.

Using her abilities to bring a plant back to life shows her caring nature. You can indicate a relaxed pose by keeping the line of the arms just slightly curved, whereas taut limbs imply tension.

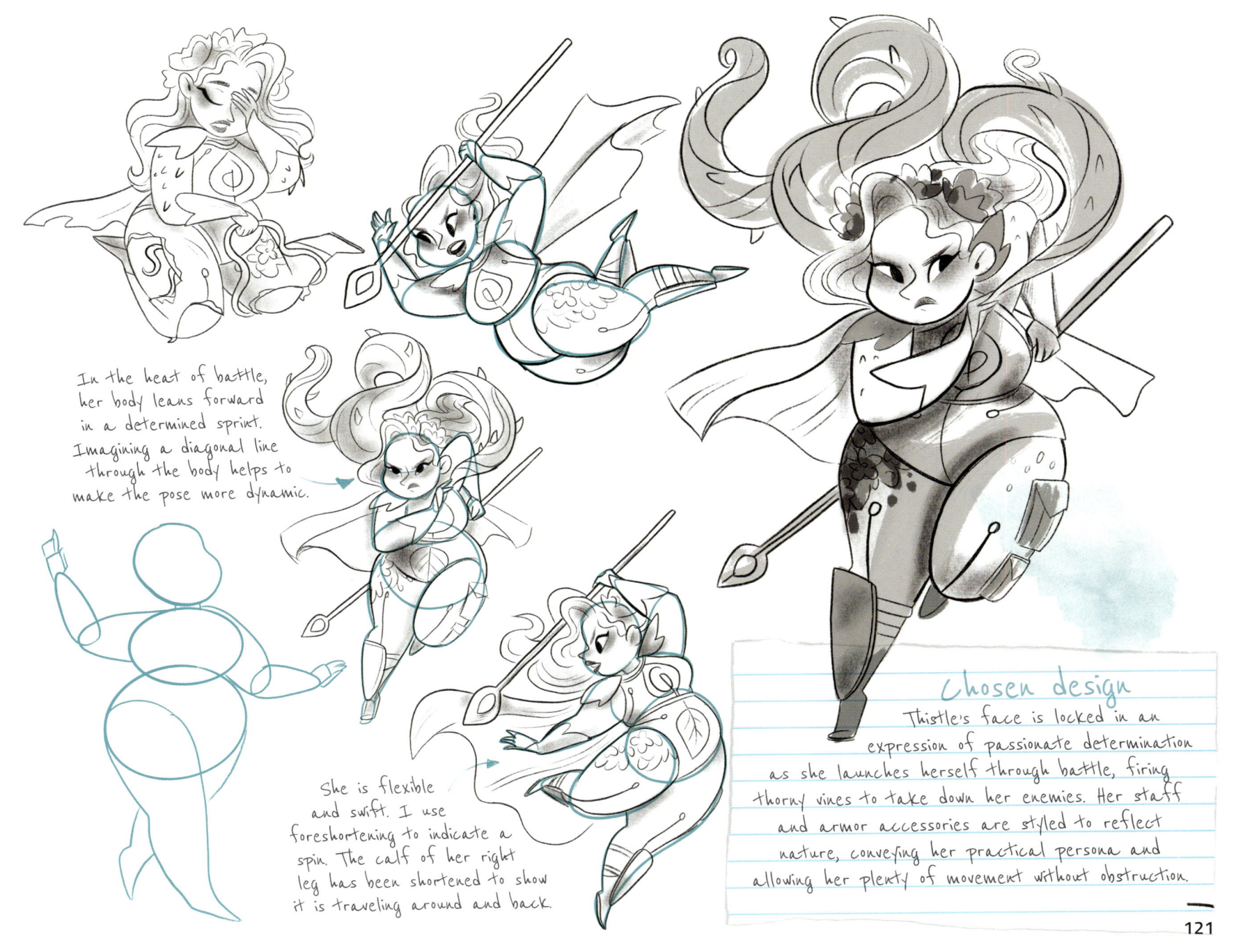

In the heat of battle, her body leans forward in a determined sprint. Imagining a diagonal line through the body helps to make the pose more dynamic.

She is flexible and swift. I use foreshortening to indicate a spin. The calf of her right leg has been shortened to show it is traveling around and back.

Chosen design

Thistle's face is locked in an expression of passionate determination as she launches herself through battle, firing thorny vines to take down her enemies. Her staff and armor accessories are styled to reflect nature, conveying her practical persona and allowing her plenty of movement without obstruction.

Botanist

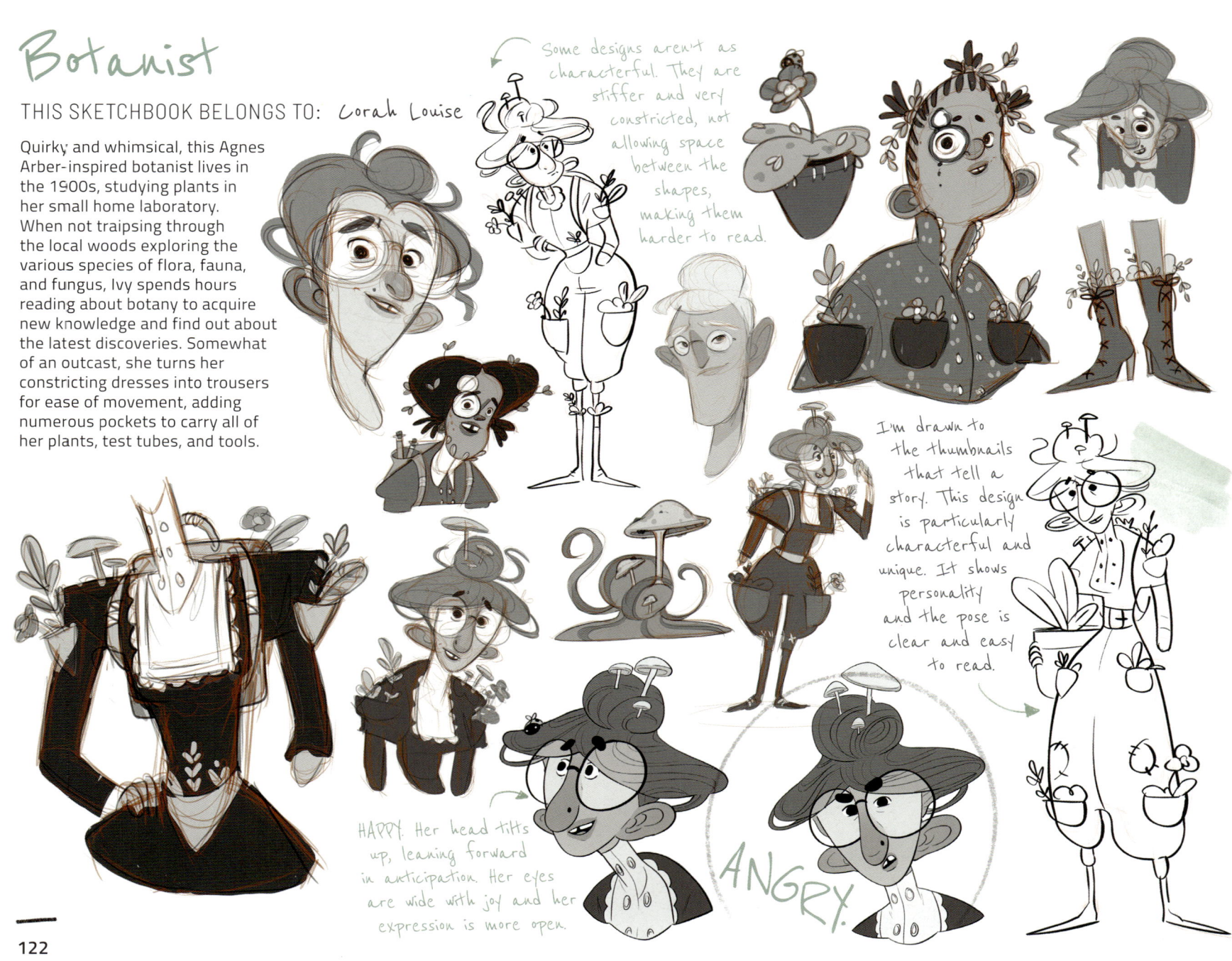

THIS SKETCHBOOK BELONGS TO: Corah Louise

Quirky and whimsical, this Agnes Arber-inspired botanist lives in the 1900s, studying plants in her small home laboratory. When not traipsing through the local woods exploring the various species of flora, fauna, and fungus, Ivy spends hours reading about botany to acquire new knowledge and find out about the latest discoveries. Somewhat of an outcast, she turns her constricting dresses into trousers for ease of movement, adding numerous pockets to carry all of her plants, test tubes, and tools.

Some designs aren't as characterful. They are stiffer and very constricted, not allowing space between the shapes, making them harder to read.

I'm drawn to the thumbnails that tell a story. This design is particularly characterful and unique. It shows personality and the pose is clear and easy to read.

HAPPY. Her head tilts up, leaning forward in anticipation. Her eyes are wide with joy and her expression is more open.

ANGRY.

122

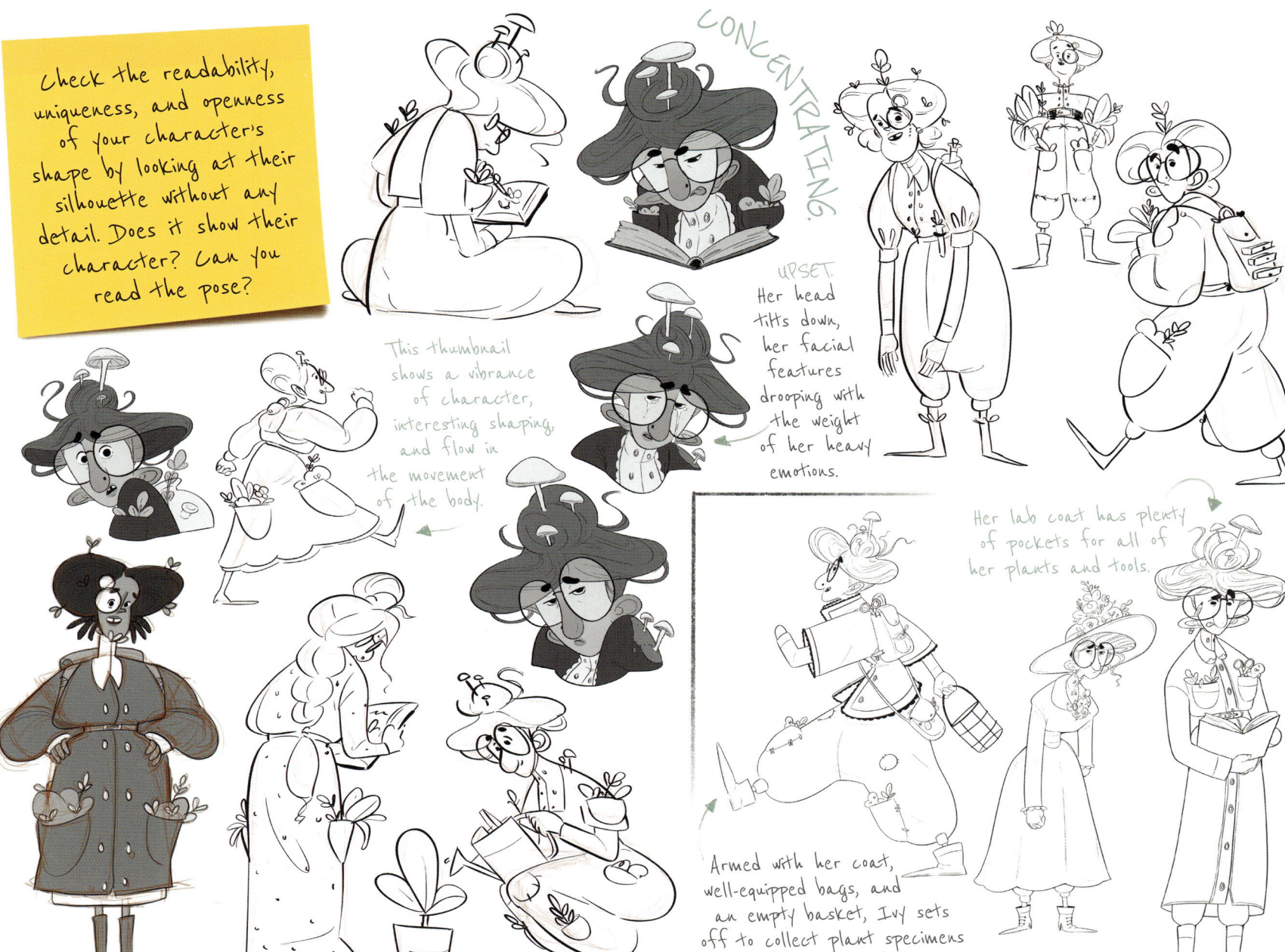

Check the readability, uniqueness, and openness of your character's shape by looking at their silhouette without any detail. Does it show their character? Can you read the pose?

CONCENTRATING.

This thumbnail shows a vibrance of character, interesting shaping, and flow in the movement of the body.

UPSET. Her head tilts down, her facial features drooping with the weight of her heavy emotions.

Her lab coat has plenty of pockets for all of her plants and tools.

Armed with her coat, well-equipped bags, and an empty basket, Ivy sets off to collect plant specimens from the woods.

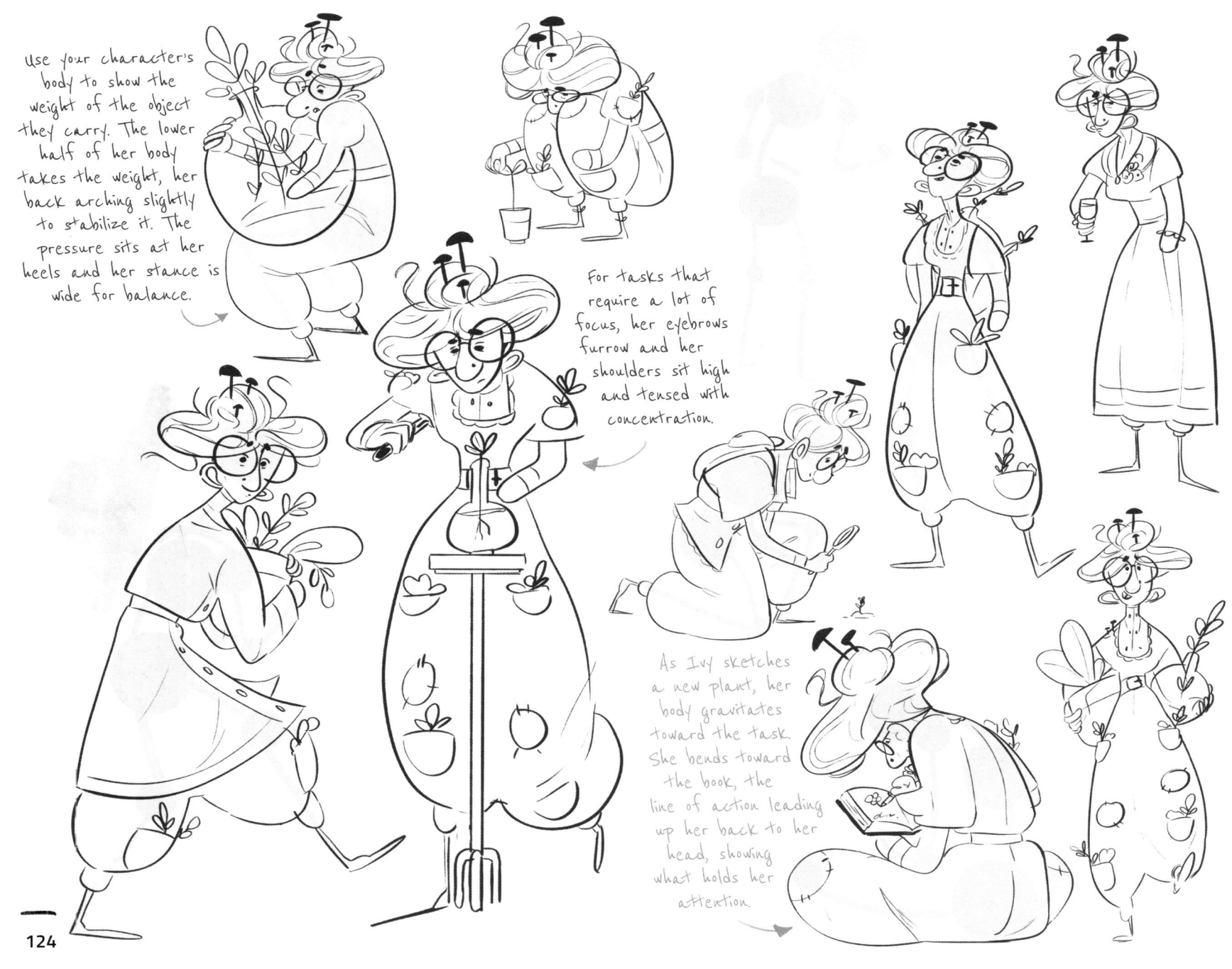

Use your character's body to show the weight of the object they carry. The lower half of her body takes the weight, her back arching slightly to stabilize it. The pressure sits at her heels and her stance is wide for balance.

For tasks that require a lot of focus, her eyebrows furrow and her shoulders sit high and tensed with concentration.

As Ivy sketches a new plant, her body gravitates toward the task. She bends toward the book, the line of action leading up her back to her head, showing what holds her attention.

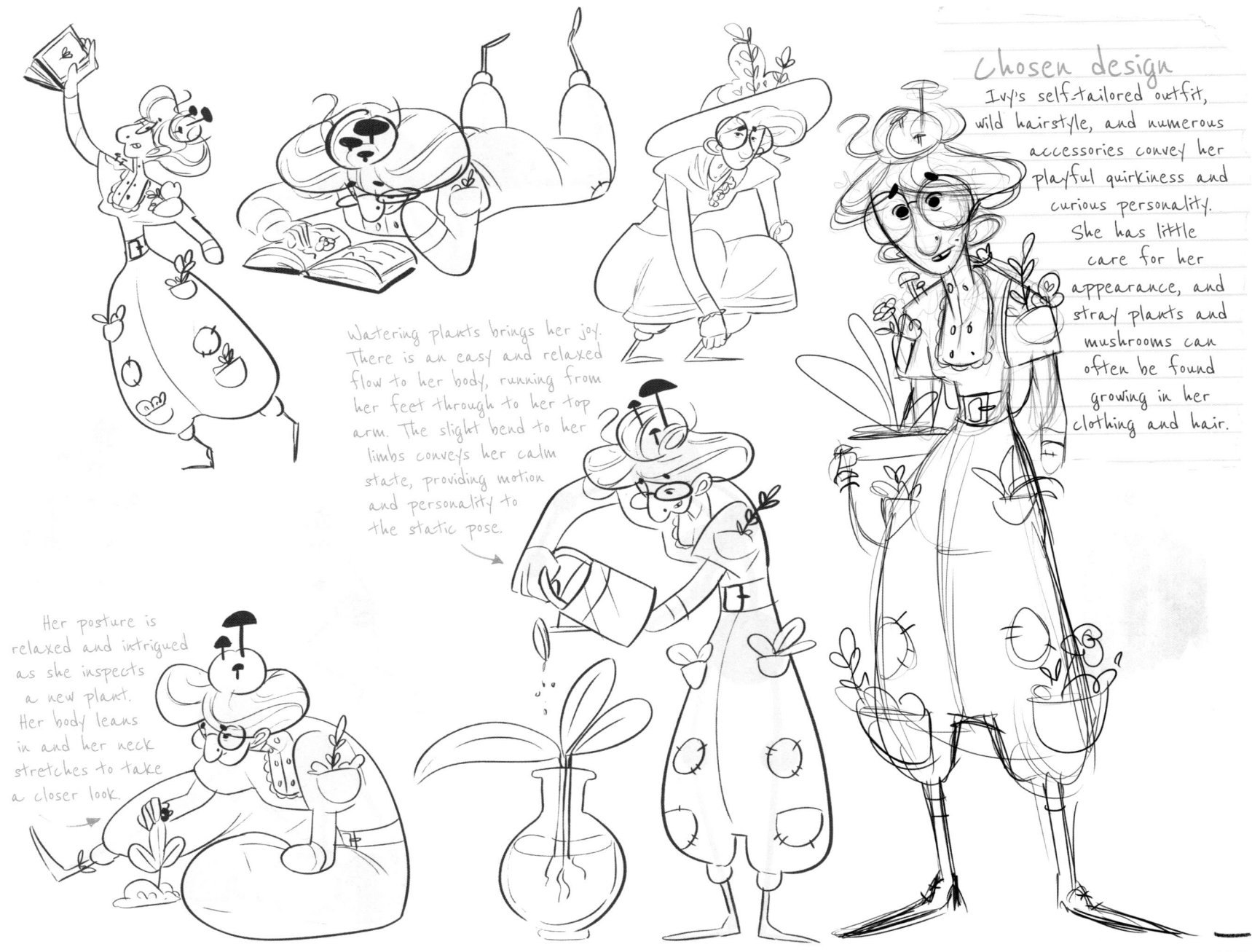

chosen design

Ivy's self-tailored outfit, wild hairstyle, and numerous accessories convey her playful quirkiness and curious personality. She has little care for her appearance, and stray plants and mushrooms can often be found growing in her clothing and hair.

Watering plants brings her joy. There is an easy and relaxed flow to her body, running from her feet through to her top arm. The slight bend to her limbs conveys her calm state, providing motion and personality to the static pose.

Her posture is relaxed and intrigued as she inspects a new plant. Her body leans in and her neck stretches to take a closer look.

Water superheroine

THIS SKETCHBOOK BELONGS TO: Gretel Lusky

Maritza lives in a small, Caribbean coastal town where she spends her free time diving, kayaking, and surfing. While out diving one day, she finds a strange artifact near a shipwreck that grants her the ability to manipulate water. Carrying the amulet with her always, she uses these abilities to protect her town and the marine life around it. She is adventurous, energetic, and curious, and has a sporty, natural look.

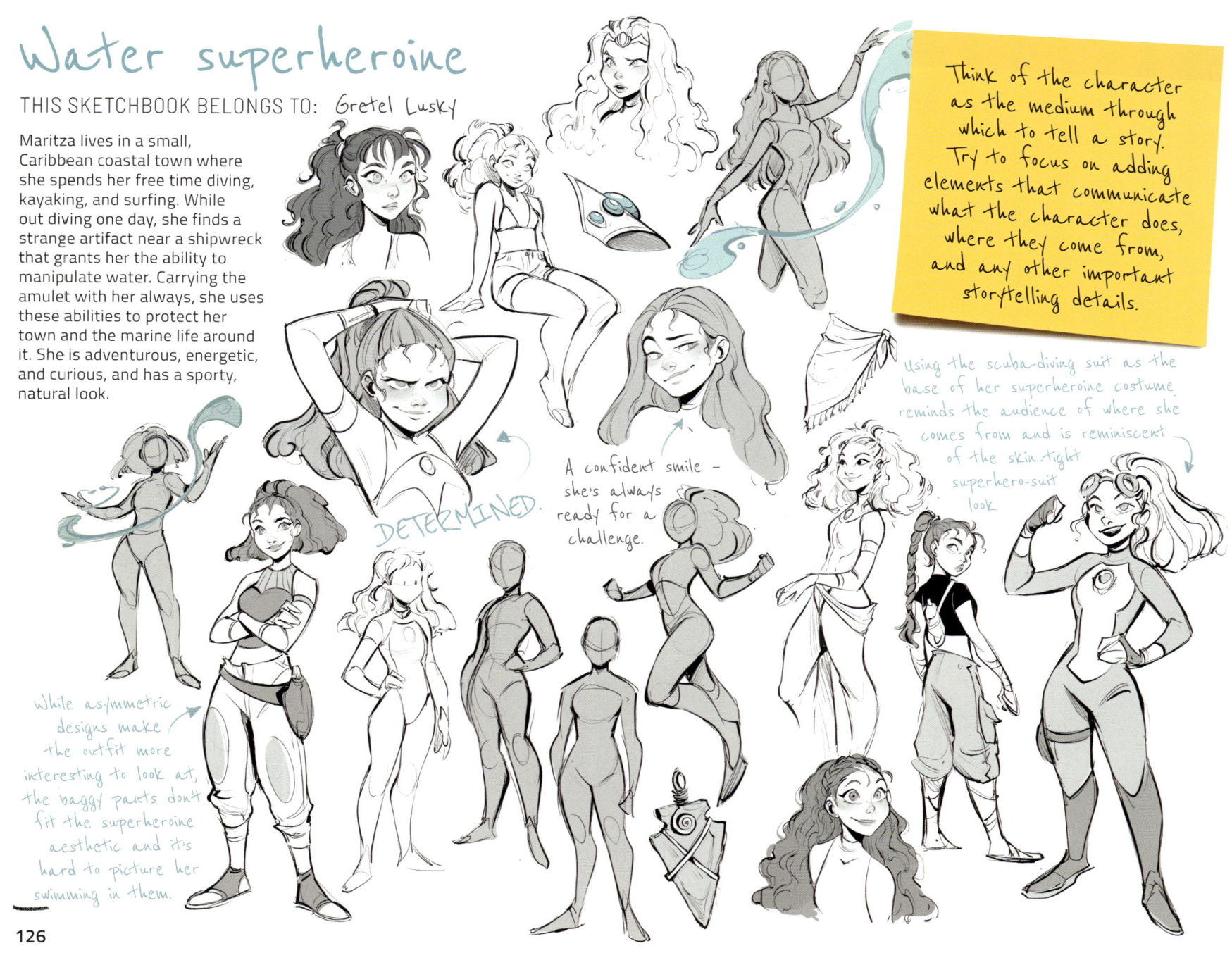

Think of the character as the medium through which to tell a story. Try to focus on adding elements that communicate what the character does, where they come from, and any other important storytelling details.

Using the scuba-diving suit as the base of her superheroine costume reminds the audience of where she comes from and is reminiscent of the skin-tight superhero-suit look.

A confident smile – she's always ready for a challenge.

DETERMINED.

While asymmetric designs make the outfit more interesting to look at, the baggy pants don't fit the superheroine aesthetic and it's hard to picture her swimming in them.

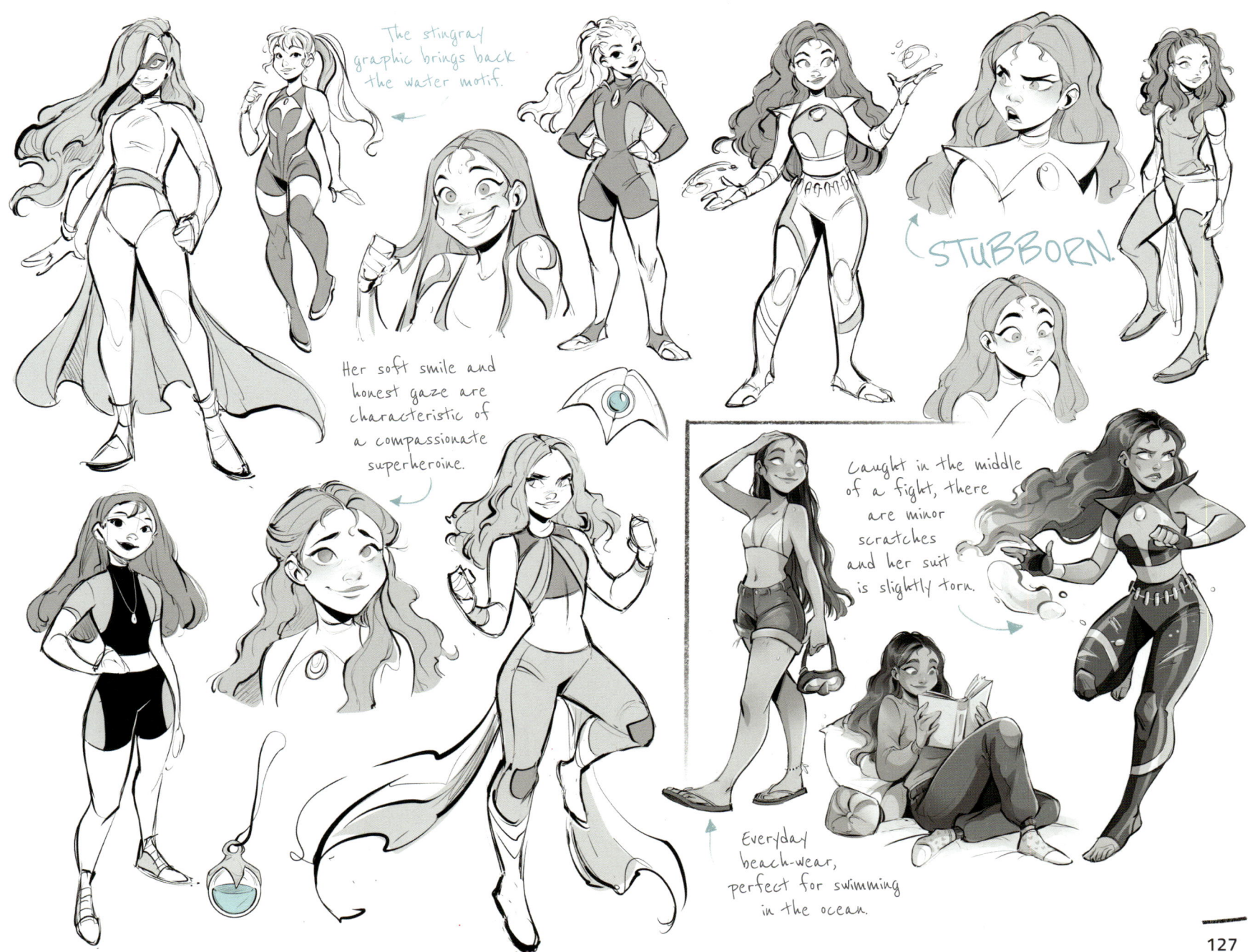

The stingray graphic brings back the water motif.

Her soft smile and honest gaze are characteristic of a compassionate superheroine.

STUBBORN.

Caught in the middle of a fight, there are minor scratches and her suit is slightly torn.

Everyday beach-wear, perfect for swimming in the ocean.

127

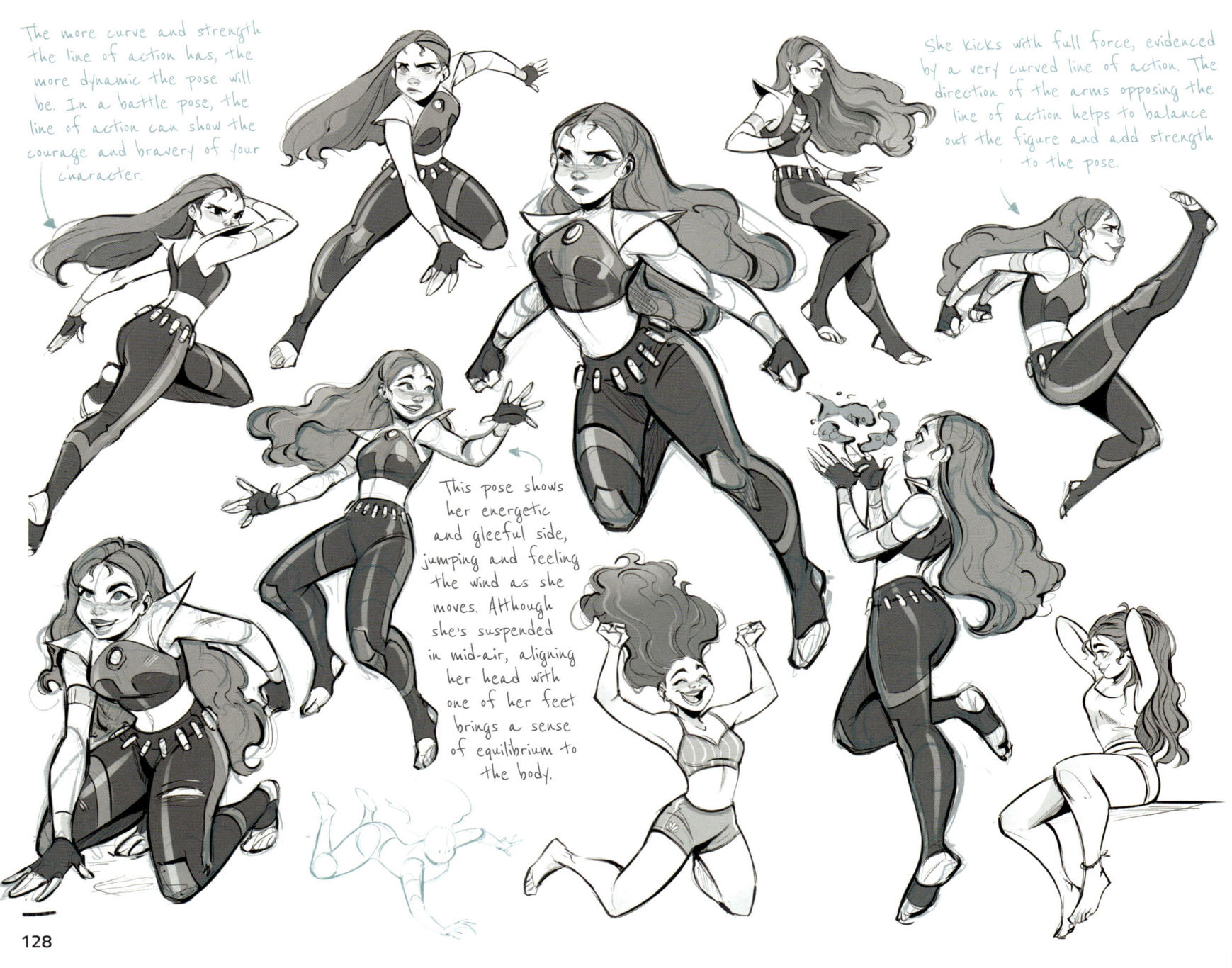

The more curve and strength the line of action has, the more dynamic the pose will be. In a battle pose, the line of action can show the courage and bravery of your character.

She kicks with full force, evidenced by a very curved line of action. The direction of the arms opposing the line of action helps to balance out the figure and add strength to the pose.

This pose shows her energetic and gleeful side, jumping and feeling the wind as she moves. Although she's suspended in mid-air, aligning her head with one of her feet brings a sense of equilibrium to the body.

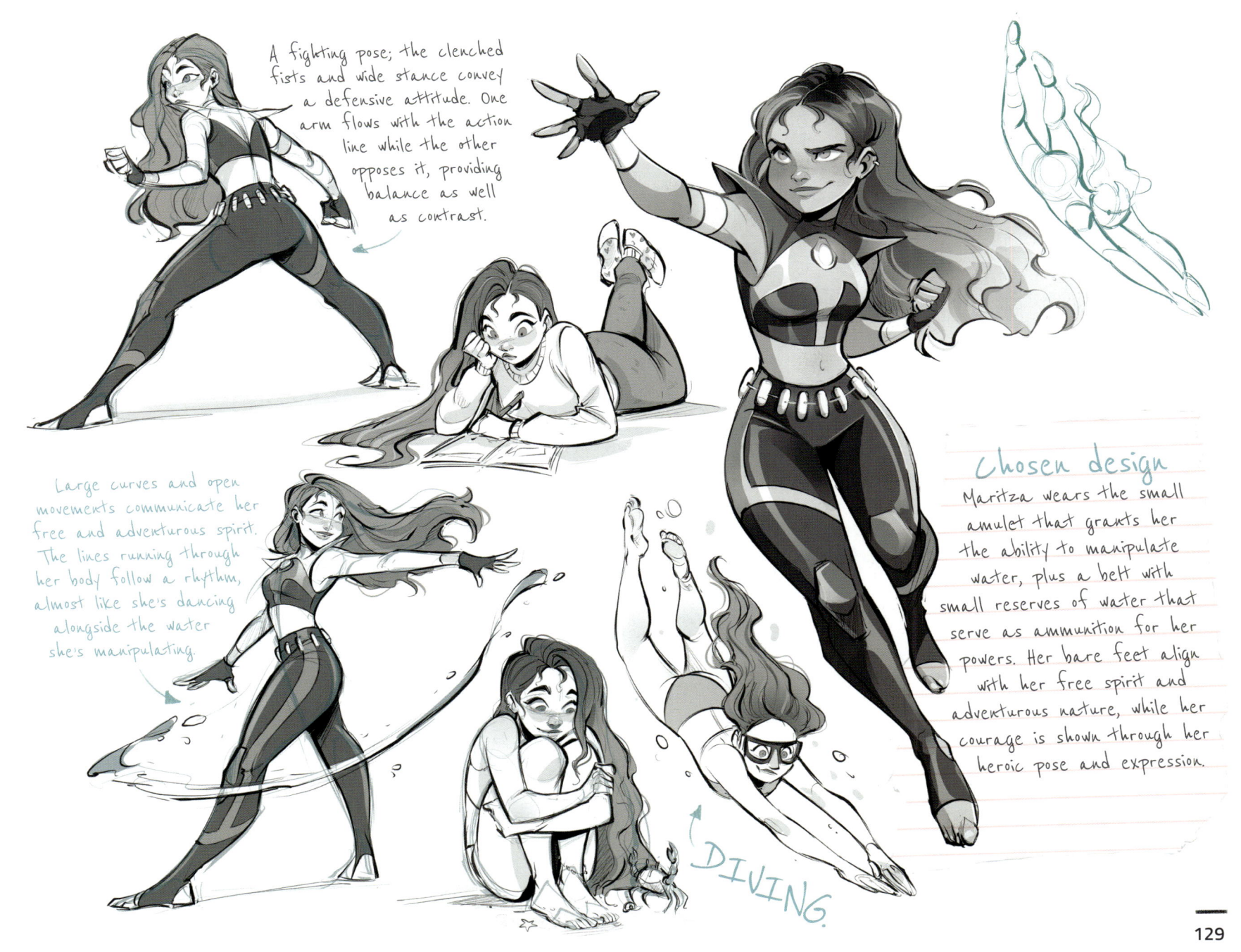

A fighting pose; the clenched fists and wide stance convey a defensive attitude. One arm flows with the action line while the other opposes it, providing balance as well as contrast.

Large curves and open movements communicate her free and adventurous spirit. The lines running through her body follow a rhythm, almost like she's dancing alongside the water she's manipulating.

DIVING.

Chosen design

Maritza wears the small amulet that grants her the ability to manipulate water, plus a belt with small reserves of water that serve as ammunition for her powers. Her bare feet align with her free spirit and adventurous nature, while her courage is shown through her heroic pose and expression.

Fairy

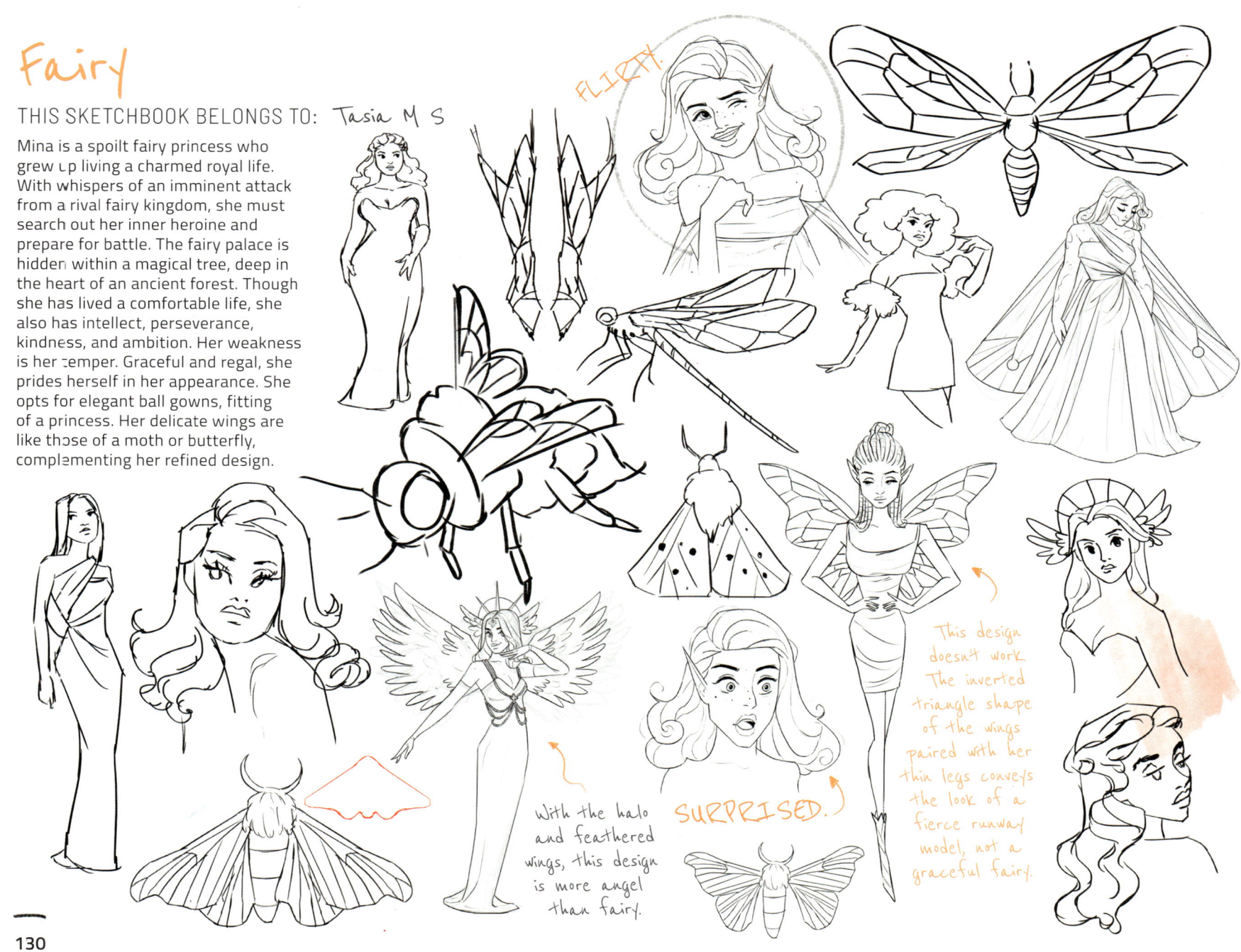

THIS SKETCHBOOK BELONGS TO: Tasia M S

Mina is a spoilt fairy princess who grew up living a charmed royal life. With whispers of an imminent attack from a rival fairy kingdom, she must search out her inner heroine and prepare for battle. The fairy palace is hidden within a magical tree, deep in the heart of an ancient forest. Though she has lived a comfortable life, she also has intellect, perseverance, kindness, and ambition. Her weakness is her temper. Graceful and regal, she prides herself in her appearance. She opts for elegant ball gowns, fitting of a princess. Her delicate wings are like those of a moth or butterfly, complementing her refined design.

FLIRT.

With the halo and feathered wings, this design is more angel than fairy.

SURPRISED.

This design doesn't work. The inverted triangle shape of the wings paired with her thin legs conveys the look of a fierce runway model, not a graceful fairy.

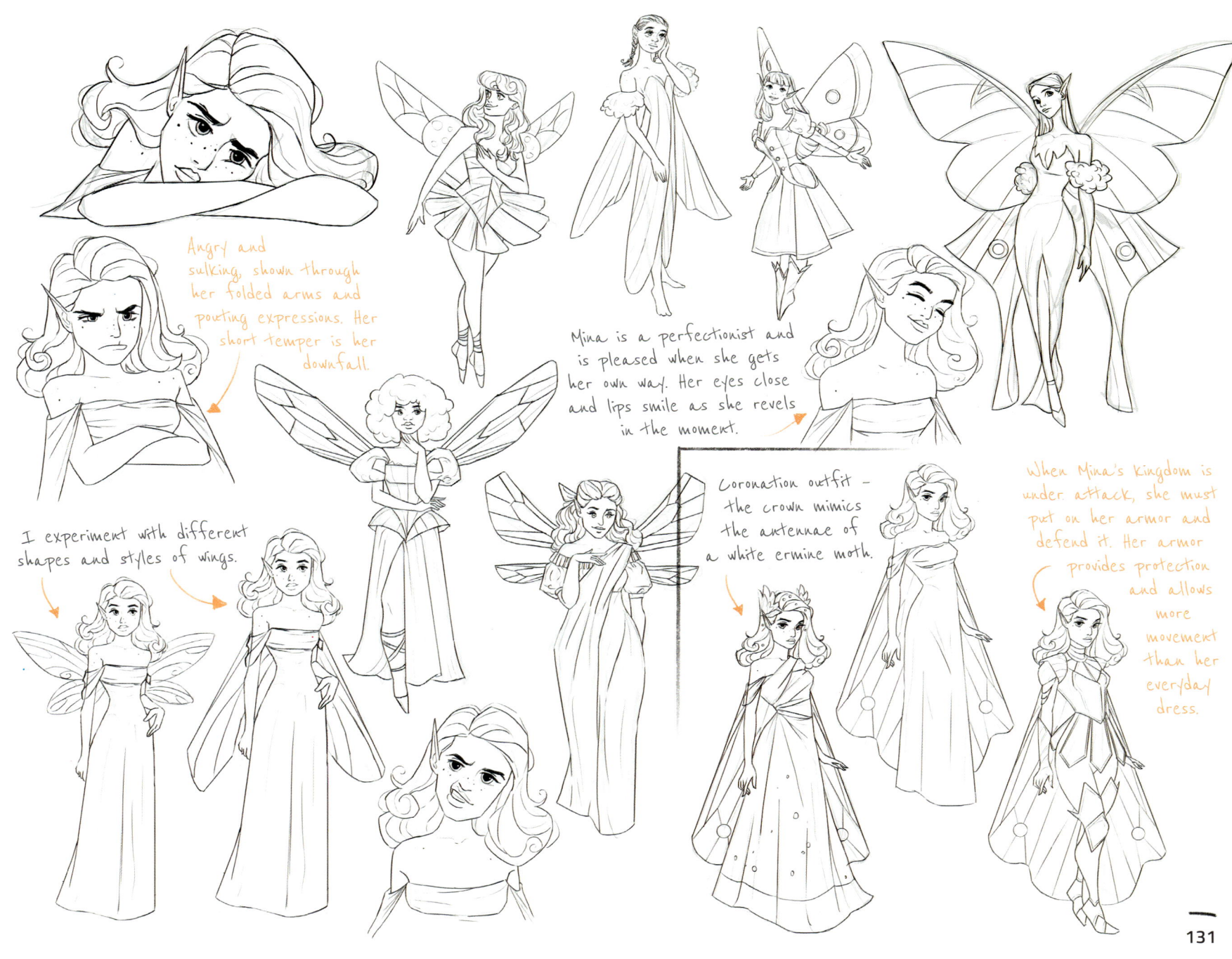

Angry and sulking, shown through her folded arms and pouting expressions. Her short temper is her downfall.

Mina is a perfectionist and is pleased when she gets her own way. Her eyes close and lips smile as she revels in the moment.

I experiment with different shapes and styles of wings.

Coronation outfit - the crown mimics the antennae of a white ermine moth.

When Mina's kingdom is under attack, she must put on her armor and defend it. Her armor provides protection and allows more movement than her everyday dress.

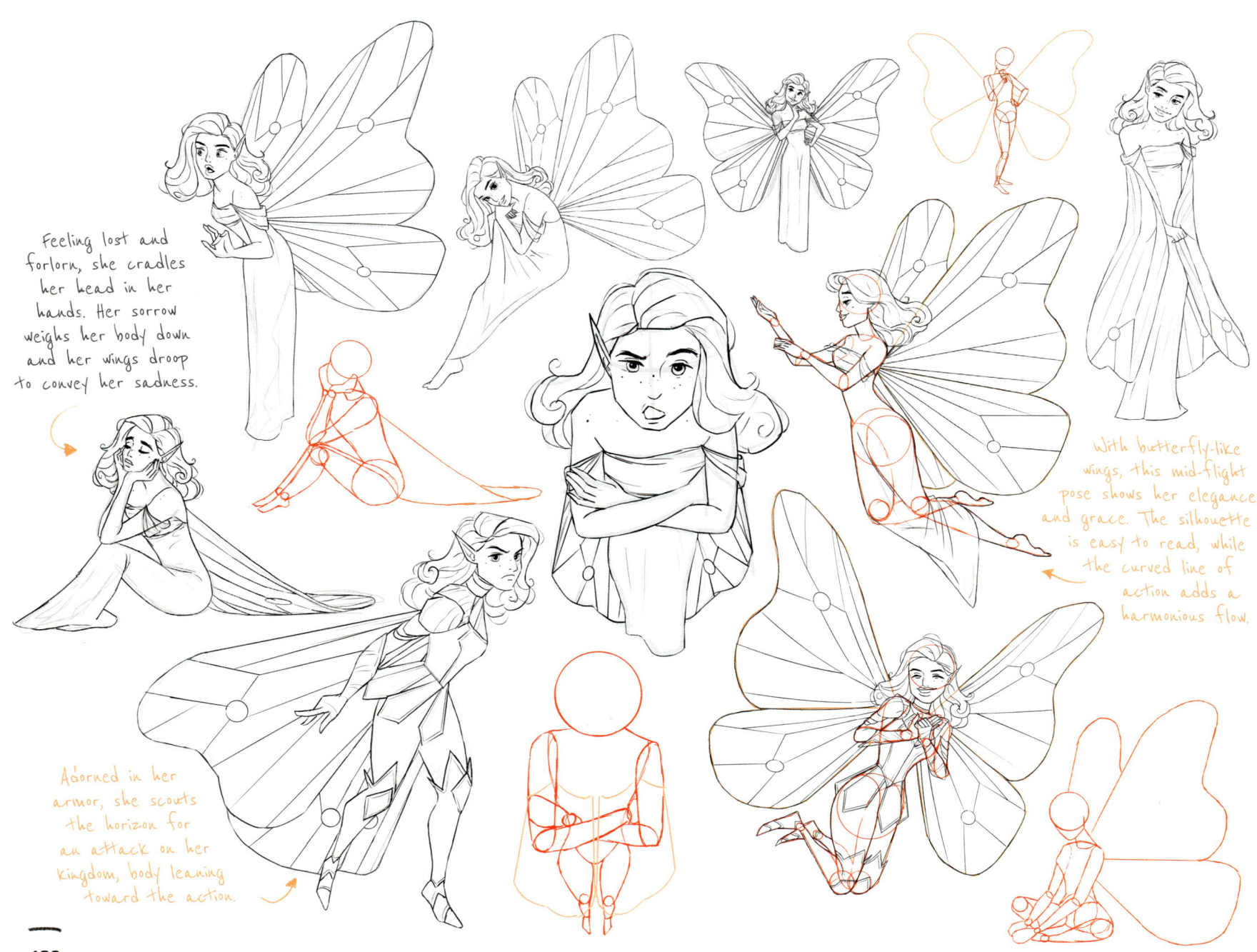

Feeling lost and forlorn, she cradles her head in her hands. Her sorrow weighs her body down and her wings droop to convey her sadness.

With butterfly-like wings, this mid-flight pose shows her elegance and grace. The silhouette is easy to read, while the curved line of action adds a harmonious flow.

Adorned in her armor, she scouts the horizon for an attack on her kingdom, body leaning toward the action.

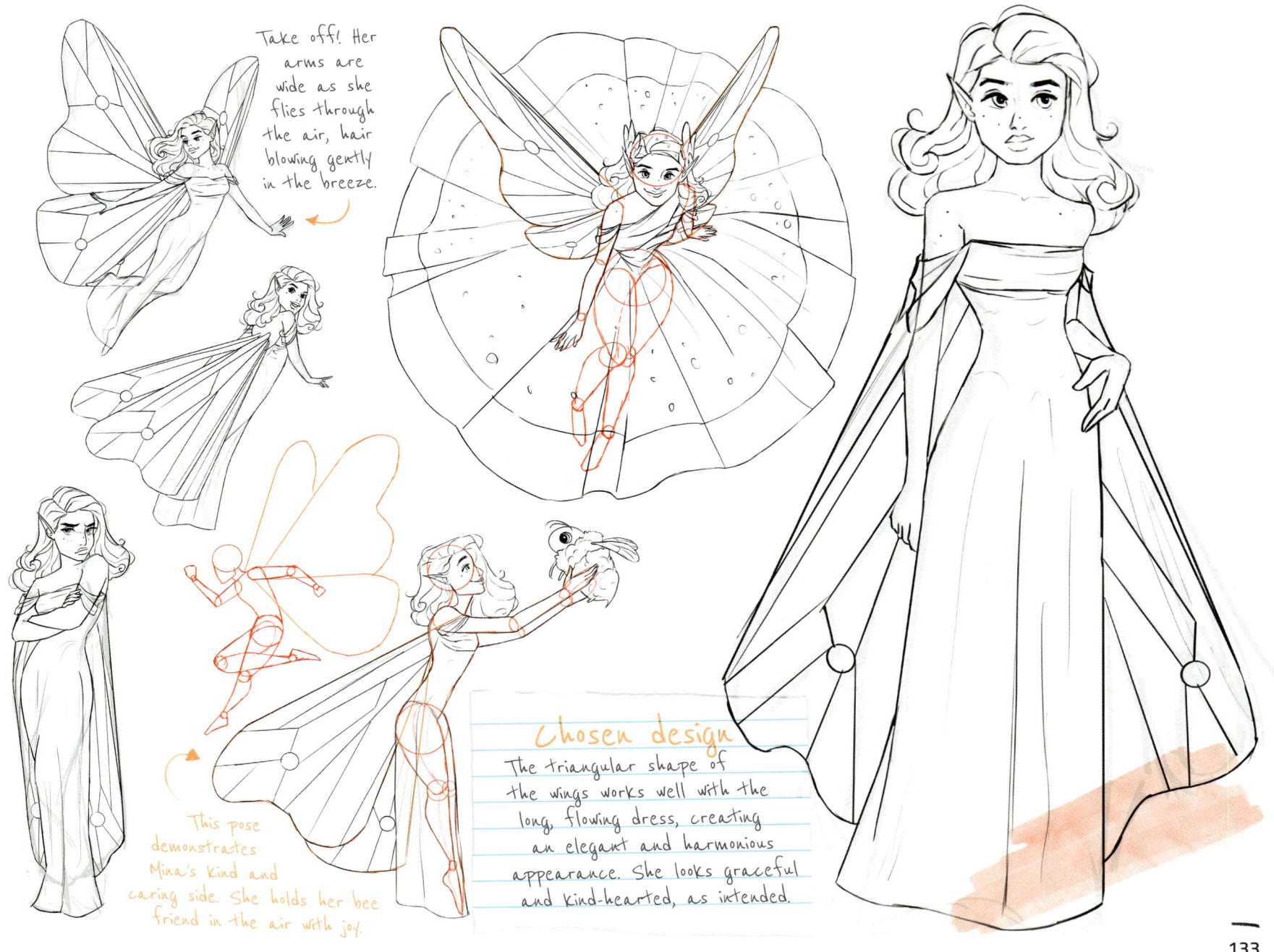

Take off! Her arms are wide as she flies through the air, hair blowing gently in the breeze.

This pose demonstrates Mina's kind and caring side. She holds her bee friend in the air with joy.

Chosen design

The triangular shape of the wings works well with the long, flowing dress, creating an elegant and harmonious appearance. She looks graceful and kind-hearted, as intended.

Vigilante

THIS SKETCHBOOK BELONGS TO: Maria Lia Malandrino

Hex comes from a future Earth where genetic manipulation has made superpowers more common. She can create pockets of temporal distortion to make herself super fast. After losing her legs in an accident where her parents died, she grew up learning to take care of herself. Due to a botched space-time bubble, she ends up in an alternate dimension of Earth where her tech doesn't work. She must learn how to survive in this old Western desert reality, becoming a post woman by day and a vigilante by night. Hex has a good sense of humor and can be charming, but is slow to let anyone close.

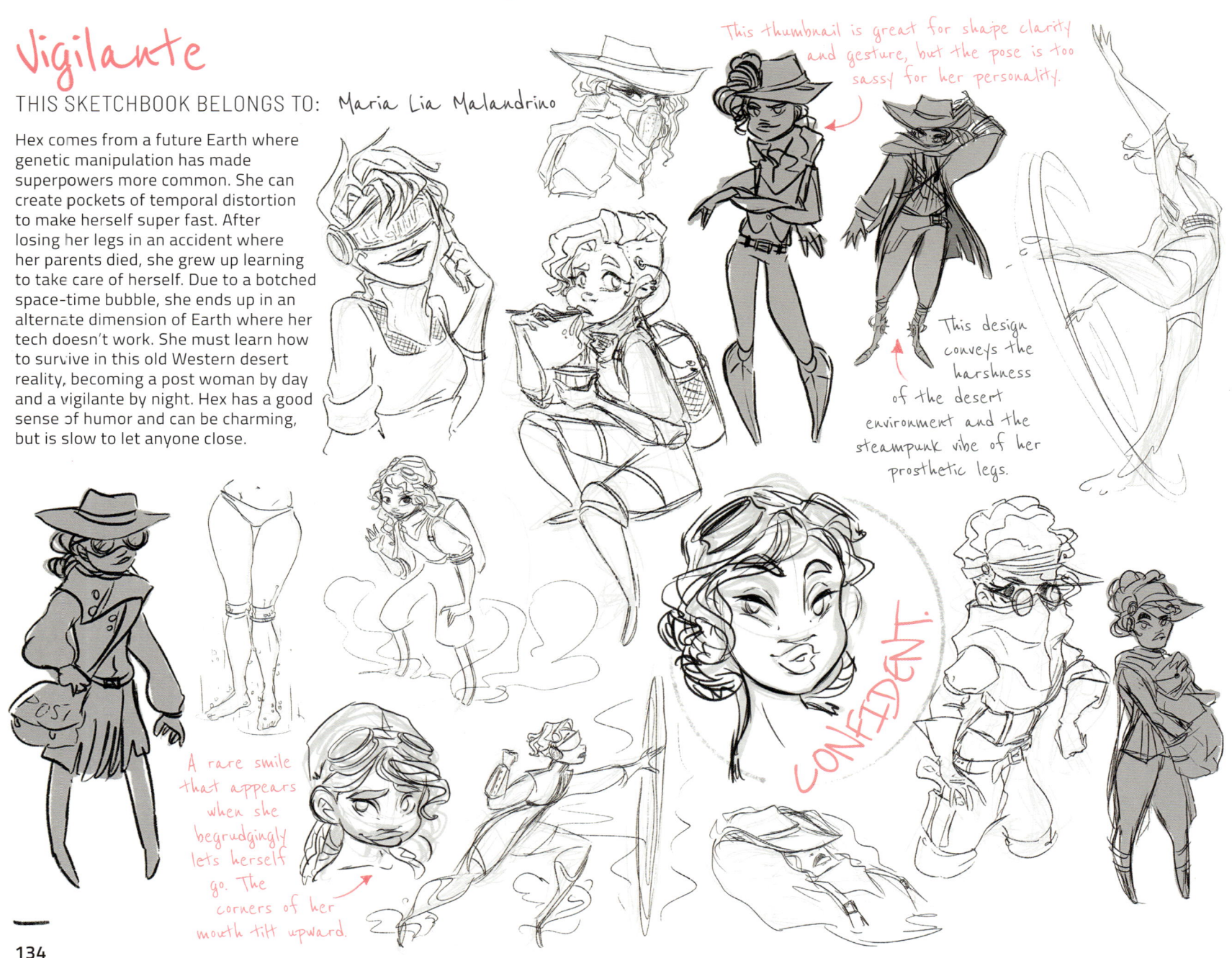

This thumbnail is great for shape clarity and gesture, but the pose is too sassy for her personality.

This design conveys the harshness of the desert environment and the steampunk vibe of her prosthetic legs.

CONFIDENT.

A rare smile that appears when she begrudgingly lets herself go. The corners of her mouth tilt upward.

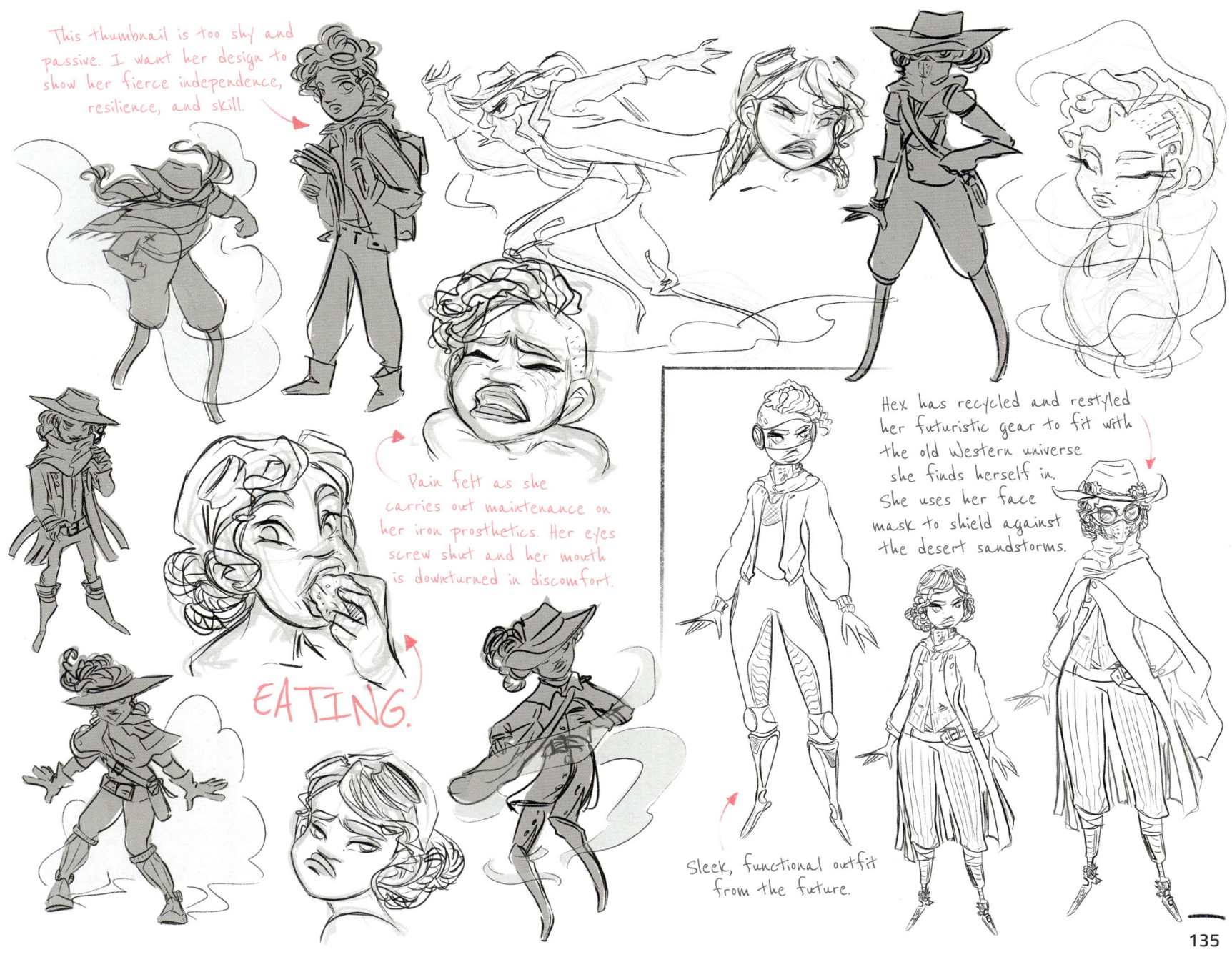

This thumbnail is too shy and passive. I want her design to show her fierce independence, resilience, and skill.

Pain felt as she carries out maintenance on her iron prosthetics. Her eyes screw shut and her mouth is downturned in discomfort.

EATING.

Hex has recycled and restyled her futuristic gear to fit with the old Western universe she finds herself in. She uses her face mask to shield against the desert sandstorms.

Sleek, functional outfit from the future.

135

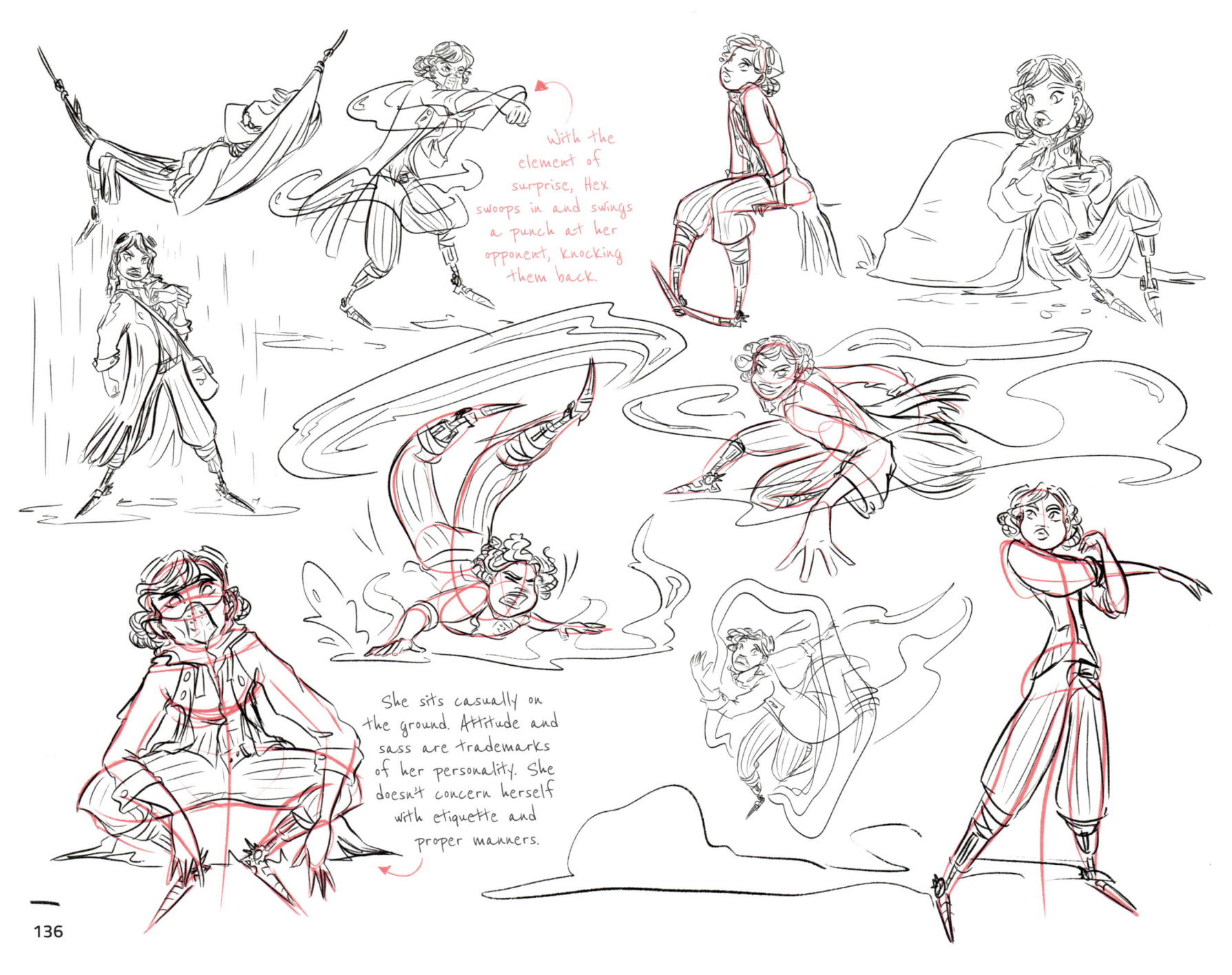

With the element of surprise, Hex swoops in and swings a punch at her opponent, knocking them back.

She sits casually on the ground. Attitude and sass are trademarks of her personality. She doesn't concern herself with etiquette and proper manners.

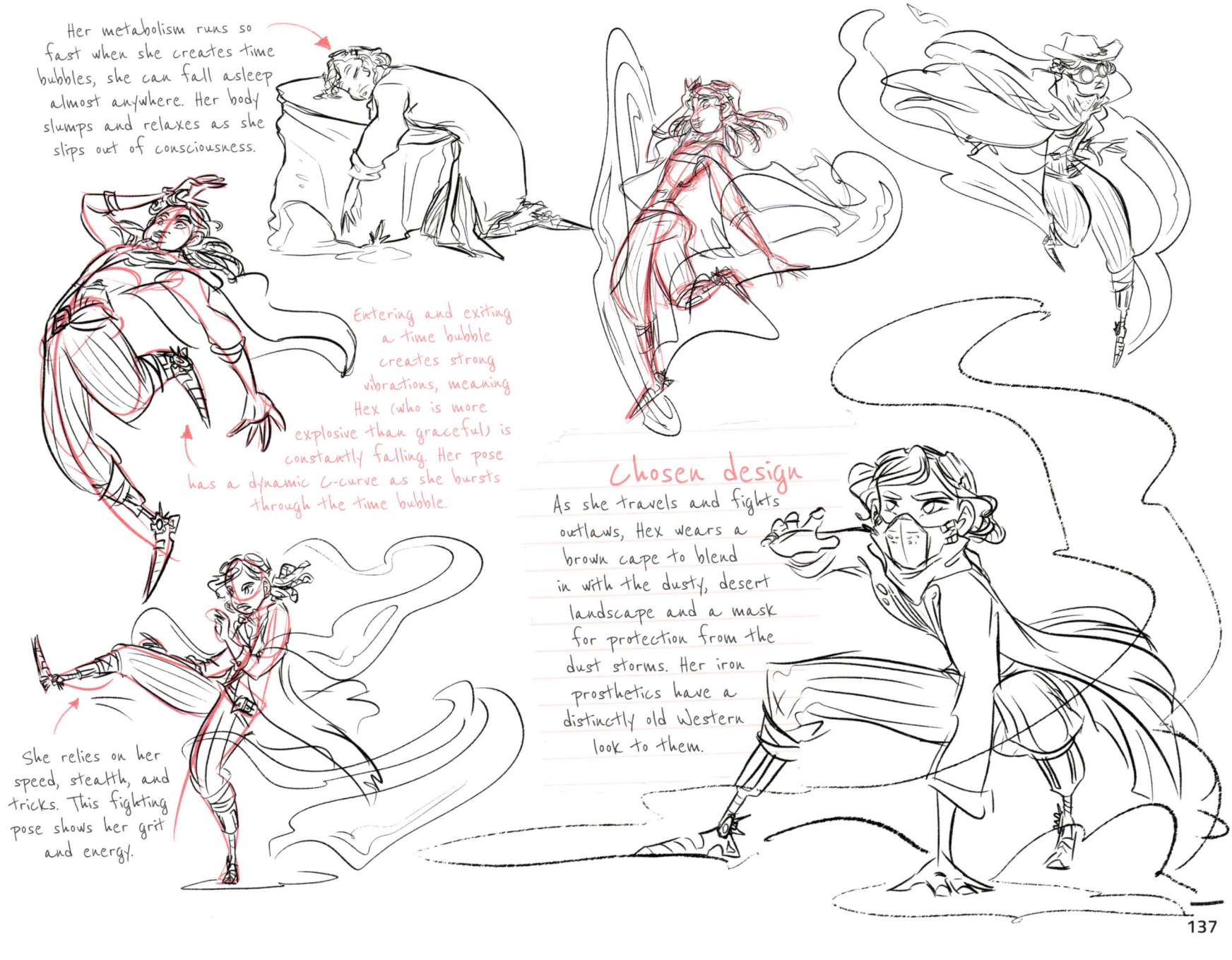

Her metabolism runs so fast when she creates time bubbles, she can fall asleep almost anywhere. Her body slumps and relaxes as she slips out of consciousness.

Entering and exiting a time bubble creates strong vibrations, meaning Hex (who is more explosive than graceful) is constantly falling. Her pose has a dynamic C-curve as she bursts through the time bubble.

She relies on her speed, stealth, and tricks. This fighting pose shows her grit and energy.

Chosen design

As she travels and fights outlaws, Hex wears a brown cape to blend in with the dusty, desert landscape and a mask for protection from the dust storms. Her iron prosthetics have a distinctly old Western look to them.

Wild West outlaw

THIS SKETCHBOOK BELONGS TO: Marvi Manzoni

Set in the Wild West, Sawyer is an outlaw trying to find her place in the world. After being cast out by society, she became an outlaw to survive and found herself in a Robin Hood-type role, taking from the rich to give back to the poor and other outcasts like herself. Though small in stature, she is bold, independent, and fearless, and often wears male clothing to conceal her gender. She is an impulsive character with a soft heart.

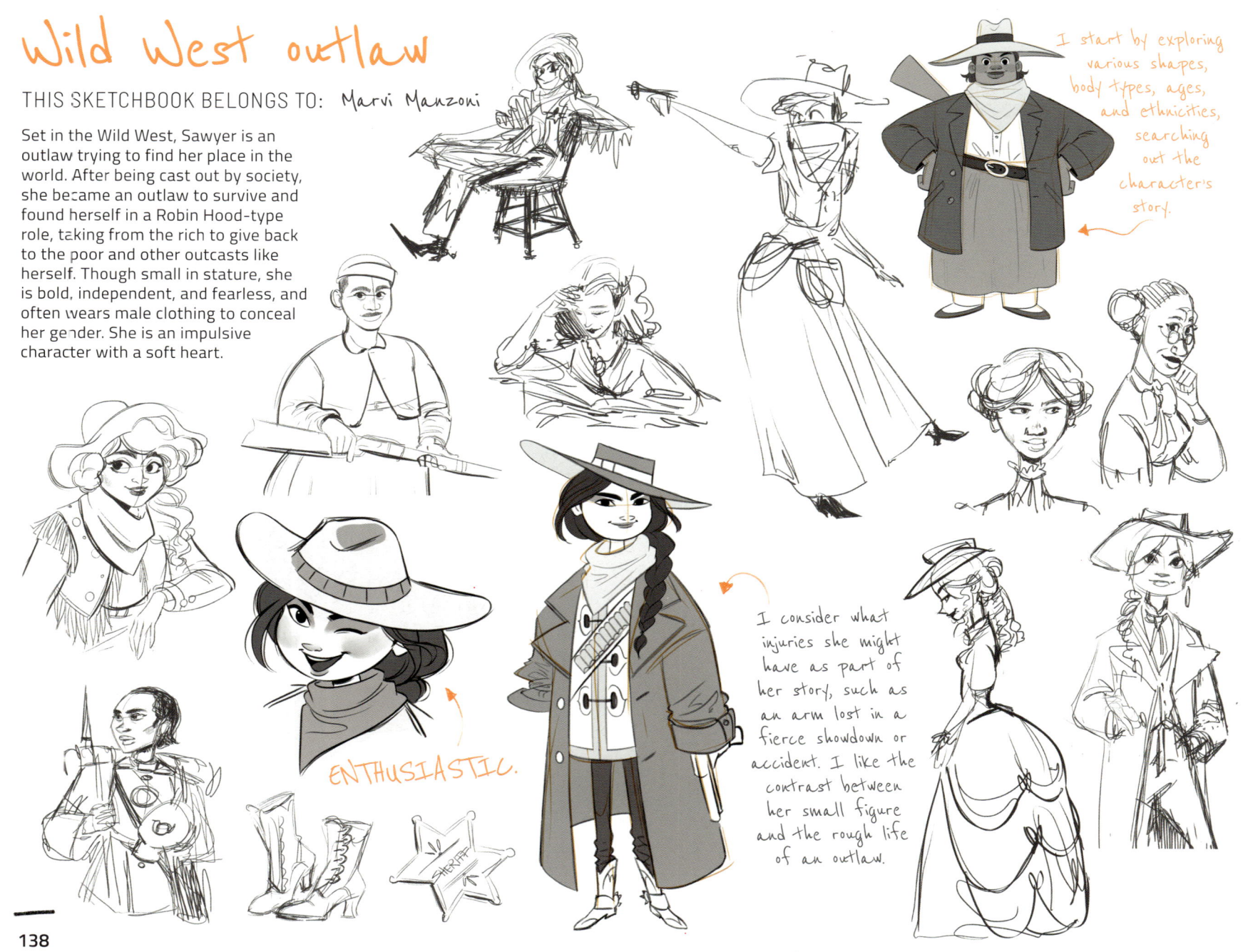

I start by exploring various shapes, body types, ages, and ethnicities, searching out the character's story.

ENTHUSIASTIC.

I consider what injuries she might have as part of her story, such as an arm lost in a fierce showdown or accident. I like the contrast between her small figure and the rough life of an outlaw.

138

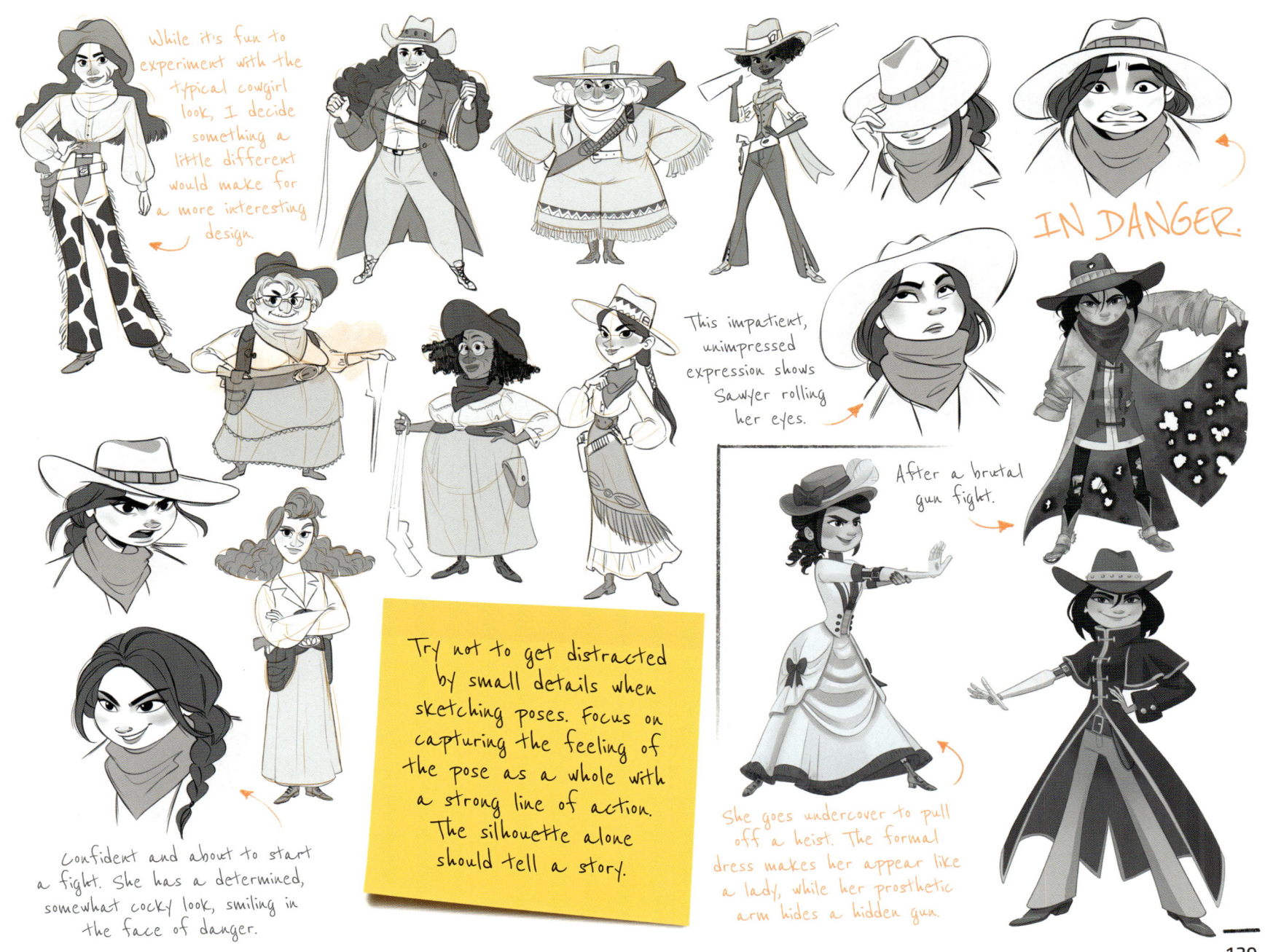

While it's fun to experiment with the typical cowgirl look, I decide something a little different would make for a more interesting design.

IN DANGER.

This impatient, unimpressed expression shows Sawyer rolling her eyes.

Try not to get distracted by small details when sketching poses. Focus on capturing the feeling of the pose as a whole with a strong line of action. The silhouette alone should tell a story.

After a brutal gun fight.

Confident and about to start a fight. She has a determined, somewhat cocky look, smiling in the face of danger.

She goes undercover to pull off a heist. The formal dress makes her appear like a lady, while her prosthetic arm hides a hidden gun.

139

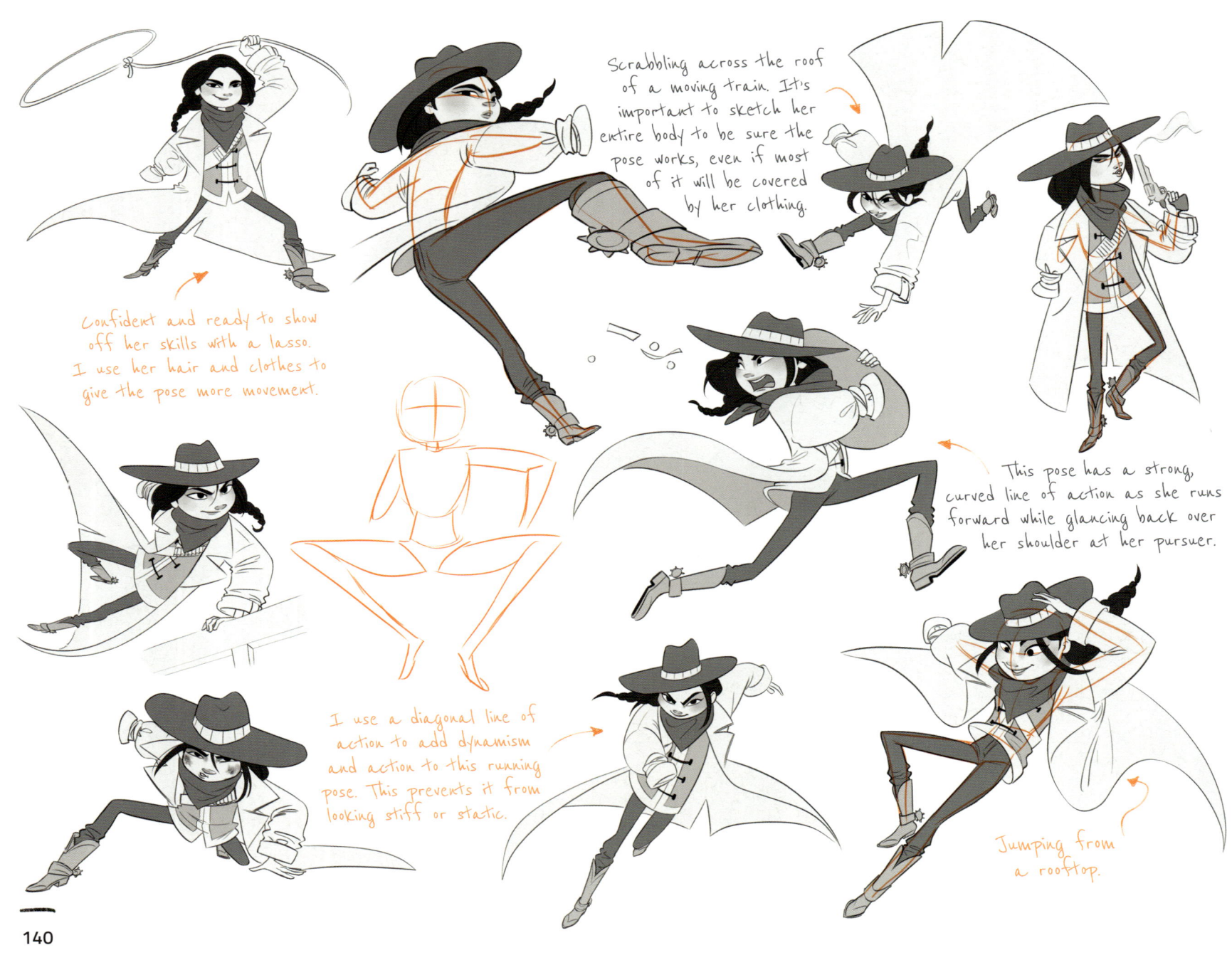

Confident and ready to show off her skills with a lasso. I use her hair and clothes to give the pose more movement.

Scrabbling across the roof of a moving train. It's important to sketch her entire body to be sure the pose works, even if most of it will be covered by her clothing.

This pose has a strong, curved line of action as she runs forward while glancing back over her shoulder at her pursuer.

I use a diagonal line of action to add dynamism and action to this running pose. This prevents it from looking stiff or static.

Jumping from a rooftop.

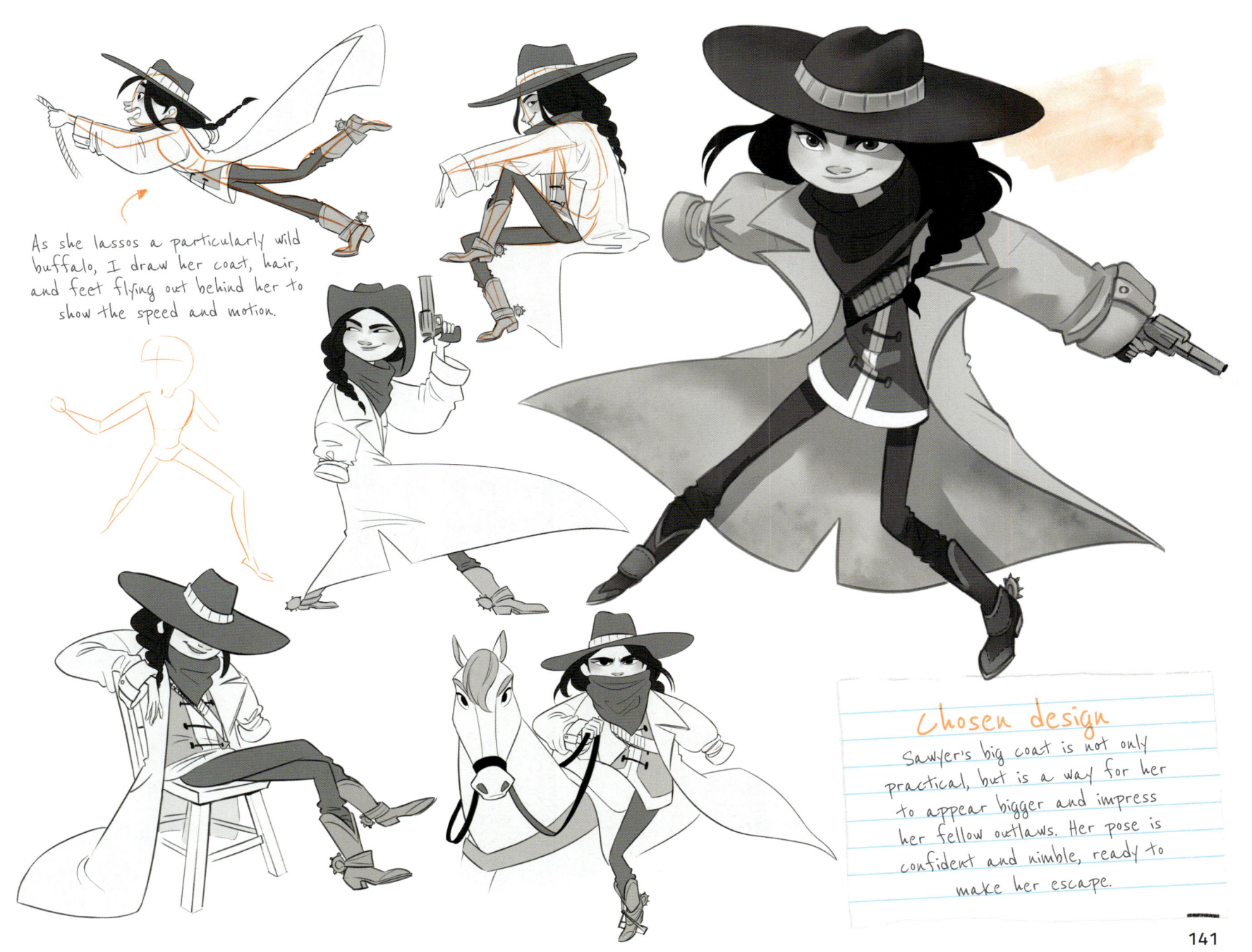

As she lassos a particularly wild buffalo, I draw her coat, hair, and feet flying out behind her to show the speed and motion.

Elfin archer

THIS SKETCHBOOK BELONGS TO: Ana Marija

Laeanna is an elfin archer. The daughter of a wood elf and human king, she has shorter and less pointed ears than the average elf. She has a graceful figure like her elf mother, and silky straight hair like her father. Next in line to rule the kingdom, she is strong-minded and brave, but also has doubts about whether she is good enough. These fears only make her stronger as she sets out to prove she is up to the challenge. A talented archer, Laeanna is ready to use her bow and arrow to protect her people.

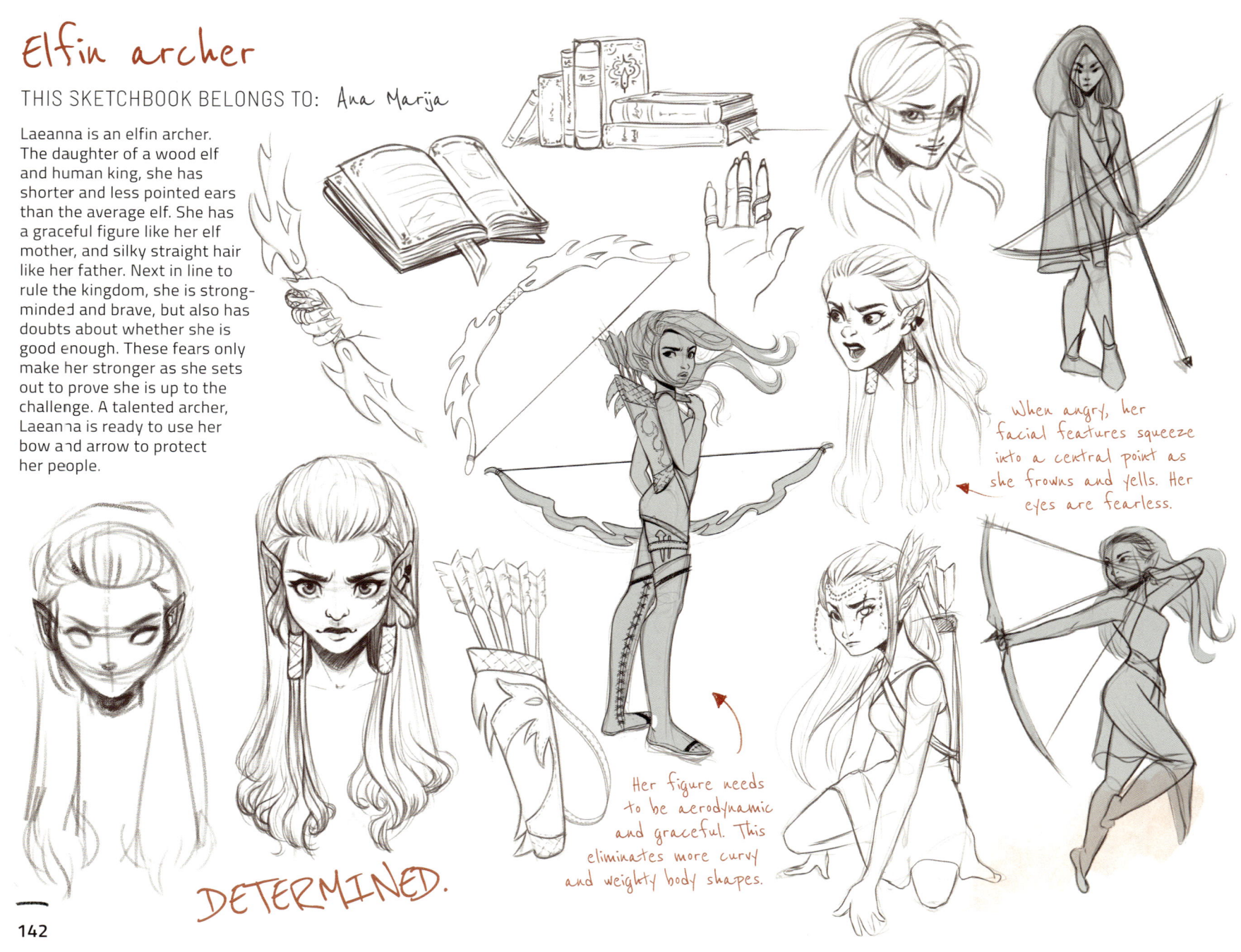

When angry, her facial features squeeze into a central point as she frowns and yells. Her eyes are fearless.

Her figure needs to be aerodynamic and graceful. This eliminates more curvy and weighty body shapes.

DETERMINED.

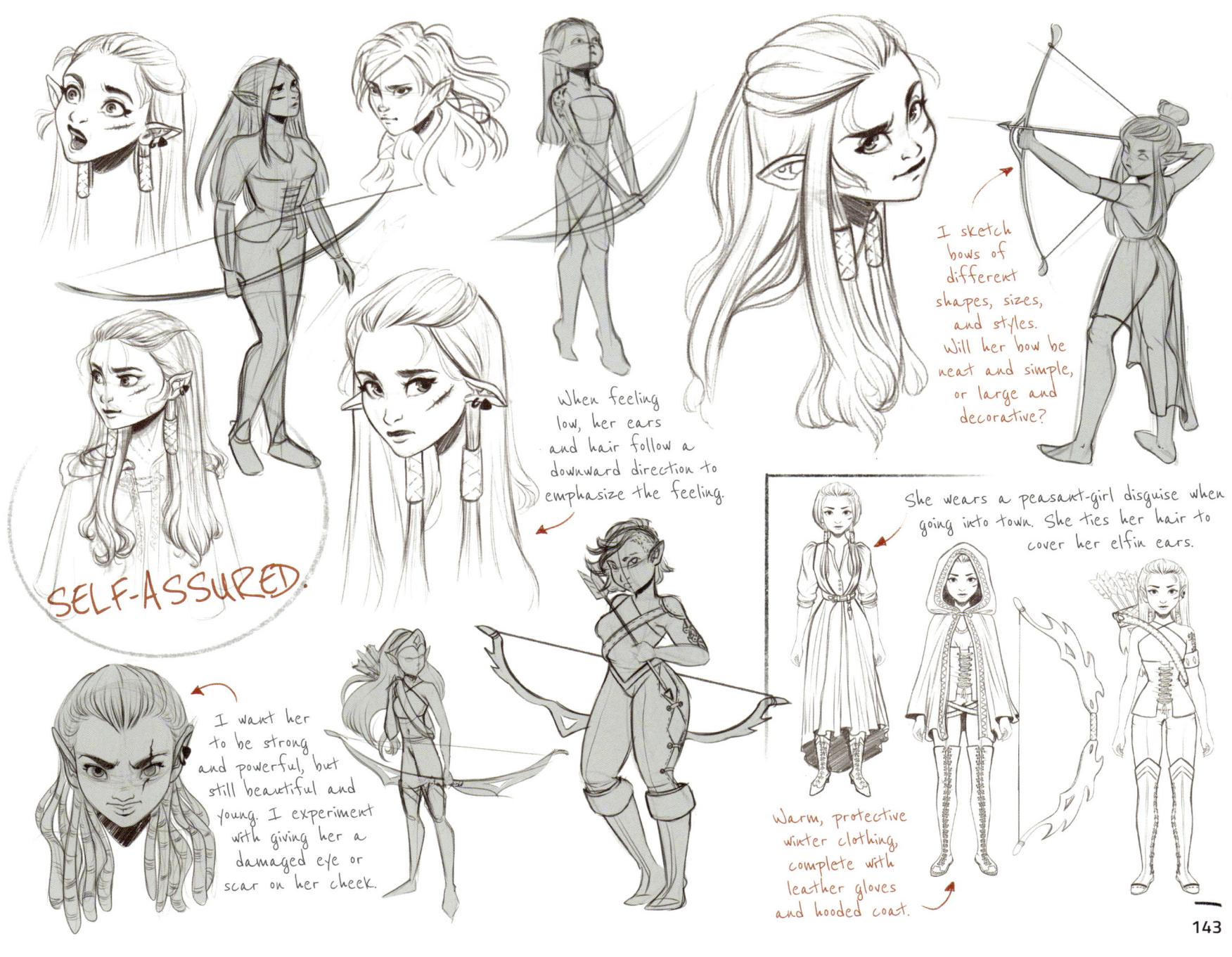

SELF-ASSURED.

When feeling low, her ears and hair follow a downward direction to emphasize the feeling.

I sketch bows of different shapes, sizes, and styles. Will her bow be neat and simple, or large and decorative?

She wears a peasant-girl disguise when going into town. She ties her hair to cover her elfin ears.

I want her to be strong and powerful, but still beautiful and young. I experiment with giving her a damaged eye or scar on her cheek.

Warm, protective winter clothing, complete with leather gloves and hooded coat.

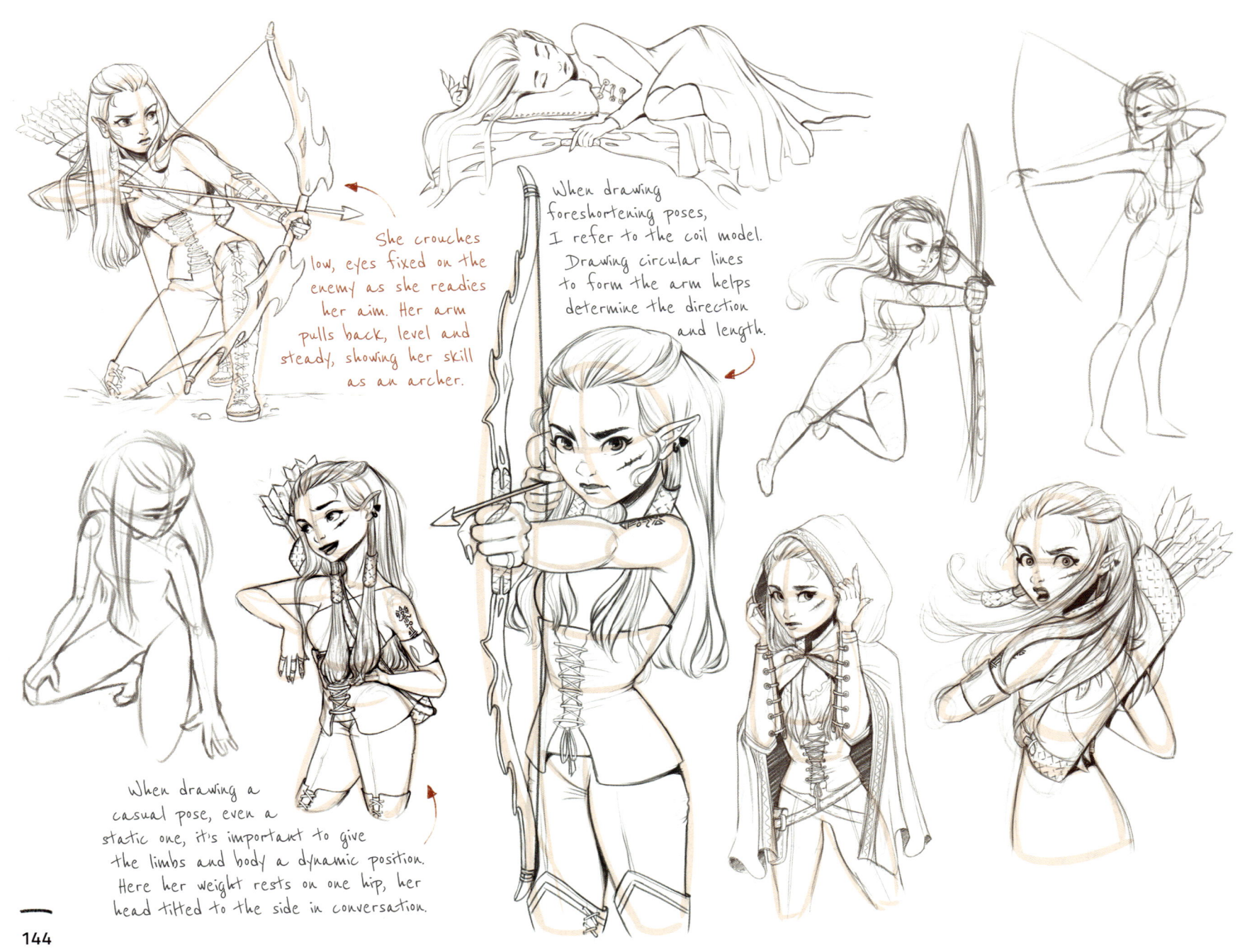

She crouches low, eyes fixed on the enemy as she readies her aim. Her arm pulls back, level and steady, showing her skill as an archer.

When drawing foreshortening poses, I refer to the coil model. Drawing circular lines to form the arm helps determine the direction and length.

When drawing a casual pose, even a static one, it's important to give the limbs and body a dynamic position. Here her weight rests on one hip, her head tilted to the side in conversation.

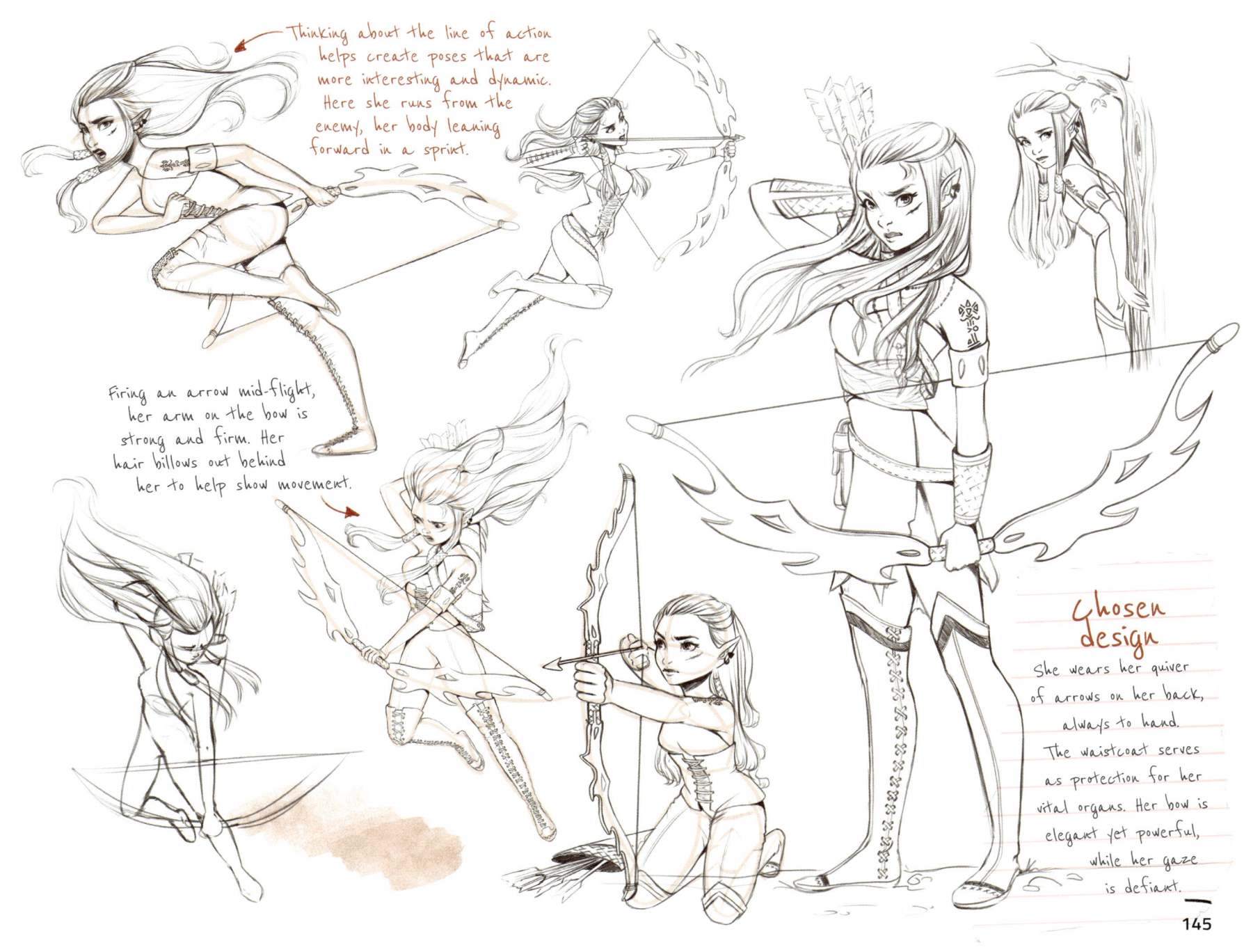

Thinking about the line of action helps create poses that are more interesting and dynamic. Here she runs from the enemy, her body leaning forward in a sprint.

Firing an arrow mid-flight, her arm on the bow is strong and firm. Her hair billows out behind her to help show movement.

Chosen design

She wears her quiver of arrows on her back, always to hand. The waistcoat serves as protection for her vital organs. Her bow is elegant yet powerful, while her gaze is defiant.

Rock star

THIS SKETCHBOOK BELONGS TO: Valentina Millosevich

This rockstar loves being the center of attention. A talented musician, Jett expresses her individuality through her music and is most at home on stage, performing to her adoring fans. Rebellious and unapologetic, she brings an alternative version of femininity, wearing punk clothing, piercings, and tattoos, including her signature leather jacket. Strong-willed and proud of the path she's forged for herself in a male-dominated industry, she hopes to inspire future generations of rebel girls to follow their dreams.

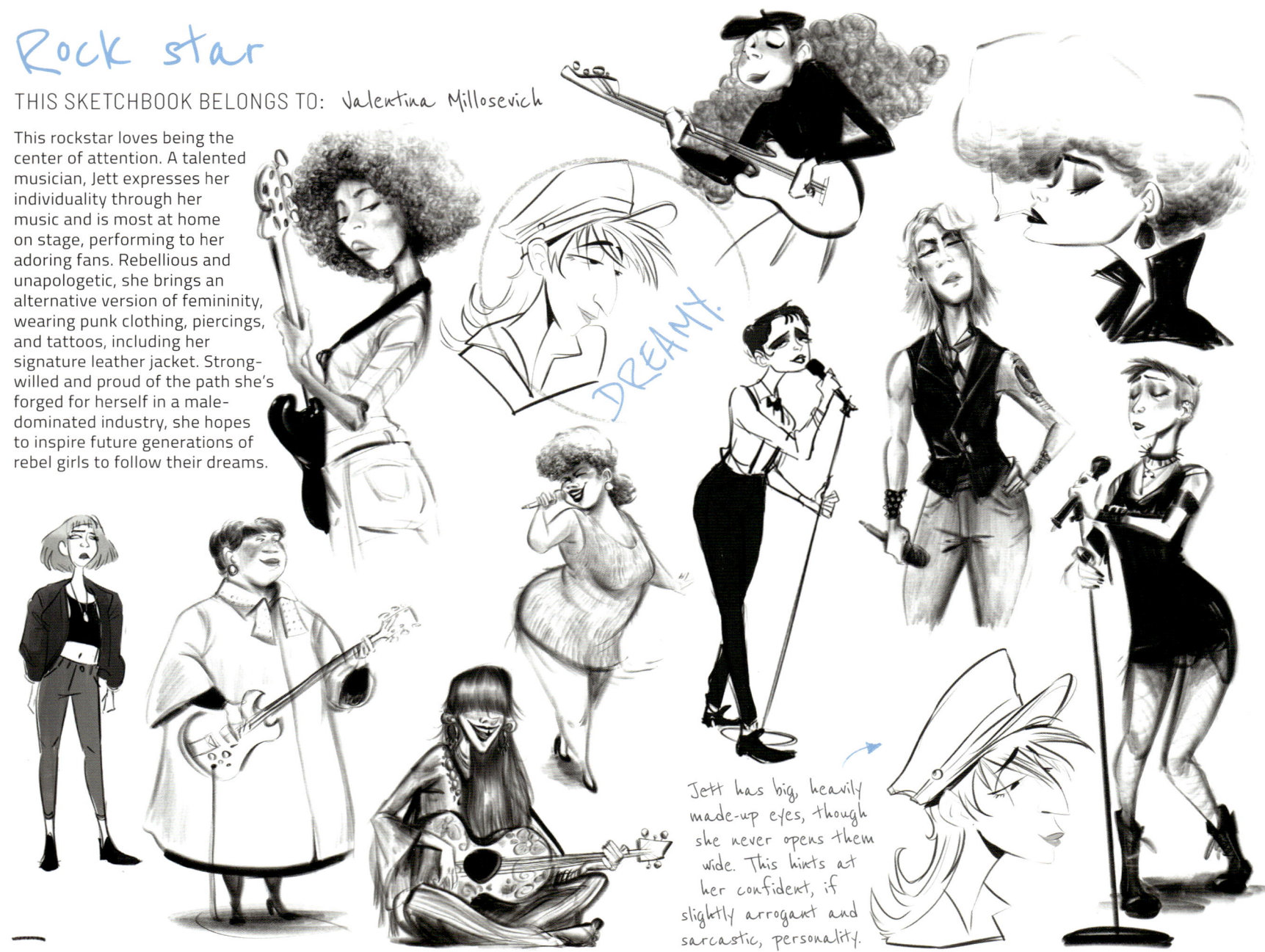

DREAMY.

Jett has big, heavily made-up eyes, though she never opens them wide. This hints at her confident, if slightly arrogant and sarcastic, personality.

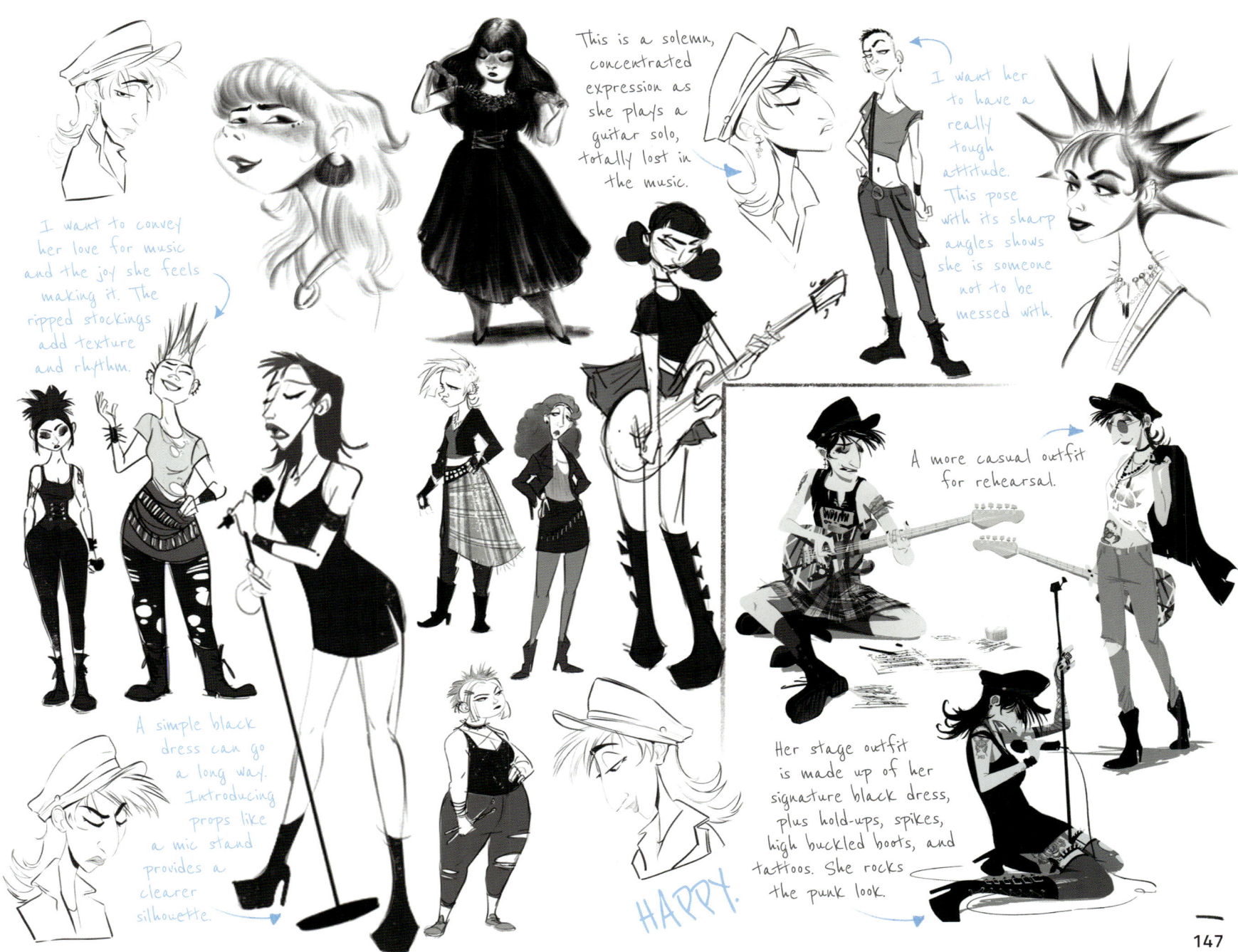

This is a solemn, concentrated expression as she plays a guitar solo, totally lost in the music.

I want her to have a really tough attitude. This pose with its sharp angles shows she is someone not to be messed with.

I want to convey her love for music and the joy she feels making it. The ripped stockings add texture and rhythm.

A simple black dress can go a long way. Introducing props like a mic stand provides a clearer silhouette.

A more casual outfit for rehearsal.

Her stage outfit is made up of her signature black dress, plus hold-ups, spikes, high buckled boots, and tattoos. She rocks the punk look.

HAPPY.

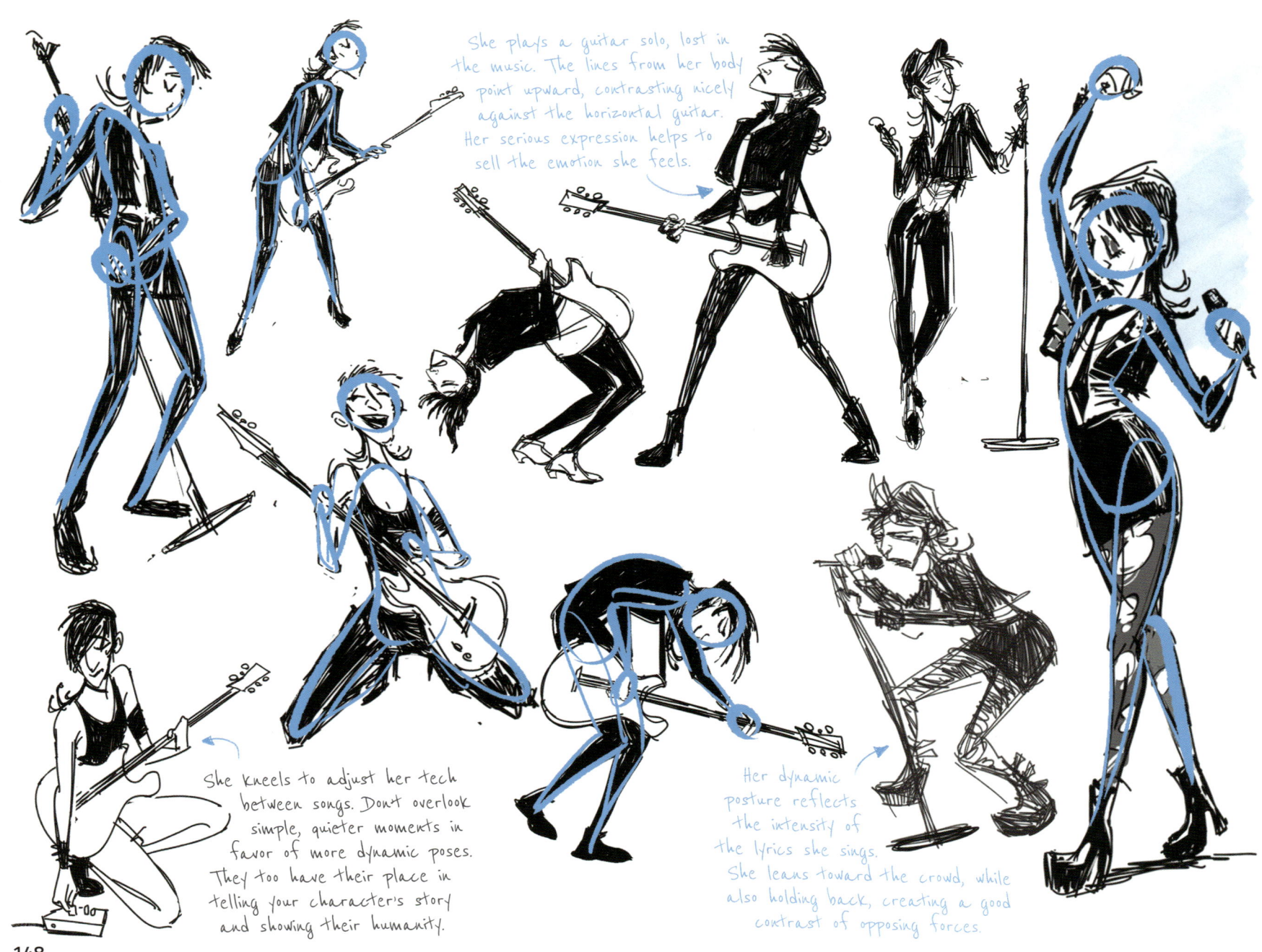

She plays a guitar solo, lost in the music. The lines from her body point upward, contrasting nicely against the horizontal guitar. Her serious expression helps to sell the emotion she feels.

She kneels to adjust her tech between songs. Don't overlook simple, quieter moments in favor of more dynamic poses. They too have their place in telling your character's story and showing their humanity.

Her dynamic posture reflects the intensity of the lyrics she sings. She leans toward the crowd, while also holding back, creating a good contrast of opposing forces.

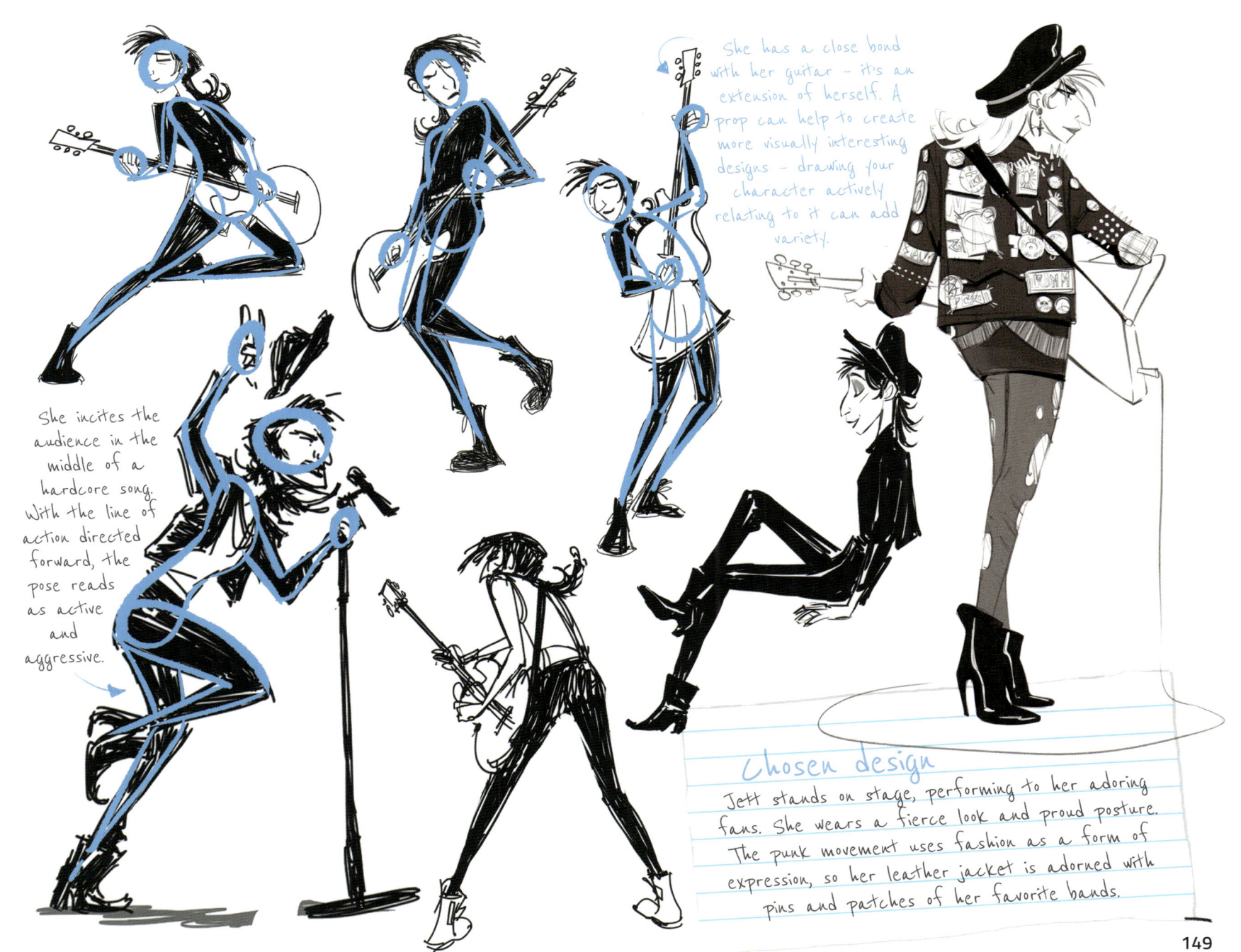

She has a close bond with her guitar – it's an extension of herself. A prop can help to create more visually interesting designs – drawing your character actively relating to it can add variety.

She incites the audience in the middle of a hardcore song. With the line of action directed forward, the pose reads as active and aggressive.

Chosen design

Jett stands on stage, performing to her adoring fans. She wears a fierce look and proud posture. The punk movement uses fashion as a form of expression, so her leather jacket is adorned with pins and patches of her favorite bands.

Pirate

THIS SKETCHBOOK BELONGS TO: Oliver Ödmark

This 18th century pirate strikes fear into those who cross her. Captain of her own ship, Ola is a free spirit and a seasoned traveler. Bold, courageous, and deadly, she's a skilled sailor and sails her ship across the seven seas in search of adventure, commanding a loyal crew of buccaneers.

I use references for inspiration when sketching the initial designs, looking at 18th century clothing from different cultures around the world, mixing them up to convey the character as rootless and well-traveled.

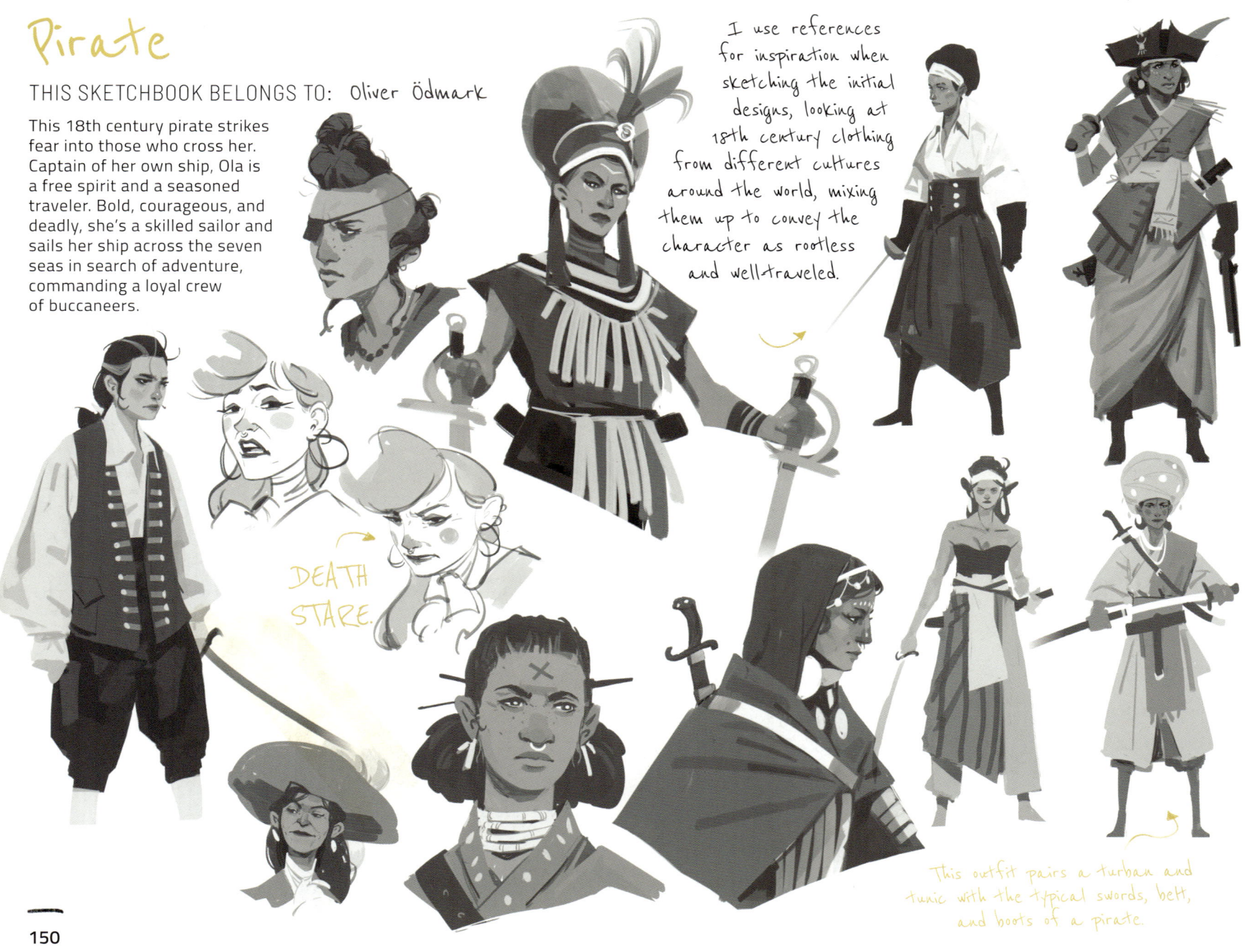

DEATH STARE.

This outfit pairs a turban and tunic with the typical swords, belt, and boots of a pirate.

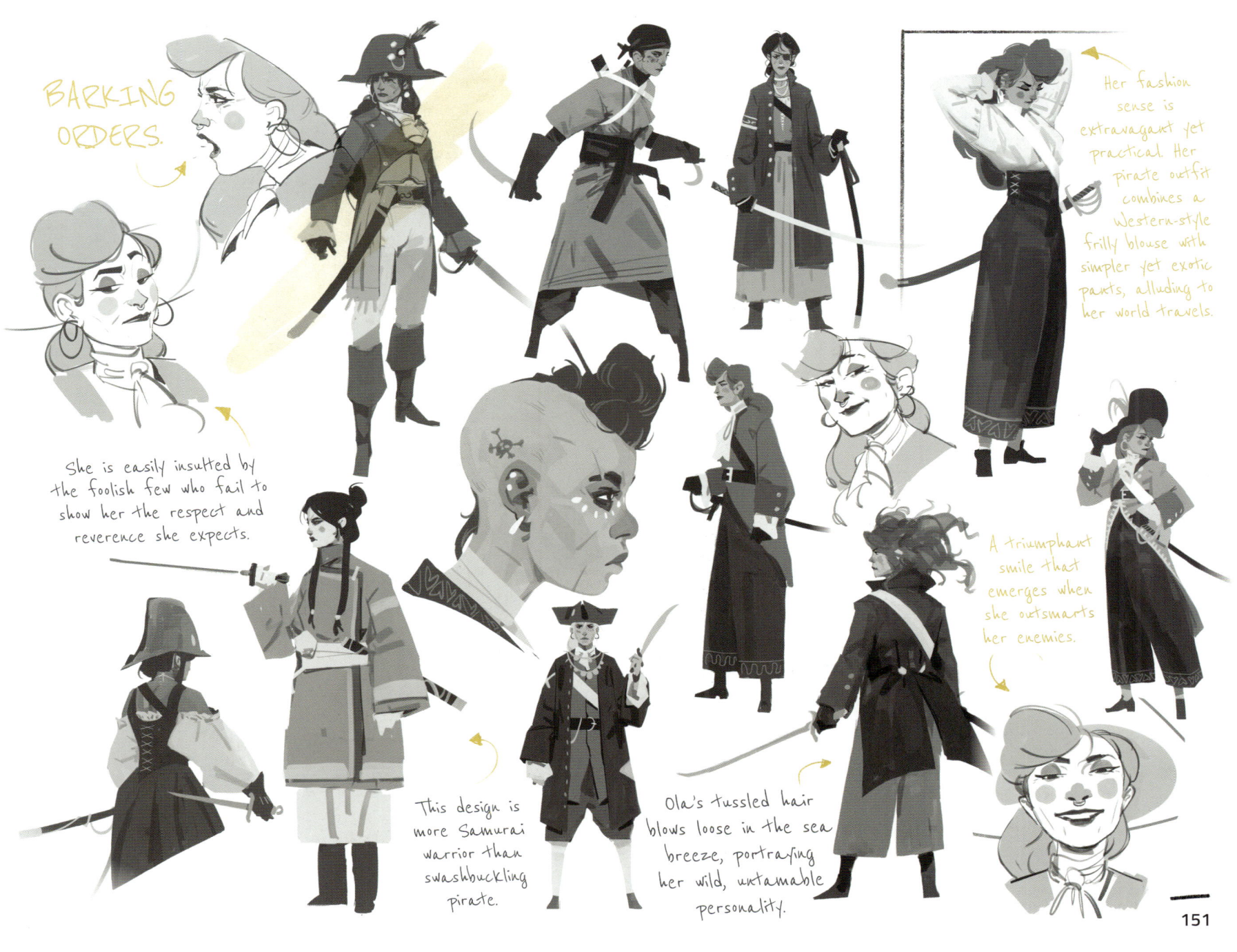

BARKING ORDERS.

She is easily insulted by the foolish few who fail to show her the respect and reverence she expects.

Her fashion sense is extravagant yet practical. Her pirate outfit combines a Western-style frilly blouse with simpler yet exotic pants, alluding to her world travels.

A triumphant smile that emerges when she outsmarts her enemies.

This design is more Samurai warrior than swashbuckling pirate.

Ola's tussled hair blows loose in the sea breeze, portraying her wild, untamable personality.

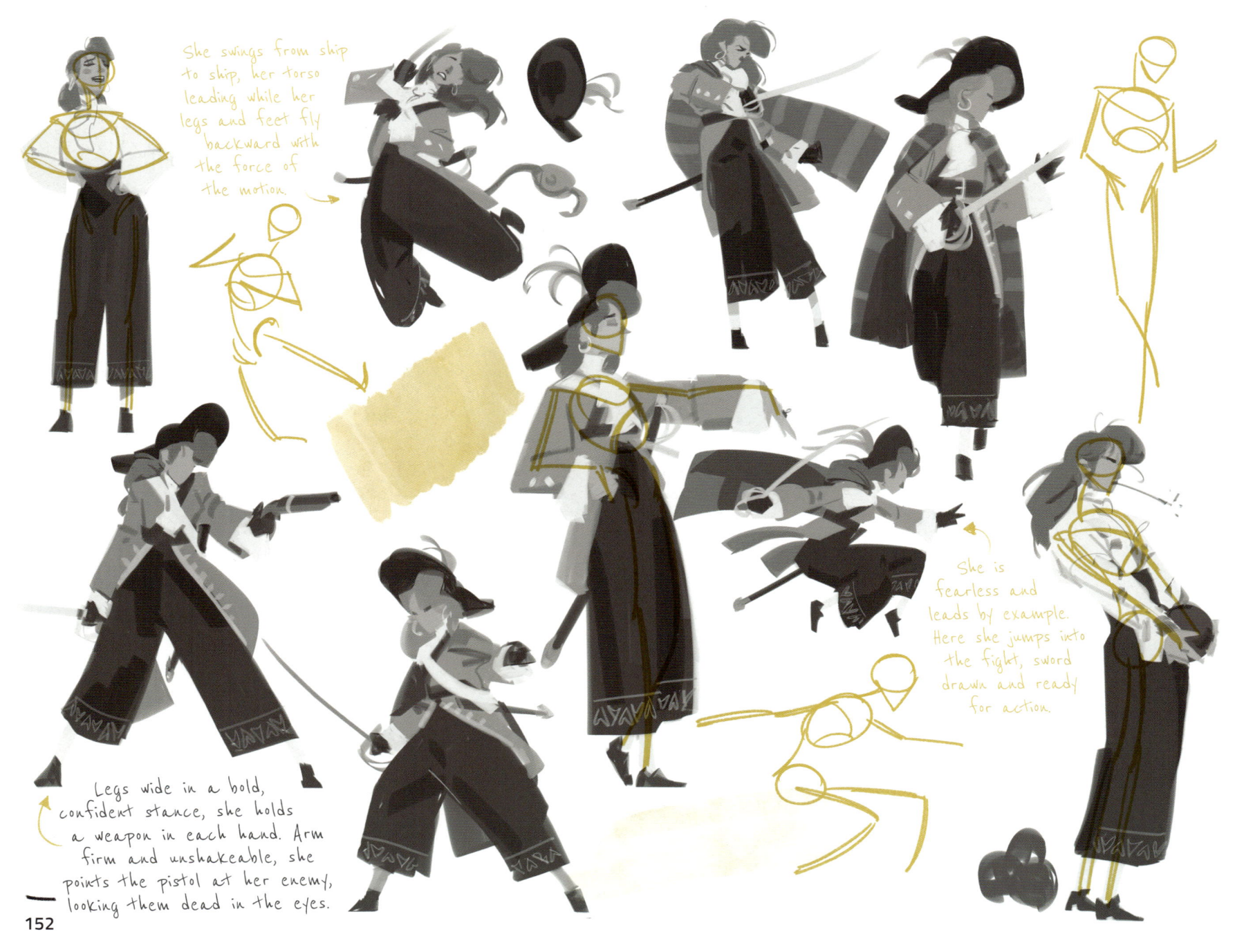

She swings from ship to ship, her torso leading while her legs and feet fly backward with the force of the motion.

She is fearless and leads by example. Here she jumps into the fight, sword drawn and ready for action.

Legs wide in a bold, confident stance, she holds a weapon in each hand. Arm firm and unshakeable, she points the pistol at her enemy, looking them dead in the eyes.

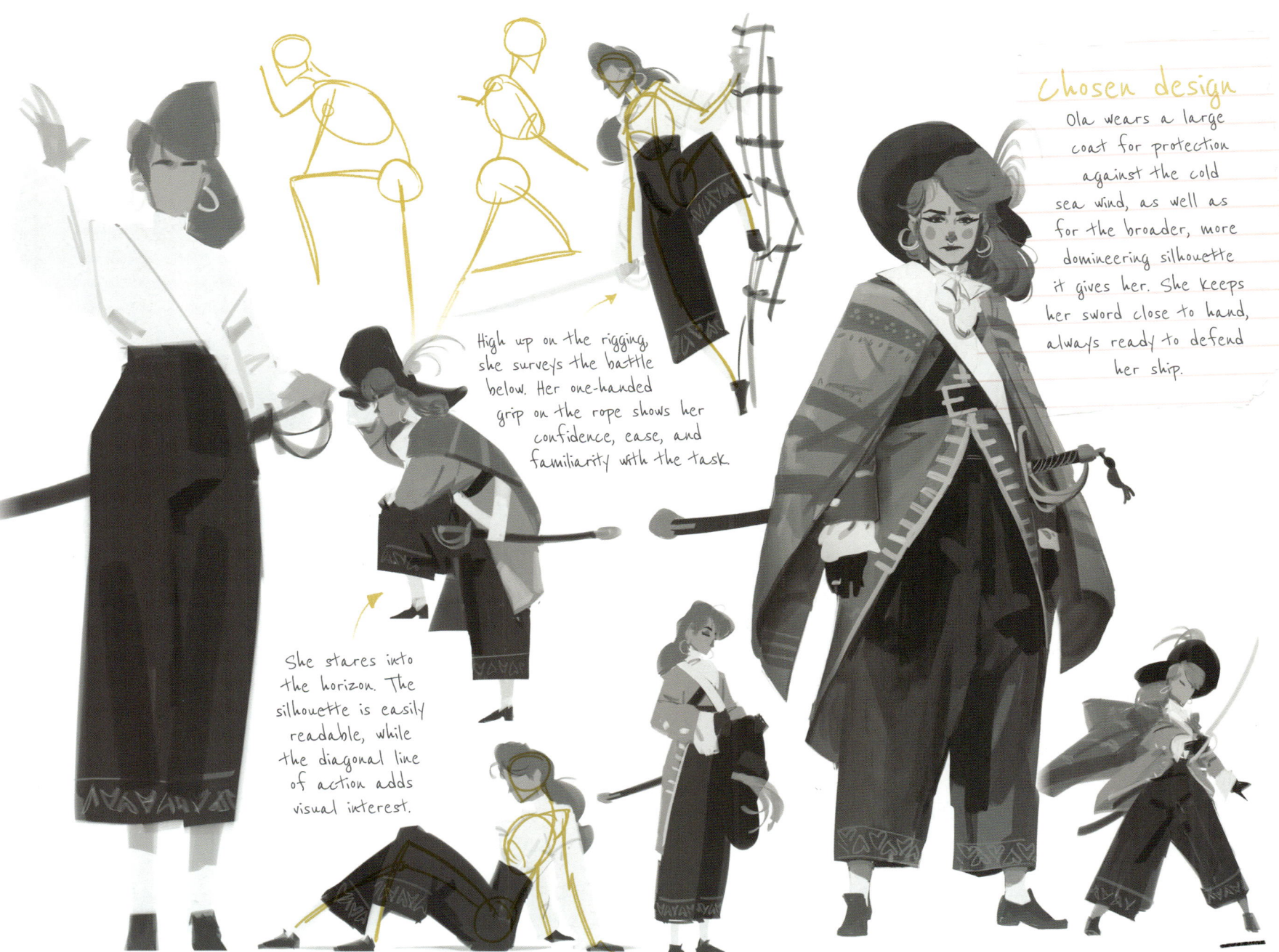

Ola wears a large coat for protection against the cold sea wind, as well as for the broader, more domineering silhouette it gives her. She keeps her sword close to hand, always ready to defend her ship.

High up on the rigging, she surveys the battle below. Her one-handed grip on the rope shows her confidence, ease, and familiarity with the task

She stares into the horizon. The silhouette is easily readable, while the diagonal line of action adds visual interest.

Super-strength superheroine

THIS SKETCHBOOK BELONGS TO: Toniko Pantoja

By day, Dynamo is a high-spirited, elementary sports teacher who works to inspire the young people she teaches to pursue sports and physical activity. Fun, playful, and a friendly neighbor, she is a big kid at heart and is respected by her students. But she is also a powerful superheroine with impressive super-strength abilities. Tall, muscular, and able to lift and throw extremely heavy objects, she sees it as her duty to protect the kids she helps raise from those who would mean them harm.

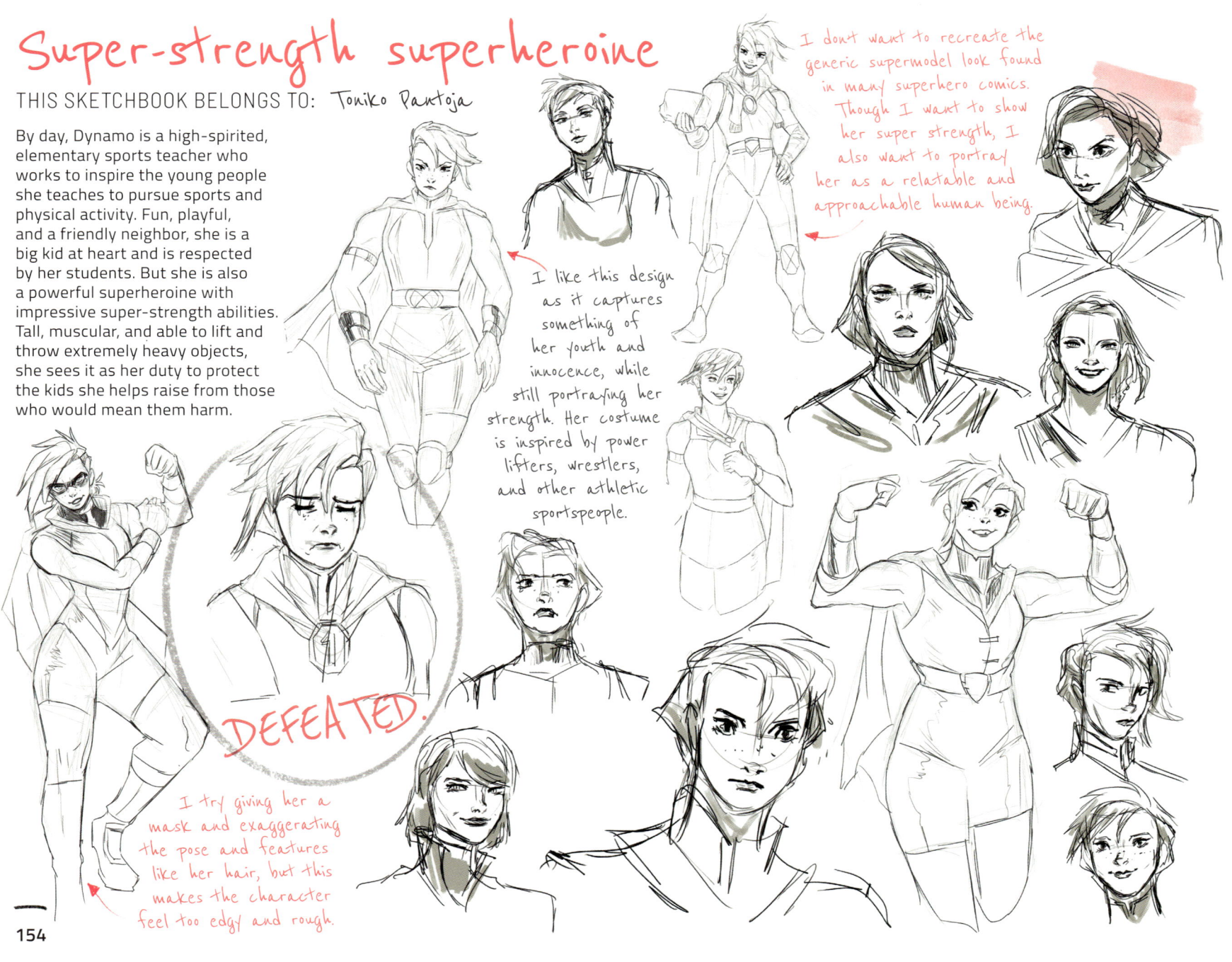

I like this design as it captures something of her youth and innocence, while still portraying her strength. Her costume is inspired by power lifters, wrestlers, and other athletic sportspeople.

I don't want to recreate the generic supermodel look found in many superhero comics. Though I want to show her super strength, I also want to portray her as a relatable and approachable human being.

DEFEATED.

I try giving her a mask and exaggerating the pose and features like her hair, but this makes the character feel too edgy and rough.

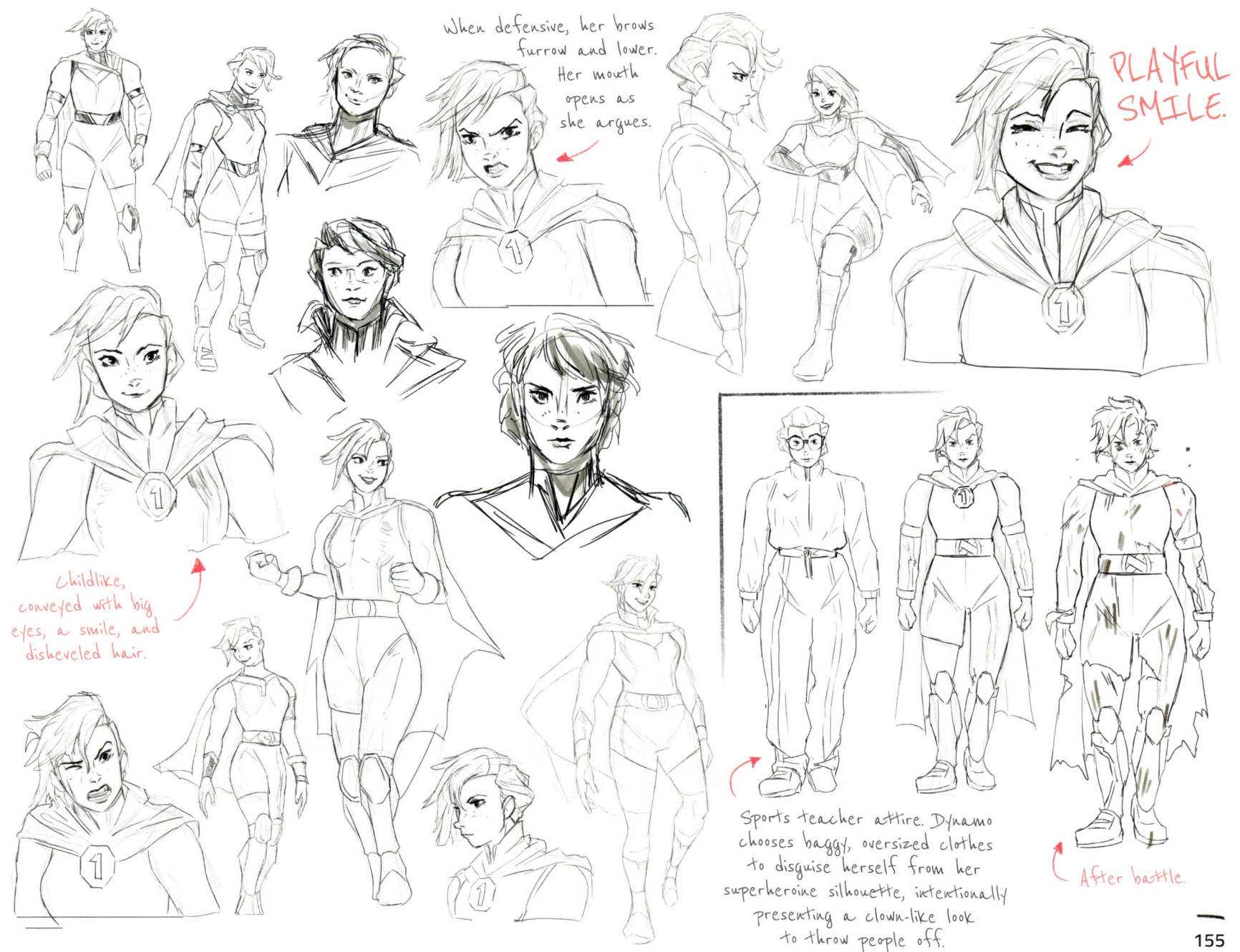

When defensive, her brows furrow and lower. Her mouth opens as she argues.

PLAYFUL SMILE.

Childlike, conveyed with big eyes, a smile, and disheveled hair.

Sports teacher attire. Dynamo chooses baggy, oversized clothes to disguise herself from her superheroine silhouette, intentionally presenting a clown-like look to throw people off.

After battle.

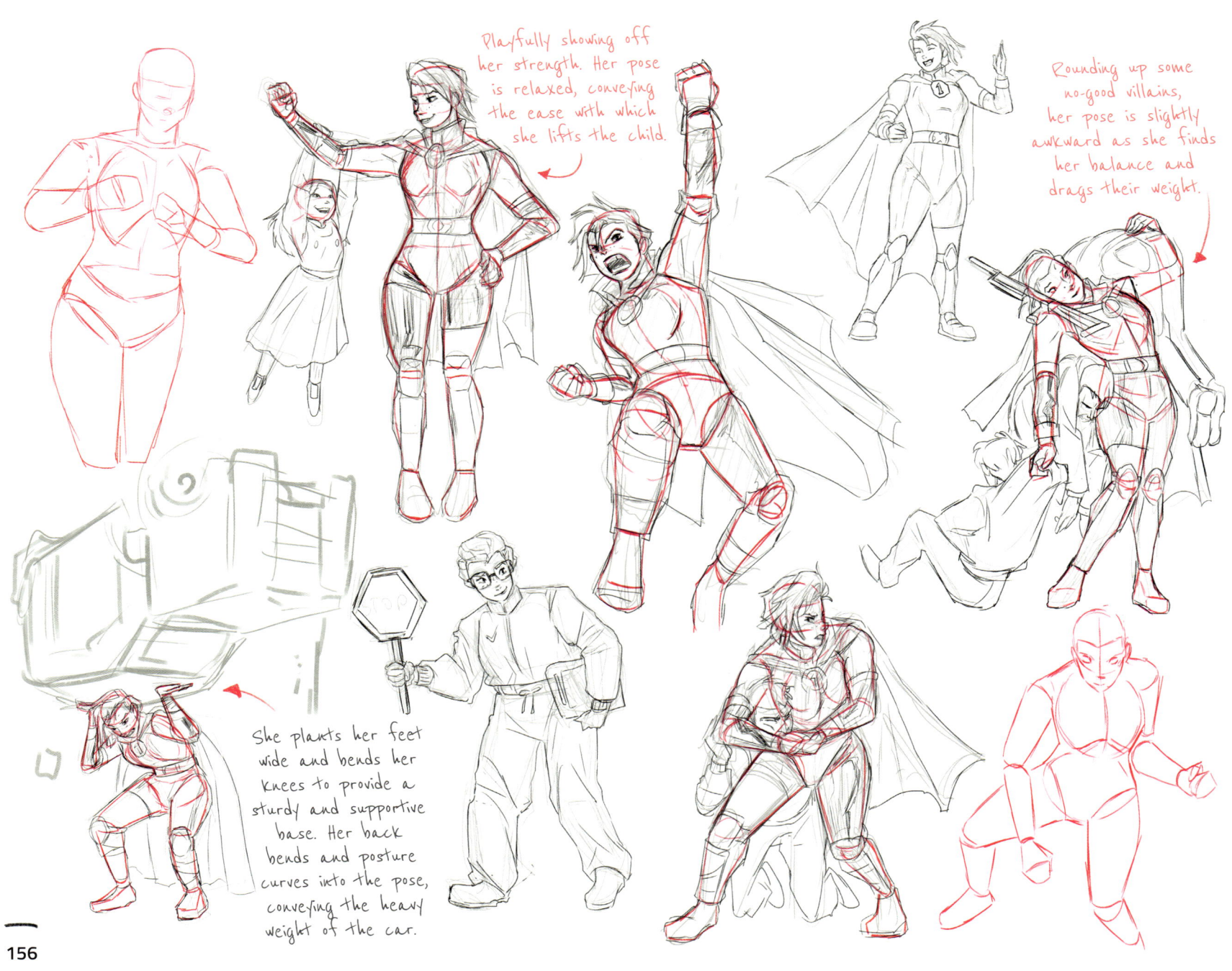

Playfully showing off her strength. Her pose is relaxed, conveying the ease with which she lifts the child.

Rounding up some no-good villains, her pose is slightly awkward as she finds her balance and drags their weight.

She plants her feet wide and bends her knees to provide a sturdy and supportive base. Her back bends and posture curves into the pose, conveying the heavy weight of the car.

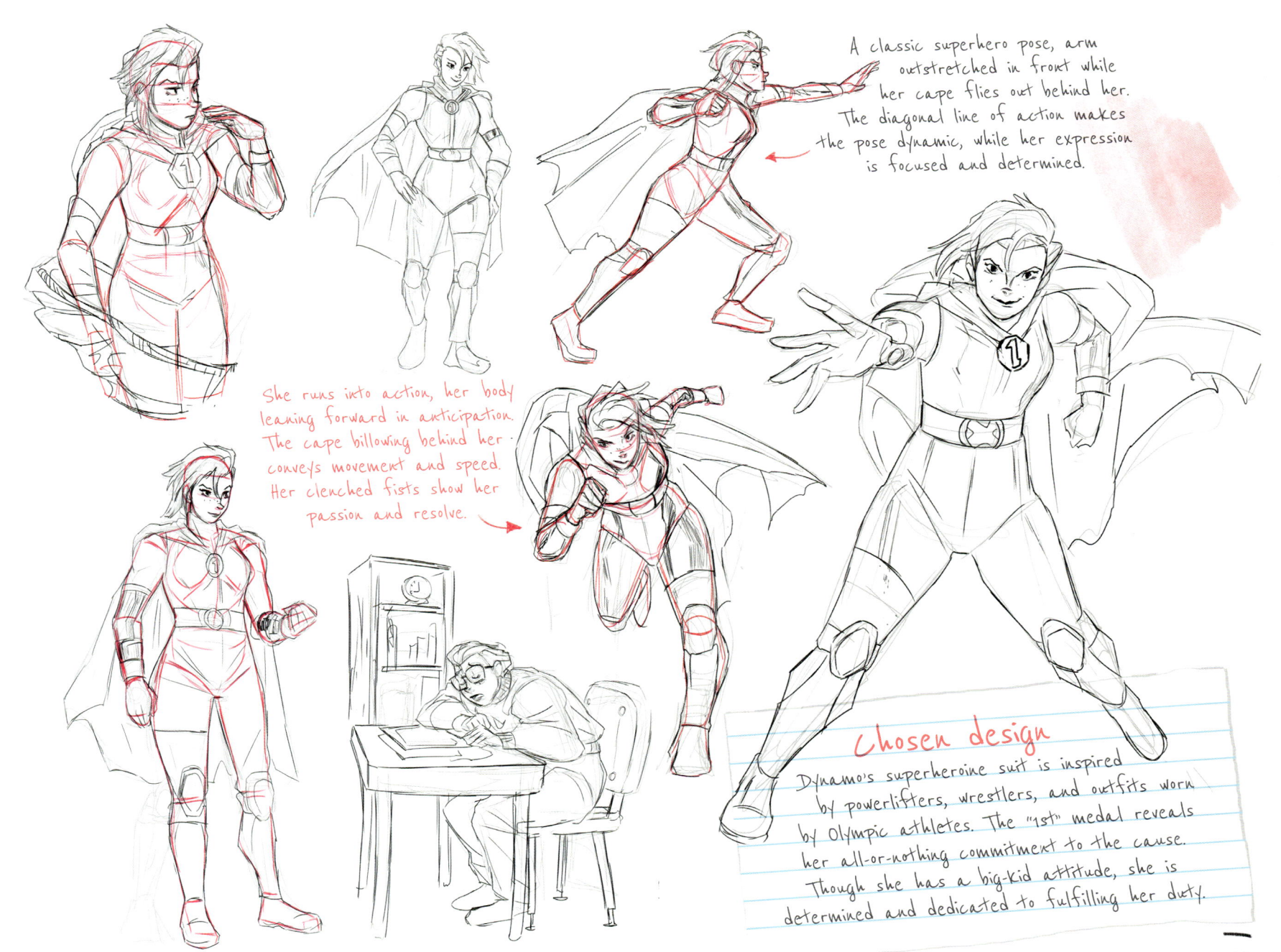

A classic superhero pose, arm outstretched in front while her cape flies out behind her. The diagonal line of action makes the pose dynamic, while her expression is focused and determined.

She runs into action, her body leaning forward in anticipation. The cape billowing behind her conveys movement and speed. Her clenched fists show her passion and resolve.

Chosen design

Dynamo's superheroine suit is inspired by powerlifters, wrestlers, and outfits worn by Olympic athletes. The "1st" medal reveals her all-or-nothing commitment to the cause. Though she has a big-kid attitude, she is determined and dedicated to fulfilling her duty.

Geisha

THIS SKETCHBOOK BELONGS TO: Yewon Park

Haku is a young geisha who grew up in a wealthy family in Japan. Elegant and graceful, she has a slender figure and enjoys dancing for her audience. She is confident, powerful, and brave, working out with a bar to improve her poise and stamina. She aims for perfection and tries to hide her weakness, often appearing stony-faced. At night, after her geisha duties are complete, she fights off underworld criminals who would bring harm to her ancient town and its people.

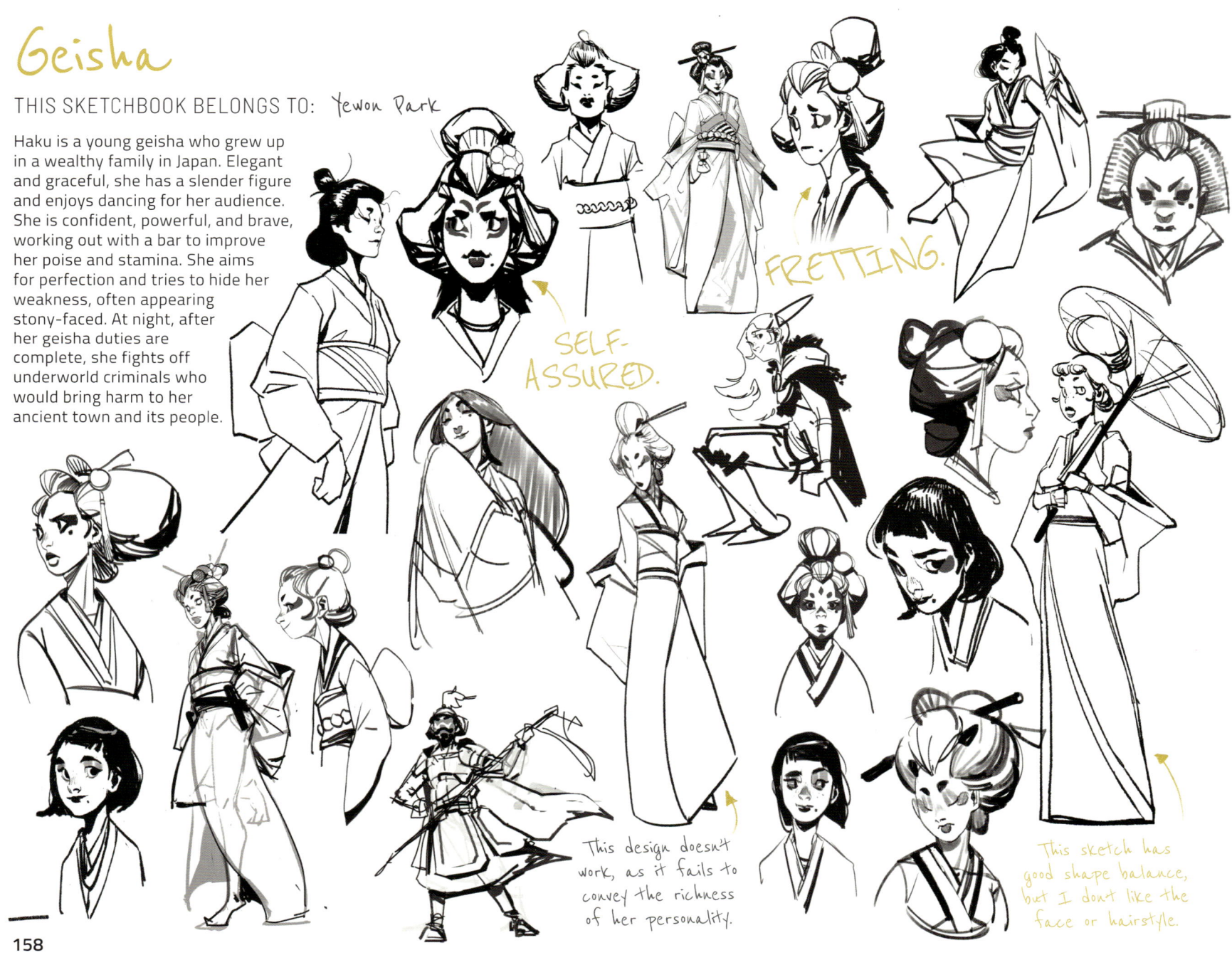

FRETTING.

SELF-ASSURED.

This design doesn't work, as it fails to convey the richness of her personality.

This sketch has good shape balance, but I don't like the face or hairstyle.

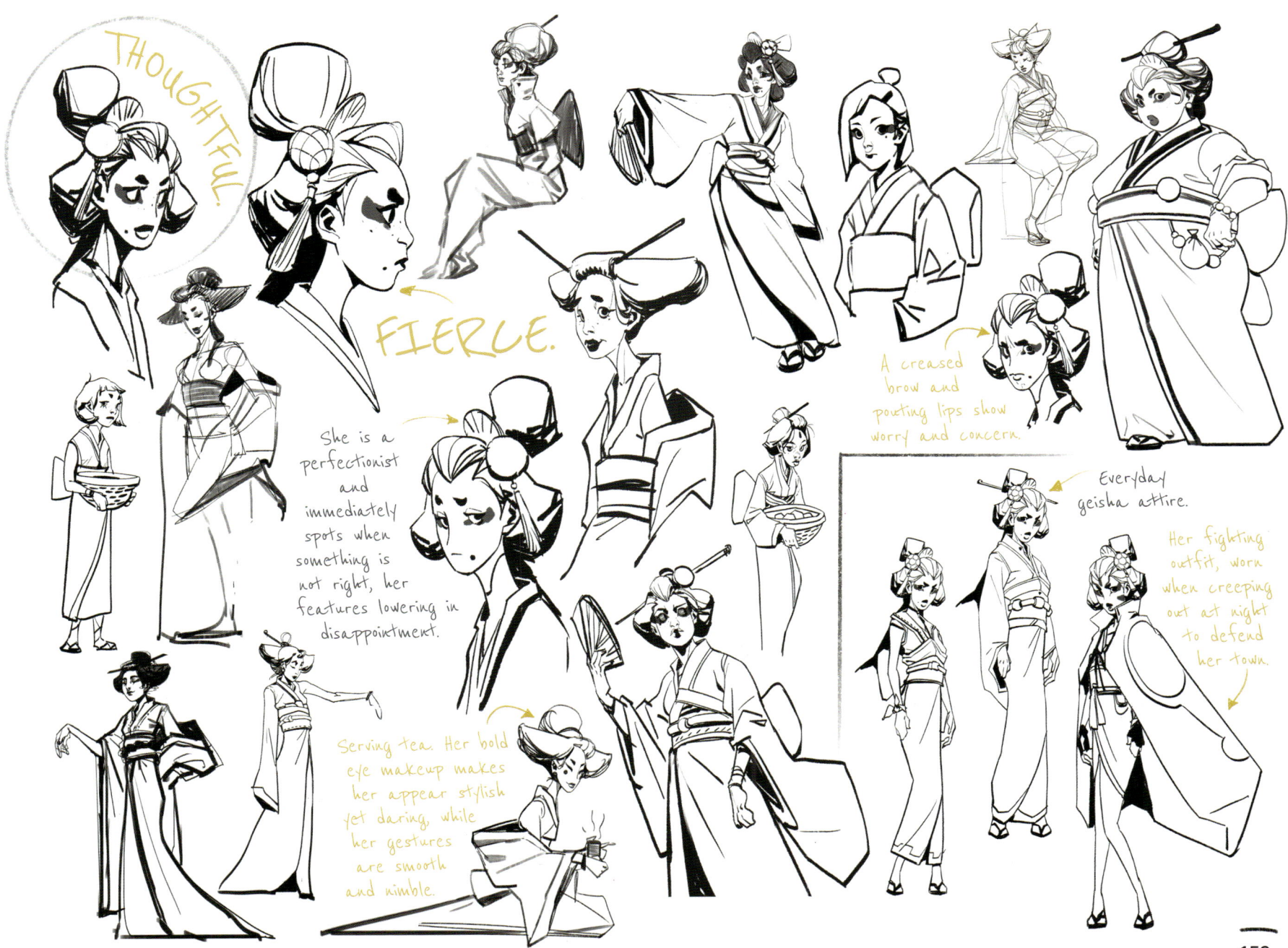

THOUGHTFUL.

FIERCE.

She is a perfectionist and immediately spots when something is not right, her features lowering in disappointment.

Serving tea. Her bold eye makeup makes her appear stylish yet daring, while her gestures are smooth and nimble.

A creased brow and pouting lips show worry and concern.

Everyday geisha attire.

Her fighting outfit, worn when creeping out at night to defend her town.

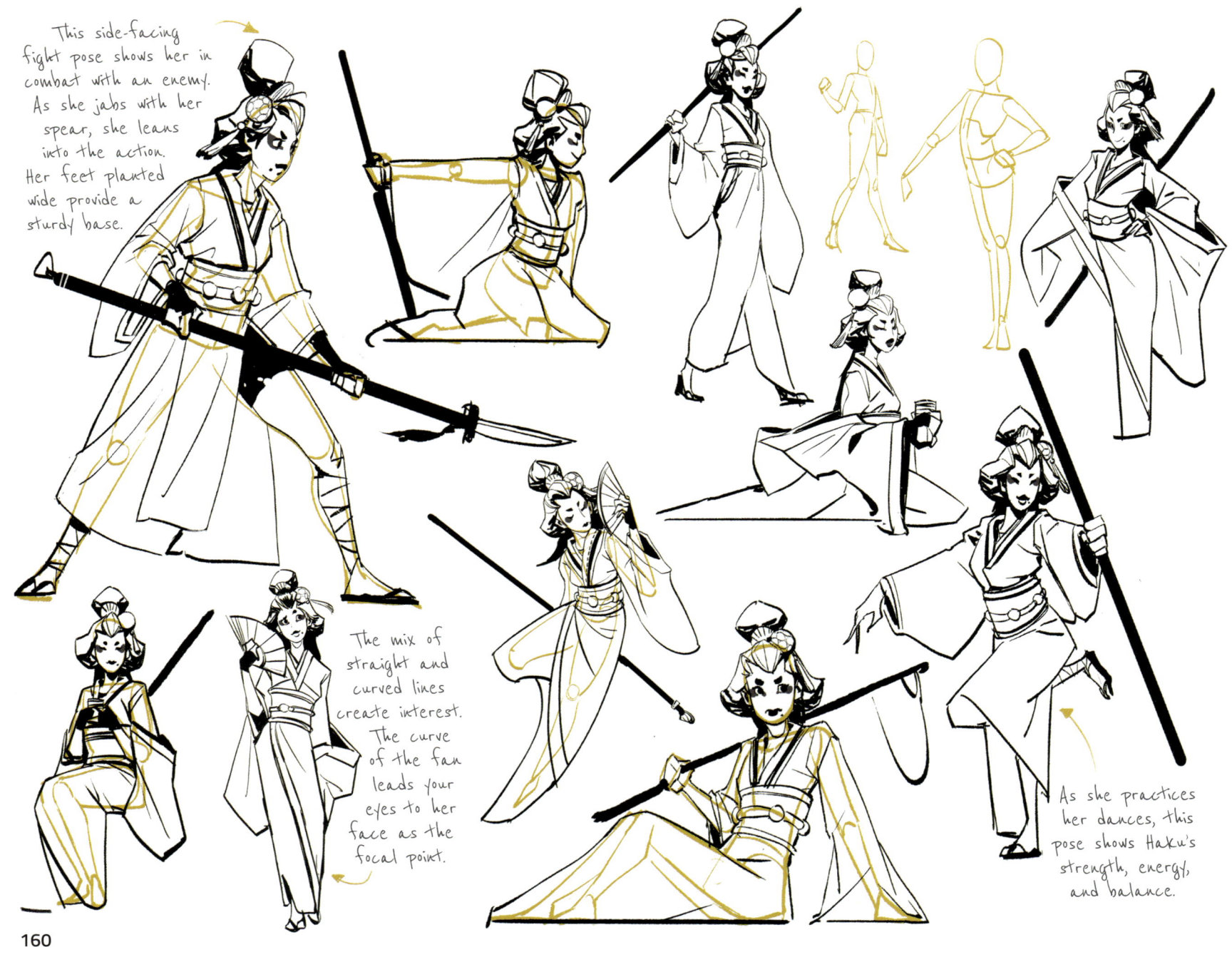

This side-facing fight pose shows her in combat with an enemy. As she jabs with her spear, she leans into the action. Her feet planted wide provide a sturdy base.

The mix of straight and curved lines create interest. The curve of the fan leads your eyes to her face as the focal point.

As she practices her dances, this pose shows Haku's strength, energy, and balance.

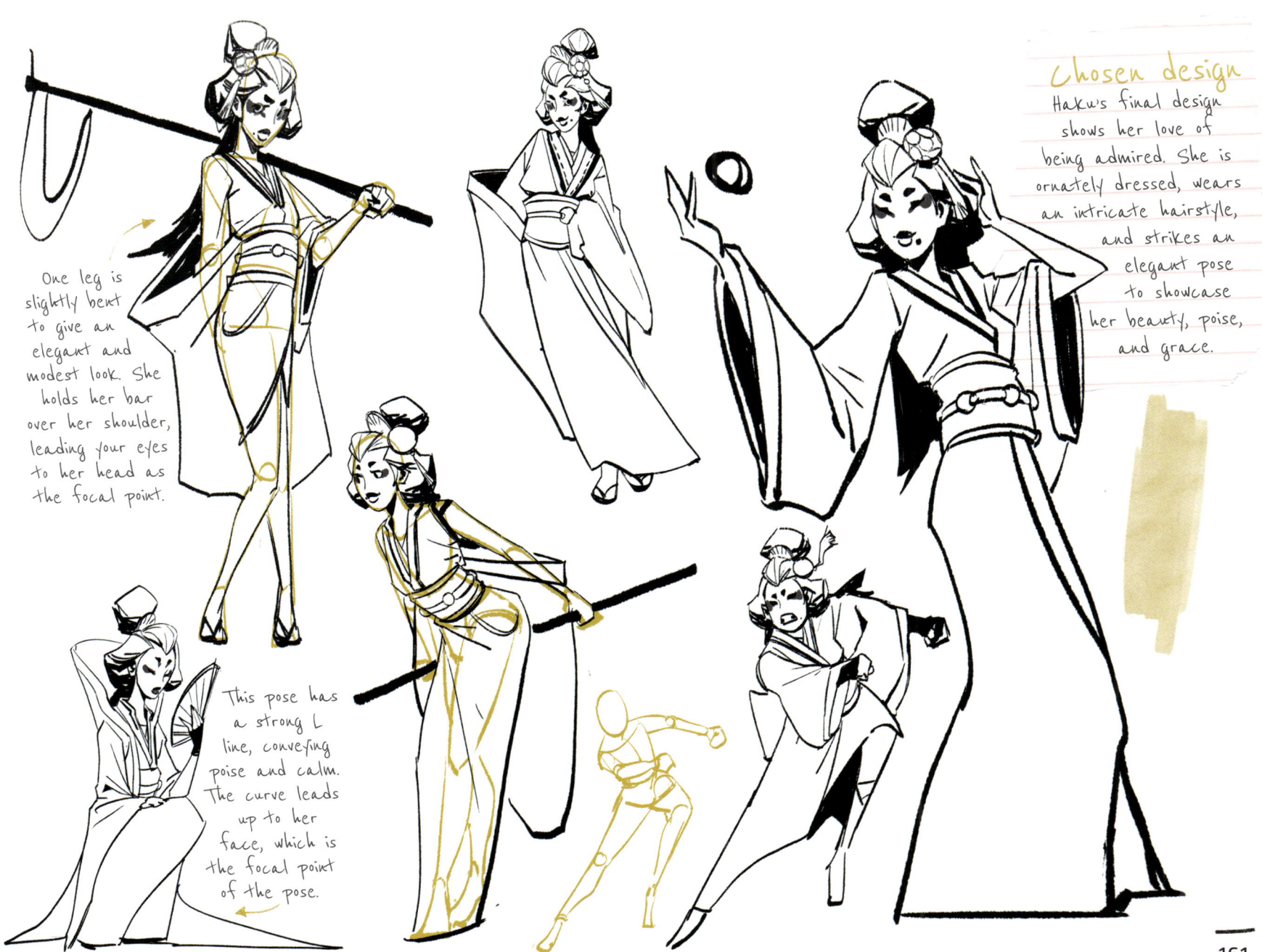

One leg is slightly bent to give an elegant and modest look. She holds her bar over her shoulder, leading your eyes to her head as the focal point.

This pose has a strong L line, conveying poise and calm. The curve leads up to her face, which is the focal point of the pose.

Haku's final design shows her love of being admired. She is ornately dressed, wears an intricate hairstyle, and strikes an elegant pose to showcase her beauty, poise, and grace.

161

Shaman

Set in ancient times, Rhea is the shaman in her mountain village. Strong, independent, and deeply connected to the natural environment, she spends her days exploring the mountains, climbing trees, healing the sick with her magical powers, and helping those in need. Curious, perceptive, and creative, she is a skilled hunter, fisher, and craftswoman. She wears animal hides and furs, along with bones, stone, and bronze jewelry.

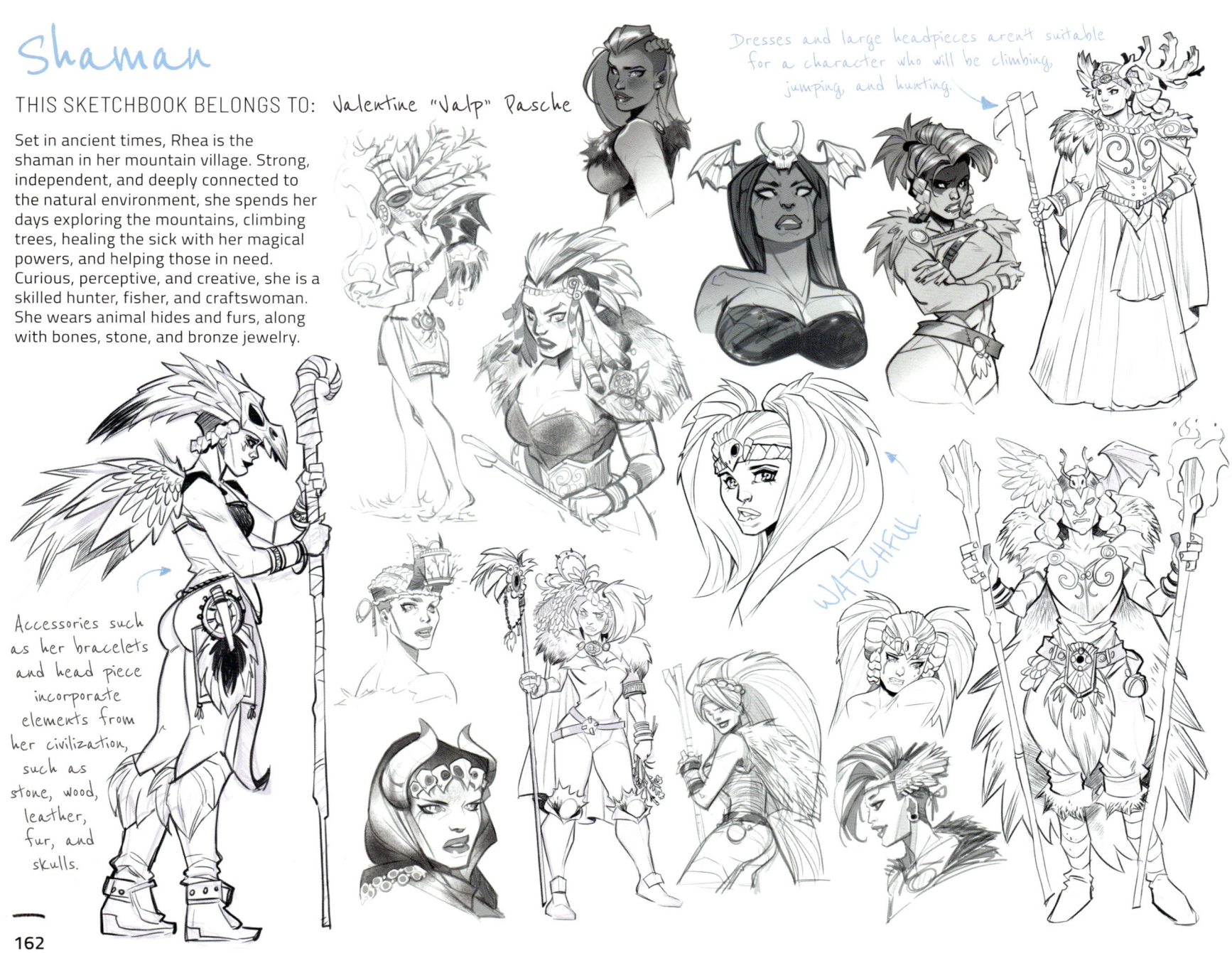

Dresses and large headpieces aren't suitable for a character who will be climbing, jumping, and hunting.

Accessories such as her bracelets and head piece incorporate elements from her civilization, such as stone, wood, leather, fur, and skulls.

WATCHFUL

162

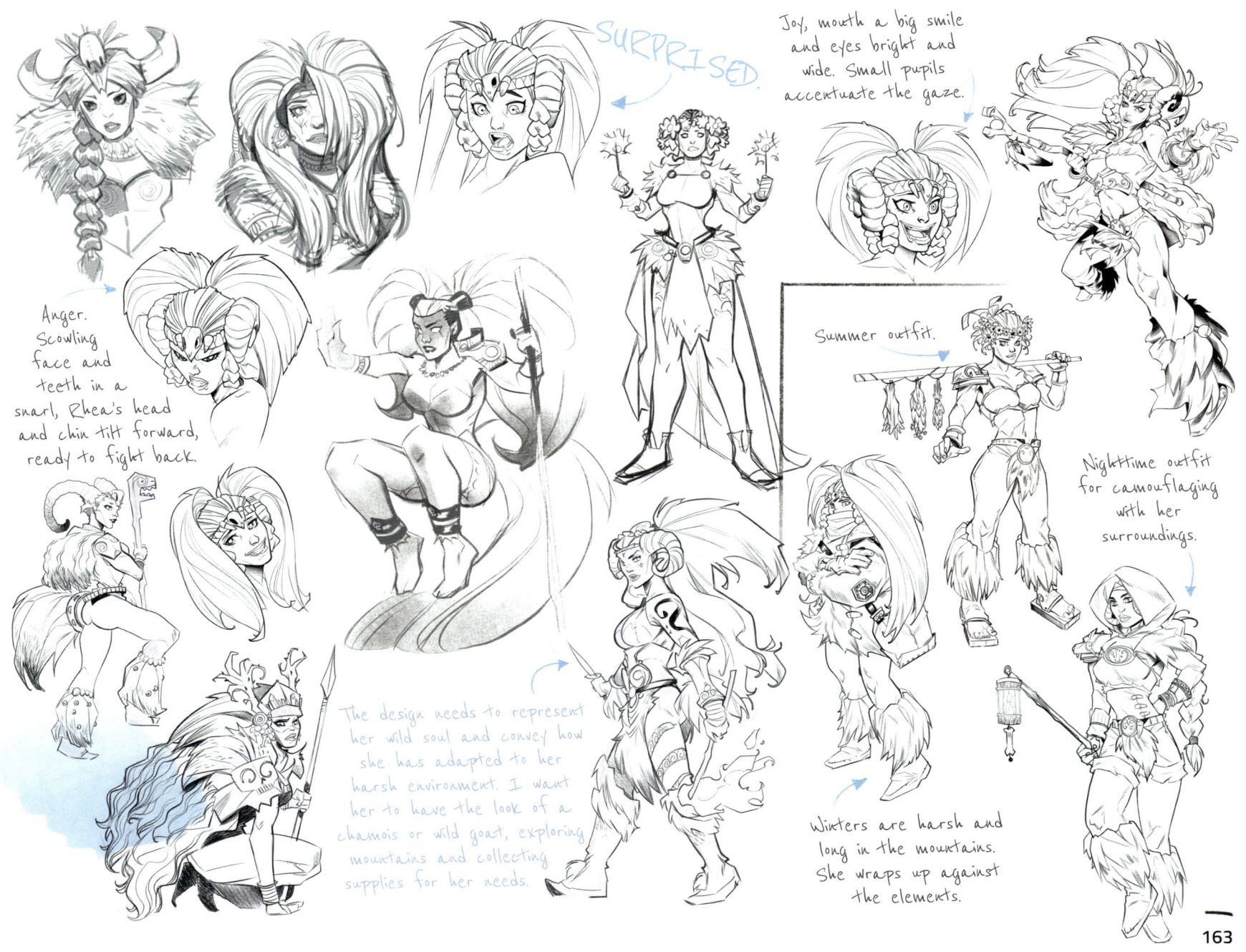

SURPRISED.

Joy, mouth a big smile and eyes bright and wide. Small pupils accentuate the gaze.

Anger. Scowling face and teeth in a snarl, Rhea's head and chin tilt forward, ready to fight back.

Summer outfit.

Nighttime outfit for camouflaging with her surroundings.

The design needs to represent her wild soul and convey how she has adapted to her harsh environment. I want her to have the look of a chamois or wild goat, exploring mountains and collecting supplies for her needs.

Winters are harsh and long in the mountains. She wraps up against the elements.

163

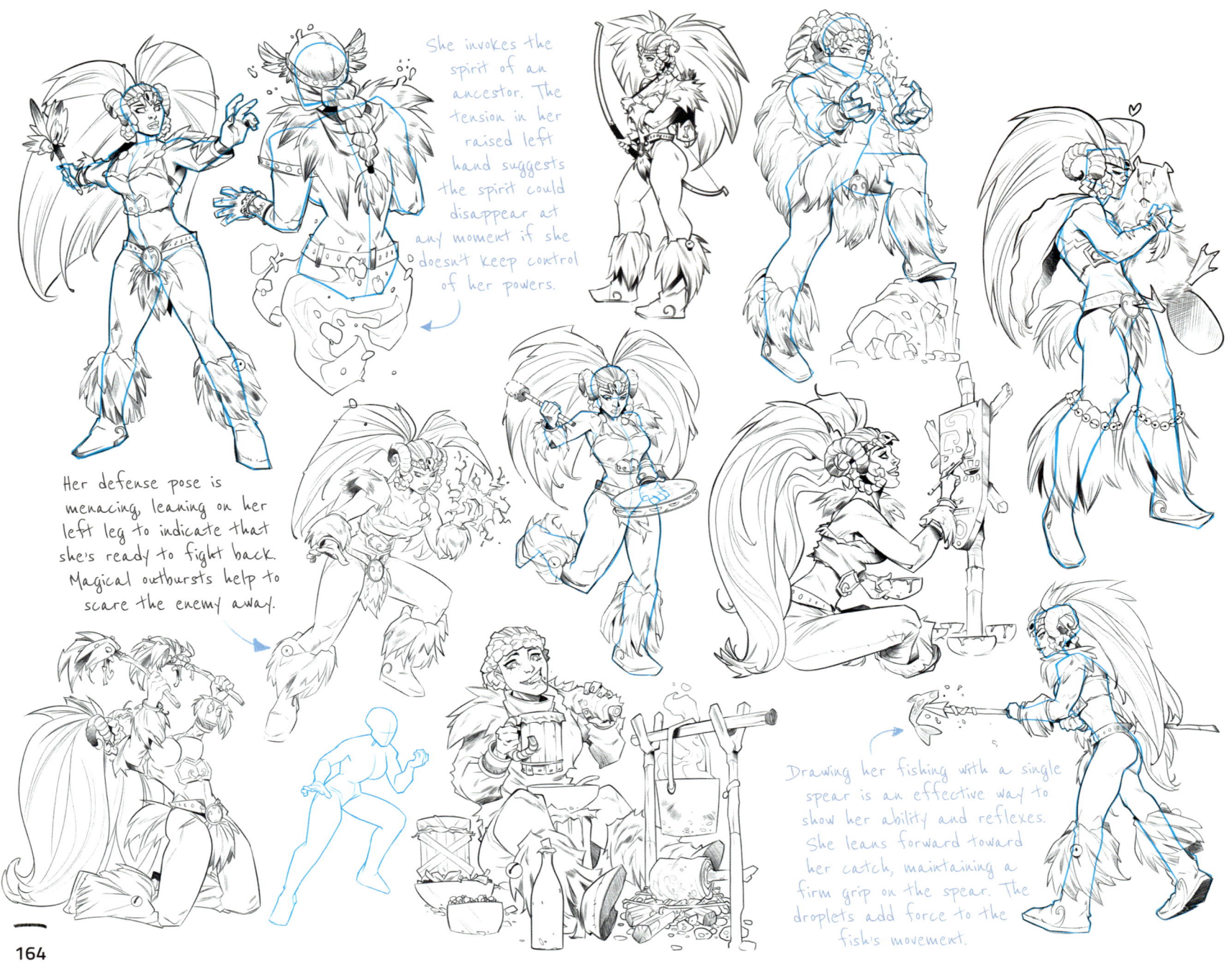

She invokes the spirit of an ancestor. The tension in her raised left hand suggests the spirit could disappear at any moment if she doesn't keep control of her powers.

Her defense pose is menacing, leaning on her left leg to indicate that she's ready to fight back. Magical outbursts help to scare the enemy away.

Drawing her fishing with a single spear is an effective way to show her ability and reflexes. She leans forward toward her catch, maintaining a firm grip on the spear. The droplets add force to the fish's movement.

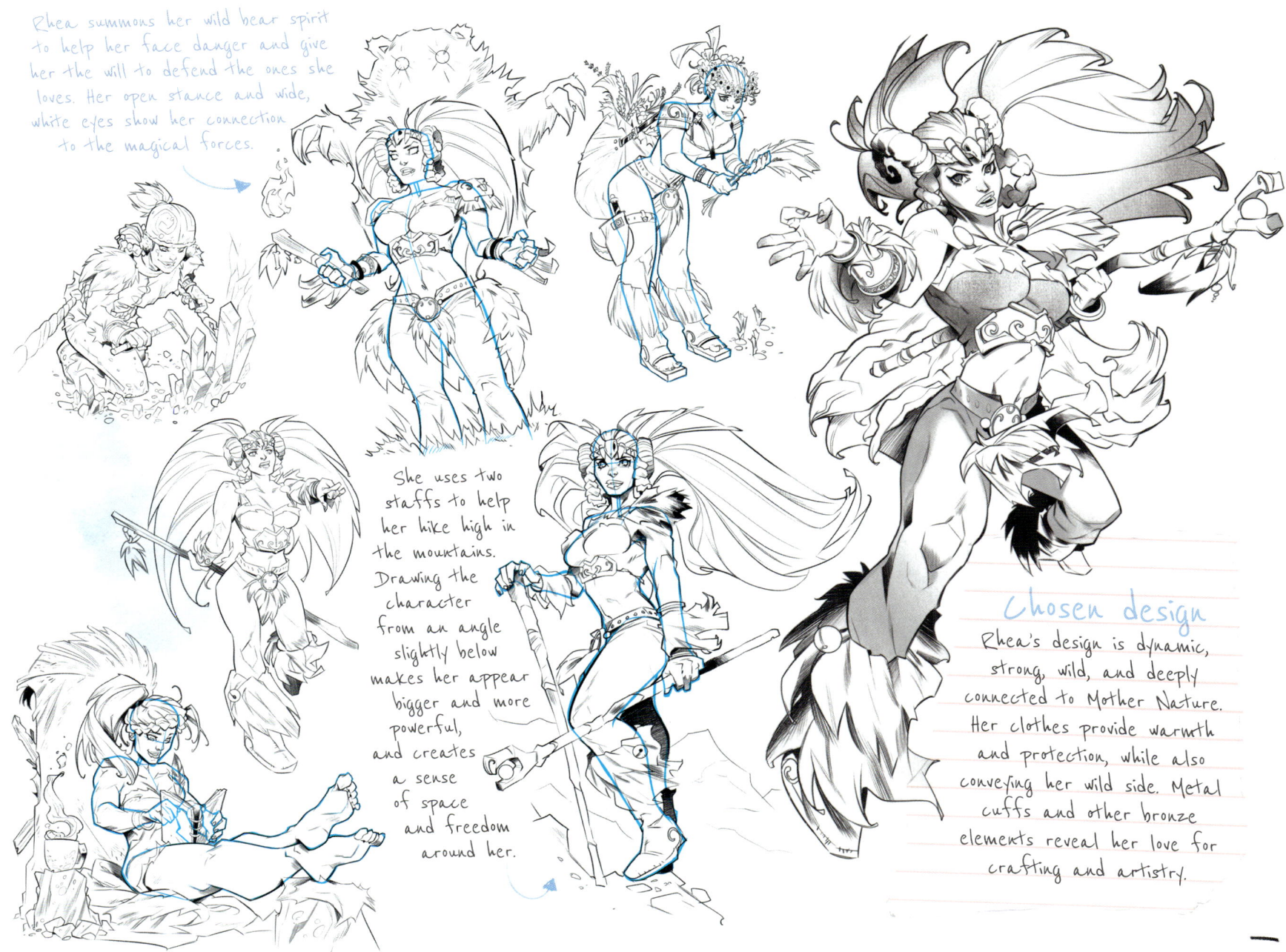

Rhea summons her wild bear spirit to help her face danger and give her the will to defend the ones she loves. Her open stance and wide, white eyes show her connection to the magical forces.

She uses two staffs to help her hike high in the mountains. Drawing the character from an angle slightly below makes her appear bigger and more powerful, and creates a sense of space and freedom around her.

Chosen design

Rhea's design is dynamic, strong, wild, and deeply connected to Mother Nature. Her clothes provide warmth and protection, while also conveying her wild side. Metal cuffs and other bronze elements reveal her love for crafting and artistry.

Gothic superheroine

One Halloween night, Willa was attacked and all of her Halloween candy stolen. She found herself in a pumpkin field and noticed some candy left inside a strange, glowing pumpkin. Not realizing it was radioactive, she ate the candy and was transformed into a Halloween superheroine! Now her mission is to protect fellow trick-or-treaters from harm. Moving secretly through the night, she decorates houses and gives out candy. Her design is gothic, dark, and mysterious.

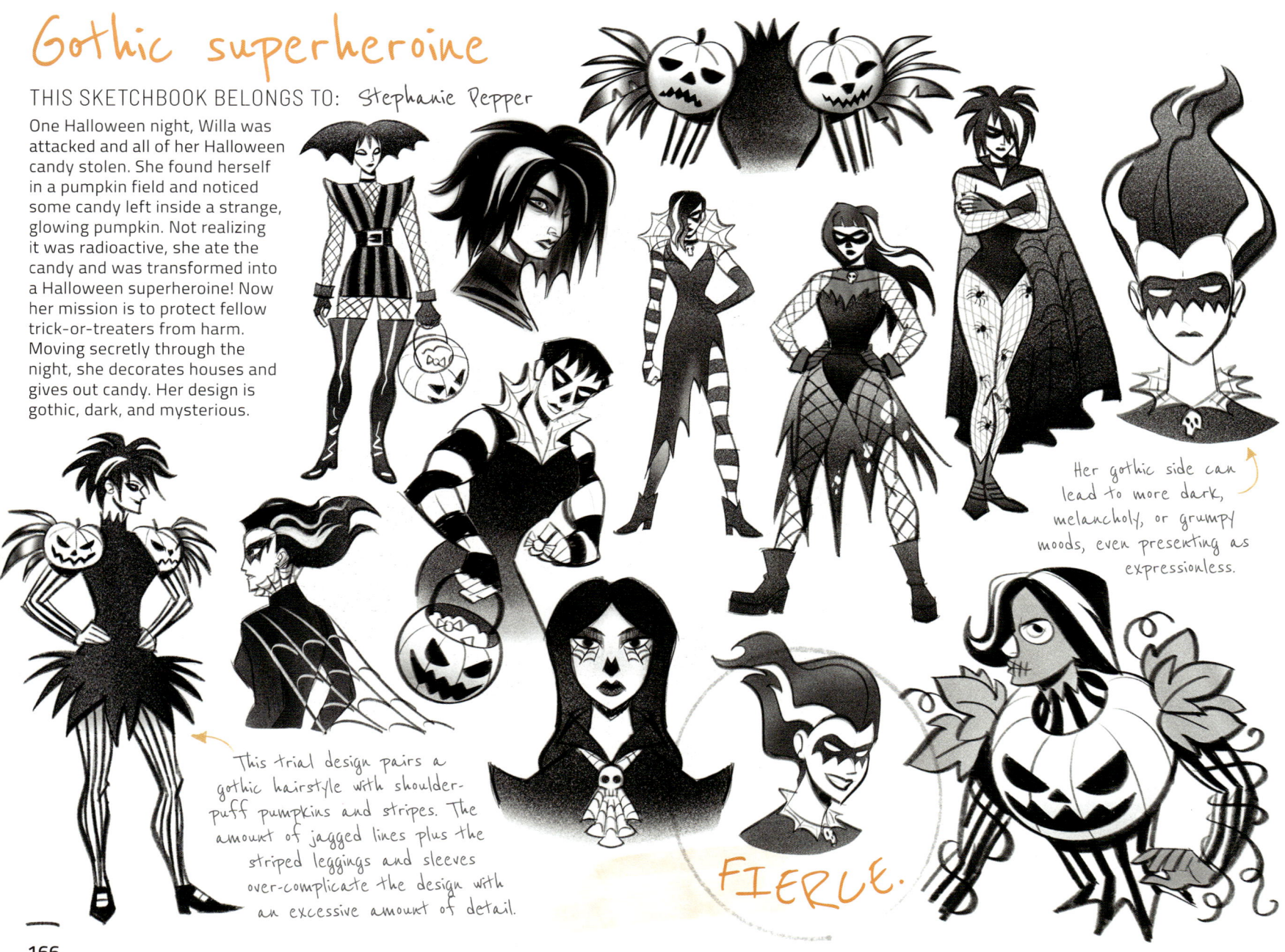

Her gothic side can lead to more dark, melancholy, or grumpy moods, even presenting as expressionless.

This trial design pairs a gothic hairstyle with shoulder-puff pumpkins and stripes. The amount of jagged lines plus the striped leggings and sleeves over-complicate the design with an excessive amount of detail.

FIERCE.

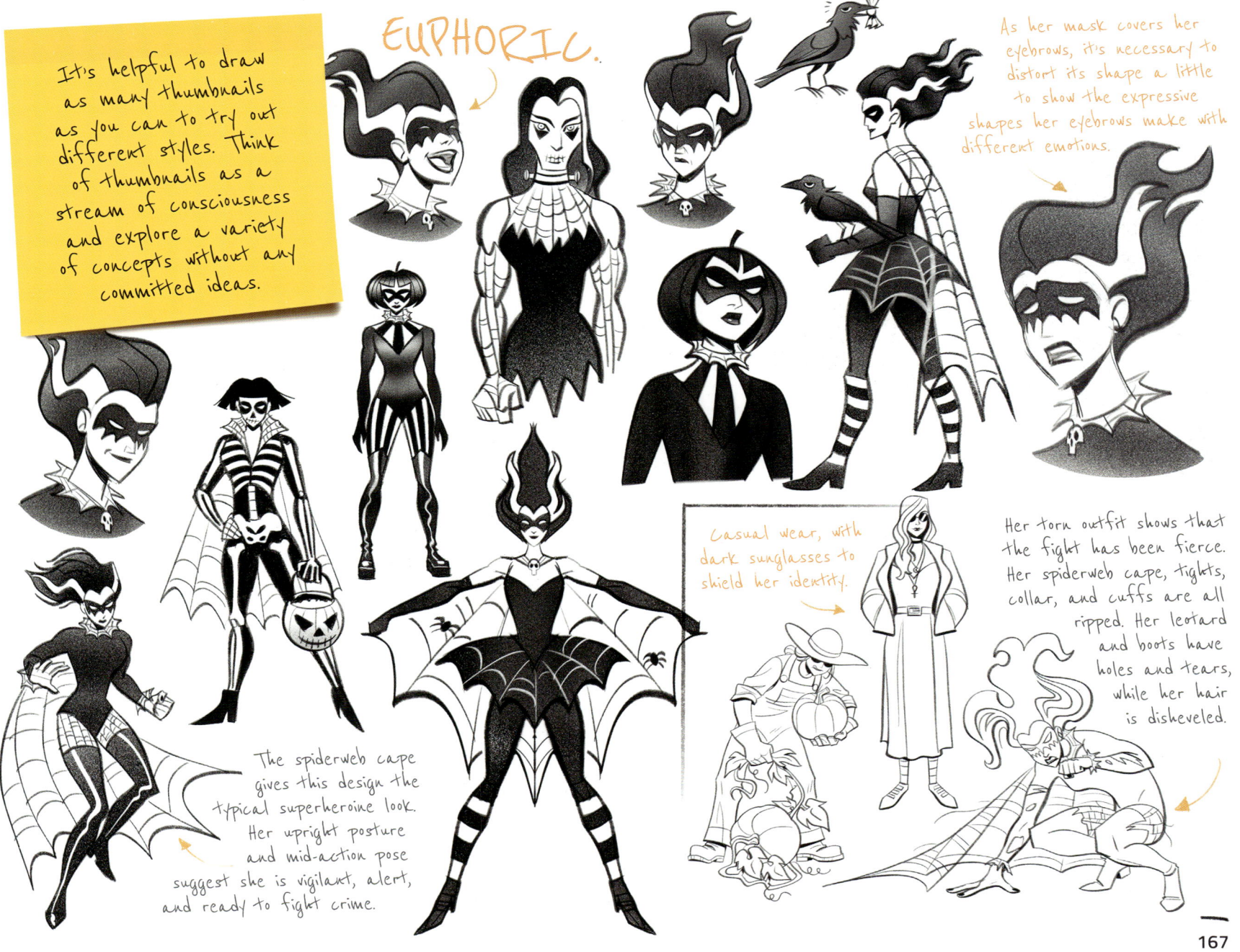

It's helpful to draw as many thumbnails as you can to try out different styles. Think of thumbnails as a stream of consciousness and explore a variety of concepts without any committed ideas.

EUPHORIC.

As her mask covers her eyebrows, it's necessary to distort its shape a little to show the expressive shapes her eyebrows make with different emotions.

The spiderweb cape gives this design the typical superheroine look. Her upright posture and mid-action pose suggest she is vigilant, alert, and ready to fight crime.

Casual wear, with dark sunglasses to shield her identity.

Her torn outfit shows that the fight has been fierce. Her spiderweb cape, tights, collar, and cuffs are all ripped. Her leotard and boots have holes and tears, while her hair is disheveled.

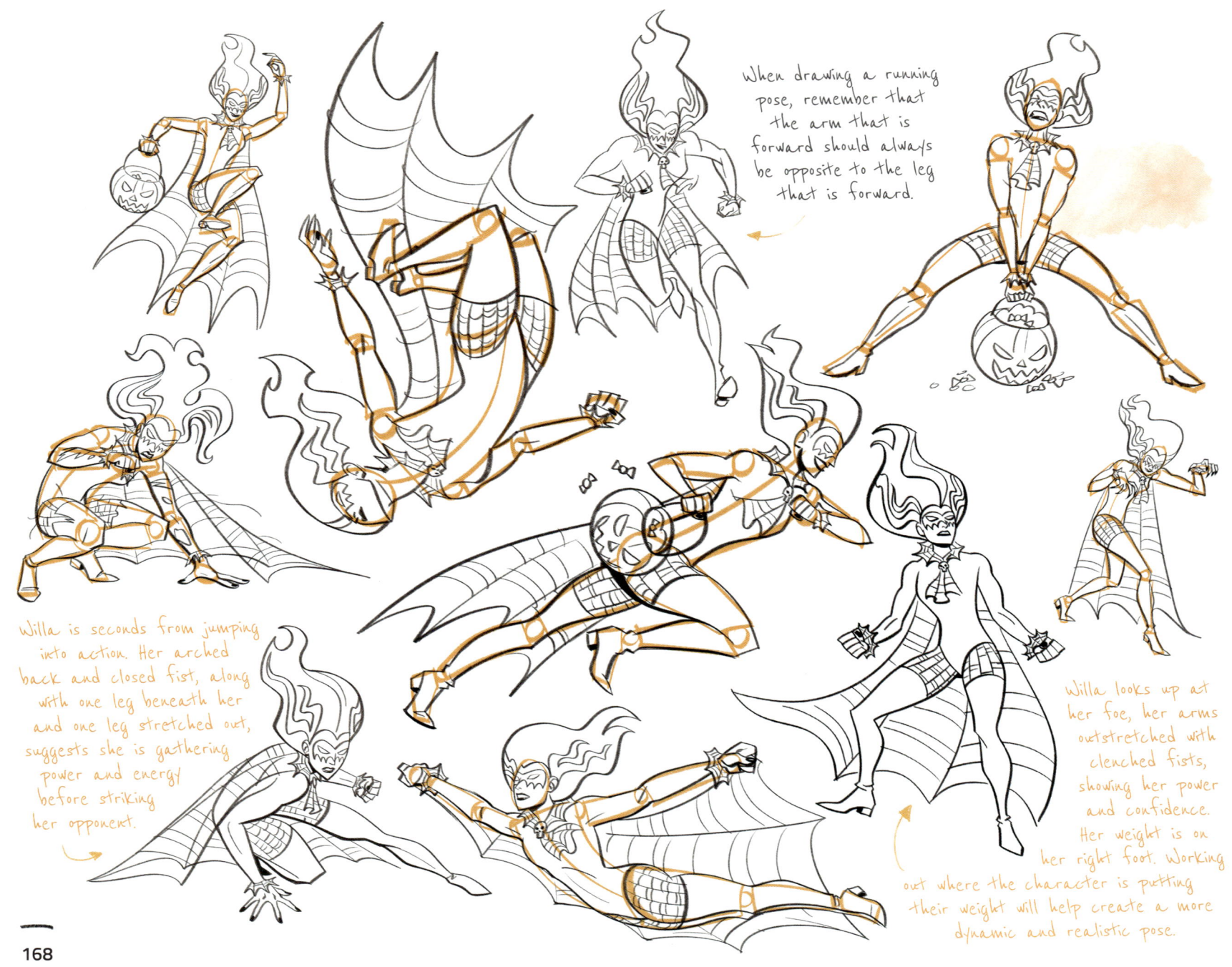

When drawing a running pose, remember that the arm that is forward should always be opposite to the leg that is forward.

Willa is seconds from jumping into action. Her arched back and closed fist, along with one leg beneath her and one leg stretched out, suggests she is gathering power and energy before striking her opponent.

Willa looks up at her foe, her arms outstretched with clenched fists, showing her power and confidence. Her weight is on her right foot. Working out where the character is putting their weight will help create a more dynamic and realistic pose.

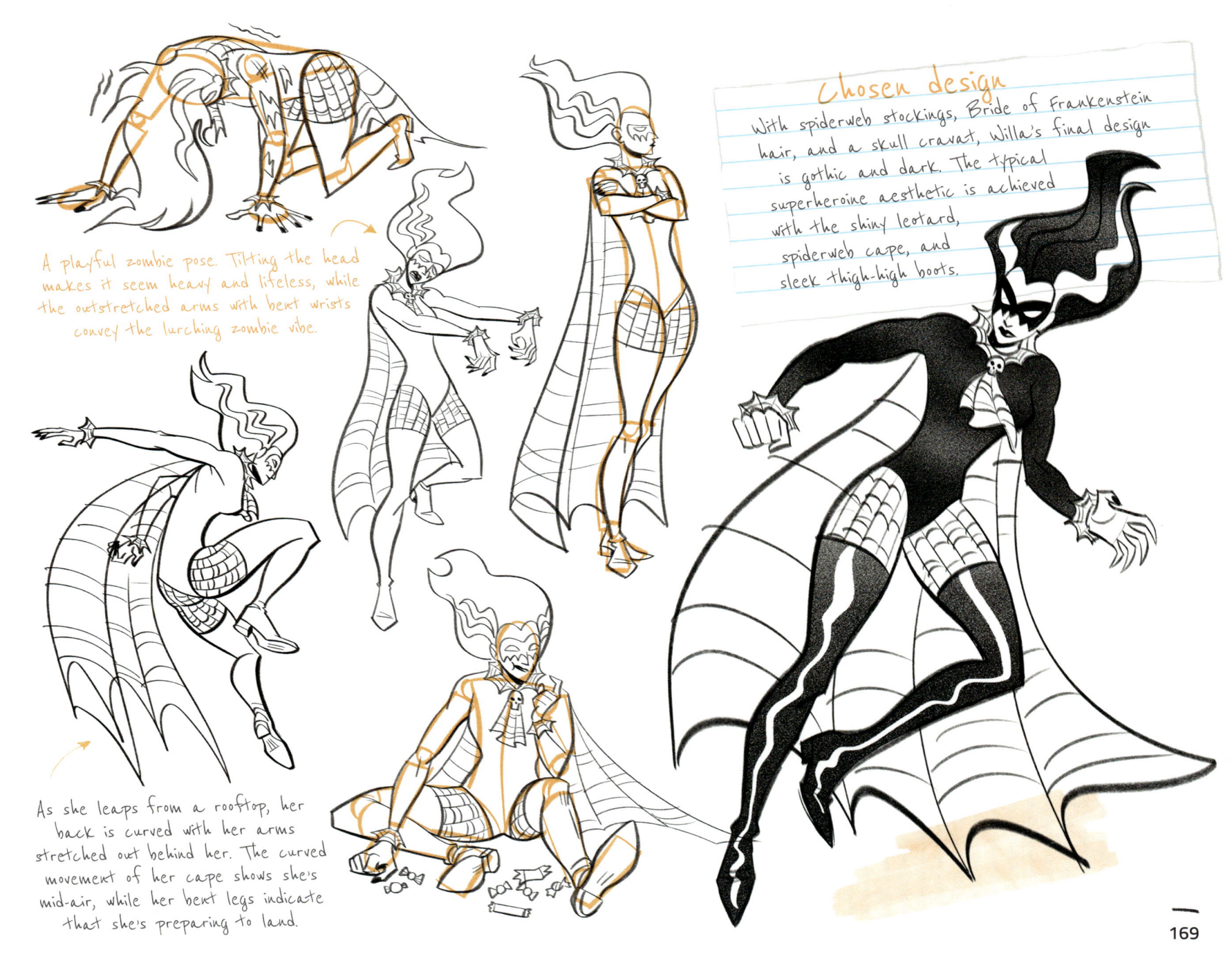

A playful zombie pose. Tilting the head makes it seem heavy and lifeless, while the outstretched arms with bent wrists convey the lurching zombie vibe.

As she leaps from a rooftop, her back is curved with her arms stretched out behind her. The curved movement of her cape shows she's mid-air, while her bent legs indicate that she's preparing to land.

With spiderweb stockings, Bride of Frankenstein hair, and a skull cravat, Willa's final design is gothic and dark. The typical superheroine aesthetic is achieved with the shiny leotard, spiderweb cape, and sleek thigh-high boots.

Rogue

THIS SKETCHBOOK BELONGS TO: Guille Rancel

Stealthy, sneaky, and astute, this rogue is inspired by Robin Hood. Raven works as a bounty hunter capturing criminals, but if she doesn't trust her client, she will do whatever she thinks is fair. The master of disguise, she will cheat and swindle when the situation requires it. With a strict moral code, she is passionate about social justice and always shares her loot with those in need. She is agile, slim, and fit, which allows her to creep about unseen.

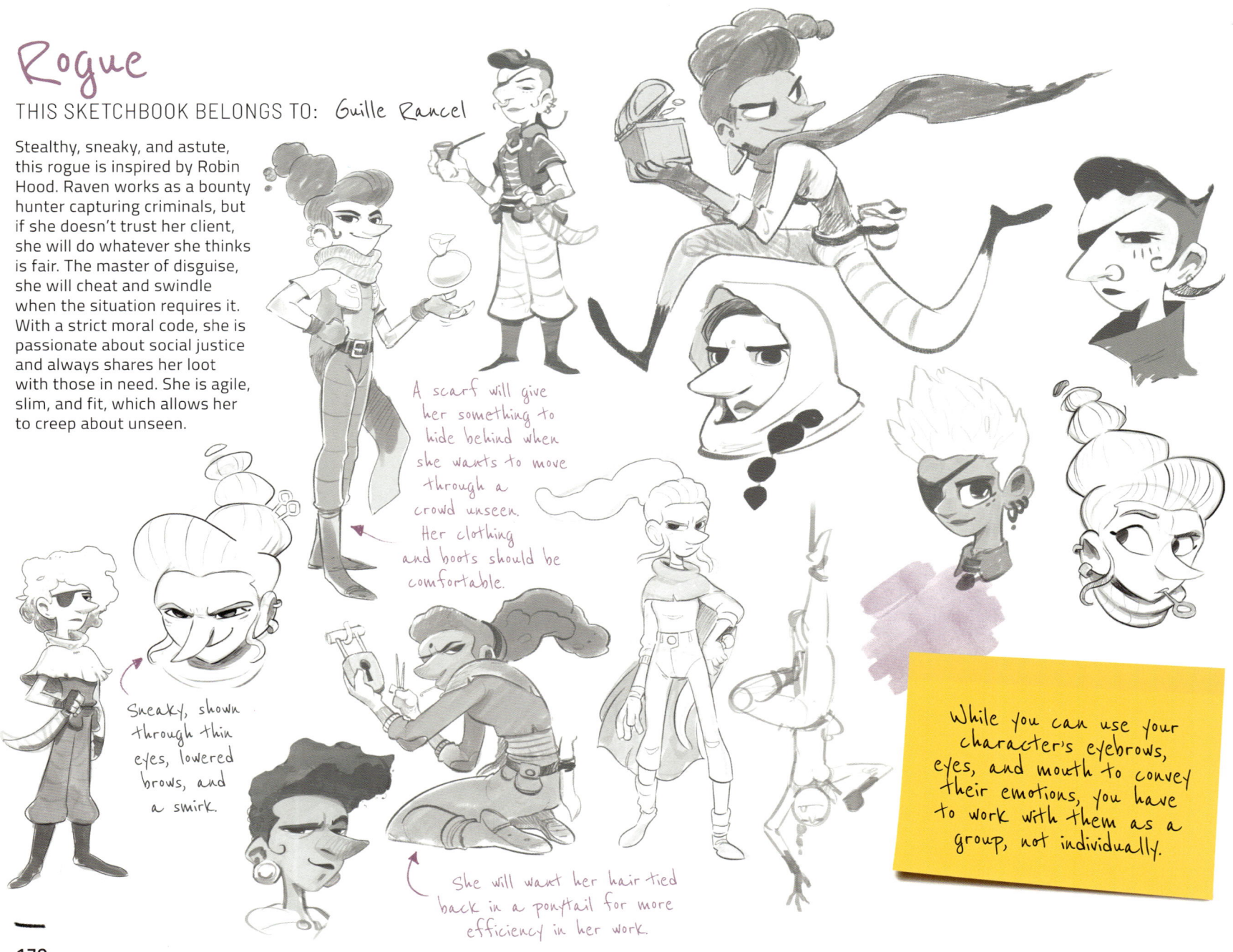

A scarf will give her something to hide behind when she wants to move through a crowd unseen. Her clothing and boots should be comfortable.

Sneaky, shown through thin eyes, lowered brows, and a smirk.

She will want her hair tied back in a ponytail for more efficiency in her work.

While you can use your character's eyebrows, eyes, and mouth to convey their emotions, you have to work with them as a group, not individually.

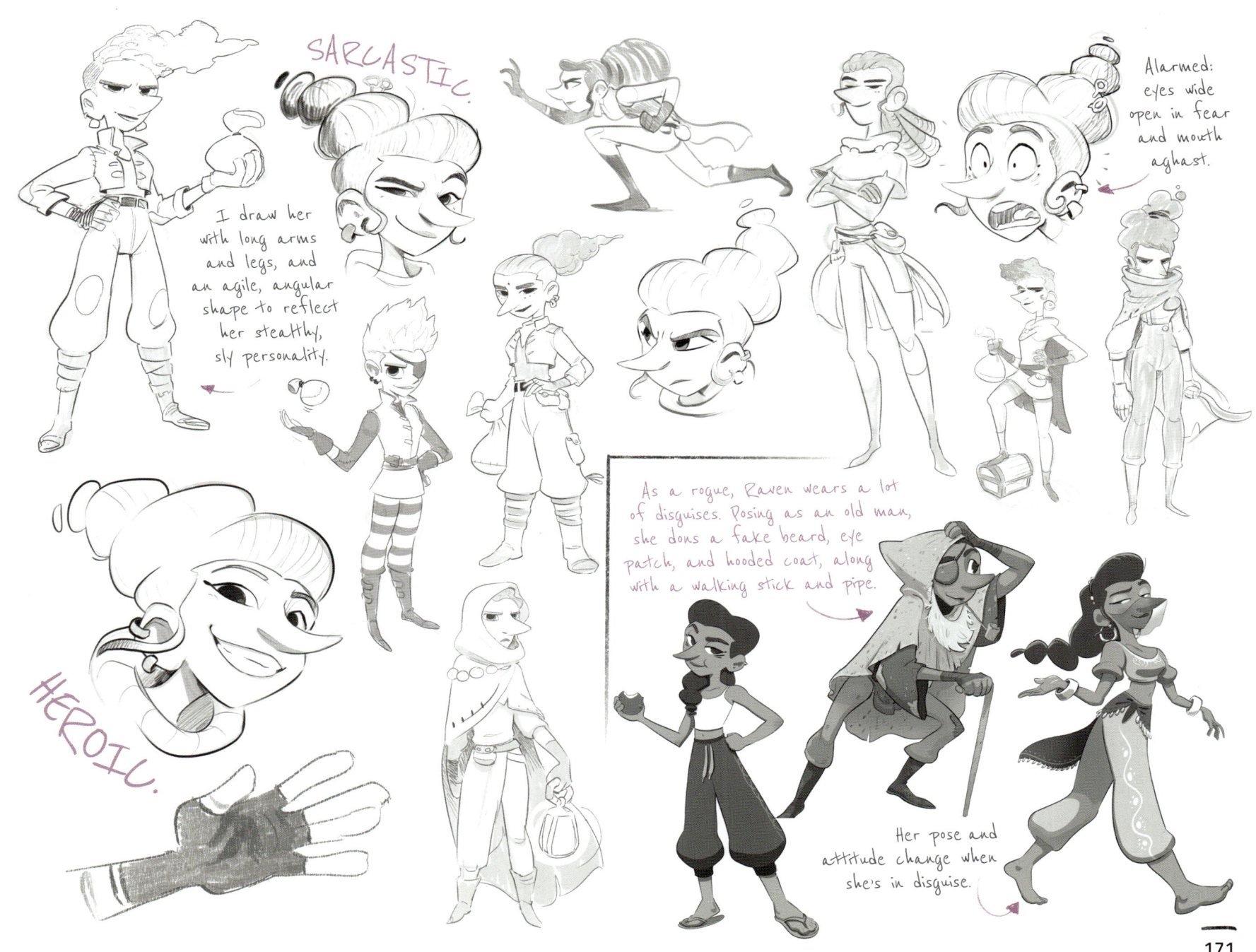

SARCASTIC.

I draw her with long arms and legs, and an agile, angular shape to reflect her stealthy, sly personality.

Alarmed: eyes wide open in fear and mouth aghast.

HEROIU.

As a rogue, Raven wears a lot of disguises. Posing as an old man, she dons a fake beard, eye patch, and hooded coat, along with a walking stick and pipe.

Her pose and attitude change when she's in disguise.

171

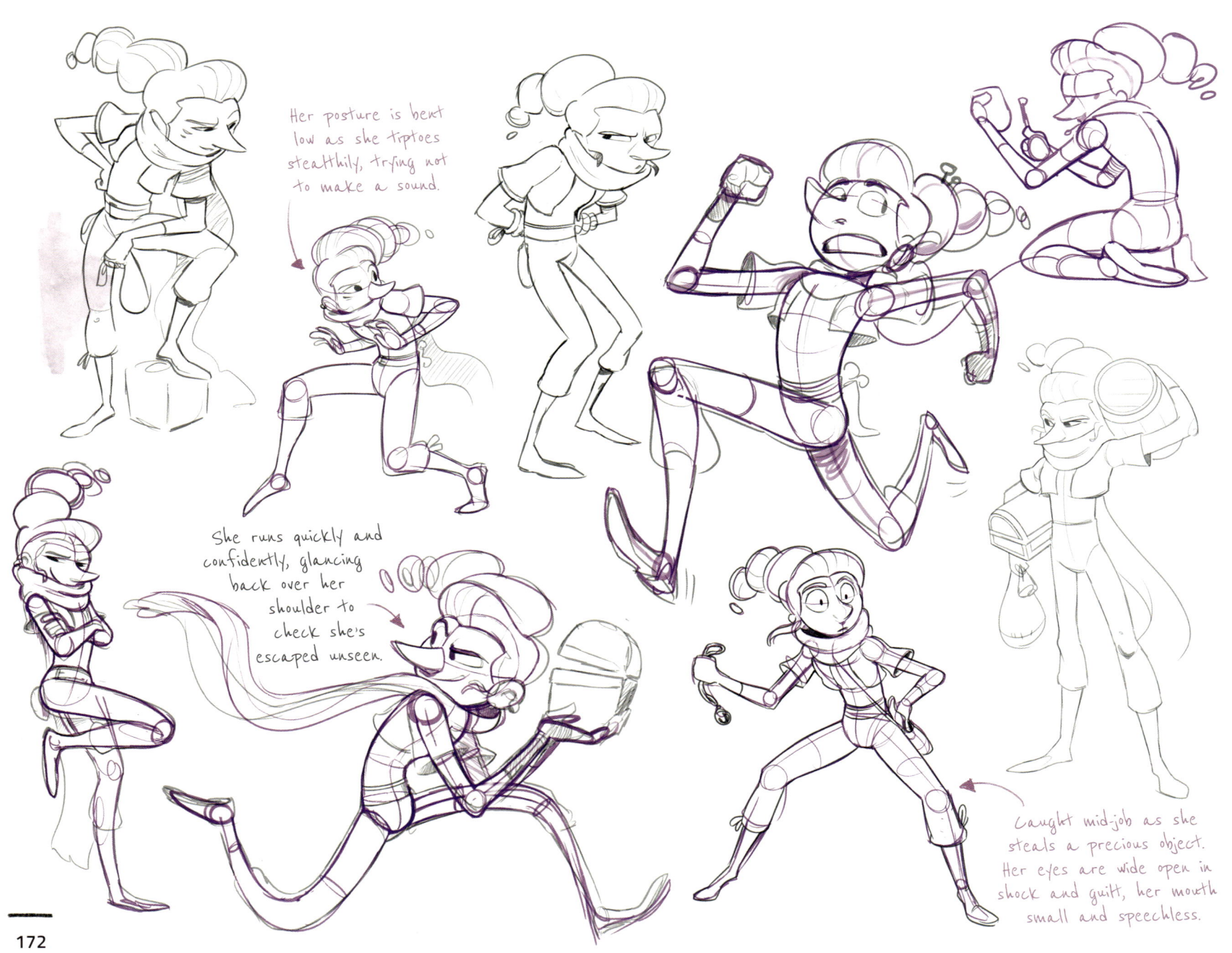

Her posture is bent low as she tiptoes stealthily, trying not to make a sound.

She runs quickly and confidently, glancing back over her shoulder to check she's escaped unseen.

Caught mid-job as she steals a precious object. Her eyes are wide open in shock and guilt, her mouth small and speechless.

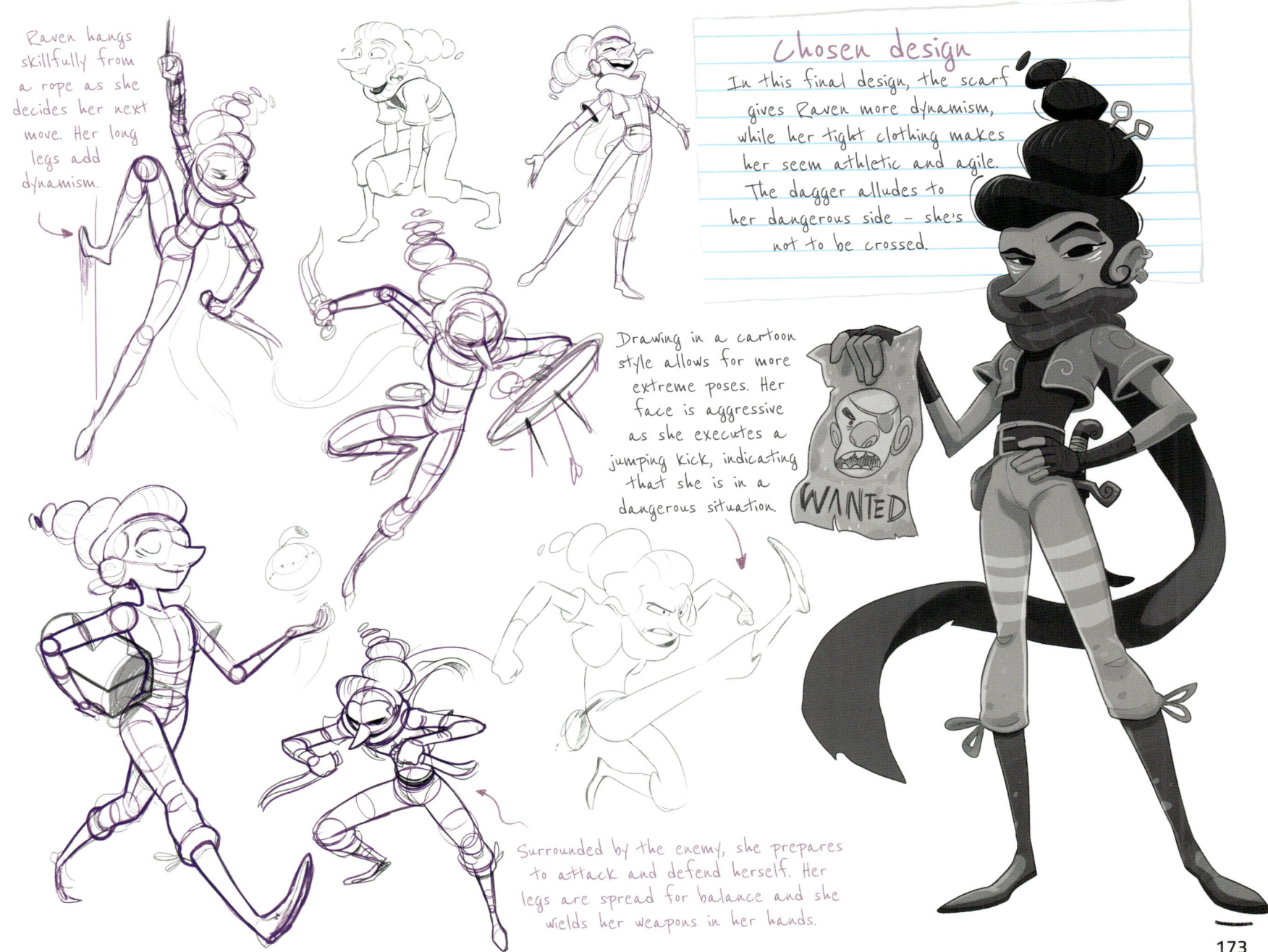

Raven hangs skillfully from a rope as she decides her next move. Her long legs add dynamism.

In this final design, the scarf gives Raven more dynamism, while her tight clothing makes her seem athletic and agile. The dagger alludes to her dangerous side – she's not to be crossed.

Drawing in a cartoon style allows for more extreme poses. Her face is aggressive as she executes a jumping kick, indicating that she is in a dangerous situation

WANTED

Surrounded by the enemy, she prepares to attack and defend herself. Her legs are spread for balance and she wields her weapons in her hands.

Aztec warrior

THIS SKETCHBOOK BELONGS TO: Almu Redondo

Coatlicue is an Aztec mother goddess, raised during times of darkness to bring forth light. She was found as a child in the jungle and grew up as an outcast. This led her to develop a deep gratitude for all living things and to fight for the pursuit of life and the miracle of creation. Creator and destroyer, she rules fire, fertility, death, and rebirth, and is mother of the sun, moon, and stars. Fierce and frightening, with serpent fangs, she is the symbol of human capacity to create, destroy, and rebuild.

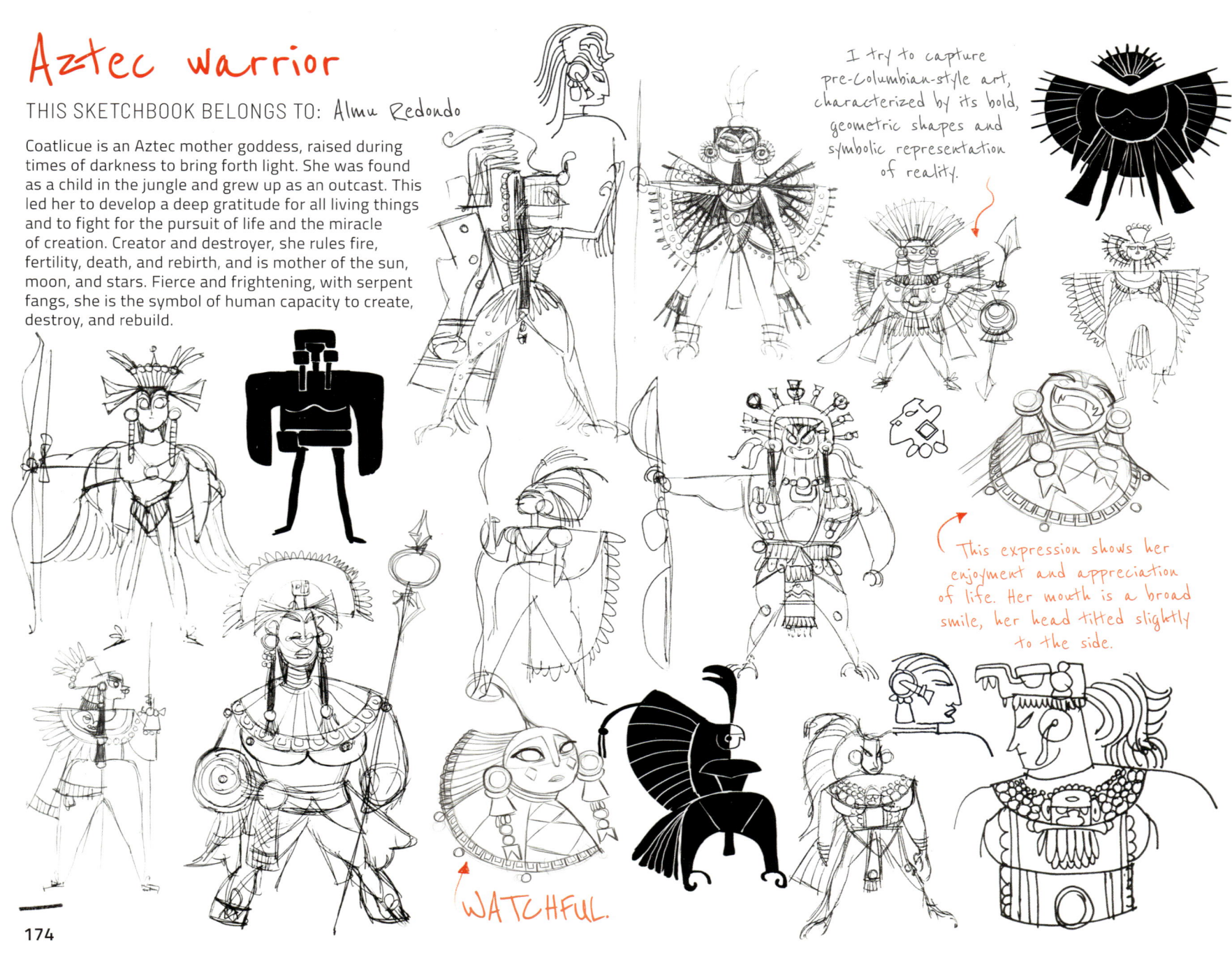

I try to capture pre-Columbian-style art, characterized by its bold, geometric shapes and symbolic representation of reality.

This expression shows her enjoyment and appreciation of life. Her mouth is a broad smile, her head tilted slightly to the side.

WATCHFUL.

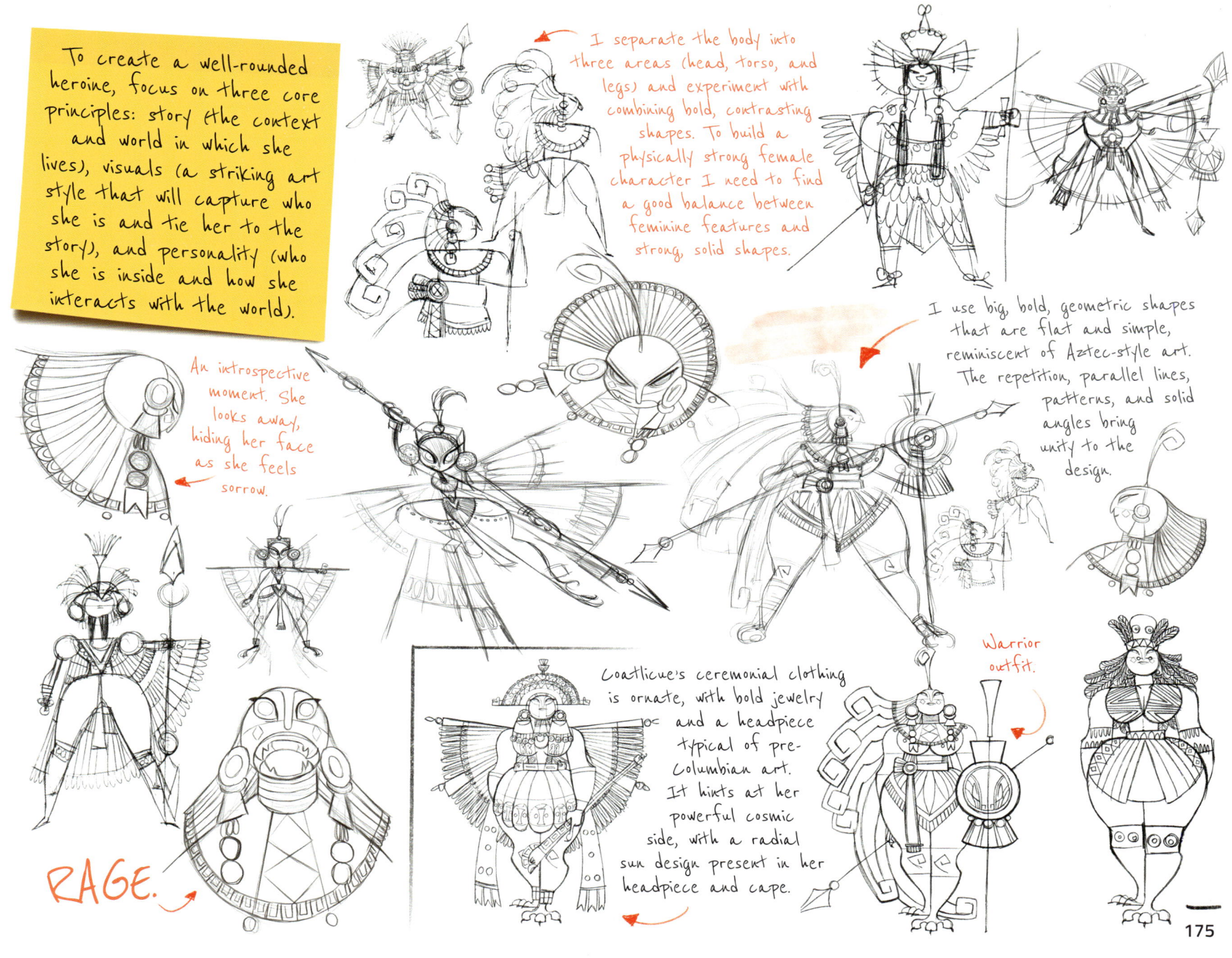

To create a well-rounded heroine, focus on three core principles: story (the context and world in which she lives), visuals (a striking art style that will capture who she is and tie her to the story), and personality (who she is inside and how she interacts with the world).

I separate the body into three areas (head, torso, and legs) and experiment with combining bold, contrasting shapes. To build a physically strong female character I need to find a good balance between feminine features and strong, solid shapes.

I use big, bold, geometric shapes that are flat and simple, reminiscent of Aztec-style art. The repetition, parallel lines, patterns, and solid angles bring unity to the design.

An introspective moment. She looks away, hiding her face as she feels sorrow.

RAGE.

Coatlicue's ceremonial clothing is ornate, with bold jewelry and a headpiece typical of pre-Columbian art. It hints at her powerful cosmic side, with a radial sun design present in her headpiece and cape.

Warrior outfit.

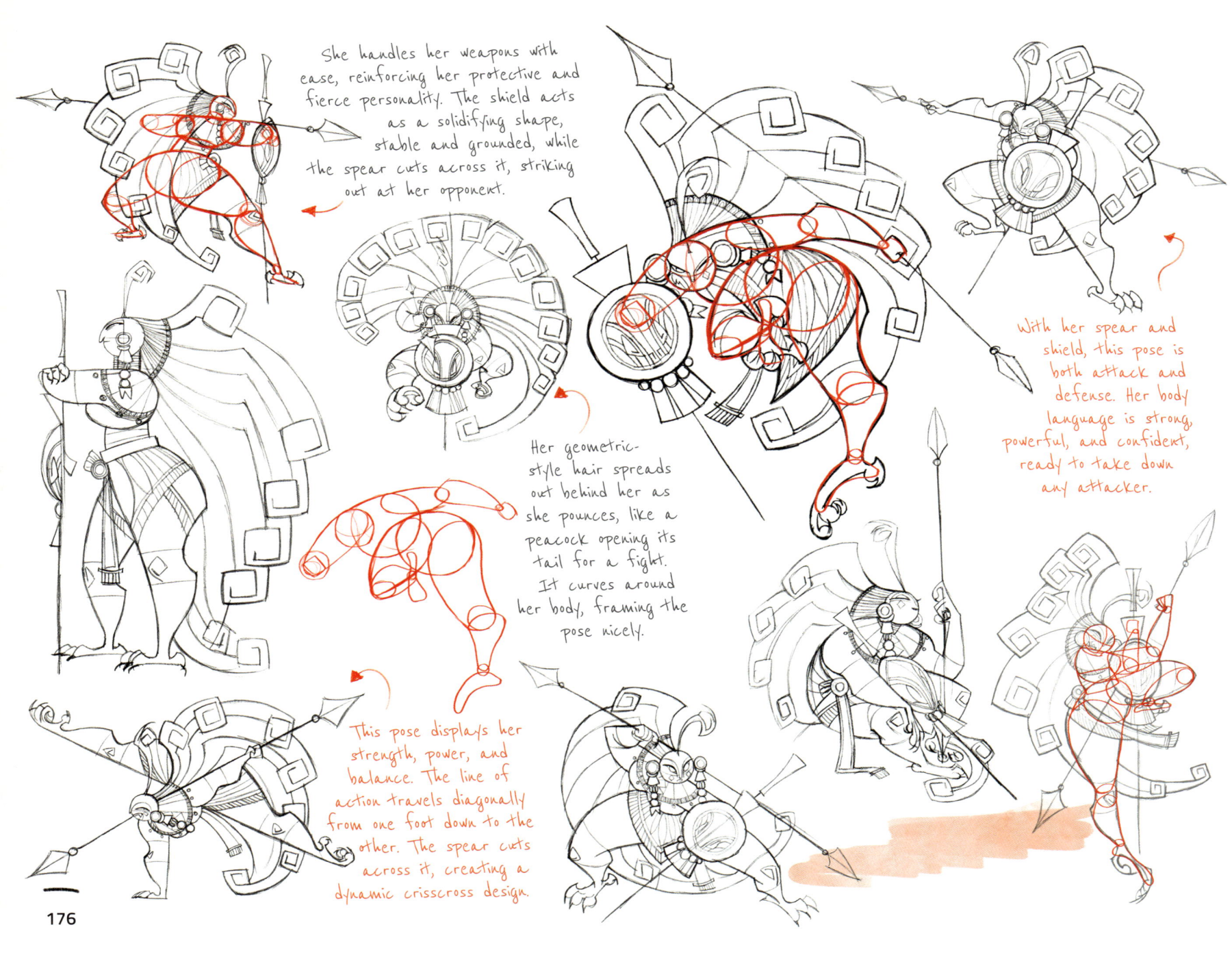

She handles her weapons with ease, reinforcing her protective and fierce personality. The shield acts as a solidifying shape, stable and grounded, while the spear cuts across it, striking out at her opponent.

Her geometric-style hair spreads out behind her as she pounces, like a peacock opening its tail for a fight. It curves around her body, framing the pose nicely.

With her spear and shield, this pose is both attack and defense. Her body language is strong, powerful, and confident, ready to take down any attacker.

This pose displays her strength, power, and balance. The line of action travels diagonally from one foot down to the other. The spear cuts across it, creating a dynamic crisscross design.

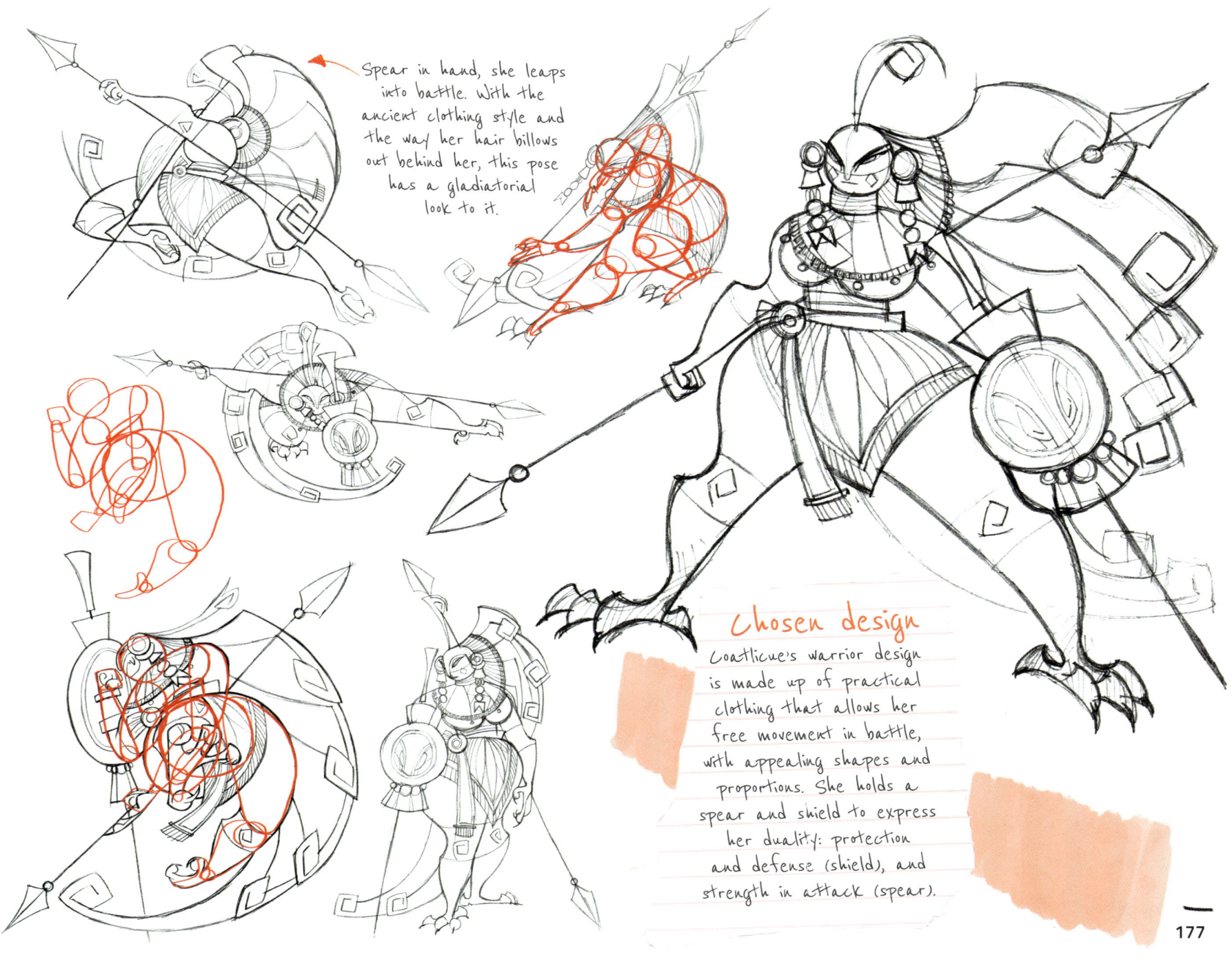

Spear in hand, she leaps into battle. With the ancient clothing style and the way her hair billows out behind her, this pose has a gladiatorial look to it.

Chosen design

Coatlicue's warrior design is made up of practical clothing that allows her free movement in battle, with appealing shapes and proportions. She holds a spear and shield to express her duality: protection and defense (shield), and strength in attack (spear).

Athlete

THIS SKETCHBOOK BELONGS TO: Joakim Riedinger

Zoe is a sixteen-year-old teen from a Parisian suburb. Her dad is from Guadeloupe and her mother was French. Zoe started volleyball at a young age after her mother's death, and plays as the opposite hitter on the court. She is quiet and introverted, and uses the volleyball court to express herself – she loves to spike the ball hard to release her energy and emotions. Passing, spiking, digging, and serving is a language she is comfortable with. She is tall and has a strong upper body and athletic figure. A loyal team player, she dreams of becoming an Olympic athlete.

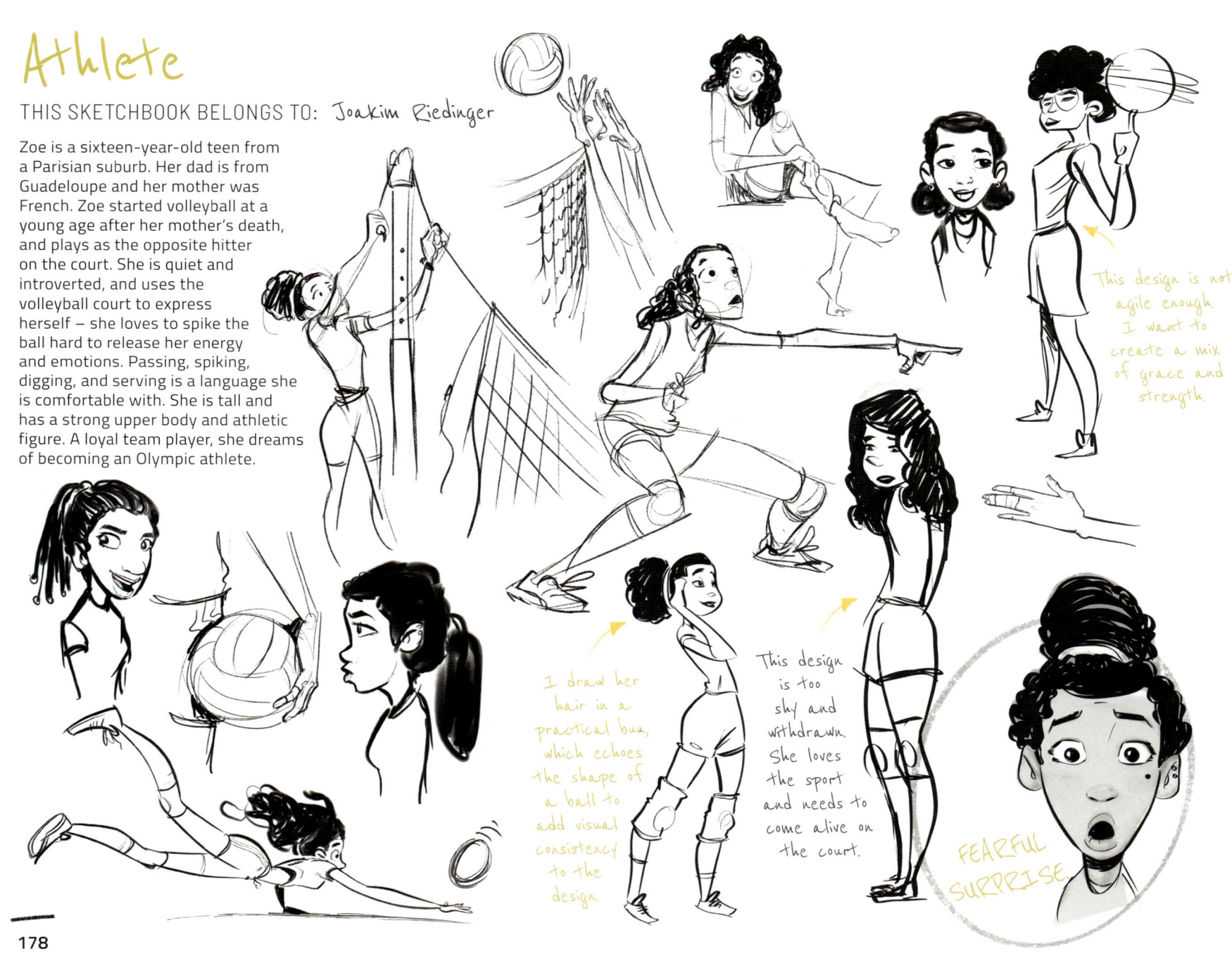

This design is not agile enough. I want to create a mix of grace and strength.

I draw her hair in a practical bun, which echoes the shape of a ball to add visual consistency to the design.

This design is too shy and withdrawn. She loves the sport and needs to come alive on the court.

FEARFUL SURPRISE.

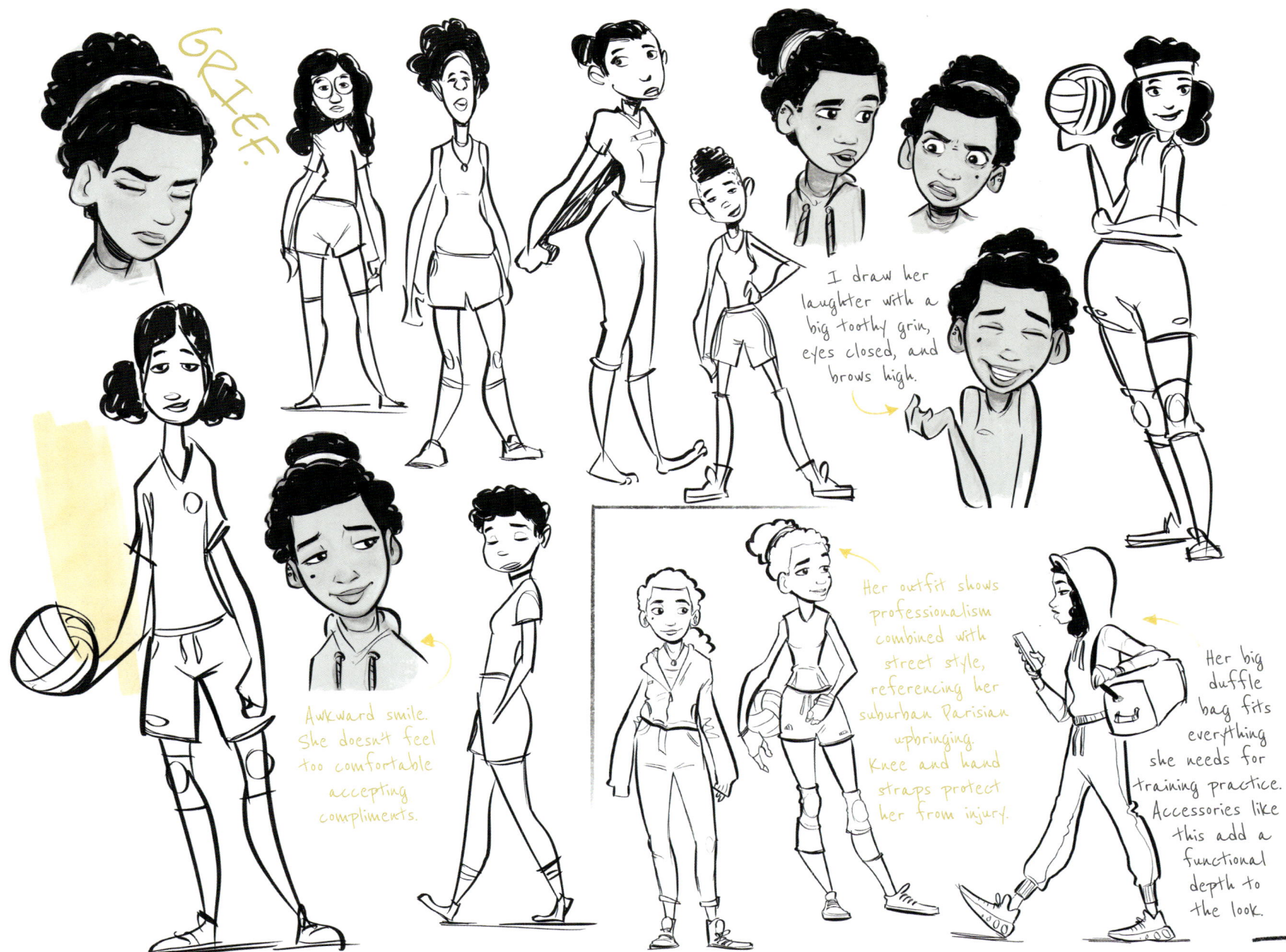

GRIEF.

I draw her laughter with a big toothy grin, eyes closed, and brows high.

Awkward smile. She doesn't feel too comfortable accepting compliments.

Her outfit shows professionalism combined with street style, referencing her suburban Parisian upbringing. Knee and hand straps protect her from injury.

Her big duffle bag fits everything she needs for training practice. Accessories like this add a functional depth to the look.

179

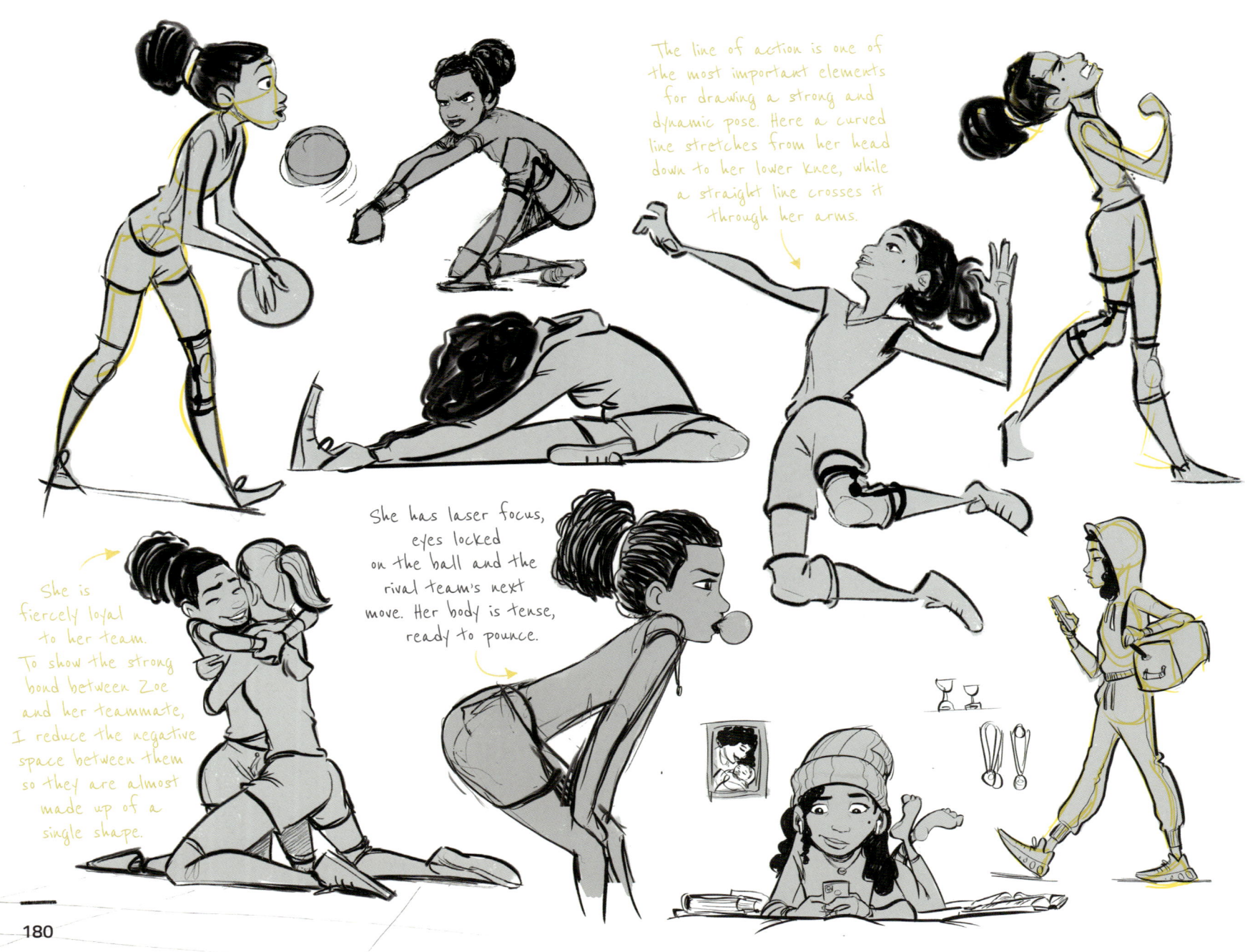

The line of action is one of the most important elements for drawing a strong and dynamic pose. Here a curved line stretches from her head down to her lower knee, while a straight line crosses it through her arms.

She is fiercely loyal to her team. To show the strong bond between Zoe and her teammate, I reduce the negative space between them so they are almost made up of a single shape.

She has laser focus, eyes locked on the ball and the rival team's next move. Her body is tense, ready to pounce.

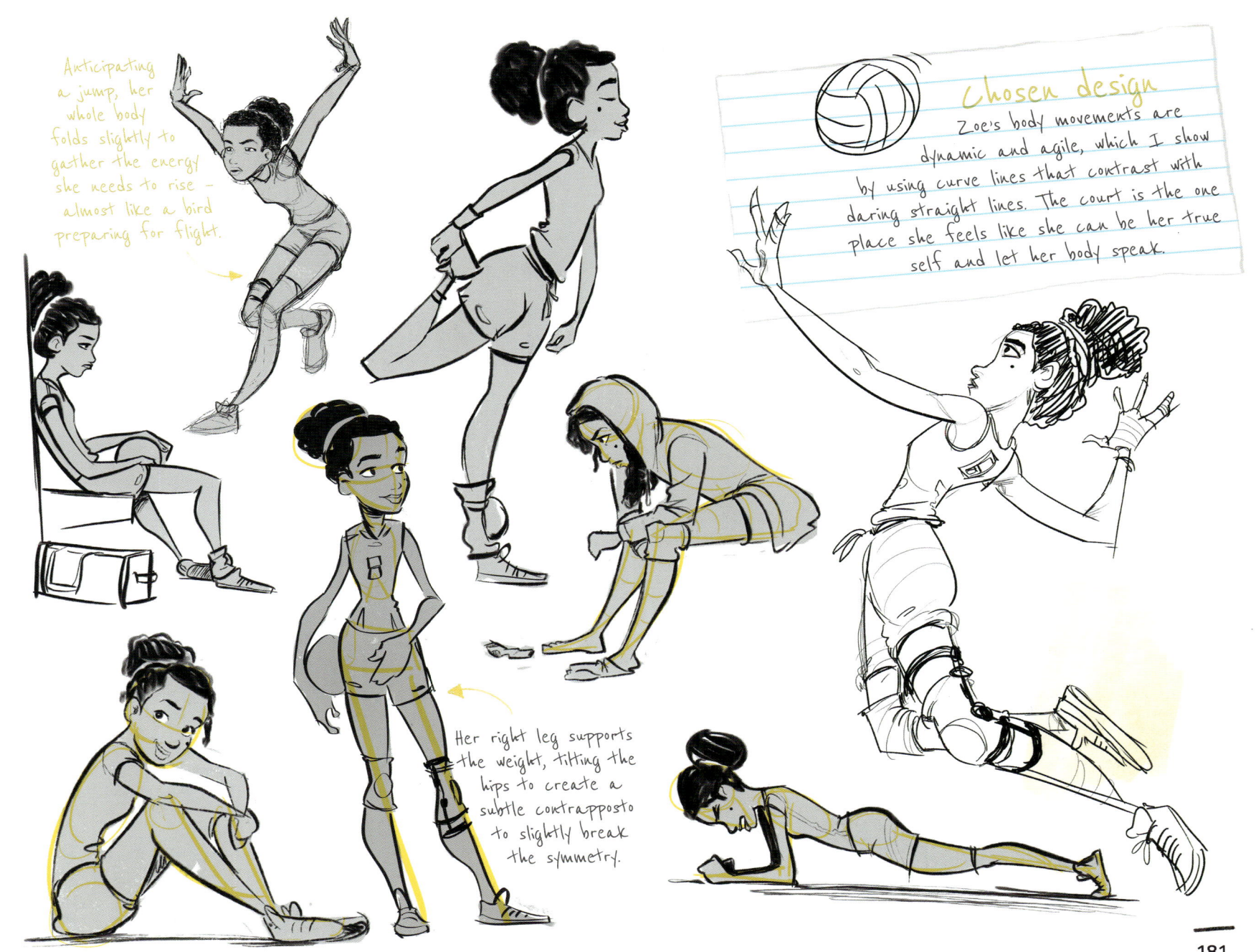

Anticipating a jump, her whole body folds slightly to gather the energy she needs to rise — almost like a bird preparing for flight.

Zoe's body movements are dynamic and agile, which I show by using curve lines that contrast with daring straight lines. The court is the one place she feels like she can be her true self and let her body speak.

Her right leg supports the weight, tilting the hips to create a subtle contrapposto to slightly break the symmetry.

Scientist

Carmella is a horticultural scientist in 1940s' Tlaxcala, Mexico, who works at the university researching plant life with medicinal uses to save lives. An Hispanic Indiana-Jones type character, her mission is to track down rare plants and flowers that could provide cures, even if it means putting her own life at risk. Intelligent, stubborn, and optimistic, her use of plants to heal is seen as magic by some in the community.

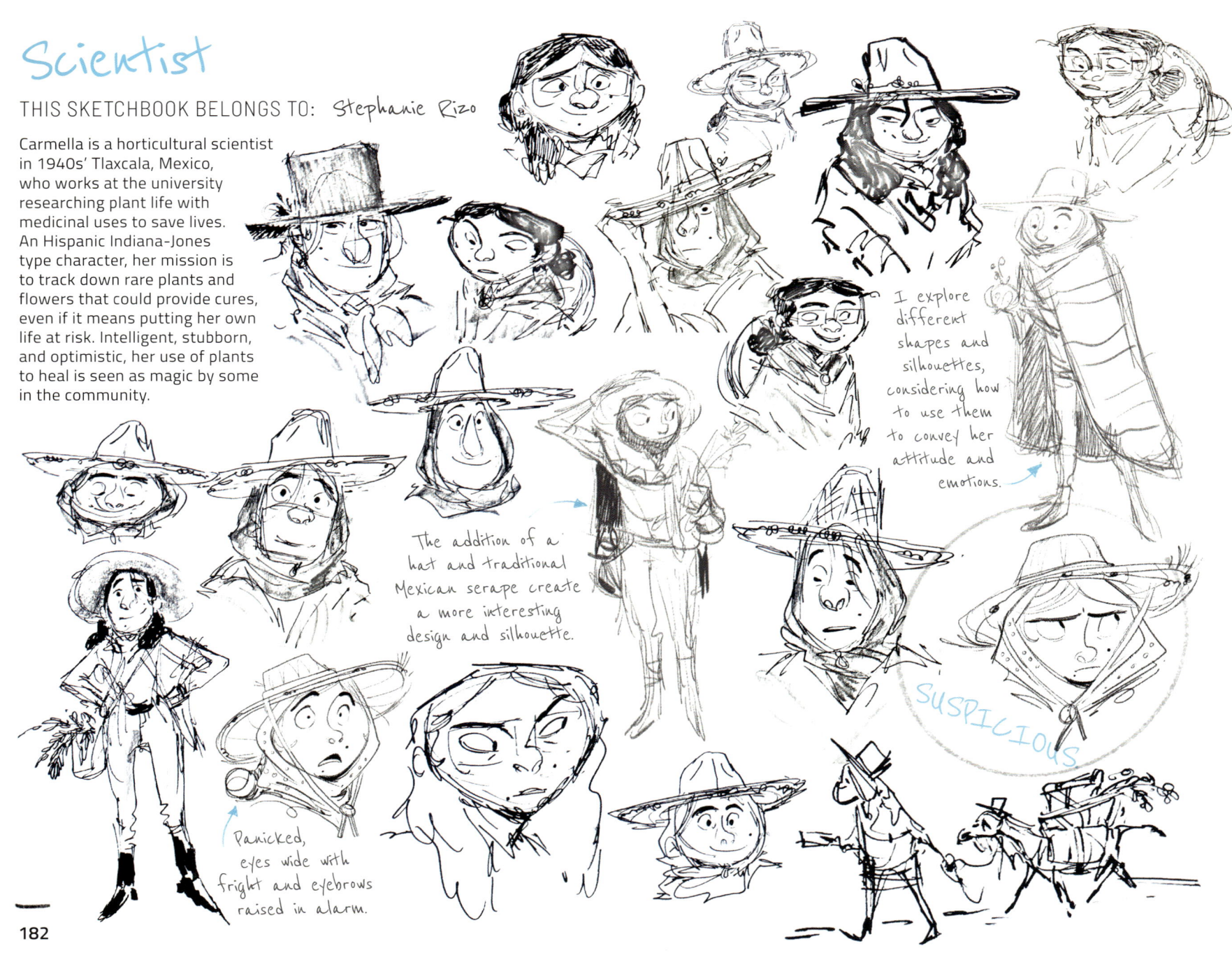

I explore different shapes and silhouettes, considering how to use them to convey her attitude and emotions.

The addition of a hat and traditional Mexican serape create a more interesting design and silhouette.

SUSPICIOUS

Panicked, eyes wide with fright and eyebrows raised in alarm.

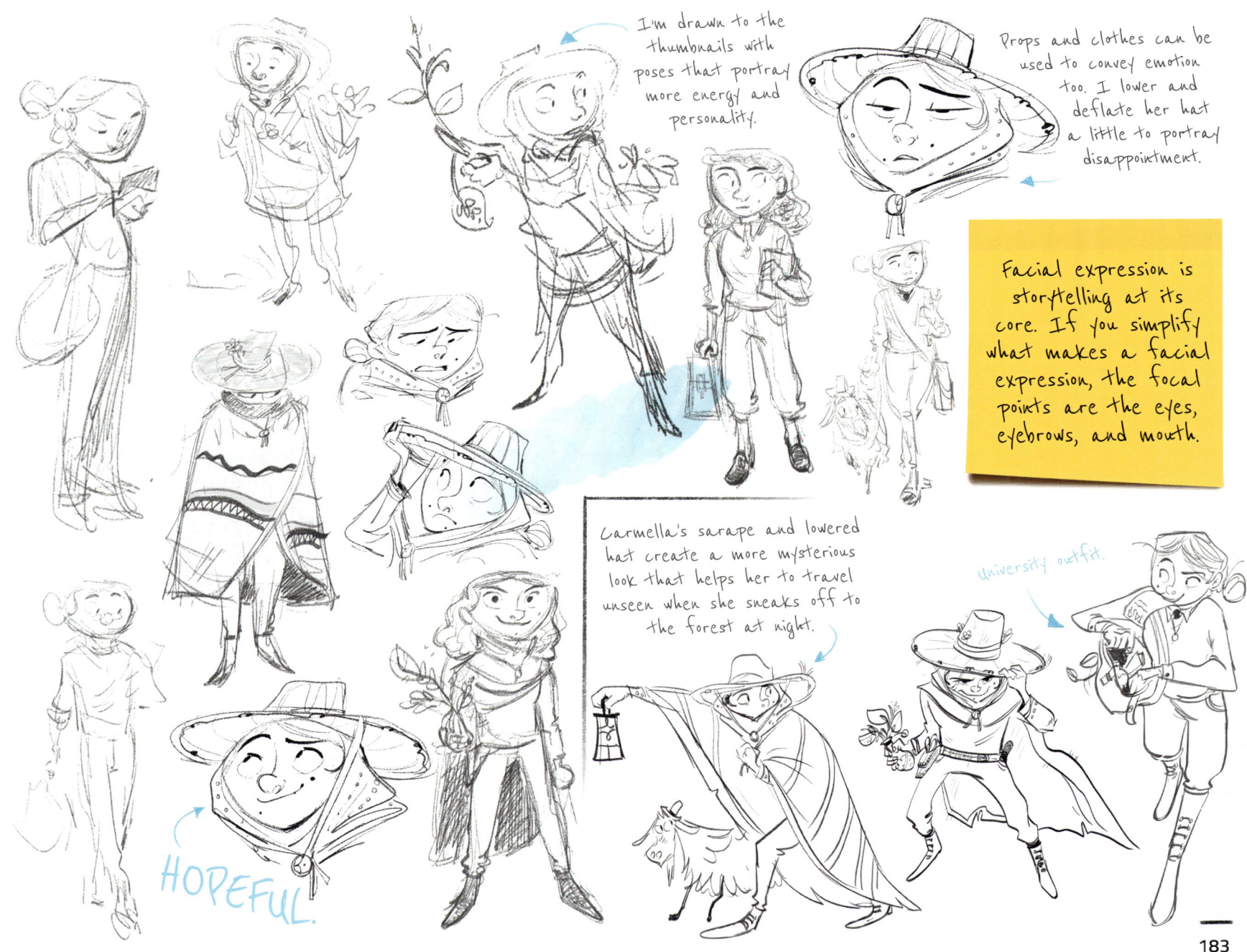

I'm drawn to the thumbnails with poses that portray more energy and personality.

Props and clothes can be used to convey emotion too. I lower and deflate her hat a little to portray disappointment.

Facial expression is storytelling at its core. If you simplify what makes a facial expression, the focal points are the eyes, eyebrows, and mouth.

Carmella's sarape and lowered hat create a more mysterious look that helps her to travel unseen when she sneaks off to the forest at night.

University outfit.

HOPEFUL.

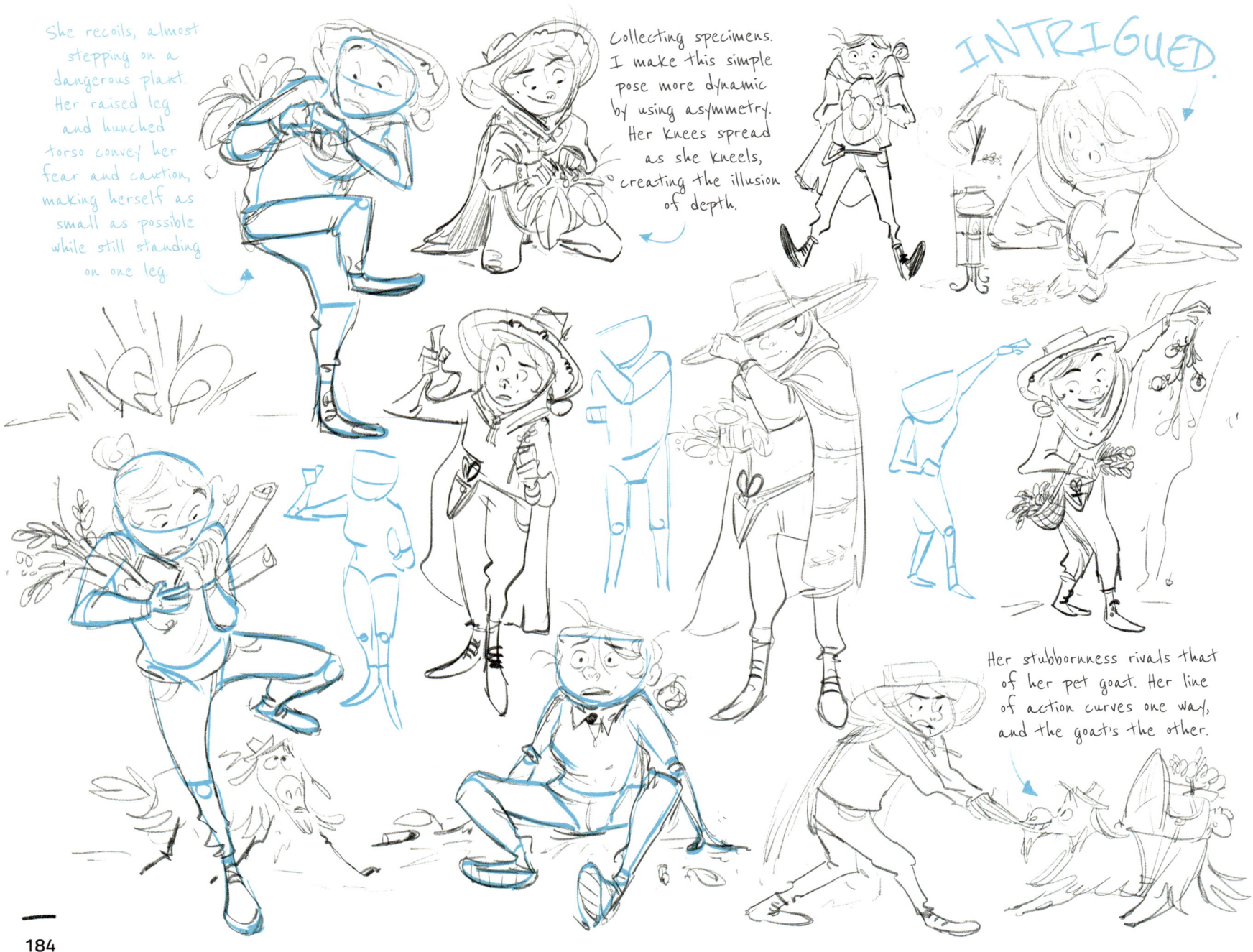

She recoils, almost stepping on a dangerous plant. Her raised leg and hunched torso convey her fear and caution, making herself as small as possible while still standing on one leg.

Collecting specimens. I make this simple pose more dynamic by using asymmetry. Her knees spread as she kneels, creating the illusion of depth.

INTRIGUED.

Her stubbornness rivals that of her pet goat. Her line of action curves one way, and the goat's the other.

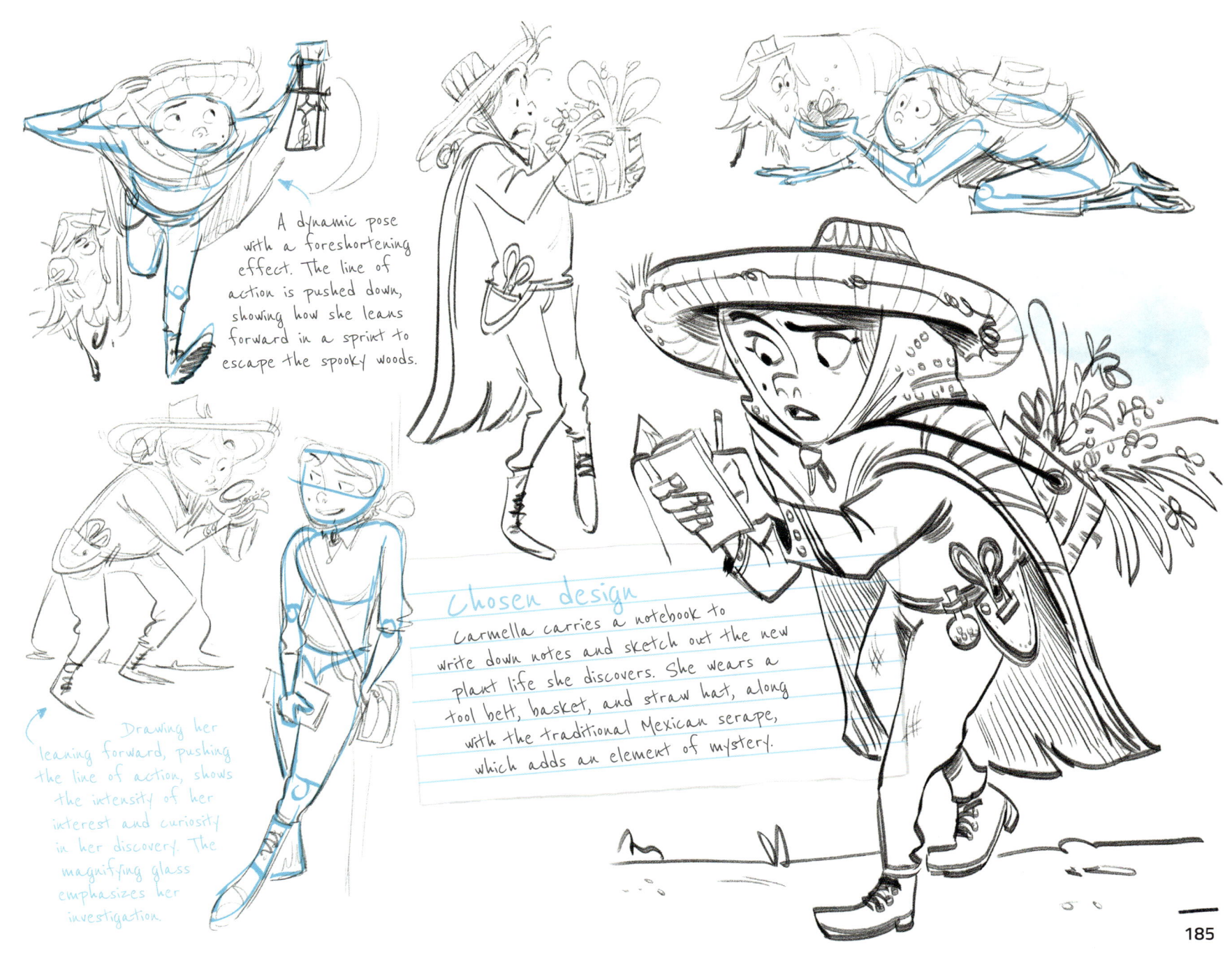

A dynamic pose with a foreshortening effect. The line of action is pushed down, showing how she leans forward in a sprint to escape the spooky woods.

Drawing her leaning forward, pushing the line of action, shows the intensity of her interest and curiosity in her discovery. The magnifying glass emphasizes her investigation.

Chosen design

Carmella carries a notebook to write down notes and sketch out the new plant life she discovers. She wears a tool belt, basket, and straw hat, along with the traditional Mexican serape, which adds an element of mystery.

Inuit hunter

Nanouk is an Inuit hunter from a northern tribe. Loyal to her people, she hunts, fishes, and farms to provide food and create the tools, weapons, and clothing they need for survival. She is fearsome, strong, and skilled, and is rarely without her spear. Living in a cold climate, she wears thick cloth and animal furs, fashioned into practical attire that allows her to hunt and move with ease.

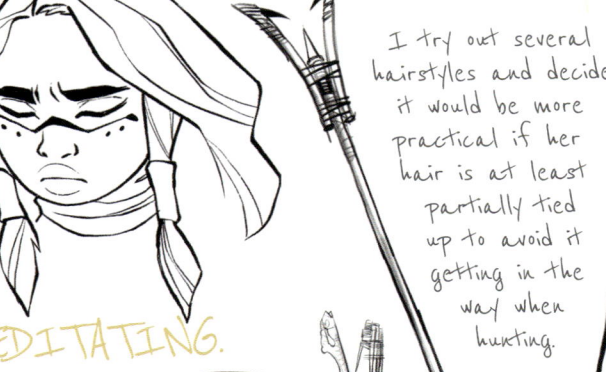

MEDITATING.

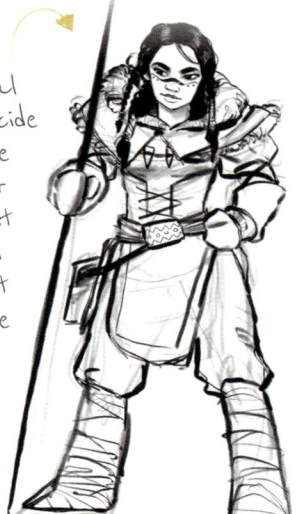

I try out several hairstyles and decide it would be more practical if her hair is at least partially tied up to avoid it getting in the way when hunting.

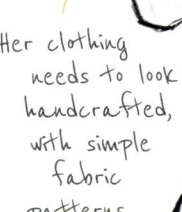

Her clothing needs to look handcrafted, with simple fabric patterns.

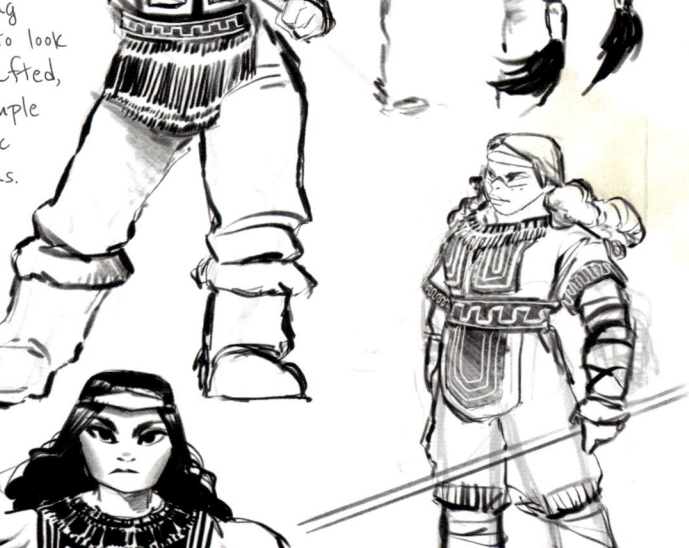

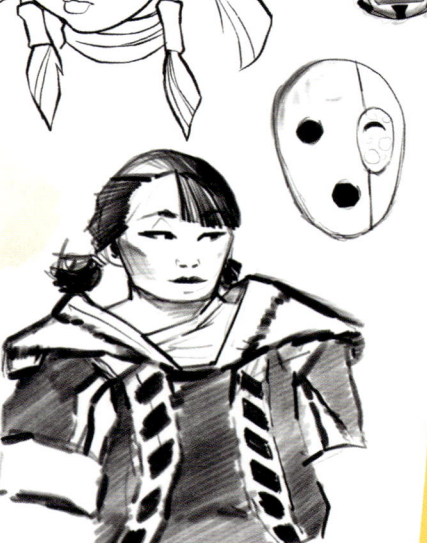

With a surprised expression, the facial features stretch out. Her eyes are wide with surprise, her mouth gaping open.

Think of the face as an elastic sheet that stretches from the top of the eyebrows to the bottom of the mouth, covering the eyes and nose with a shape like a heart. Everything is connected. When you pull one part of the face, other parts will respond.

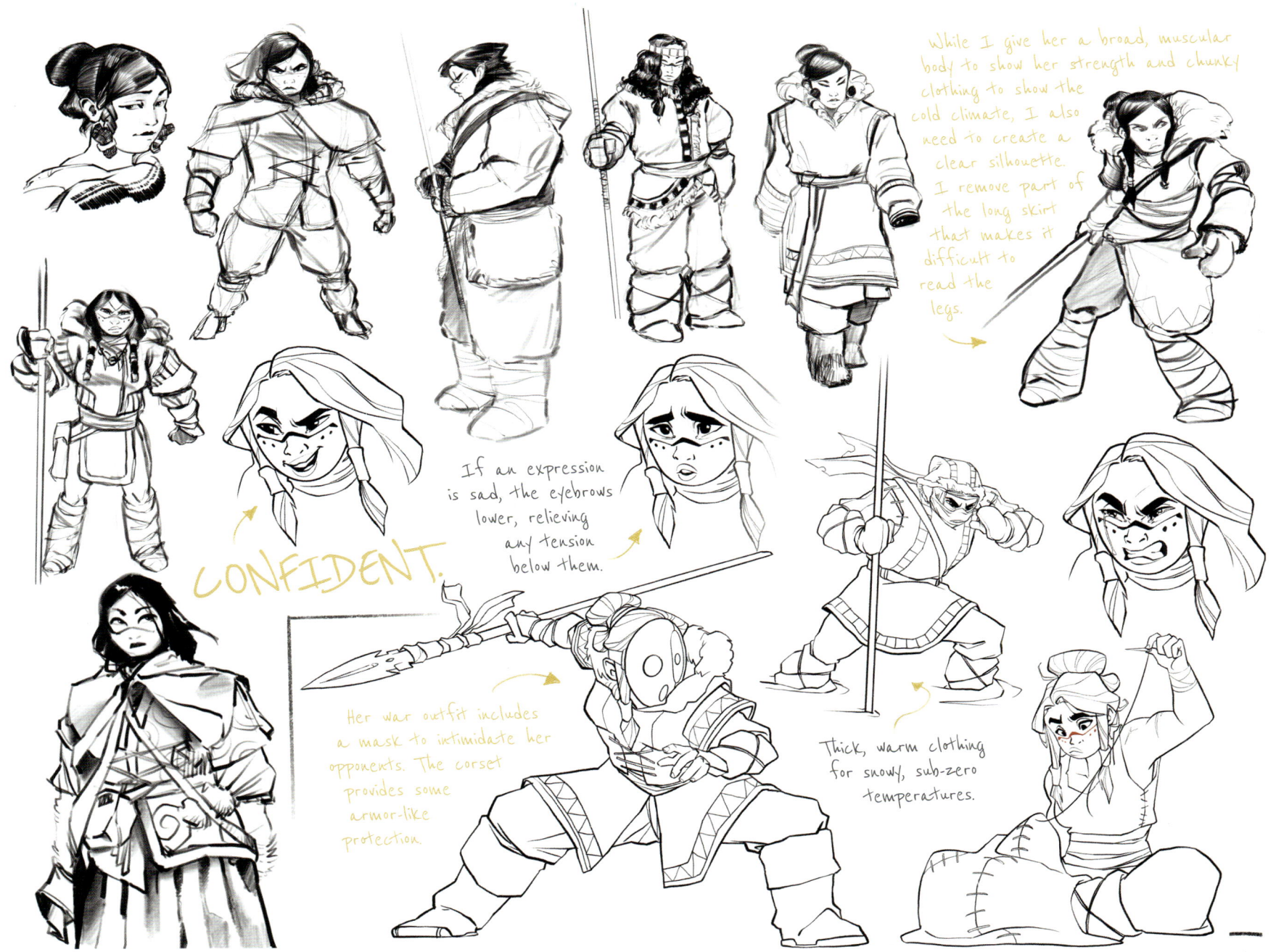

While I give her a broad, muscular body to show her strength and chunky clothing to show the cold climate, I also need to create a clear silhouette. I remove part of the long skirt that makes it difficult to read the legs.

If an expression is sad, the eyebrows lower, relieving any tension below them.

CONFIDENT.

Her war outfit includes a mask to intimidate her opponents. The corset provides some armor-like protection

Thick, warm clothing for snowy, sub-zero temperatures.

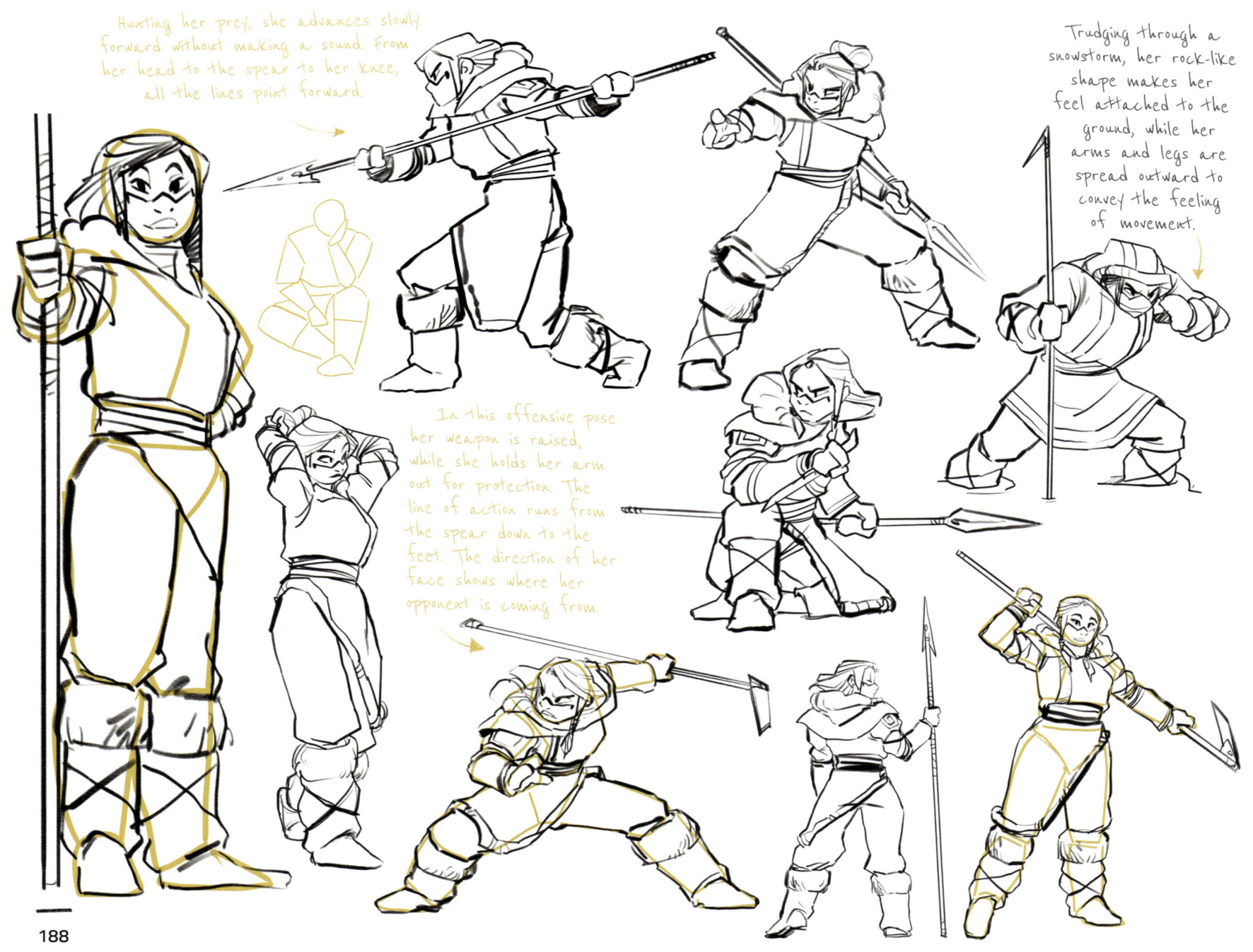

Hunting her prey, she advances slowly forward without making a sound. From her head to the spear to her knee, all the lines point forward.

Trudging through a snowstorm, her rock-like shape makes her feel attached to the ground, while her arms and legs are spread outward to convey the feeling of movement.

In this offensive pose her weapon is raised, while she holds her arm out for protection. The line of action runs from the spear down to the feet. The direction of her face shows where her opponent is coming from.

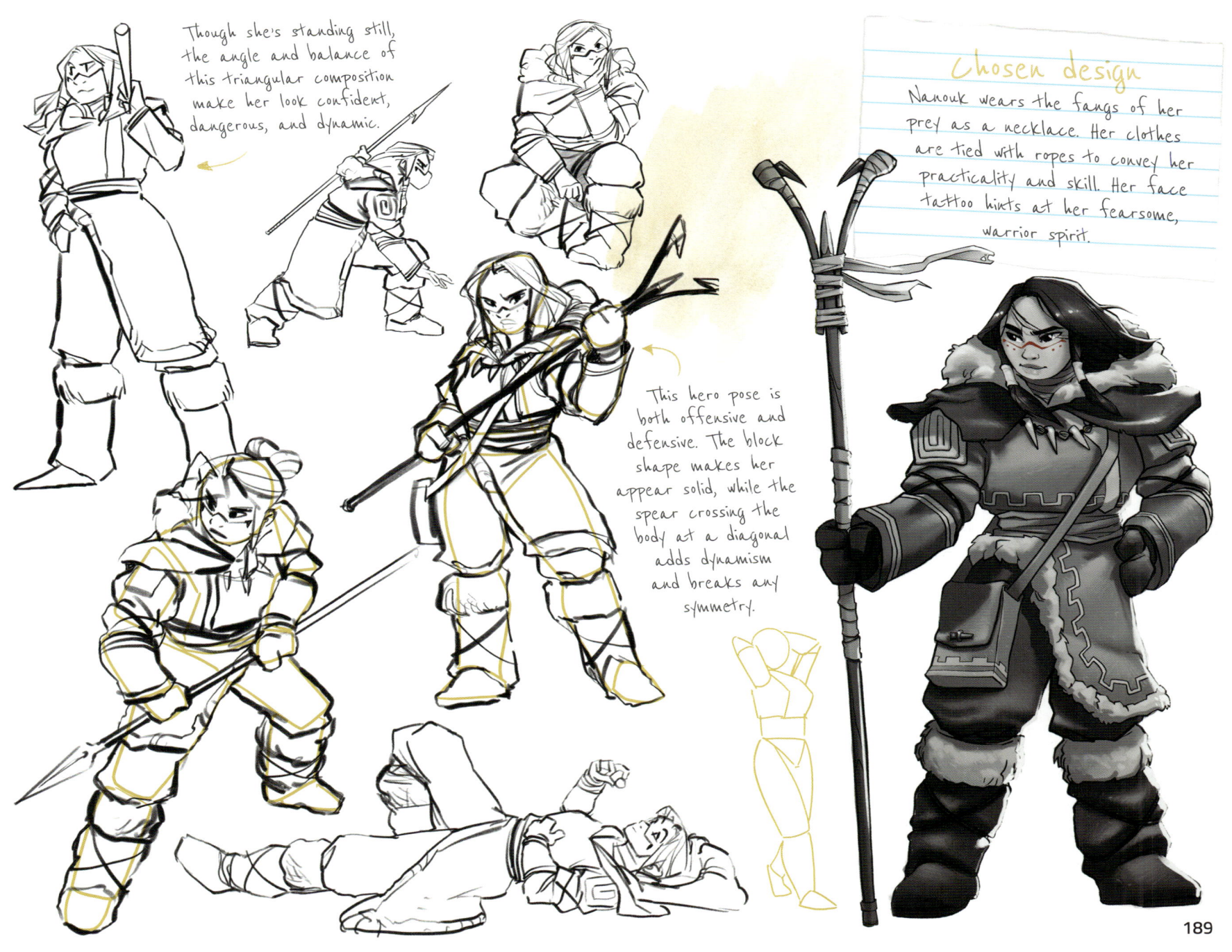

Though she's standing still, the angle and balance of this triangular composition make her look confident, dangerous, and dynamic.

Chosen design

Nanouk wears the fangs of her prey as a necklace. Her clothes are tied with ropes to convey her practicality and skill. Her face tattoo hints at her fearsome, warrior spirit.

This hero pose is both offensive and defensive. The block shape makes her appear solid, while the spear crossing the body at a diagonal adds dynamism and breaks any symmetry.

Alien warrior

THIS SKETCHBOOK BELONGS TO: Justin Runfola

In a galaxy light-years away, Milli is number 236 of 430 siblings. The women of the family are trained to become galactic heroines of the universe, while the men lead normal lives as civilians. Their species comes from a long line of warriors, celebrated for their ability to fight against evil forces in the galaxy. Curvy, short, and full-figured, Milli was kept back from training due to her physique, but an aunt trained her in secret until she was as fierce a warrior as any of her sisters. Strong-minded and courageous, she can lift 4,000 times her weight and fly through the air with ease. Having not been issued the standard royal equipment, she makes do with old, discarded equipment and armor, making her a masterful mechanic.

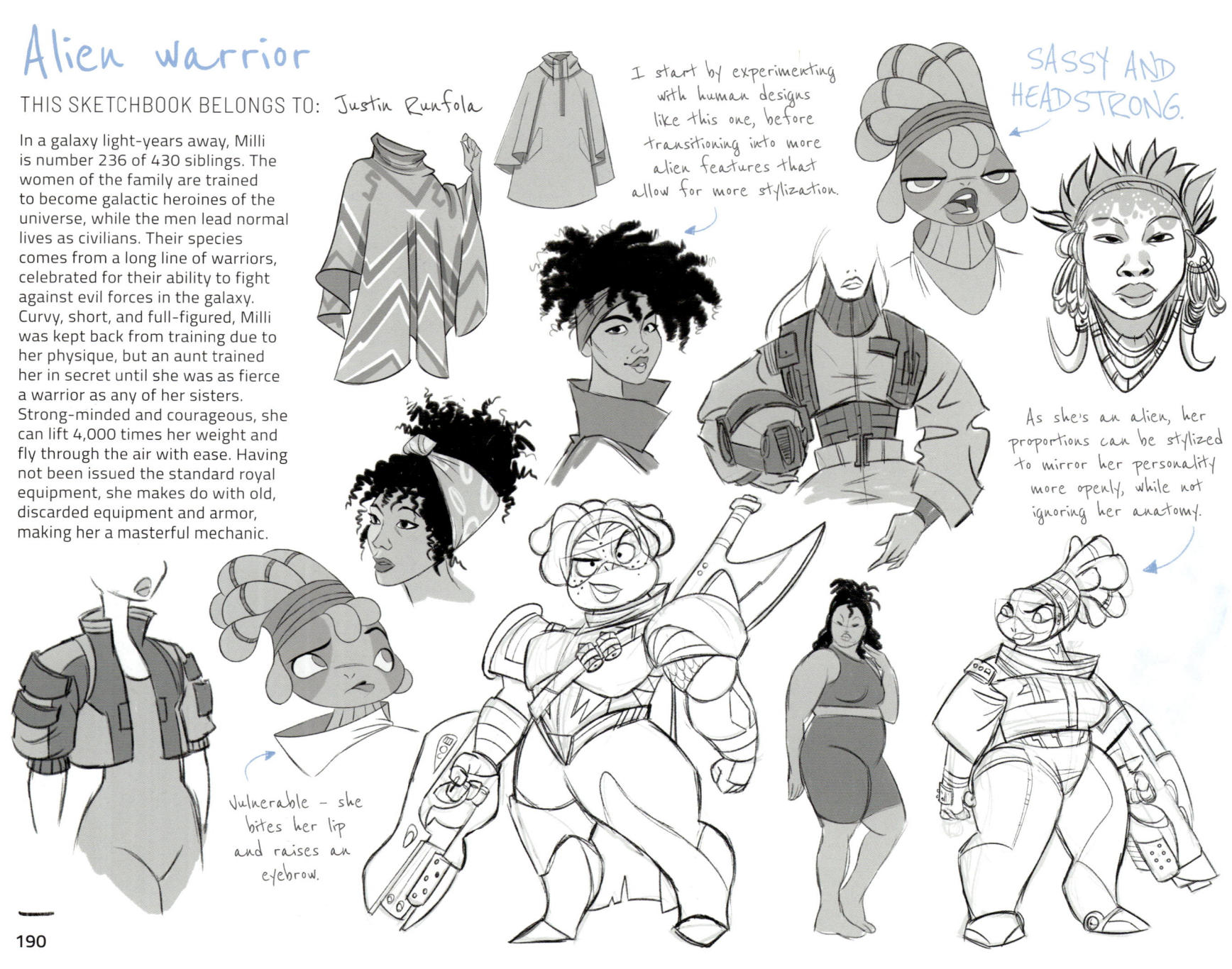

I start by experimenting with human designs like this one, before transitioning into more alien features that allow for more stylization.

SASSY AND HEADSTRONG.

As she's an alien, her proportions can be stylized to mirror her personality more openly, while not ignoring her anatomy.

Vulnerable — she bites her lip and raises an eyebrow.

190

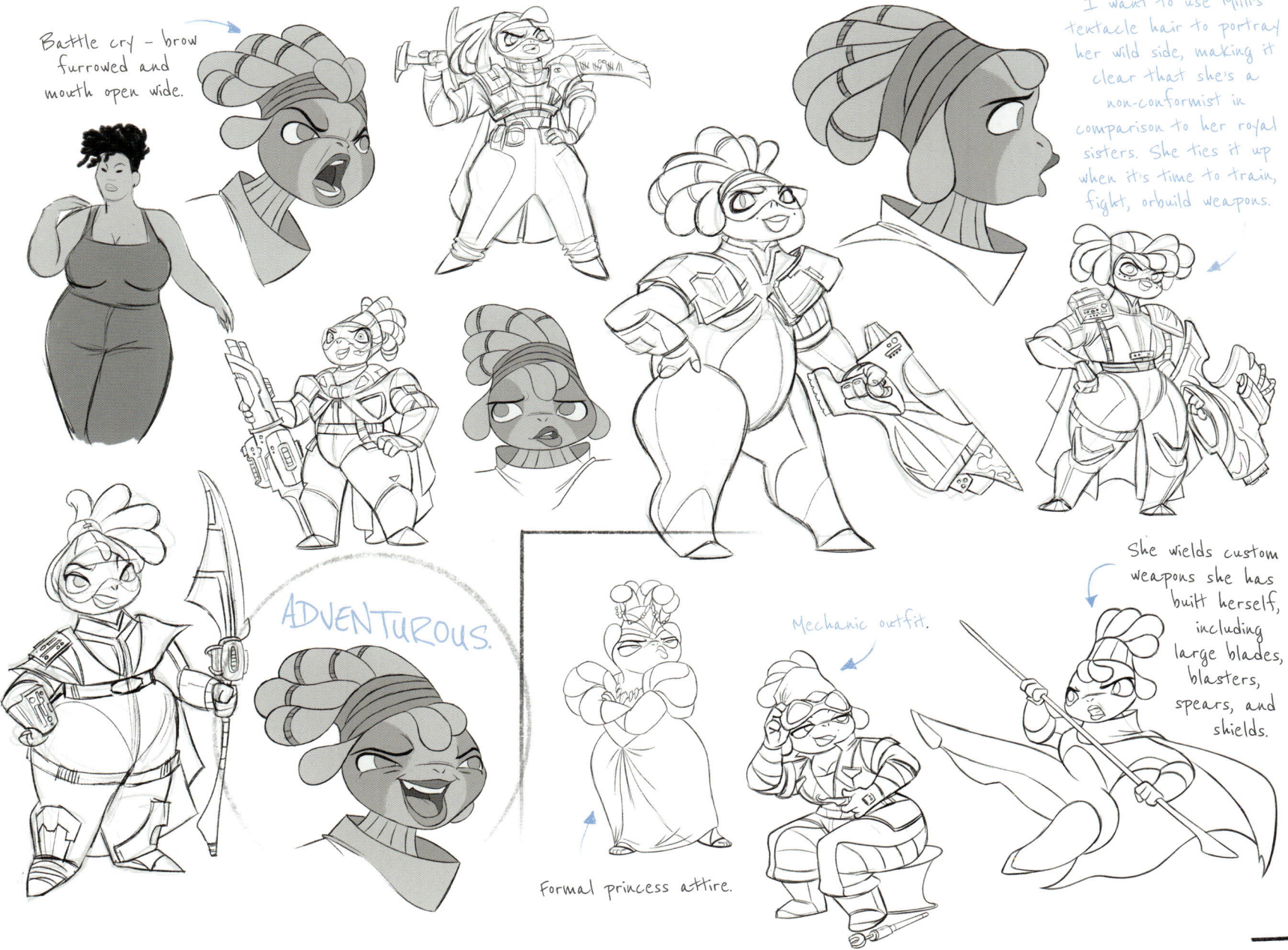

Battle cry - brow furrowed and mouth open wide.

I want to use Milli's tentacle hair to portray her wild side, making it clear that she's a non-conformist in comparison to her royal sisters. She ties it up when it's time to train, fight, or build weapons.

ADVENTUROUS.

Formal princess attire.

Mechanic outfit.

She wields custom weapons she has built herself, including large blades, blasters, spears, and shields.

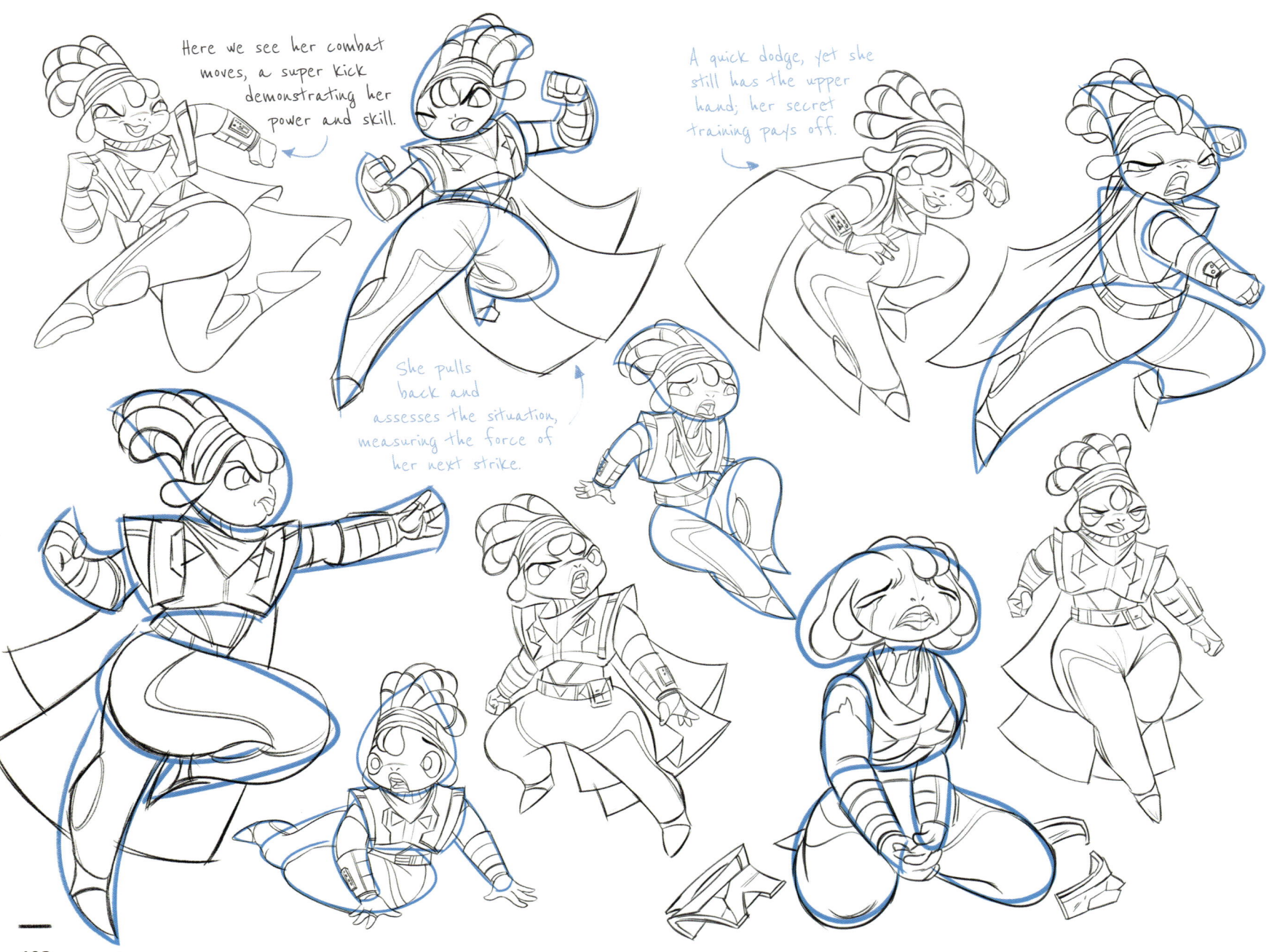

Here we see her combat moves, a super kick demonstrating her power and skill.

A quick dodge, yet she still has the upper hand; her secret training pays off.

She pulls back and assesses the situation, measuring the force of her next strike.

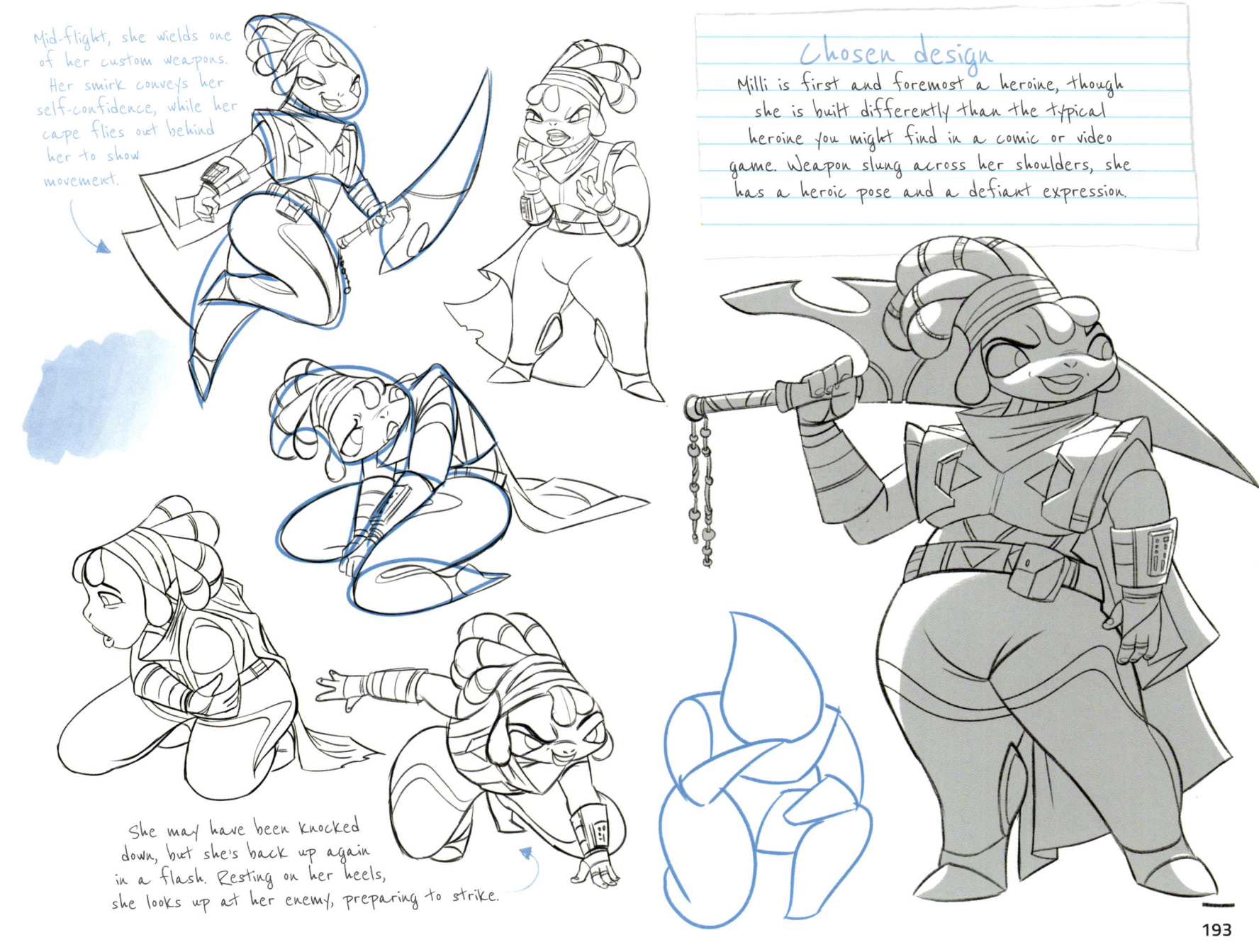

Mid-flight, she wields one of her custom weapons. Her smirk conveys her self-confidence, while her cape flies out behind her to show movement.

Milli is first and foremost a heroine, though she is built differently than the typical heroine you might find in a comic or video game. Weapon slung across her shoulders, she has a heroic pose and a defiant expression.

She may have been knocked down, but she's back up again in a flash. Resting on her heels, she looks up at her enemy, preparing to strike.

Snake charmer

THIS SKETCHBOOK BELONGS TO: Noor Sofi

Growing up in the Rajasthan region of India, Anita is a desert dweller and member of the Kalbeliya tribe, the original snake charmers and dancers who performed for royalty. She grew up learning the traditional dance of her culture and it is part of who she is. Snake charming is typically done by the men in the tribe, but Anita has learned the skill as well and sometimes dances with her cobra. Wild and untamable, she is an adventure seeker and creative thinker with a fiery spirit. She dreams of performing for the world and bringing respect and recognition for her tribe's history.

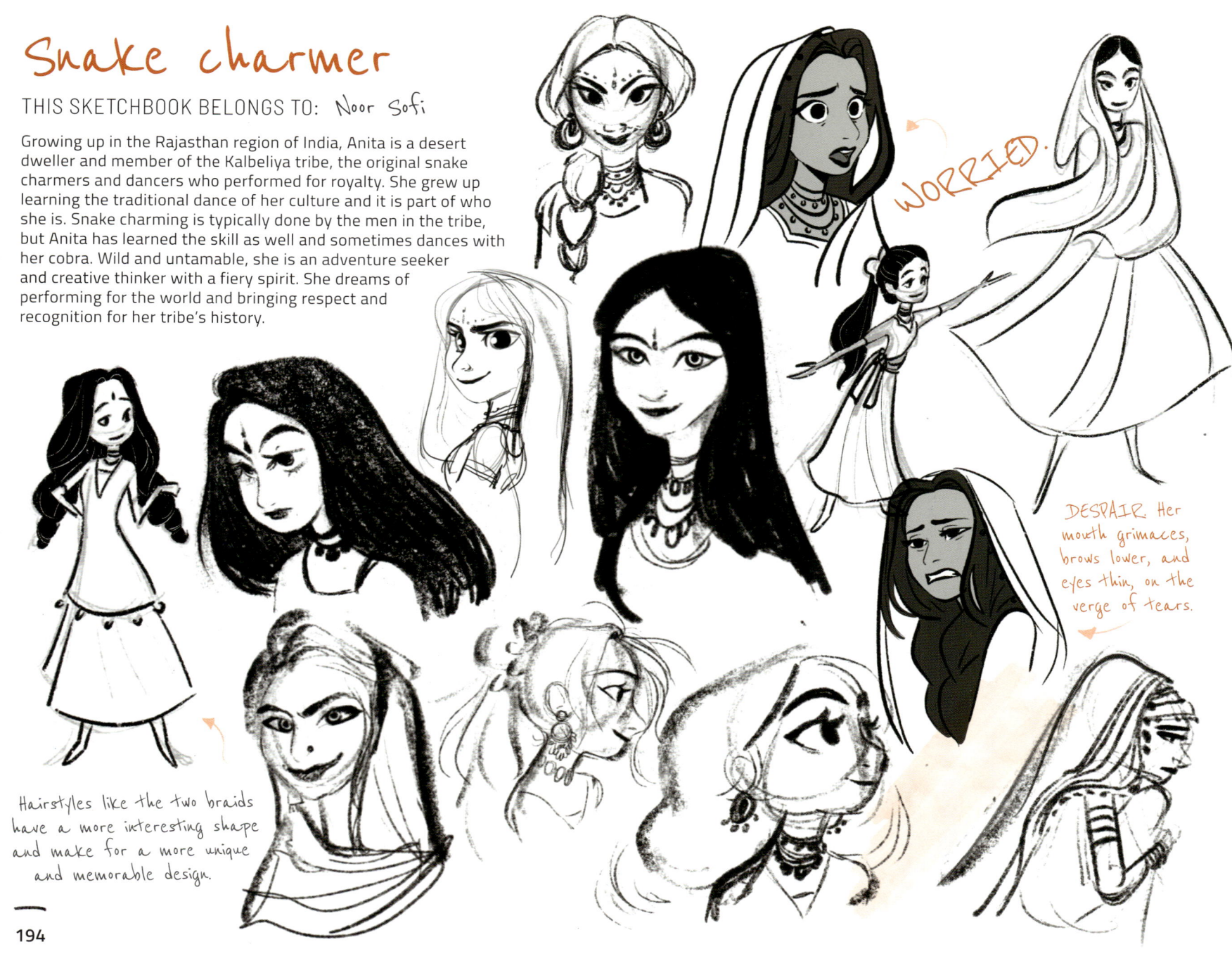

WORRIED.

DESPAIR. Her mouth grimaces, brows lower, and eyes thin, on the verge of tears.

Hairstyles like the two braids have a more interesting shape and make for a more unique and memorable design.

194

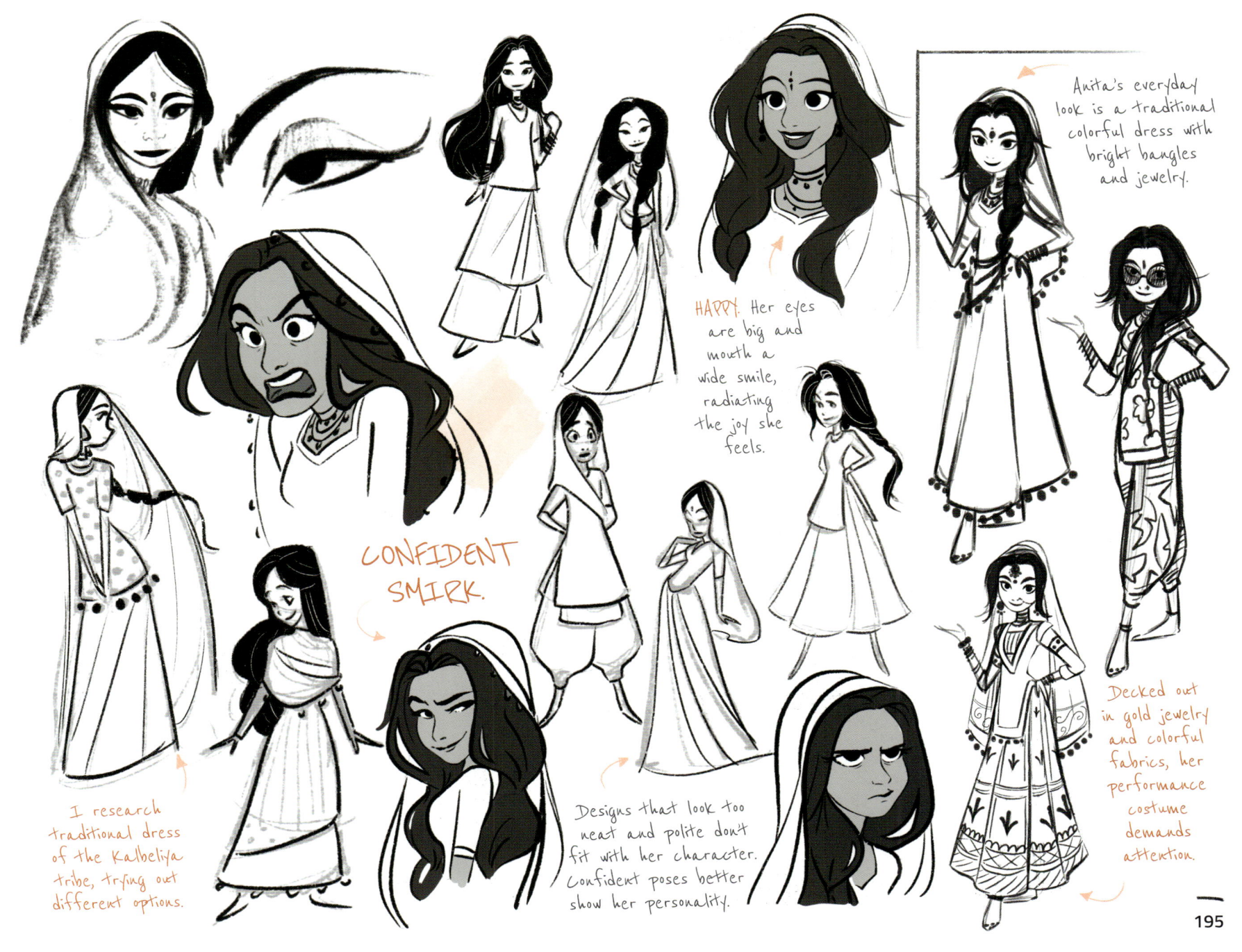

Anita's everyday look is a traditional colorful dress with bright bangles and jewelry.

HAPPY. Her eyes are big and mouth a wide smile, radiating the joy she feels.

CONFIDENT SMIRK.

I research traditional dress of the Kalbeliya tribe, trying out different options.

Designs that look too neat and polite don't fit with her character. Confident poses better show her personality.

Decked out in gold jewelry and colorful fabrics, her performance costume demands attention.

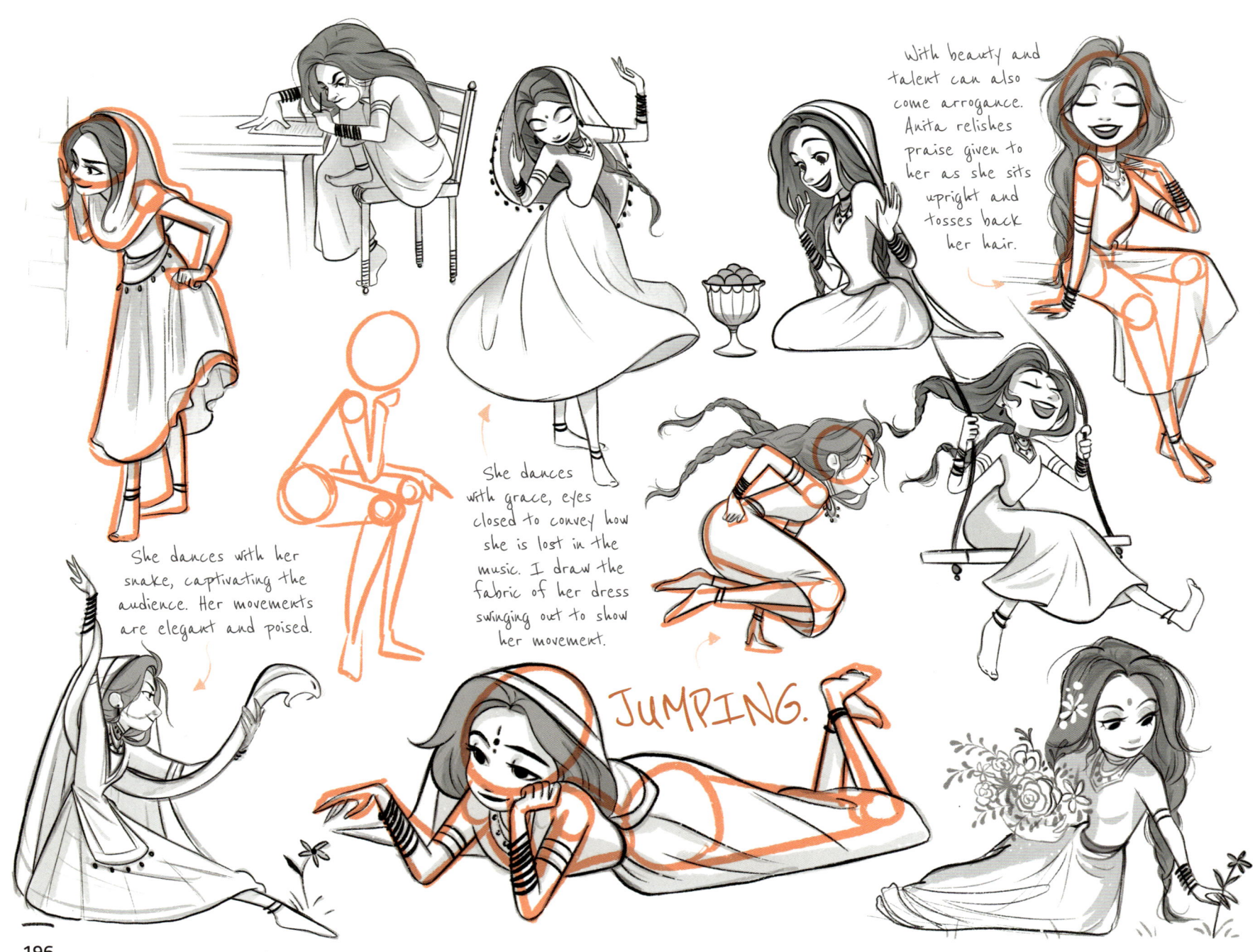

With beauty and talent can also come arrogance. Anita relishes praise given to her as she sits upright and tosses back her hair.

She dances with her snake, captivating the audience. Her movements are elegant and poised.

She dances with grace, eyes closed to convey how she is lost in the music. I draw the fabric of her dress swinging out to show her movement.

JUMPING.

196

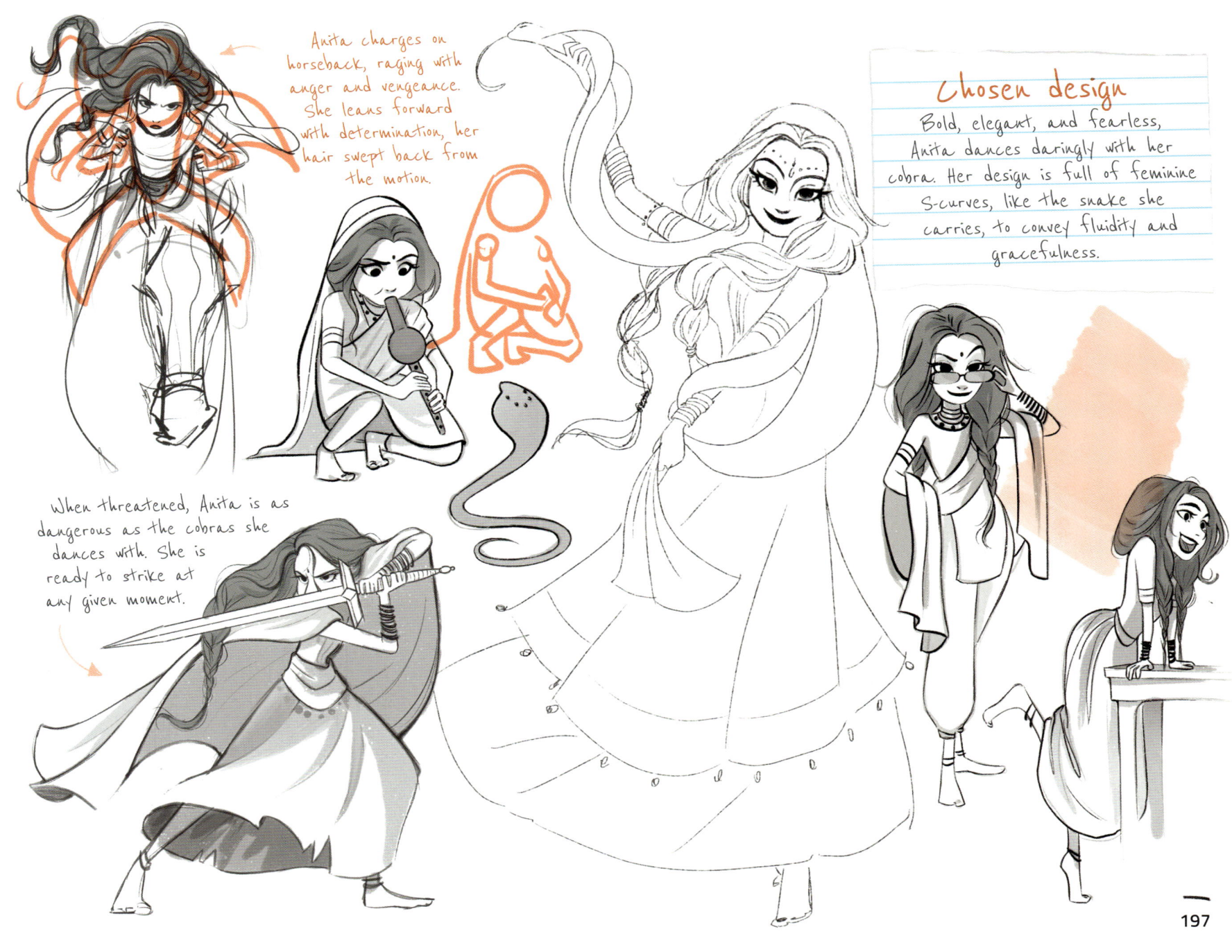

Anita charges on horseback, raging with anger and vengeance. She leans forward with determination, her hair swept back from the motion.

Chosen design

Bold, elegant, and fearless, Anita dances daringly with her cobra. Her design is full of feminine S-curves, like the snake she carries, to convey fluidity and gracefulness.

When threatened, Anita is as dangerous as the cobras she dances with. She is ready to strike at any given moment.

Energy superheroine

THIS SKETCHBOOK BELONGS TO: Eva Stöcker "EvaYabai"

Nina lost her arm in a car accident as a child and has experienced phantom pain ever since. One day she discovered the ability to transform the phantom pain into a super flexible arm made from fiery energy. She found other people who had also developed superpowers through special genomes and became part of their secret society to fight against evil forces. Agile, strong, intelligent, and cunning, she doesn't try to hide her arm but embraces the power that comes with it.

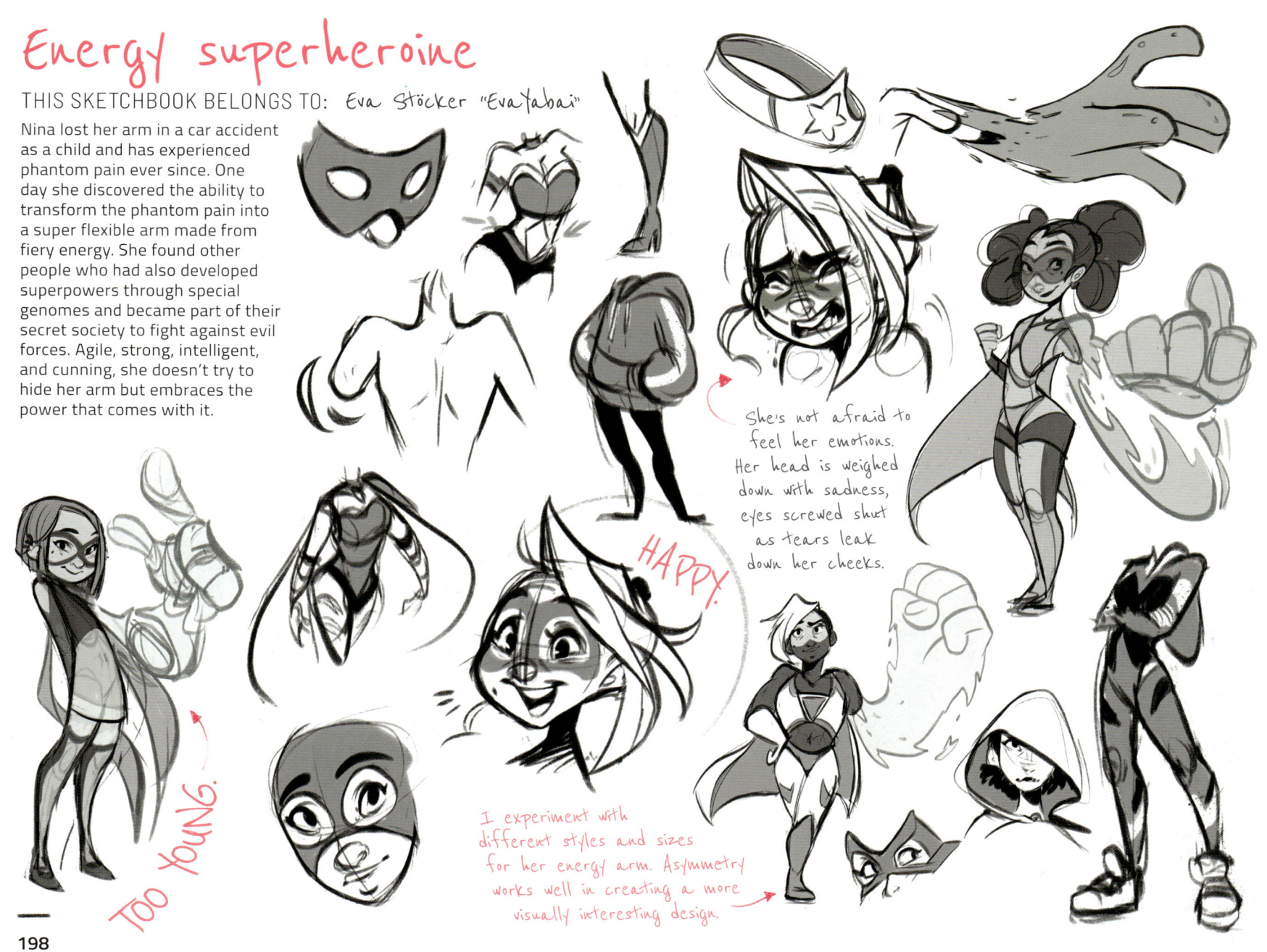

She's not afraid to feel her emotions. Her head is weighed down with sadness, eyes screwed shut as tears leak down her cheeks.

HAPPY!

TOO YOUNG.

I experiment with different styles and sizes for her energy arm. Asymmetry works well in creating a more visually interesting design.

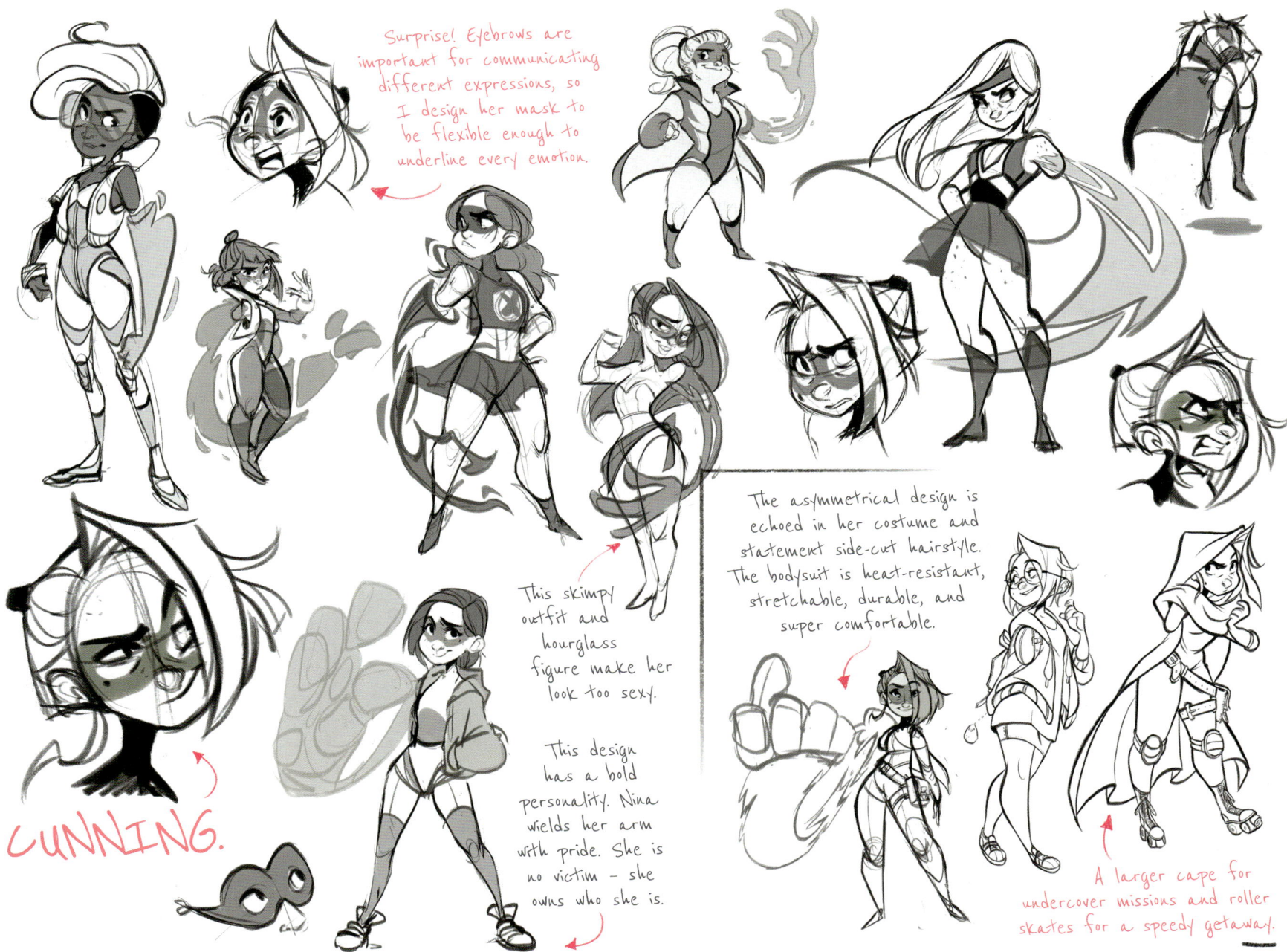

Surprise! Eyebrows are important for communicating different expressions, so I design her mask to be flexible enough to underline every emotion.

The asymmetrical design is echoed in her costume and statement side-cut hairstyle. The bodysuit is heat-resistant, stretchable, durable, and super comfortable.

This skimpy outfit and hourglass figure make her look too sexy.

This design has a bold personality. Nina wields her arm with pride. She is no victim — she owns who she is.

CUNNING.

A larger cape for undercover missions and roller skates for a speedy getaway.

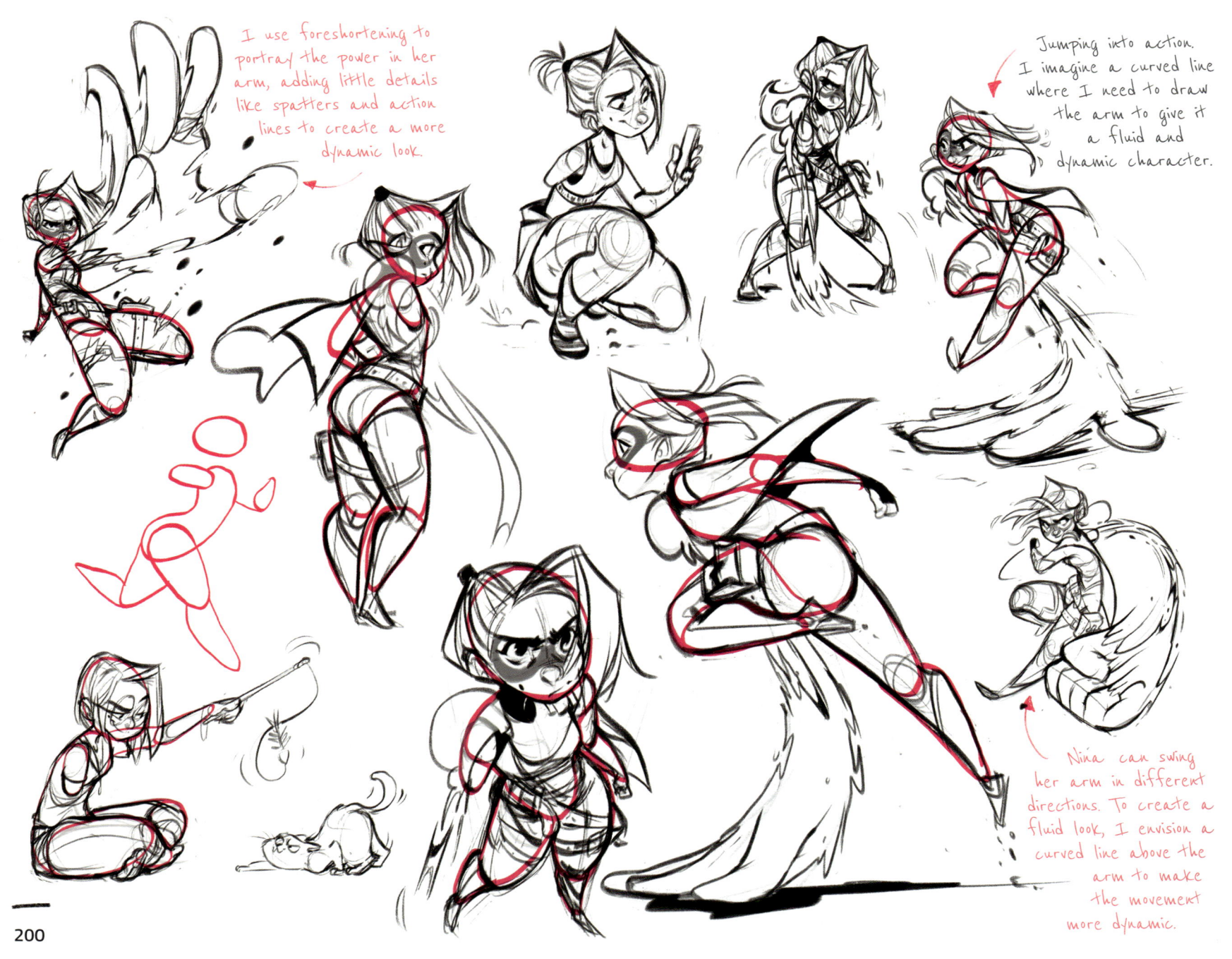

I use foreshortening to portray the power in her arm, adding little details like spatters and action lines to create a more dynamic look.

Jumping into action. I imagine a curved line where I need to draw the arm to give it a fluid and dynamic character.

Nina can swing her arm in different directions. To create a fluid look, I envision a curved line above the arm to make the movement more dynamic.

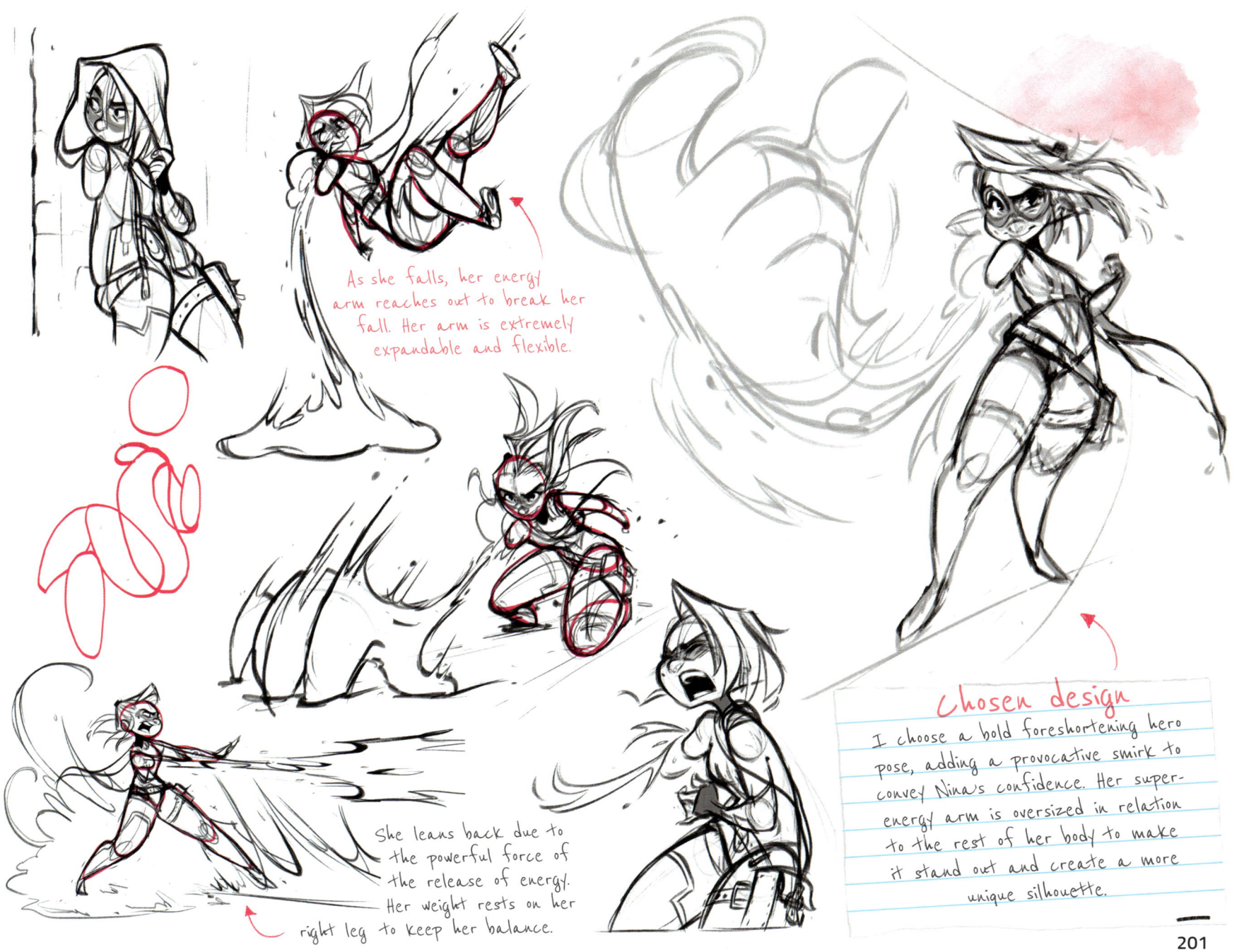

As she falls, her energy arm reaches out to break her fall. Her arm is extremely expandable and flexible.

She leans back due to the powerful force of the release of energy. Her weight rests on her right leg to keep her balance.

chosen design

I choose a bold foreshortening hero pose, adding a provocative smirk to convey Nina's confidence. Her super-energy arm is oversized in relation to the rest of her body to make it stand out and create a more unique silhouette.

Alien empress

THIS SKETCHBOOK BELONGS TO: Gary Villarreal

Deorah is a powerful alien empress from a purple bloodline of Caranians, known for their intelligence and peaceful ways. Their home planet is a jungle utopia surrounded by the vast Urakan desert, which provides essential minerals. Deorah is naturally loving and empathetic, but is also direct and knows when to be authoritative when things get out of hand. She can be recognized by her ornate royal garments, ceremonial jewelry, and large decorative headpiece.

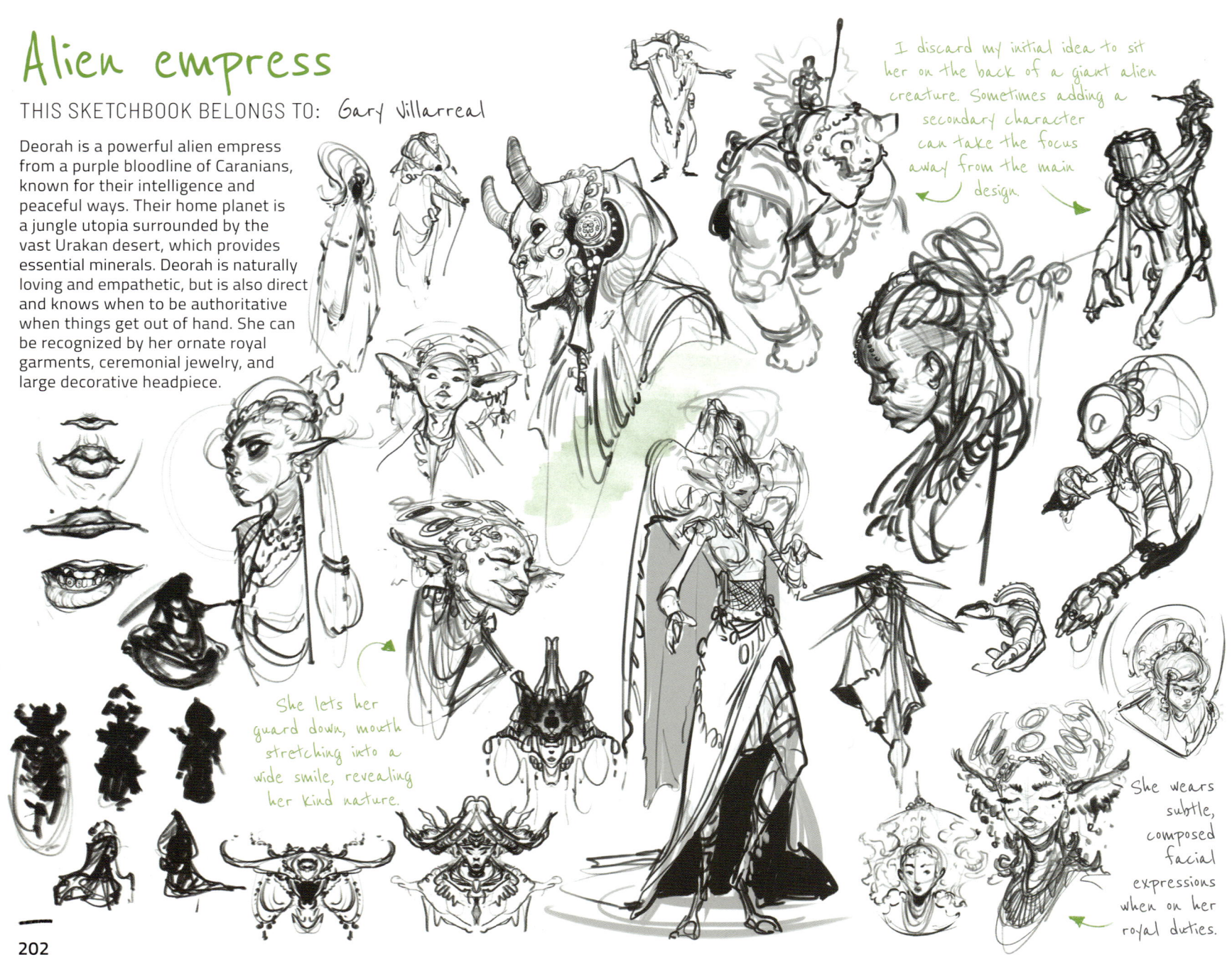

I discard my initial idea to sit her on the back of a giant alien creature. Sometimes adding a secondary character can take the focus away from the main design.

She lets her guard down, mouth stretching into a wide smile, revealing her kind nature.

She wears subtle, composed facial expressions when on her royal duties.

202

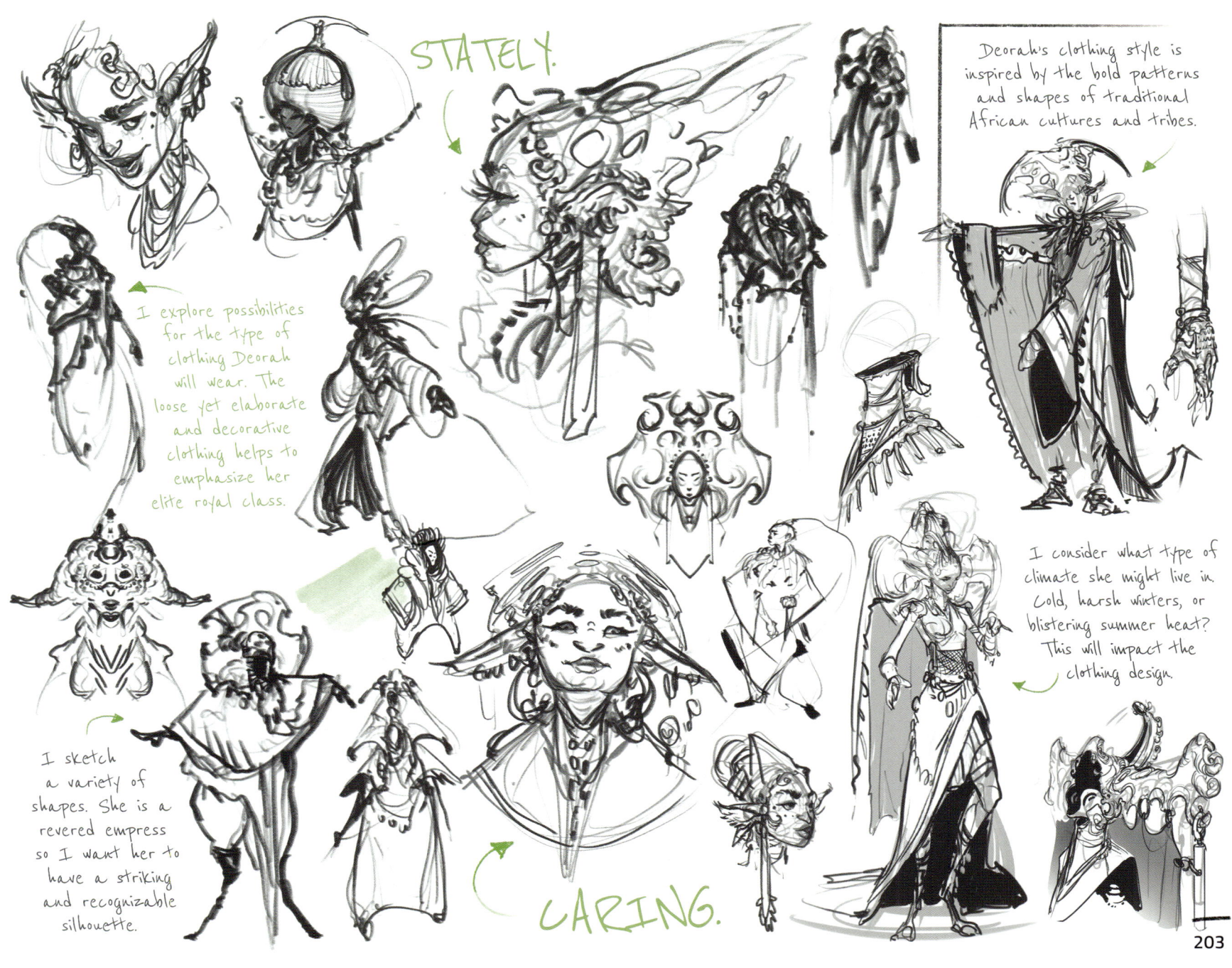

STATELY.

Deorah's clothing style is inspired by the bold patterns and shapes of traditional African cultures and tribes.

I explore possibilities for the type of clothing Deorah will wear. The loose yet elaborate and decorative clothing helps to emphasize her elite royal class.

I consider what type of climate she might live in. Cold, harsh winters, or blistering summer heat? This will impact the clothing design.

I sketch a variety of shapes. She is a revered empress so I want her to have a striking and recognizable silhouette.

CARING.

203

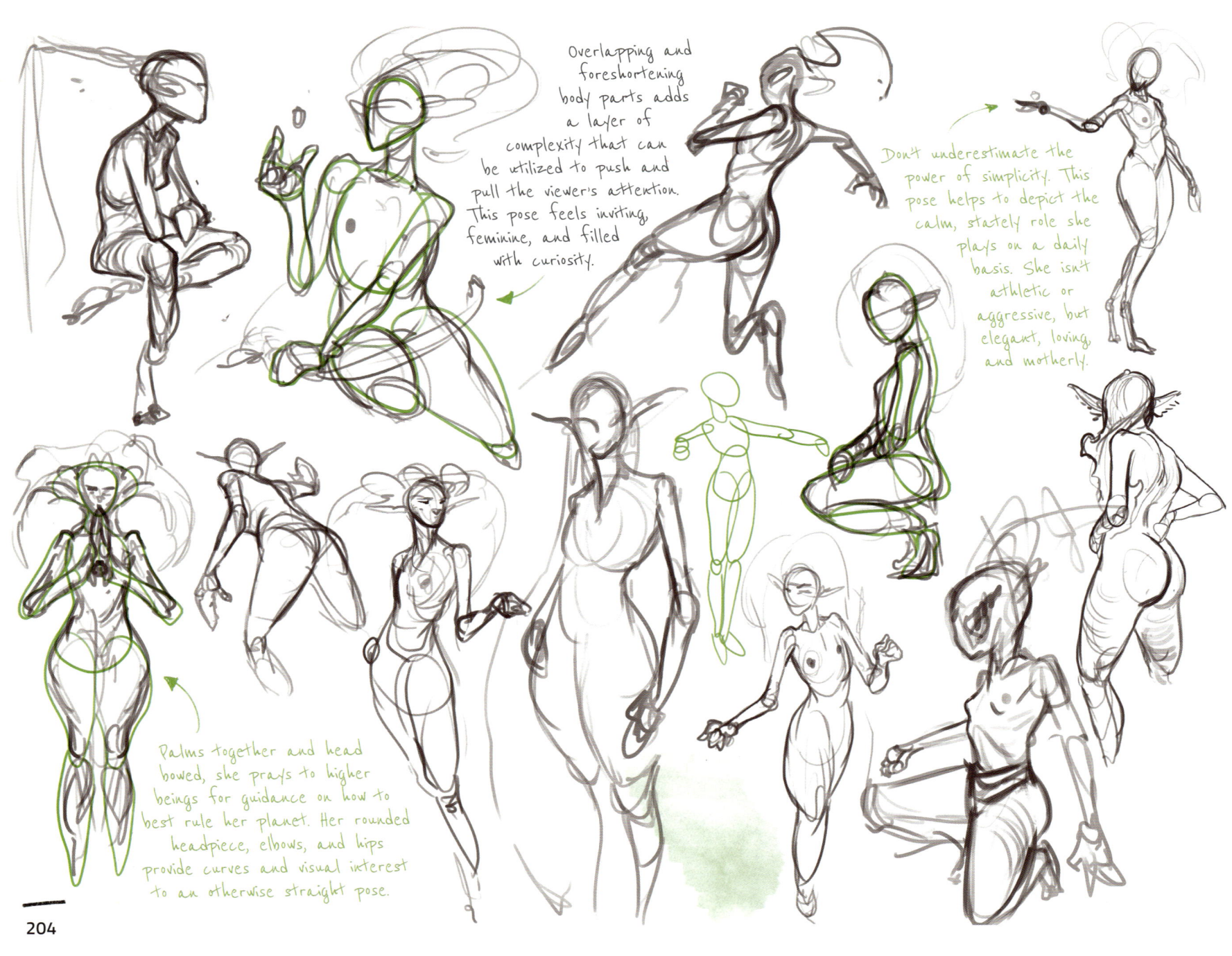

Overlapping and foreshortening body parts adds a layer of complexity that can be utilized to push and pull the viewer's attention. This pose feels inviting, feminine, and filled with curiosity.

Don't underestimate the power of simplicity. This pose helps to depict the calm, stately role she plays on a daily basis. She isn't athletic or aggressive, but elegant, loving, and motherly.

Palms together and head bowed, she prays to higher beings for guidance on how to best rule her planet. Her rounded headpiece, elbows, and hips provide curves and visual interest to an otherwise straight pose.

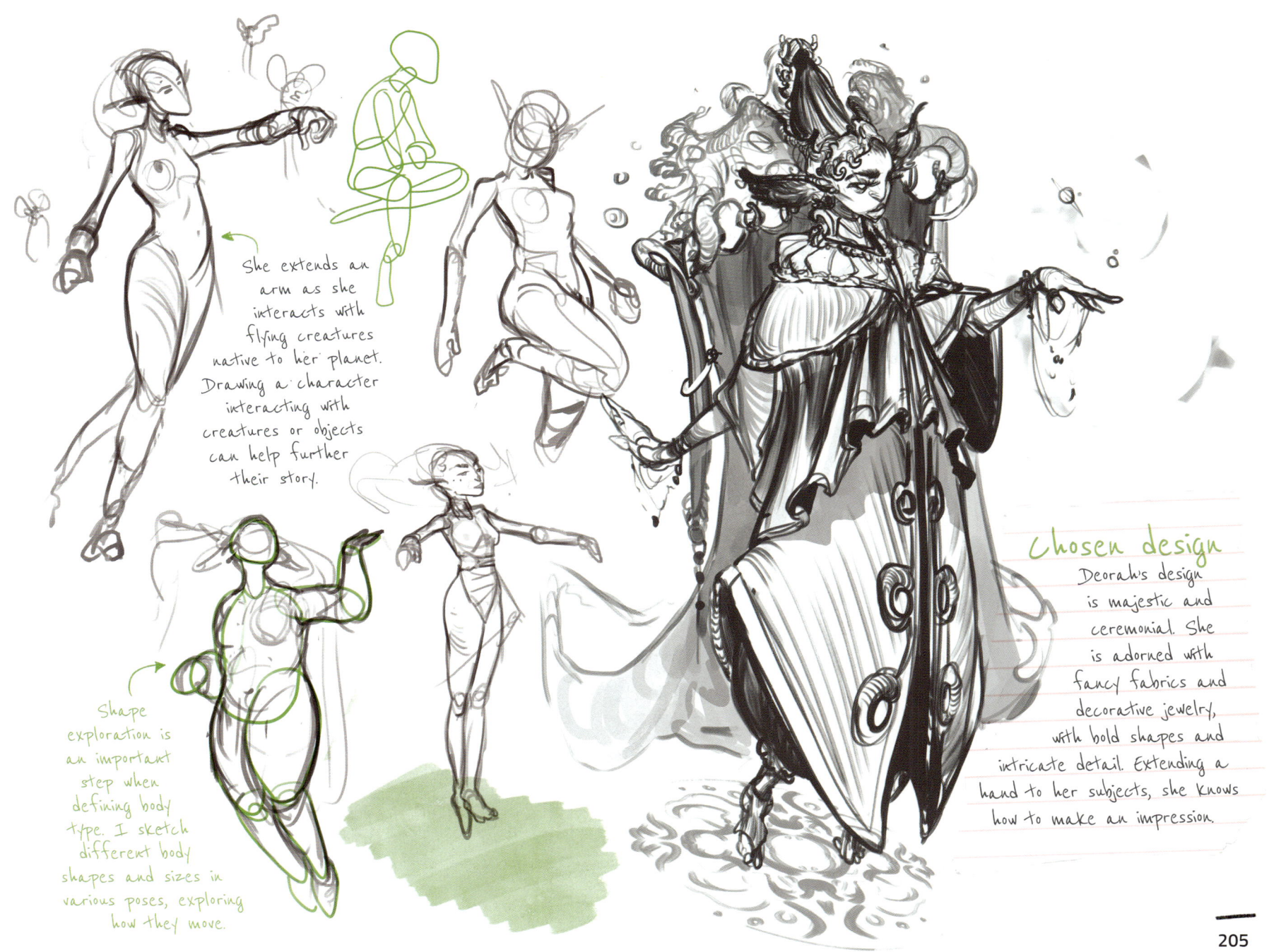

She extends an arm as she interacts with flying creatures native to her planet. Drawing a character interacting with creatures or objects can help further their story.

Shape exploration is an important step when defining body type. I sketch different body shapes and sizes in various poses, exploring how they move.

Chosen design
Deorah's design is majestic and ceremonial. She is adorned with fancy fabrics and decorative jewelry, with bold shapes and intricate detail. Extending a hand to her subjects, she knows how to make an impression.

Elfin princess

THIS SKETCHBOOK BELONGS TO: Erika Wiseman

Anais is a rebellious elfin princess who longs for adventure. She has long, curly hair that she leaves long and untamed. Her go-to clothes are comfortable enough to adventure in, yet smart enough that others can infer her royal lineage. Though she doesn't go looking for trouble, her mischievous nature often leads her to it! She possesses magical abilities that allow her to influence nature. Using these abilities she is able to traverse the forest with ease. She loves the thrill of discovering something new!

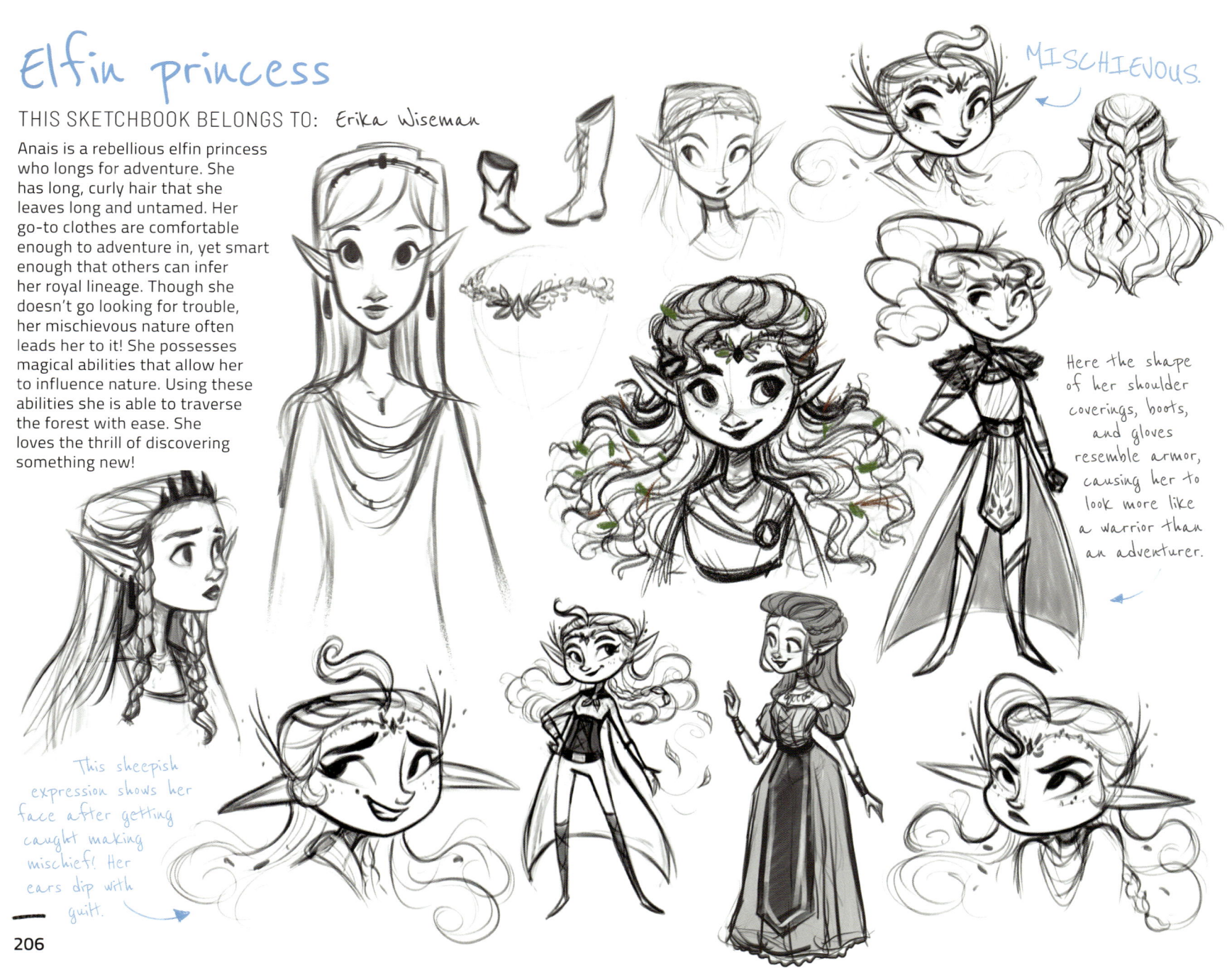

MISCHIEVOUS.

Here the shape of her shoulder coverings, boots, and gloves resemble armor, causing her to look more like a warrior than an adventurer.

This sheepish expression shows her face after getting caught making mischief! Her ears drip with guilt.

206

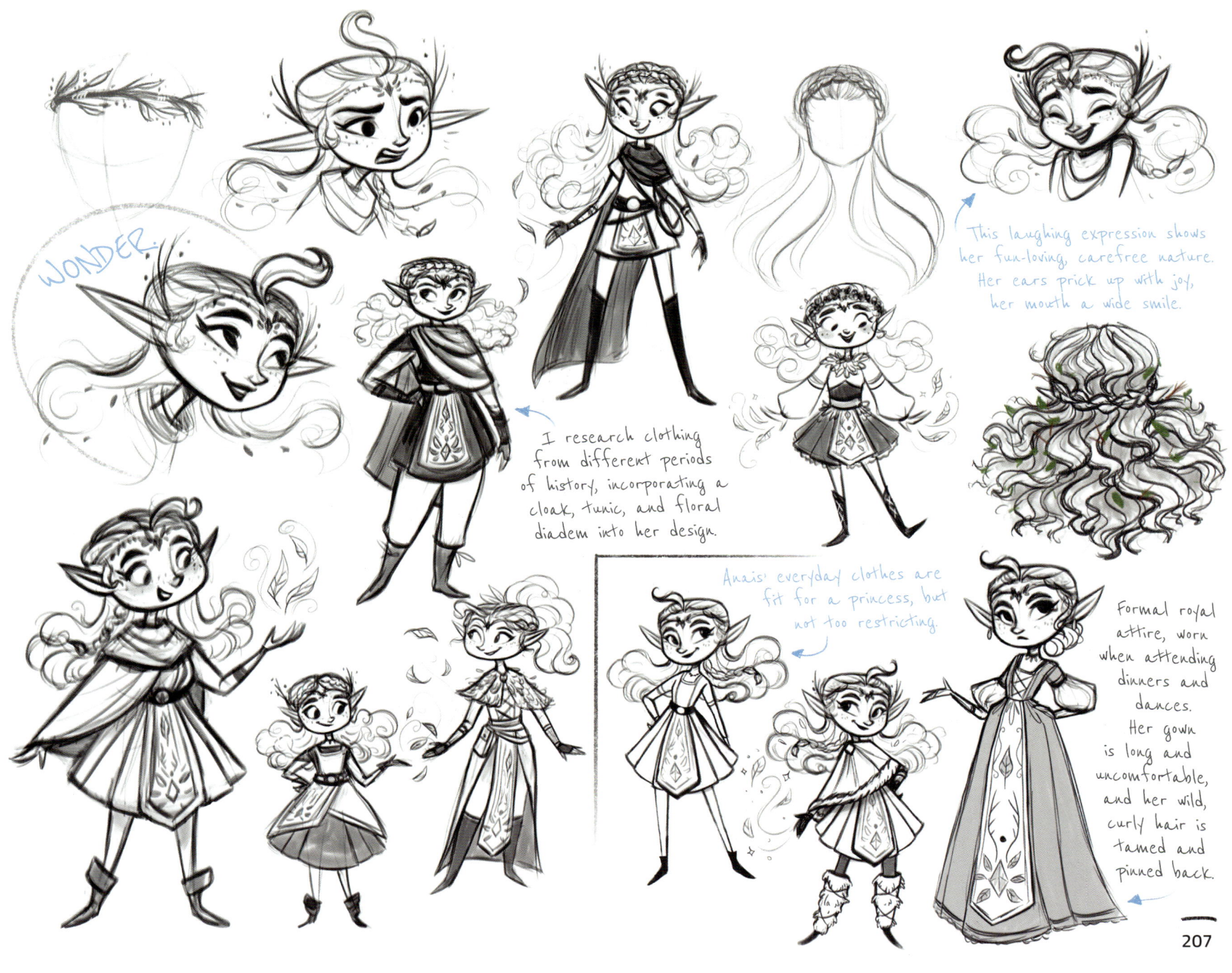

WONDER

This laughing expression shows her fun-loving, carefree nature. Her ears prick up with joy, her mouth a wide smile.

I research clothing from different periods of history, incorporating a cloak, tunic, and floral diadem into her design.

Anais' everyday clothes are fit for a princess, but not too restricting.

Formal royal attire, worn when attending dinners and dances. Her gown is long and uncomfortable, and her wild, curly hair is tamed and pinned back.

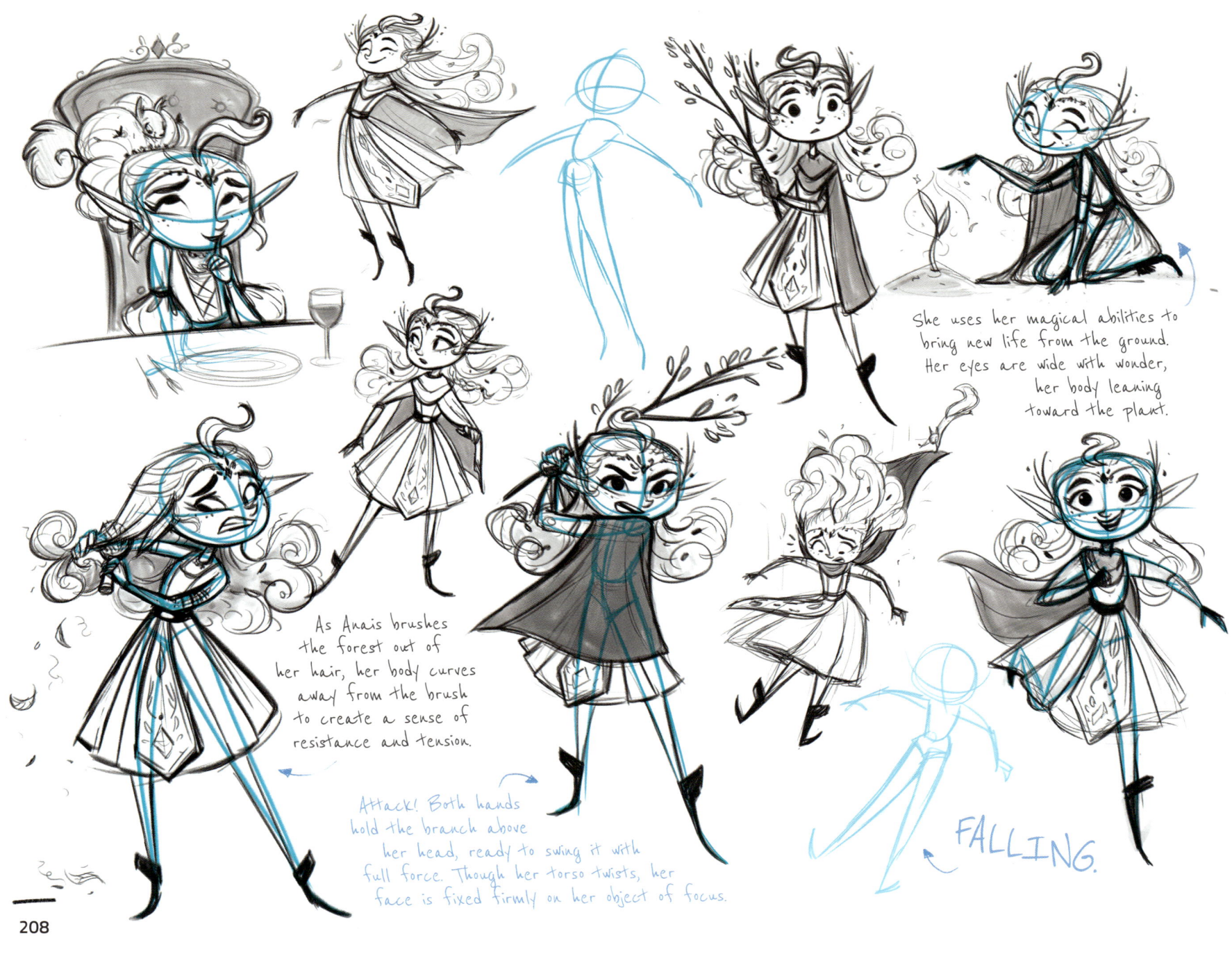

She uses her magical abilities to bring new life from the ground. Her eyes are wide with wonder, her body leaning toward the plant.

As Anais brushes the forest out of her hair, her body curves away from the brush to create a sense of resistance and tension.

Attack! Both hands hold the branch above her head, ready to swing it with full force. Though her torso twists, her face is fixed firmly on her object of focus.

FALLING.

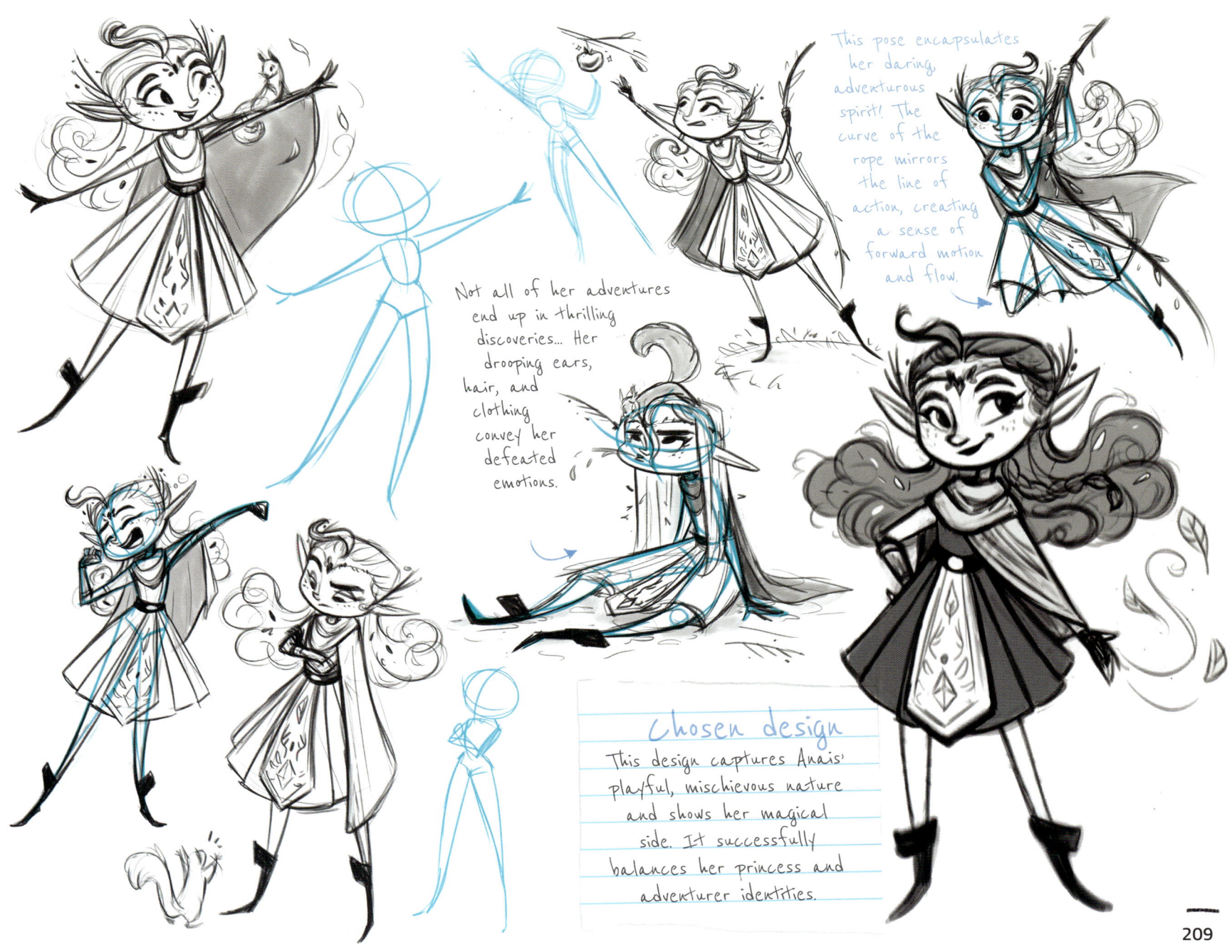

This pose encapsulates her daring, adventurous spirit! The curve of the rope mirrors the line of action, creating a sense of forward motion and flow.

Not all of her adventures end up in thrilling discoveries... Her drooping ears, hair, and clothing convey her defeated emotions.

Chosen design

This design captures Anais' playful, mischievous nature and shows her magical side. It successfully balances her princess and adventurer identities.

Contributors

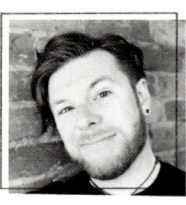

Martin Abel
Independent artist
martinabelart.com

Martin is an Australian artist who works on board games, creates YouTube content, and scribbles fantasy art. He wants to live in a magical faerie realm, but only if there is pizza and coffee.

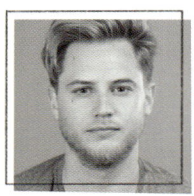

Chris Ables
Character designer, illustrator & visual development artist
chrisablesart.com

Chris is a Los Angeles-based illustrator and visual development artist with over ten years' experience working in the animation, film, television, and publishing industries.

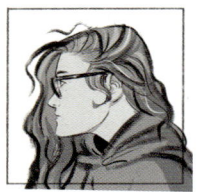

Amagoia Agirre
Illustrator
lacont.artstation.com

Amagoia is a freelance illustrator and comic artist based in Spain. She is currently working on various illustrated books and comics, as well as personal projects.

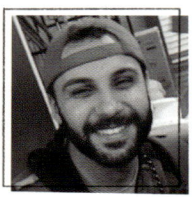

Ahmed Aldoori
YouTuber & concept artist
ahmedaldoori.com

Ahmed graduated from ArtCenter College of Design, California, before going on to work as a concept artist. He runs a YouTube channel where he shares tutorials, podcasts, and reviews.

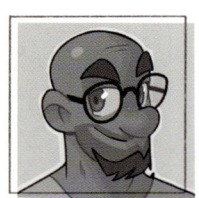

Dado "dadotronic" Almeida
2D artist
dadoalmeida.com

Inspired by 90s video-game artwork, Dado's artwork is a celebration of this golden era, as well as an attempt to transform his nostalgia into something fresher for the new generation.

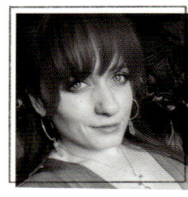

Olga "Asu Rocks" Andriyenko
Character designer, illustrator, concept & story artist
asurocks.de

Olga has been drawing characters and stories all her life. After a successful career in games, she now focuses on animation and telling her own stories.

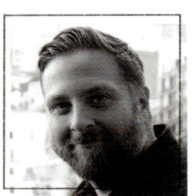

Brett Bean
Character designer & comic artist
brettbean.com

Brett is the creator of the *Zoo Patrol Squad* series. His work has been featured in film, TV, games, and comics for Disney, DreamWorks, Riot Games, Jim Henson's Creature Shop, Marvel, Penguin Books, Scholastic, and more.

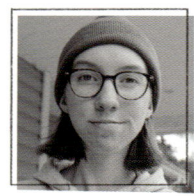

Allison Berg
Character & visual development artist
allisonberg2.wixsite.com/portfolio

Allison is a freelance character designer and visual development artist. She is currently studying at the University of Victoria, Canada, majoring in Computer Science and minoring in Visual Arts.

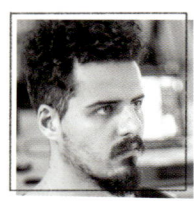

Tano Bonfanti
Concept artist
artstation.com/tanobonfanti

Tano is a concept artist based in Santa Fe, Argentina, working for the entertainment industry. He studied architecture before pursuing a career in concept art and loves games and movies.

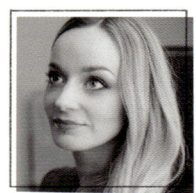

Laura Braga
Comic book artist
instagram.com/laura_braga.art

Laura attended the International School of Comics and the Disney Academy. She has worked as a storyboard artist, illustrator, and colorist, and as a comic book artist for DC Comics, Archie Comics, and Marvel.

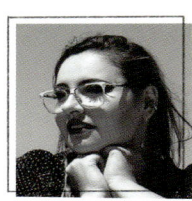

Devon Bragg
Background designer & character designer
devonbraggart.myportfolio.com
Originally from Maryland, Devon currently works for Nickelodeon studio in California as a background designer on *Middlemost Post*. She enjoys character designing, background painting, and developing shows.

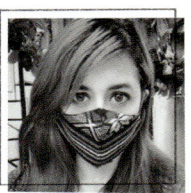

Eva Cabrera
Comic artist & illustrator
behance.net/evacabrera
Eva is a Latina comic artist, Will Eisner and GLAAD Award nominee, and co-founder of the Mexican studio Boudika Comics. She likes magic and nature, and shares her experiences on YouTube.

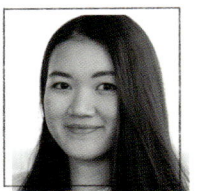

Laura Catrinella
Illustrator & character designer
lauracatrinella.com
Born and raised in Indonesia, Laura pursues her career as an illustrator and character designer. She currently works in a game studio and lives in Vancouver with her two dachshunds.

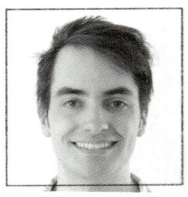

Thomas Chamberlain - Keen
Character concept artist
artstation.com/tck
Thomas is a character concept artist at Playground Games, working on the next *Fable*. He loves all things creative, including music, carving, crocheting, and cooking.

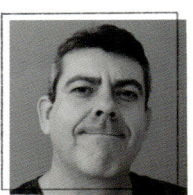

Sandro Cleuzo
Character designer & animator
inspectorcleuzo.blogspot.com
Sandro is a Brazilian self-taught animator and character designer. He has worked on many films, including *Anastasia*, *The Emperor's New Groove*, *Fantasia 2000*, *Mary Poppins Returns*, and *Klaus*.

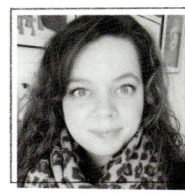

Sarah Conradsen
Illustrator
sarahconradsen.com
Sarah is a children's book illustrator and character designer working in print and animation.

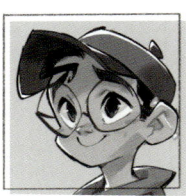

Russell Del Socorro
Character designer
artstation.com/russelldelsocorro
Russell is a Toronto-based character designer and illustrator for animation and video games.

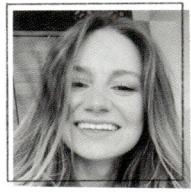

Magdalina Dianova
Character designer
instagram.com/magdalina.dianova
Magdalina is a self-taught character designer working in the animation industry and creating Patreon content. Besides drawing, she also loves playing her guitar, baking, and climbing.

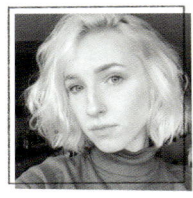

Jackie Droujko
Character designer
jackiedroujko.com
Jackie is a character designer based in Vancouver, currently working on a Netflix animated feature. Clients include DreamWorks TV, Warner Brothers, Lucasfilm, and more.

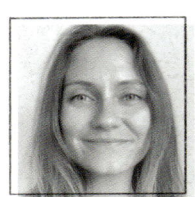

Marta García Navarro "MARGANA"
Freelance illustrator
instagram.com/margana_mgn
MARGANA is a Spanish illustrator and character designer based in Madrid. She has designed concept characters for a video game, illustrated several children's books, and taken portrait commissions.

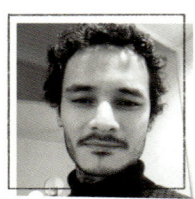

Leo Gómez "The Chulo"
Illustrator, filmmaker & writer
instagram.com/thechuloart
Leo is an illustrator from Colombia, moving into independent filmmaking in Paris.

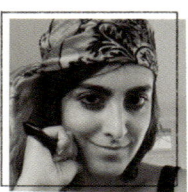

Taraneh Karimi
Principal artist
taraneh.me
Born in Iran, Taraneh started her career as a graphic designer before moving into digital illustration and work as a concept artist in the game industry. She lives in the Netherlands.

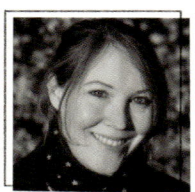

Margaux Kindhauser
Comic book writer, illustrator & art school teacher
instagram.com/margauxmara
Margaux started as a comic book artist on the French series *Clues*. She currently works as an art teacher, as well as working on her graphic novel series *Spirite*.

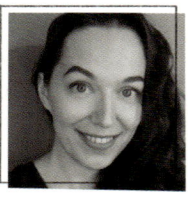

Lisanne Koeteeuw
Illustrator & character artist
instagram.com/lizzie_sketches
Lisanne is an illustrator and character artist living in the Netherlands. She loves sketching, telling stories, and drawing hair and ball gowns way poofier than they have any right to be.

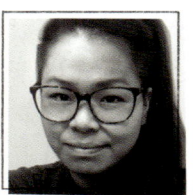

Cassey Kuo
Storyboard artist
kckuo.com
With a love of movement and anatomy, Cassey is a story artist for animation, currently working at Titmouse, Inc. She has also worked as a visual development artist and character designer.

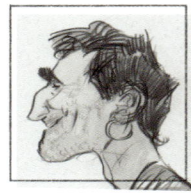

Jordi Lafebre
Author, artist & character designer
jordilafebre.format.com
Born in Barcelona, Jordi has worked as an illustrator and artist for books and animation, and has several graphic novels of his own. He believes every image has a story to tell.

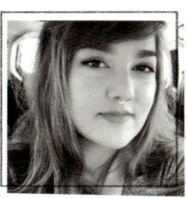

Jacquelin de Leon
Illustrator & comic artist
jacquelindeleon.com
Jacquelin is an illustrator from San Jose, California, who graduated with a BFA in illustration from Laguna College of Art and Design. She draws mystical characters full of vibrant colors.

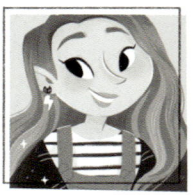

Saoirse Lou
Illustrator
saoirselou.com
Saoirse is a UK-based children's illustrator. She loves making quirky, colorful artwork for children's books and has a keen interest in nature and mythology, which often appear in her illustrations.

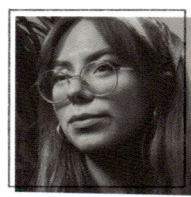

Corah Louise
Illustrator & character designer
corahlouise.com
Corah is a freelance illustrator and character designer from the UK, designing characters, telling stories, and creating products for her shop from a small office above a library.

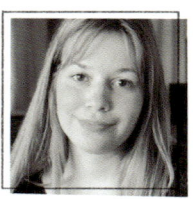

Gretel Lusky
Illustrator & comic book artist
gretellusky.com
Gretel is an illustrator and character designer who worked in animation before moving to the comic book industry. She has worked on projects for clients including DC Comics, Marvel, IDW, and Netflix.

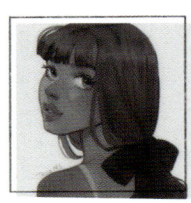

Tasia M S

Illustrator

tasiams.com

Tasia is a freelance illustrator and animator from Johannesburg, South Africa. She has been drawing since she could hold a pencil and has studied 3D and 2D animation.

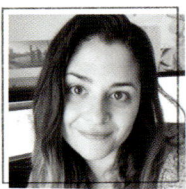

Maria Lia Malandrino

Illustrator & story artist

mlmillustration.com

Maria is an Italian illustrator and freelancer. She has worked as a character designer for toys and merchandise for numerous clients, including Disney, Hachette, and Sweet Cherry.

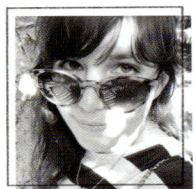

Marvi Manzoni

2D Design Supervisor

marvimanzoni.com

Marvi works at Brown Bag Films as 2D Design Supervisor. She enjoys baking for her friends in her free time.

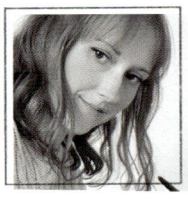

Ana Marija

Visual development artist & character designer

instagram.com/madebyinkyjar

Ana is a digital artist who has designed characters for book publishing, video games, and animation. She enjoys creating back stories for her characters to help them come alive.

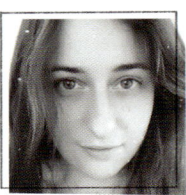

Valentina Millosevich

Visual development artist

artofval.com

Valentina is an Italian visual development artist who strives to fill her life with art, characters, and new worlds. She loves to travel and draws inspiration from her surroundings.

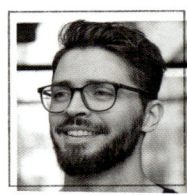

Oliver Ödmark

Senior concept artist

artstation.com/oliverodmark

Oliver grew up in the Swedish countryside. He has worked as a concept artist in the games industry for over ten years, specializing in character design.

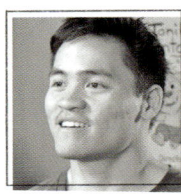

Toniko Pantoja

2D animator, story artist & character designer

tonikopantoja.com

Toniko is a story artist, 2D animator, and character designer for the animation industry. He currently works full-time as a story artist for feature and television.

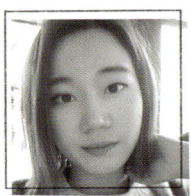

Yewon Park

Visual development artist

yewon-park.info

Yewon graduated from ArtCenter College of Design and has worked in visual development, background, and character design for game, animation, and TV studios, including Blizzard Entertainment and DreamWorks Animation.

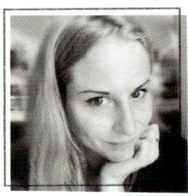

Valentine "Valp" Pasche

Comic artist, variant cover artist, writer & colorist

instagram.com/valentinepasche

Valp has worked in the French comic book industry since 2001 and has published many series as a comic artist. She has also worked as a variant cover artist for Marvel and for role-playing games.

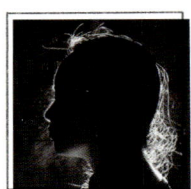

Stephanie Pepper

Illustrator

stephaniepepper.com

Stephanie is an American illustrator with a love for character design. She studied Illustration at the School of Visual Arts, New York, and currently resides in Australia.

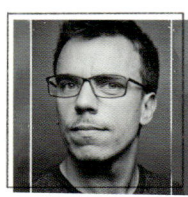

Guille Rancel
Character designer & illustrator

instagram.com/guillerancel

Guille's recent work includes *Emi The Dream Catcher* and *Sorunne* comic books. His work has been featured in *Character Design Quarterly*, *Masters of Anatomy*, *Storytime Magazine,* and *ImagineFX,* plus B-Water Animation and Animation Mentor .

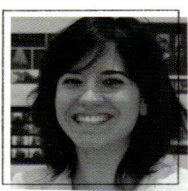

Almu Redondo
Art director

almuredondo.com

Almu is a Spanish art director, concept artist, and storyboarder. She has worked for Cartoon Saloon, Riot Games, Axis Studios, Disney, and Universal.

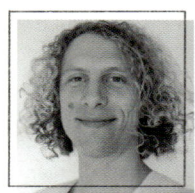

Joakim Riedinger
Lead animator & concept artist

jouak.com

Joakim is a French animator who has worked on projects including *Spider-Man: Into the Spider-Verse*, *Minions*, and *Game of Thrones*. He was nominated for an Annie Award for his work on *Spider-Man: Far From Home*.

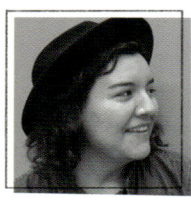

Stephanie Rizo
Character designer & story artist

stephanierizo.com

Stephanie is a Mexican-American character designer and story artist from southern California. She studied narrative illustration at Orange Coast College. She has worked for Sony, Nickelodeon, Warner Bros, and Disney.

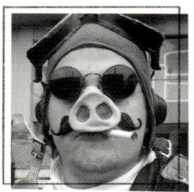

Renato Roldan Ramis
Concept artist

instagram.com/renato3xl

Renato started his career as an animator, character designer, and storyboard artist. For the last seven years he has been working as an art director, before joining Bandai Namco as a concept artist.

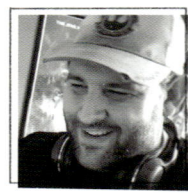

Justin Runfola
Character designer

justinrunfola.com

Justin graduated with a BFA in illustration from Ringling College of Art and Design. He worked as an editorial illustrator before making the transition into animation as a designer.

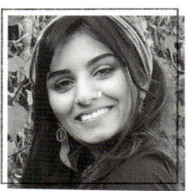

Noor Sofi
Visual development artist

noorsofi.com

Noor is a visual developer based in Burbank, California. She currently works at TAIKO Animation Studios and aspires to create her own stories in her spare time.

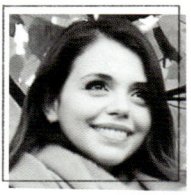

Eva Stöcker "EvaYabai"
Senior art director & illustrator

instagram.com/evayabai

Eva is an advertising art director living with her two cats in Berlin, Germany. She loves to draw and create characters in her free time.

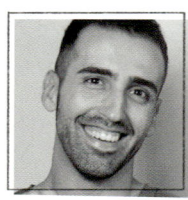

Gary Villarreal
Senior concept artist

instagram.com/villarrte

Gary is a senior concept artist in the film and game industry. He is well known for his traditional work, storytelling, character design, and unique rendering style.

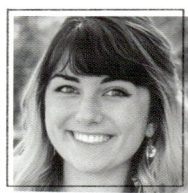

Erika Wiseman
Illustrator & character designer

instagram.com/erikathegoober

Erika is a freelance illustrator and character designer. She's passionate about creating fun, relatable characters and helping other artists grow and develop their skills.

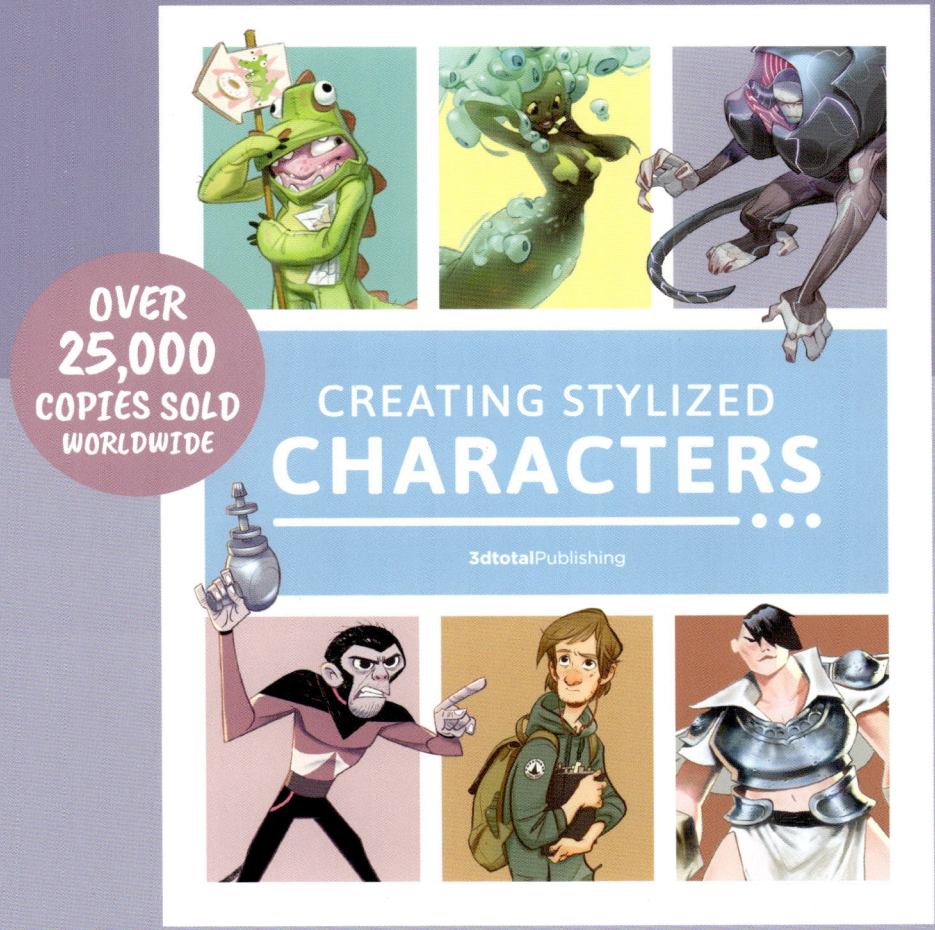

CREATING STYLIZED
CHARACTERS

3dtotalPublishing

Delve into the vibrant, exciting world of character design with *Creating Stylized Characters*!
Join professional illustrators, animators, and comic artists as they demonstrate how to exaggerate form and proportion. Sharing in-depth and industry-informed knowledge of creating fun and memorable characters, this book teaches essential creative skills that are applicable to both digital and traditional media. Learn how to design exciting heroes, villains, and monsters, as well as about key concepts such as gesture, color, poses, and expressions.

Available at shop.3dtotal.com

3dtotalPublishing

3dtotal Publishing is a trailblazing, creative publisher specializing in inspirational and educational resources for artists.

Our titles feature top industry professionals from around the globe who share their experience in skillfully written step-by-step tutorials and fascinating, detailed guides. Illustrated throughout with stunning artwork, these best-selling publications offer creative insight, expert advice, and essential motivation. Fans of digital art will enjoy our comprehensive volumes covering Adobe Photoshop, Procreate, and Blender, as well as our superb titles based around character design, including *Fundamentals of Character Design* and *Creating Characters for the Entertainment Industry*. The dedicated, high-quality blend of instruction and inspiration also extends to traditional art. Titles covering a range of techniques, genres, and abilities allow your creativity to flourish while building essential skills.

Well-established within the industry, we now offer over 100 titles and counting, many of which have been translated into multiple languages around the world. With something for every artist, we are proud to say that our books offer the 3dtotal package:

LEARN · CREATE · SHARE

Visit us at 3dtotalpublishing.com

3dtotal Publishing is part of 3dtotal.com, a leading website for CG artists founded by Tom Greenway in 1999.